SOUTHERN LITERARY STUDIES

Fred Hobson, Editor

DESIRE VIOLENCE & DIVINITY
IN MODERN SOUTHERN FICTION

KATHERINE ANNE PORTER

FLANNERY O'CONNOR

CORMAC McCARTHY

WALKER PERCY

GARY M. CIUBA

LOUISIANA STATE UNIVERSITY PRESS

BATON ROUGE

Published by Louisiana State University Press
Copyright © 2007 by Louisiana State University Press
All rights reserved
Manufactured in the United States of America
Louisiana Paperback Edition, 2011

DESIGNER: Michelle A. Garrod
TYPEFACE: Minion Pro, AdvertRough
TYPESETTER: The Composing Room of Michigan, Inc.

LIBRARY OF CONGRESS CATALOGING-IN-PUBLICATION DATA

Ciuba, Gary M.
  Desire, violence, and divinity in modern southern fiction : Katherine Anne Porter, Flannery
O'Connor, Cormac McCarthy, Walker Percy / Gary M.Ciuba.
    p. cm.
  Includes bibliographical references and index.
  ISBN-13: 978-0-8071-3175-6
  1. American literature—Southern States—History and criticism. 2. American literature—
20th century—History and criticism. 3. Violence in literature. 4. Desire in literature.
5. Porter, Katherine Anne, 1890–1980—Criticism and interpretation. 6. O'Connor, Flannery—
Criticism and interpretation. 7. McCarthy, Cormac, 1933– —Criticism and interpretation.
8. Percy, Walker, 1916– —Criticism and interpretation. I. Title.
  PS261.C48 2006
  810.9'3552—dc22

2005033975

ISBN: 978-0-8071-3863-2 (paper : alk. paper)

    Material in chapter 3 was published previously as "'Like a Boulder Blocking Your Path': Scandal
and Skandalon in Flannery O'Connor," The Flannery O'Connor Bulletin 26–27 (1998–2000): 1–23.
Used by permission.
    Material in chapter 4 was published previously as "McCarthy's Enfant Terrible: Mimetic Desire
and Sacred Violence in Child of God," in Sacred Violence: A Reader's Companion to Cormac
McCarthy, edited by Wade Hall and Rick Wallach (El Paso: Texas Western Press, 1995), 77–85. Used
by permission.

amazon.co.uk

Thank you for shopping at Amazon.co.uk!

Invoice for
Your order of 21 April 2014
Order ID 203-3263002-5819529
Invoice number DZrj6zNRN
Invoice date 21 April 2014

Billing Address
Sophie Riley
14 St Annes Road
Newquay, Cornwall TR7 2SA
United Kingdom

Shipping Address
Sophie Riley
7 Anchor Road
Coleford
RADSTOCK BA3 5PB
United Kingdom

Qty	Item	Our Price (excl. VAT)	VAT Rate	Total Price
1	**Desire, Violence, & Divinity in Modern Southern Fiction: Katherine Anne Porter, Flannery O'Connor, Cormac McCarthy, Walker Percy (Southern Literary Studies)** Paperback. Ciuba, Gary M. 0807138630 (** P-1-F74B143 **)	£11.88	0%	£11.88

Shipping charges £2.75

Subtotal (excl. VAT) 0% £2.75
Total VAT £14.63
Total £0.00
 £14.63

Conversion rate - £1.00 : EUR 1.22

This shipment completes your order.

You can always check the status of your orders or change your account details from the 'Your Account' link at the top of each page on our site

Thinking of returning an item? PLEASE USE OUR ON-LINE RETURNS SUPPORT CENTRE.

Our Returns Support Centre (www.amazon.co.uk/returns-support) will guide you through our Returns Policy and provide you with a printable personalised return label. Please have your order number ready (you can find it next to your order summary, above). Our Returns Policy does not affect your statutory rights.

Amazon EU S.a.r.L, 5 Rue Plaetis, L-2338, Luxembourg
VAT number : GB727255821

Please note - this is not a returns address - for returns - please see above for details of our online returns centre

To Patricia Rogan

CONTENTS

ACKNOWLEDGMENTS

In "Herman Melville," Walker Percy was inspired by Hawthorne's friendship with the author of *Moby Dick* to reflect on the communal enterprise of writing. "As lonely as is the craft of writing, it is the most social of vocations," Percy claimed. "No matter what the writer may say, the work is always written to someone, for someone, against someone." I am pleased to acknowledge here what one of Melville's 1851 letters to Hawthorne called the "[i]neffable sociabilities" of writing.

Kent State University helped to underwrite this book through sponsoring my Faculty Professional Development leaves as well as my Research and Creative Activity appointments. Diana Culbertson, my former colleague at Kent State, first motivated me to think about violence and the sacred in southern literature. Robert Brinkmeyer, Susan Donaldson, Jill Peláez Baumgaertner, and Noel Polk contributed valuable professional support at a critical moment while I was working on this book.

Louisiana State University Press gave this project the most congenial of homes. Candis LaPrade welcomed the manuscript and supervised its review with the kind of warm encouragement that every writer would like to receive. Fred Hobson, editor of the Southern Literary Studies Series, and John Desmond of Whitman College provided readings that at once made me re-envision the text and believe in it all over again. Marie Blanchard, copyeditor for this project, brought greater clarity, fluency, and consistency to my writing. John Easterly, executive editor at Louisiana State University Press, and Lee Sioles, managing editor, oversaw the publication process with wise attention.

So many family members and friends live in the background of this book as well as on its pages. Richard Giannone and Frank D'Andrea have been exemplary in their ongoing faith and generosity. My mother Anne Ciuba, my brothers Raymond Ciuba and Mark Ciuba, as well as Julie Suchodolski, Agnes Rogan, the late John Rogan, and Margy Conway have kept me grounded in the larger life of family. My sons Junio, Giovane, Thiago, Jonathan, João, and André have opened my heart further to much of what I discuss in this study.

Thanks to you all.

Patricia Rogan, my wife, has daily offered me the most ineffable of sociabilities. She is truly the "someone" to whom, for whom, and with whom this book was written.

DESIRE, VIOLENCE, AND DIVINITY
IN MODERN SOUTHERN FICTION

THE HANGED MAN AT OLD SARDIS CHURCH
The Culture of Violence and the Violence of Culture in the South

On July 5, 1933, in Clinton, South Carolina, the body of Norris Bendy was found, according to the *Atlanta Constitution* of the next day, "at Old Sardis church on the Calhoun highway. It was lying on the ground." Bendy, a thirty-five-year-old "Laurens county negro," had been arrested for striking Marvin Tollis, a twenty-two-year-old truck driver, during a Fourth of July altercation. Shortly after midnight, Bendy was "spirited" away from the Clinton jail by four white men, but Sheriff Columbus Owens subsequently claimed that he could not identify the abductors or trace the route that their car traveled. A few hours later when Bendy's body was found by a deputy sheriff, it had been shot once and beaten extensively. Bendy's arms and legs were bound, and his neck was circled by a rope. "Sheriff Owens said it appeared he had been hanged," the newspaper reported. "The body was cut down and removed to the church."

The account of Norris Bendy's murder reads like a bit of newspaper marginalia. It is surrounded by reports of injury and death caused by truck accidents, of plans to celebrate the long tenure of the Episcopal bishop of Tennessee, of a forthcoming meeting of the Georgia Association of Commercial Secretaries in Elberton. Its brevity and lack of the sensational details that journalists sometimes reported to convey their outrage over mob violence make the piece seem as if Bendy barely deserves notice. Indeed, when a follow-up article was printed on July 7, the victim was incorrectly identified as "Norris Dendy." The two articles about Bendy—each a barely six-inch-long column—are no more than minor notes in the larger story of 3,762 victims lynched in America between 1889, when such records began to be kept, and late 1933. In South Carolina, where Senator Coleman L. Blease boasted in 1930 that as governor he had not used the militia to protect African Americans against such killings and had asked not to be informed until the morning after a suspect was captured, readers might have interpreted the article out of apathy or animosity: an "uppity Negro" got what was coming to him.

However, such a reading would not have been unanimous in 1933. Governor Ibra C. Blackwood reflected a shift in popular sentiment when he described Bendy's death as "a murder—not a lynching" in the July 7 *Atlanta Constitution*. Blackwood even assigned state constables to help local authorities investigate the case, and the newspaper noted that South Carolina's last officially recognized lynching took place in 1930. At the end of 1933 the *New York Herald-Tribune* found evidence that mob violence was diminishing in America, for only seventeen people had been lynched as of December 3. The decline in such mock justice suggests that a different interpretation of the newspaper account might have been reached by readers who noted the arrest of Bendy but not of Tollis, the sheriff's failure to guard his prisoner, the summary execution by an anonymous crowd, and the ferocity of the assault on Bendy's flesh. They might have discerned that Norris Bendy was the victim of gradually escalating fury, which spread, like a contagion, from Marvin Tollis to the officers of the law and finally to the lynch mob that left a hanged body in the church yard.[1]

Since 1933 readers have become even more schooled in the hermeneutics of suspicion so that they are accustomed to look for what has been slanted, silenced, or suppressed in such reports about mob violence. Commenting on how texts of persecution are interpreted, René Girard observes that when scholars review accounts of seventeenth-century witchcraft trials, they do not believe that the accused women and men actually killed their neighbor's cow or son. Rather, readers perceive how the community has mythologized those whom it seeks to exclude because of their differences. Girard normally writes about the continental novel, Greek drama, the Bible, or Shakespeare, but when he offers another example of the way that accounts of victimization may get interpreted, he draws it this time from the American South:

> If you read, for instance, a newspaper report of a lynching in the South in 1933, when you see certain telltale signs in the text, you will know [that the murdered was a victim of false allegations and collective violence]; but a historian a thousand years from now—he may not know. The truth will lie only in a novel written by someone named William Faulkner. Then the sound historians will say that we should not believe the novel; we have the press, we have all the documents. In fact, however, it is only the novel that puts together all the signs. ("Discussion" 228)

Girard's affirmation of Faulkner overlooks many other writers who also disclose such scapegoating. In particular, it overlooks the vigorous tradition of African American novelists from William Wells Brown to John Wideman that, according to Trudier Harris, has exposed how white Americans have sought to exorcise blackness. However, Girard's tribute to Faulkner is helpful in the way it celebrates the crucial role that the fiction writer, especially in the South, can play in helping to understand violence and the texts of violence. Whereas Girard can imagine twentieth-century readers of a newspaper account about a 1933 lynching, like that of Norris Bendy, as detecting the victimization, he views such interpretation as becoming more problematic with the passage of years. However, to read how Charles Bon is excluded by Thomas Sutpen in *Absalom, Absalom!,* how Darl Bundren is seized and confined to the asylum in *As I Lay Dying,* how Lucas Beauchamp is nearly lynched in *Intruder in the Dust,* or how Joe Christmas is shot and castrated in *Light in August* is to uncover a violent process that a reader in the future may find obscured in a newspaper report. Fiction, for Girard, may reveal the facts about systematic persecution and execution that the historical record conceals.

If the articles on Norris Bendy's execution are read by way of Girard's theories about killing and cultural formation, by way of the critical vision that Girard identifies in Faulkner's fiction, "certain telltale signs in the text" become more noticeable, require to be "put together," and raise questions about mimesis, mob fury, and religion. Is there a similarity between the African American Bendy and the white Tollis that may be as significant as their obvious differences? What is the connection between such possible resemblance and their violent encounter? How is the fight between the two related to the vigilante execution? And why—why is the hanged body of Bendy left lying on the ground at Old Sardis church?

DEMYSTIFYING VIOLENCE IN THE SOUTH

Of the 1,886 lynchings in the United States from 1900 to 1930, almost 90 percent took place in the South (Brearley 679). The death of Norris Bendy three years later in South Carolina confirmed with one more victim the South's reputation for violence that had been noted in travel accounts from the late eighteenth century (Ayers 9) and that had become well established by the 1830s. Wayfarers from the North and from England recorded so many brawls, duels, and stabbings in their logs and narratives that to have omitted note of southern violence would have been almost more remarkable than to have reported it. Some nineteenth-century southerners argued that their bloody notoriety was more the invention of northern journalists than a verifiable fact and countered that mobs and criminals actually made the North a more dangerous locale (Bruce 3–4). However, statistics challenge the claim that Dixie's reputation for quarrels and killings resulted purely from regional bias. Mortality figures from the 1850 census indicate that the South's murder rate was seven times that of the North (Bruce 242n.). Early scholarly attempts to tally southern homicides confirm the propensity for violence. In 1880 H. V. Redfield, whose research in newspapers and official records pioneered the study of southern violence, found that southerners in the benchmark states of Texas, Kentucky, and South Carolina "kill one another at a rate about eighteen hundred per cent. greater than does the population of New England" (13). One year after Bendy's death H. C. Brearley reported that from 1920 to 1924 the homicide rate in the South was slightly over two and a half times that for the rest of the country (681).[2]

Such a tradition of violence provides an even larger context for the questions raised by the newspaper accounts of Norris Bendy's murder. It requires that this lynching be read against the background of how imitative desire, bloodshed, and religion have long been intertwined in the South. When Girard credits Faulkner's fiction with telling the truth about hangings, he implies that it understands victimization in a way that differs markedly from traditional attempts to explain killings in the South or in America at large. D. H. Lawrence's famous description of "the essential American soul" as "hard, isolate, stoic, and a killer" acknowledged how violence had become part of a national mythology (68). The license for such individual aggression and for collective fury in America has been traced back to the country's bloody origins. Richard Slotkin claims that the Puritan wars with Native Americans established the archetypal countryman as the hunter who seeks regeneration through violence (178–79). And Richard Maxwell Brown contends that the American Revolution provided the often-imitated example for how violence is justified in reaching a supposedly honorable end (42). Since the South has become notorious as the most violent region of this violent country, commentators have repeatedly tried to identify some distinctive feature to explain its propensity for conflict and carnage. They have explored whether its violence might be traced to class structure, rural lifestyles, poverty, struggles to modernize, anomie, child-rearing practices, or peculiar qualities of interpersonal relationships. They have viewed the violence as the legacy of slavery, the frontier, Celtic settlers, and an obsession with honor.

Clarence Cason even attributed the hot tempers to the hot temperatures. "The climate of the South also has an effect upon the nervous systems of the inhabitants," he claimed in *90° in the Shade*. "They like pepper in their food, strong coffee, and the excitement of fights" (12).[3]

Girard's studies in mimesis and murder point inquiries into southern violence beyond the Mason-Dixon line, beyond even American history. They suggest that such hostility should be understood not only as a problem of a particular region or nation but also as an example of a generative mechanism at work in all culture. To view southern violence as cultural rather than just local does not deny that there are specific causes for such aggression that are endemic to the South. Instead, such an approach seeks to analyze and connect these regional factors in terms of the larger work of culture. It seeks to answer John Shelton Reed's objection to many theories about southern violence—"the origins of the trait cannot explain its persistence"—by focusing on the underlying dynamics that lead to violence regardless of the immediate cause (141). Finally, it seeks to explore how violence is related to one of the chief products of southern culture, modern southern fiction. Since Girard's theories about violence and culture developed from his study of novels and drama, he regards imaginative writing as playing a critical role in understanding the culture of victimization. Literature can reveal how desire may lead to violence, how violence may climax in scapegoating, and how scapegoating may generate the culture that disguises and deifies its origins in desire. Such analysis and excavation is the story behind so many of the stories from the twentieth-century South.

Girard's study of literature and culture has led him to argue that violence, like the kind that led to the murder of Norris Bendy, originates not in the self alone but in what he calls interdividuality, the mimetic relationship between the self and the other.[4] This psychosocial approach rejects explanations of violence that attribute it to some fundamental human instinct. In *Beyond the Pleasure Principle* Freud theorized that the self is driven to regress toward absolute peace, toward an inorganic state, ultimately toward death. However, the self avoids its own destruction, as Freud claimed in *Civilization and Its Discontents*, by diverting these potentially suicidal urges outward into attacking others. Whereas Freud understood thanatos as being redirected by eros, Konrad Lorenz studied how a similar instinct for violence actually promoted survival in the animal kingdom. In *On Aggression* he argued that animals resort to force as an evolutionary adaptation to defend territory, to guarantee the perpetuation of the fittest, and to establish hierarchy. Humans share these same inborn impulses to fight, according to Lorenz, but whereas other animals limit violence through appeasement rituals, humans have lost the mechanisms that might keep them from intraspecific aggression. Girard criticizes the concept of instinctual violence because, whether psychoanalytic or ethological, it predestines individuals to being ruled by some force beyond their control. Moreover, it conceals how imitation may lead to conflict and makes such contention seem one-sided rather than generated by mutual rivalry ("Discussion" 124–25). Whether the instinct is viewed as serving death or life, Girard argues that such theories about inborn drives divert attention from the way that violence originates in the mimesis that both attracts and obstructs models and disciples (*Things Hidden* 409–15).[5]

Rather than emphasizing the innate origins of violence, Girard has more in common with theorists who posit the interpersonal basis for violence. For example, he would agree with Leonard Berkowitz, who contends that violence comes about as one possible response to frustration. Berkowitz has studied how thwarted individuals may direct their anger toward harming the actual obstacles to their goals or displace their rage onto similar and easily accessible individuals. Girard would agree with Albert Bandura, who emphasizes the lifelong role of modeling in all social learning, especially in aggression. Bandura argues that aggression results from imitation of violent examples and that such assault is more likely when doing injury has already brought rewards to the model and perpetrator. And Girard would agree with James Gilligan, whose work with prisoners, particularly with those judged criminally insane, has convinced him that violence is caused by attempts to replace acute shame with a conviction of pride, power, and honor (110). Reaching similar conclusions from principles in "self theory," Gerda Siann contends that when individuals feel devalued, they may use force to assert the self and humiliate others (241–42). Although Girard draws his early insights from literature rather than from interviews, field studies, and experimental observation, he resembles these theoreticians in maintaining that violence may result when the self confronts some obstacle, that violence reflects a desire to affirm the frustrated self, and that violence may provoke further counterviolence. What Girard contributes to such clinical and laboratory research is a vivid understanding of how violence may be caused and spread by mimetic desire.

Girard's analysis of modern continental fiction has directed him away from a purely linear concept of desire. Romantics view desire as originating spontaneously in the autonomous self. Even if Deleuze and Guattari recognize the collective nature of desire, they long in *Anti-Oedipus* for a return to a schizo-phrenic state of solitary and unmediated desire. Freudians, on the other hand, emphasize desire as finding a goal in cathexis. Even if Lacan understands self-formation in terms of the other, he imagines desire as arising out of the loss of the phallus (*Things Hidden* 402–9). In *Deceit, Desire, and the Novel* Girard fo-cuses on neither the subject nor the object of desire but on the triangle that they form with a mediator. Girard posits a compelling sense of unfulfillment at the center of the subject. It lacks, and so it longs. Such metaphysical desire leads to mimetic desire. As the self seeks to fill up this emptiness, it takes as a model some individual who seems to possess the fullness of being for which the subject yearns. The self desires according to that other rather than to itself, wants what another wants—love, power, wealth, celebrity, success, godhead—because the other wants it. Subtitled *The Self and Other in Literary Structure*, Girard's first book explores how fiction from Cervantes to Proust reveals the social con-struction of desire.

Because such imitation is potentially destructive, Girard's work sometimes gives the misleading impression that all mimesis, all desire, is evil. However, at its best, this emulation can lead to fulfillment, for it provides the self with mod-els of physical, spiritual, ethical, and intellectual excellence that can be happily copied. In such positive mimesis the model does not cling to the ideal as an ex-clusive possession but allows it to be shared or duplicated, and the disciple does not want to eliminate or replace the model but re-present it.[6] Yet if mimetic de-sire may consummate in co-presence and communion, it may also degenerate into resentment and rivalry and outright aggression. The disciple may view the model not just as the pattern for desire but as an actual obstruction to the de-sired end, and this impediment may only intensify the disciple's desire for what has been denied. The model, in turn, may view the disciple as a threat to its jeal-ously guarded well-being and ardently defend that status against any usurper. As desire gets doubled, the disciple's imitation makes the model view its posi-tion or possession as even more valuable, and the model's attempt to preserve its distinction exasperates and exacerbates the envious disciple. When such dou-bles confront each other, often in mutual frustration, they tend to lose their fo-cus on the original object of desire and become obsessed with the other as rival and obstacle. The result is that they may strike out in violence to eliminate their counterparts and to affirm the singular mastery of the self.[7]

In *Violence and the Sacred* Girard pursues the widespread effects of such im-itative antagonism. Influenced by his studies in anthropology and Greek tragedy, he expands a literary theory about how mimetic desire works in the European novel into a cultural theory about how violence animates the primitive, ancient, and modern worlds. Girard contends that violence, which is begun in mimesis, is perpetuated through mimesis. Violence invites duplication, for a raised fist typically provokes a raised fist in return. Violence also replicates itself, for the user is often forced by some counterforce to use more and greater force. Each outburst generates ever greater reprisals; each reprisal incites new and always escalating outbursts until the original dissimilarities between model and disciple begin to be eradicated in reciprocal antagonism. The two become what the model dreaded and what the disciple only desired in an entirely different way—the same.

This mimetic rivalry may convulse an entire community. Since desire is spread by imitation and imitation is spread by desire, the model-disciple relationship may expand beyond any single pair of doubles and get reproduced throughout a group. As desire circulates, the disciple copies the model, the copy, in turn, is copied by others, and the reduplication provides further models for further disciples. New or variant forms of imitative desire may generate their own family of doubles so that mimesis gradually becomes rampant. When selves increasingly come to resemble each other, the sheer multiplicity of the mimicry risks proliferating the same kind of envy that fuels individual antagonisms. Models and disciples, indeed models as disciples and disciples as models, may resort to aggression to establish a degree of distinction, to claim that they alone have the right to the contested plenitude. As the conflict between doubles becomes continually redoubled, the progression may eventually produce a mob in which everyone is fighting everyone else to prove that he or she is not everyone else but the sole truly sublime self. Laws might once have restricted the aggression; rituals might once have provided an outlet for such hostility. However, during what Girard calls "the sacrificial crisis," no code of conduct and no secondhand offering can limit the mimetic antagonism. What replaces the initial desire for the contested ideal is the desire for violence. Although violence seems like the ultimate signifier of absolute difference, it actually collapses differences, for it makes all the same by making all into warring doubles. There is no longer any distinction; there is only mimesis on a mass scale, only the imitation of violence.

This chaos may spiral toward the community's destruction, or the clash and confusion may end in its own confounding and herald the community's salvation. Girard contends that the mimesis which gave rise to violence may climax in a violent act of mimesis. The society in conflict may collectively turn its hostility and hysteria against a randomly chosen member who is representative of the strife-filled group. Just as the upheaval began when competing members imitated a desire to gain something, it ends when collaborating members imitate another desire to get rid of someone. Mutual antagonists copy the violence done by one of their own and against one of their own, polarize their fury onto a surrogate, and turn the violence against all into the violence against the lone object of communal exclusion. Since all the members of a society in crisis have become the doubles of each other, a "single victim can be substituted for all the potential victims" (*Violence* 79). This surrogate is often found among those who are already marginalized for physical, social, economic, psychological, or sexual reasons, inasmuch as any difference draws attention to itself in a world where all other distinctions have been effaced and replaced by violence. However, the choice of victim is purely arbitrary. There is no causal connection between the crisis and the one killed. Indeed, Girard claims that crimes are often invented to mediate between the two and to magnify the heinous significance of the innocent individual. To avoid confronting how purely wanton is this murder, the community typically views its double and victim as a monster deserving to be slaughtered. For if the actual randomness were acknowledged, the scapegoating would no longer work. Society must regard the victim as responsible for the menace in order for it to regard the elimination of the victim as the means to safety. However, the result of this delusion is that the red-handed polity never really rids itself of the true cause of its violence—mimetic desire.

Through such victimization the imperiled community gains a new and dubious order. Members find unanimity through focusing their scattered hostilities on a common enemy, tranquility through venting their internecine desires on a mutual foe, and impunity through executing a collective outcast whom no one will try to avenge. Since the killing of this surrogate restores peace to society, the slain outsider may later come to be viewed not just as accursed but as sacred. The victim thus gets remembered as the bearer of an ambiguous duality—the cause of the malevolent violence that nearly destroyed the community and the source of the beneficent violence that saved it. Gathered around this paradoxical founding figure, the community recovers its former stability, but because members have never confronted their own responsibility for the violence, the peace is merely temporary. It lasts only until some further mimetic conflict erupts and requires yet one more victim to reestablish the new order once again.

The social mechanism of scapegoating repeats what Girard imagines as the formative moment of culture itself. Girard posits a series of such primal murders as marking the evolutionary passage into the human world. He imagines that a group of hominids at war with itself eventually overcame the patterns of dominance and submission that normally provided instinctual restraints against intraspecific violence. The band fought its way to near destruction, yet it averted collective self-slaughter when it discovered renewal through slaying one of its own. Culture emerged in the wake of such repeated movements toward hominization. The violence that began in mimetic desire, spread through mimetic desire, and climaxed in mimetic desire was finally institutionalized through mimetic desire. The regenerative bloodshed provided not only the peaceful aftermath for the development of culture but also the fundamental pattern for what culture at once contained and commemorated.

Since culture was born out of the primordial killing, Girard views this newly civil and civilizing order with stark candor. His analysis of how mimetic desire may lead to the sacrificial crisis parallels Hobbes's famous description in *Leviathan* (chapter 13) of how the equal abilities and similar hopes of fearful, selfish individuals may lead to competition, violence, and war. But whereas Hobbes believed in the commonwealth that formed when covenanters renounced force and deeded power to the sovereign state, Girard writes no apologia for culture as the successor to warring nature. Rather, he boldly rewrites Rousseau's social contract. The collective enterprise depends not on reasonable citizens working together for the common good but on once-infuriated partisans conspiring to hide their common evil. The heirs of post-Enlightenment humanism and liberalism might like to imagine culture as opposed to violence (Barker [viii]), but Girard recognizes that the work of culture is as dual as violence itself. It has to deny, forget, or conceal the founding murder so that the community does not dissolve when members confront the bloody and aleatory origins of their bonds. However, it also has to recall and re-enact this bloodshed lest the community risk being overwhelmed by such a crisis again.

Primitive culture accomplished this paradoxical task of suppressing and expressing its primal slaughter by ingenious indirection. It paid so much attention to the originary violence that it memorialized the process of surrogate victimage in its fundamental institutions, yet it remembered the exclusion at second hand so that the primordial scapegoating was represented but never completely re-presented. Taboos and laws, for example, acknowledged the violence by trying to prevent its recurrence; they stipulated complex precautions against and clear penalties for the rivalry that might once again ravage the community. Myths retold the story of the primal victimization but from the biased perspective of the apparently innocent victimizers, who once united to rid the community of a monstrous threat to its well-being. Kingship and priesthood developed when prospective victims came to enjoy enough time before being killed to gain the efficacy in life that the community would normally attribute to them in death. Human sacrifice staged a version of the original victimization, and animal husbandry provided substitute victims for human sacrifice. Rituals repeated such sacrifices in a formalized style, and theater repeated the rituals in a yet more stylized form. Medicine used the basic principle of surrogate victimage—violence against violence—in drugs and surgery that attacked the flesh to combat illness. Even language found its beginnings in the premise behind the whole process of producing culture. Since the victim was the representative double of everyone in the community, this primal substitution established the pattern for all later symbolism. Every sign is but a surrogate, and behind each is the scapegoat.

Ultimately, the single moment of slaughter and salvation generated the duality of the sacred. Girard views primitive religion not as a response to some authentic manifestation of the holy but as a human deception to serve societal needs. Since violence had culminated in collective murder, the community removed such fury from everyday use and reserved it as the privileged realm of the gods. This consecration of wrath at once tried to prevent it from disrupting the social order in the future and to disguise how it had once erupted on earth in the past. Yet such a distinction between the sacred and the profane was fundamentally spurious, for the transcendent amounted to no more than the old violence under a new and glorified sign. The sacred was the difference without a difference—the violence of human nondifferentiation given the appearance of ultimate alterity.

Much as the victim ended the conflict by taking the place of every antagonist for every other antagonist, the sacred took the place of the victim. The "sacred" was nothing but a misnomer—the name that the community gave its imposture to hide and hypostatize its violence. This bloody godhead displayed a countenance as contradictory as the process that generated it. Just as the model might impede and entice, just as scapegoating transformed a scorned outcast into the redeemer of a fractious community, the Janus-faced sacred assumed both the maleficent and beneficent aspects of violence. It forbade and beckoned, hurt and healed, ruined and renewed. The custodian of this ambivalent rage and raging ambivalence was religion. Pretending to feed the divine appetite for vio-lence, the cult kept mimetic antagonism from overwhelming the community by instituting a holy and wholly acceptable channel for such strife. It was sacrifice. Religion established that there was legitimate violence—that of gods, priests, and later, the sacred state—and illegitimate violence, the appropriation of this sacrosanct fury for private goals that violated the social order.

Desire, violence, and divinity are thus shape-shifting names for the same mimesis. Look away, and one signifier metamorphoses into the other that it echoes through alliteration and assonance. Desire becomes violent, violence becomes divinized, and divinity becomes desired. Like mirrors upon mirrors, desire, violence, and divinity give back themselves to themselves but under the appearance of being unique and distinct. All of these protean doubles are dual—each attracting and opposing—and all redouble themselves, often in dis-placed ways that belie their actual likeness and perpetuate the illusion of dif-ference. The result is a circle that is truly vicious. Desire may lead model and disciple toward violence in their quest for divinity. The violence that the dou-bles commit may cause mimetic desire for further violence as opponents seek to emulate the sacred. The divinity that the rivals desire so violently is only the apotheosis of their own violent desire. This identity amid what seems so unlike and unrelated ultimately collapses the Girardian triangle of the interdividual re-lationship. If desire is itself triangular, a relationship involving subject, object, and mediator, it also forms part of a triangle whose object is divinity and whose mediator is violence. Each member of the threesome generates the other by re-producing itself so that trinity turns into duality, and duality into the single phe-nomenon of mimesis.

Girard has explored the workings of desire, violence, and divinity so com-prehensively that his work has been hailed as "something like the unified field theory for the humanities" (Bailie 4). Drawing upon fiction, religion, psychol-ogy, sociology, ethnology, and anthropology, Girard offers not only provocative interpretations for these individual disciplines but also a broader reading of the culture that encompasses all of them. Scholars who have applied his theories to theology, scriptural studies, psychology, philosophy, economics, violence stud-ies, and literature have further expanded the potential range of his work and perhaps also suggested its increasing validity.[8] However, precisely because Gi-rard's literary criticism and cultural critique read across the differences that are used to erect departmental divisions and specializations, his work has some-times been challenged for being totalizing and reductionist.[9] In response, Girard claims that scapegoating is not a rigid pattern into which he tries to fit every observation but "a dynamic principle of genesis and development that can operate as a hermeneutic tool" ("Discussion" 106). He uses this interpretive strategy with enormous agility so that his analyses of rituals, myths, fiction, tragedy, and Scripture contribute a diverse and complicated body of evidence to his ever more persuasive synthesis.

Girard's project is wide-ranging, interdisciplinary, and integrative, but it generally avoids simplifications because of a restless, tentative spirit of inquiry that resembles the impulse behind deconstruction. Indeed, Andrew J. McKenna has demonstrated in rigorous detail how Girard's critique of the violence in culture parallels Derrida's critique of the violence in Western thought. These likenesses point to what usually saves Girard from the naiveté of overly ambitious systematizations—a sensitivity to the evasions and ambiguities that receive no attention in such grandiose schemes, a recognition of how the differences that define systems may swiftly break down and dissolve into each other, an awareness of how demythologizing may easily turn into remythologizing. At his best, Girard avoids totalization because he reads from the margins of texts and cultures. He looks beyond the social and theoretical structures that seem so all-encompassing and looks for the one who has not been part of the totality, the single figure around whom the whole matrix of denial and deception has been configured, the victim. And precisely because Girard focuses on this outcast, he understands that what is excluded and occluded amounts not to an endless series of deconstructive deferrals but, plainly and simply, to murder.

Girard's work helps to reveal the mimetic desire, escalating violence, and mock-divinity in the communal killing of Norris Bendy. Although the initial article in the *Atlanta Constitution* never mentions that Marvin Tollis was white, its reference to Bendy as "Negro" inscribes the difference that gets implicitly challenged in the fight and finally reaffirmed through the lynching. The omission, the first of many, illustrates Girard's objection that a newspaper article might not clearly disclose the victimization, especially for a reader in the future. The emphasis on race—and race alone—frames Bendy as a black man who dared to act as if the equal, the double, of a man whose superior color was taken for granted. It suggests that Tollis was a white man who found his supremacy challenged by his black rival. If the article had mentioned that both were truckers and both had driven picnickers to Lake Murray, the threat of similarity might have seemed even more obvious, and the elision of differences even more ominous (Ginzburg 197–98). But such resemblances are almost beside the point, for the only resemblance that matters is that Bendy violated the hierarchy of color and, as if he himself were white, struck his racial equal.

The Fourth of July provided a fitting cultural context for the fight between doubles. Girard views such holiday celebrations as the ritualized remnants of the sacrificial crisis. The festivities authorize a special dispensation, a violation of everyday customs and constraints that recalls the chaos before scapegoating. The national feast of July 4, in particular, grants this freedom on a day that celebrates America's declaration of freedom. In "Picnic and Sporting Events to Feature Atlanta's July 4," the front-page story of the *Constitution* on Independence Day detailed this holiday liberty by reporting plans for fireworks, barbecues, beauty contests, wrestling matches, and trips to the mountains or the beaches. Bendy and Tollis came into conflict amid this festive permissiveness, when the distinctions that governed daily life had broken down, yet there was one inviolate difference in 1933 South Carolina, and it was based on race. Lynchings were not infrequent on the Fourth of July (Harris xi). Indeed, in Margaret Walker's *Jubilee* two black women, accused of poisoning members of their masters' families, are hanged between the morning picnics and evening fireworks (98–104). On Independence Day or on any other day there was no freedom for a black man like Bendy to clash with a white man like Tollis as if the two were equals. When the judicial system intervened in the South Carolina conflict, it ended the mimetic rivalry between Bendy and Tollis and reestablished the hierarchy from which there was no holiday. The African American was arrested. After the law pre-judged him, mob law reinforced the prejudice with a vengeance. Already marginalized by race and imprisonment, Bendy became the victim of a society furiously seeking to reassert the racist order briefly threatened by the Fourth of July struggle.

The body of Norris Bendy was found at Old Sardis church. Although the location may seem particularly blasphemous, racist mobs often left their victims at such sanctuaries. Named after one of the seven Christian communities addressed at the beginning of Revelation, Old Sardis was not just a house of worship but a church of churches. To leave the slain Bendy on such sacred ground was to sanctify his killing, to transform it into a cultic offering, perhaps even to claim that Christianity condoned such murders. Girard's work suggests an even more complicated reading of this sacrificial scene. The consecration of violence at Old Sardis might be viewed as foundering on the very attempt to appropriate the sacred. Meant to flaunt the violence of the victimizers, the corpse in the churchyard signified how the innocent victim died, as of old, once again at Old

Sardis. The body with a rope around its neck recalls another body hanged on another tree, the victim that was so crucial for the early Christians at Sardis. The lynchers, as much as those who crucified Jesus, knew not what they did.

If Girard is right in claiming that society conceals the victimization that founds it, the desire, violence, and divinity in the lynching of Norris Bendy reveal a dynamic that extends beyond Clinton, South Carolina, to the South at large. The 1933 killing provides a perspective on the entire culture that the victimizers might have imagined as enshrined at Old Sardis. It suggests that the South may be an example of what Marvin Wolfgang and Franco Ferracuti term a "subculture of violence," a community where aggression is an acceptable, expected, and even obligatory response to what seems like provocation (158–61). Arguing along such lines, Raymond Gastil has termed the South a "regional culture of violence" (416), and Sheldon Hackney has tried to identify what is distinctive about this particularly belligerent section of America: "a southern world view that defines the social, political, and physical environment as hostile and casts the white southerner in the role of the passive victim of malevolent forces" (924).[10] Such interpretations of the South help to explain the murder of Norris Bendy as a violent response to the fear that the traditional racist order may one day be forever violated. Yet to view the South as a subculture or regional culture of violence risks implying that it is anomalous rather than exemplary, as if southern culture were violent and the rest of culture were not. Girard's work makes clear how readily the moral superiority of those outside the South can translate such a distinction into a reason for accusation and exclusion. The rest of the country may easily turn the South, as Charles Roland notes, into "a scapegoat, a 'moral lightning rod' for grounding any bolts of guilt that might otherwise have hit outside the regional strike zone. Some critics even went so far as to blame the South for the racial difficulties occurring elsewhere during the 1960s" (190). Walker Percy notices the same regional tendency to indict the other and acquit the self when he comments about such reciprocity, "Sectionalism allows each section to dispense itself by using the other as a scapegoat" (*Signposts* 81). Girard's exposure of scapegoating helps to reveal much about southern culture, yet it also serves as a warning against making the South the victim of a self-righteous North, East, or West. Rather than viewing the South as exceptional in being a subculture of violence, it might be more accurate to regard the South as a culture of violence because of the violence of culture itself.[11] Like all culture, it represses traces of its originary violence even as it habitually recalls, repeats, and reenacts them. Behind southern beliefs and behaviors, customs and values, rituals and institutions can be found a violence as primordial as the founding murder—violence dreaded, violence desired, violence displaced, violence denied, violence deified.

VIOLENCE DREADED AND DESIRED

Just as the culture of victimization recognizes that violence might always plunge society into another sacrificial crisis, the South developed an acute sense of the mayhem that forever needed to be kept at bay. This awareness of potential chaos can be traced back to even before the Civil War, for, as Dickson Bruce has shown, the antebellum South held a classical view about the unruliness of the passions. Believing that such fierce emotions needed to be controlled but not eliminated, southerners came to fear in the other the eruption that was always possible in themselves. Since they were so anxious about being vulnerable and so suspicious of the other's intent, southerners tended to strike out when wronged, snubbed, or even threatened (Bruce 70). This distrust of fellow southerners was only exacerbated by defensiveness before those regarded as interlopers in the South. Because the South continually felt itself under attack from "abolitionists, the Union Army, carpetbaggers, Wall Street and Pittsburgh, civil rights agitators, the federal government, feminism, socialism, trade-unionism, Darwinism, Communism, atheism, daylight-saving time, and other by-products of modernity" (Hackney 924–25), it developed a "siege mentality" as a protective response. The resulting paranoia was nothing but mimetic rivalry magnified and multiplied; the enemy might be everyone and everywhere.

Since such internal and external foes threatened the individual and regional sense of difference, the South erected a culture founded on dissimilarity as a bulwark against violence. Its courtesies and hierarchies enacted sometimes exquisite and sometimes savage hyperdistinctions so that the proper degree of separation was preserved between potential foes. Lancelot Lamar, Percy's murderous gentleman in the novel that bears his name, understands precisely how manners provide an alternative to violence when he explains, "Either one shakes hands with someone or one ignores him or one kills him" (149). The formalities of politeness crafted nuanced zones for amenable coexistence; racism, sexism, and classism carved out more blatantly and brutally the social space that was deemed necessary to ward off upheaval. All of these deferences and divisions sought to minimize mimetic rivalry by establishing that no sort of southerner was ever the exact double of another. Blacks were not the same as whites, wives were not the same as husbands, tenant farmers were not the same as plantation owners, and gentlemen were not the same as scoundrels. By keeping every southerner in a distinct place through protocol, custom, or pure force, the culture sought to stifle the strife that might arise when equals believe each has the right to some contested plenitude. The white male world, fearful of such conflict, established a network of careful rules and refinements so that it could try to live in peace. If the culture could just separate, designate, and discriminate enough, the South could regulate violent mutuality out of existence.[12]

Whereas such restrictions sought to repress violence through a highly formalized order, the rites of the Old South tried to express violence through an array of ordered forms. Girard claims that from its beginning, culture has developed indirect ways to keep surrogate victimage from recurring. These methods sought to direct the hostilities of the community into safe and secondhand reenactments of the primal crisis, killing, and re-creation. So, too, did the South tame and translate its violence. For example, what Ted Ownby describes as the culture of manhood, which reigned in the South until the Civil War, regulated quarrels through the complex protocol of duels—formal letters of inquiry, intervening negotiations about time and place as well as position and weapons, the mediation of seconds, the elimination of potential advantages (Bruce 31–39). It found equivalents in the hunt and cockfight for the way animal sacrifice once transferred violence onto an acceptable victim. It displaced antagonism into gambling, circuses, oath-taking, oratory, militarism, and such ritualized competition as tournaments, corn shuckings, fodder pullings, log rollings, and hog killings. The evangelical culture that increasingly took hold in the postbellum South sought to limit the expression of violence even further. It opposed the culture of manhood through championing a gentler cult of self-restraint and harmony with others. Its intensified campaign in the late nineteenth and early twentieth century to prohibit the drinking of alcohol, to pass new or more stringent antiswearing laws, and to ban sports on the Sabbath might seem like a genteel crusade for an overly scrupulous religious code (Ownby 170–77). Yet the moral rectitude of evangelical culture was driven by a less provincial impulse than legislating piety and domesticity. It typified the way culture has regularly tried to eliminate any occasion of excess, lest violence erupt and escalate again toward catastrophe.

If much of southern culture restricts or redirects violence, Girard's work suggests that the origins of such violence might be found in imitation. The foremost model for any southerner is culture itself, for it supplies every member with compelling paradigms to follow. "Culture," as Mary Douglas recognizes, "in the sense of the public, standardised values of a community, mediates the experience of individuals. It provides in advance some basic categories, a positive pattern in which ideas and values are tidily ordered. And above all, it has authority, since each is induced to assent because of the assent of others" (38–39). For each southerner the region serves as a powerful and exemplary "other," forming the self into being by offering attractive models for desire that have the lure of communal approval. Family, friends, colleagues, and church members live out a template that socializes the self into discipleship southern-style. Ownby appreciates exactly how this mimesis might promote violence today when he writes that "early in life Southerners learn from television, from their elders, from the movies and, more than ever before, from the music of their own region that they live in a part of the country where people are willing to fight if the situation seems to call for it, and they learn to be somewhat belligerent when criticized" (ix). From pop culture to high culture—and even to the seemingly sublime forms of cultic practice—the South has cultivated models that perpetuate an ethos of violence.

TV, movies, and music mediate violence indirectly, but Redfield's 1880 study recognized how a more immediate kind of modeling might foster southern violence. It observed that "boys imitate their elders, arm themselves for self-defence or to resist so-called insults, and season themselves to deeds of violence" (160). Redfield's was a classic southern explanation. More than a century earlier, in *Notes on the State of Virginia* Jefferson outlined such a mimetic theory of violence when he noticed how the young were influenced by viewing cruelty toward slaves:

> Our children see this [mistreatment], and learn to imitate it; for man is an imitative animal. This quality is the germ of all education in him. From his cradle to his grave he is learning to do what he sees others do. . . . The parent storms, the child looks on, catches the lineaments of wrath, puts on the same airs in the circle of smaller slaves, gives a loose to his worst of passions, and thus nursed, educated, and daily exercised in tyranny, cannot but be stamped by it with odious peculiarities. The man must be a prodigy who can retain his manners and morals undepraved by such circumstances. (162)

Schooled in Aristotelian psychology to view humans as mimetic creatures, Jefferson wrote an almost Girardian analysis of how children duplicated the violent ideal of their slaveholding parents. Although all children in the Old South were expected to be aggressive in their play, boys, in particular, saw modeled in all of their male relatives that to be a man was to use a knife, a whip, and a gun. They were early encouraged to ride, hunt, and shoot, and they found ready opportunities to imitate adult violence in their mistreatment of African Americans. Slaves provided children with "a convenient scapegoat, a means to vent frustrations and test boundaries of acceptable conduct toward inferiors" (Wyatt-Brown 152). And the more that children viewed such violence as justified and rewarded, the more they were likely to view it as acceptable for imitation. Much as Jefferson recognized how pervasive and long lasting might be the effects of slavery, Charles Dickens lamented in *American Notes* that imitating the violence of slavery might go beyond any single act or moment to become the pattern for aggression in completely unrelated aspects of children's later lives (221). Since slavery allowed masters to give free reign to their passions, its example legitimatized the use of similar violence to control obstreperous wives, unruly children, and fractious citizens. A farmer who spoke to Frederick Law Olmsted during his travels in the South echoed Jefferson when he declared that slavery made the wealthy white owners "passionate and proud and ugly, and it made the poor people mean" (229). "Is it not partially the result of this," Olmsted wondered about such brutality, "that self-respect seldom seems to suggest to an angry man at the South that he should use anything like magnanimity? that he should be careful to secure fair play for his opponent in a quarrel?" (281).

Girard's work provides a radical answer to this question. Although Girard would agree that violence can be perpetuated by modeling, he explores the origin of such imitation by shifting the focus from the medium—violent mass media, violent parents, violent masters—to the phenomenon of mediation. He directs inquiry not just toward who might be the models but toward how the modeling works. He thus moves beyond sometimes simplistic theories about copycat violence to expose the dynamics that generate such doubling and aggression. What lies behind the imitation of southern violence is the violence of imitation itself, the mimetic struggle that joins subject, object, and mediator in the kind of bloody triangle that ended in the death of Norris Bendy.

The class-conscious South of Jefferson's slaveholders thrived on such imitation. As J. M. Huizinga explains in discussing medieval culture, mimesis is basic to the aristocracy, for the elite seek to achieve the ideals of hero and sage through the "imitation of an ideal past. The dream of past perfection ennobles life and its forms, fills them with beauty and fashions them anew as forms of art" (30). The culture of the planter, deeply feudal in spirit, was as derivative and nostalgic as Huizinga's Middle Ages. Its mimesis was not even inhibited by the fact that few of Virginia's original settlers could trace a direct bloodline to English nobility. Most planters, as W. J. Cash wrote in demythologizing the southern legend of manorial aristocracy, gained their status through industry and imitation. Once these enterprising families had amassed a fortune in the New World, they found a model for deportment in the smattering of gentry with a longer-established pedigree (7–8, 61–65). Later aristocrats imitated the imitators so that every white-columned plantation, every piece of family silver, every sir and servant took its repeated place in a tradition of simulacra. This mimetic lineage was such an accepted part of everyday life that Eudora Welty's Shelley Fairchild is astonished when she suddenly glimpses the genealogy of model and disciple in the early-twentieth-century South of *Delta Wedding*. Shelley recognizes the imitation behind planter culture after watching her future brother-in-law Troy Flavin shoot the finger of a black field hand who brandishes an ice pick at him. She reflects on how Troy has performed the role as if he were a natural-born overseer, even though this son of the hill country was hardly a native of the Delta: "Suppose a real Deltan, a planter, were no more real than that. Suppose a real Deltan only imitated another Deltan. Suppose the behavior of all *men* were actually no more than this—imitation of other men. But it had previously occurred to her that Troy was trying to imitate her father. (Suppose her *father* imitated . . . oh, not he!) Then all men could not know any too well what they were doing" (196). Behind Troy's violence is mimetic rivalry, and behind that imitation is yet still further imitation of the aristocratic code. Shelley's father is aptly named Battle Fairchild because he embodies the pugnacious ethic that Troy has copied right up to this bloody moment of conflict. Battle's daughter hardly wants to consider that her true-born Deltan sire might be just a facsimile and not the self-begotten source, the model of all mastery at Shellmound. She finds it more reassuring to deny the series of reflections upon reflections that undermines any notion of patriarchal originality. Shelley thinks her way backward from a moment of bloodshed to its origins in copying cultural prototypes, but she then goes beyond recognizing southern role-playing to a gasping intuition of universal mimesis that is just as unconscious as Girard claims. Although Shelley imagines that women "did know a *little* better" (196), Welty, like Katherine Anne Porter, explores how women can be caught, all unaware, in the same procession of southern doubles.

This dedication to miming the social as the personal was particularly strong among the aristocracy, but it established the model for desire in other groups.

"Negroes, 'poor whites,' and middle classes—all saw in the planter class the embodiment of what they themselves wished to be," Brearley observed (688; cf.
Cash 67, 113, 125, 266). Out of precisely such mimetic striving, Faulkner created
the titanic Thomas Sutpen in *Absalom, Absalom!* Barred from the front door of
a Virginia manor by a liveried slave, the hill-country boy reasons his way from
knee-jerk retaliation to the more studied violence of imitating the gentry. The
young outsider first considers shooting the master of the house as he swings in
his hammock. However, Sutpen concludes that just as he might fight rifles with
rifles, the most effective way of fighting the culture that excluded him was
mimesis: "But this aint a question of rifles. So to combat them you have got to
have what they have that made them do what he did. You got to have land and
niggers and a fine house to combat them with" (192). Ultimately, such mimetic
antagonism leads Sutpen to repeat the moment at the front door by excluding
his double and rival, his own son Charles Bon.

The South's traditional name for the mimesis that Sutpen disastrously pursues has been "honor." Bertram Wyatt-Brown and Edward Ayers have convinc-
ingly argued that southern violence originated in precisely such an obsession
with reputation among peers. Girard's work suggests that honor itself originated in mimesis. Whereas Puritanism and capitalism conferred upon the
northerner an innate sense of dignity, the southerner knew personal worth as
socially mediated (Ayers 19–25). The honor that was accorded through interpersonal relationships was a complex function of Girardian doubling. Since
honor meant that southerners beheld themselves as others beheld them, their
self-worth lived in the look of the other. Wyatt-Brown recognizes how honor
depended on such reflection when he describes it as "self-regarding in character. One's neighbors serve as mirrors that return the image of oneself" (15).
Honor made self-estimation into nothing but an imitation of how the southerner was esteemed by others. And since southerners desired such mimetic val-
idation, they copied the desires of the other so that they would regard themselves as especially well-favored in the looking glass of communal approval. The
result was that the community of honor was a network in which each member
was at once a model for everyone else and a disciple of everyone else.

When such honor was translated into ritualized action, it expressed itself as
the legendary manners of the South. Walker Percy aptly rendered the mimesis
behind such finely calibrated nuances of conduct when he described manners
as "a primary concern with an intercourse of gesture, a minuet of overture and
response. It is an economy of gesture which, in its accounting of debits and cred-

its, of generosity given and gratitude expected, of face and loss of face, is almost Oriental" (*Signposts* 335). Percy's formally balanced evocation of this balancing act enacts how manners depended on elaborate parallelism between complimentary images. Southerners had to match turn with counter-turn, partnering themselves to their counterparts in an elaborate dance of doubles. And if they did not reciprocate in society's ongoing call-and-response, if they did not demonstrate the requisite southern grace, the gauche offenders might be judged by those observant others as living in disgrace. When this counterview was internalized, as it was by the parvenu Sutpen before the manor door, it became shame, the negative double of honor. Shame is described by Girard as "the most mimetic of sentiments. To experience it I must look at myself through the eyes of whoever makes me feel ashamed. This requires intense imagination, which is the same as servile imitation" (*Scapegoat* 155). Dishonor was a mimetic construction, for it depended on the imitation of the other as the very precondition for selfhood.

Southerners who wanted to avoid such dishonor often sought out an equally mimetic alternative. They hoped that violence might deliver them from shame. Girard's work makes clear that as model and disciple increasingly grow to resemble and threaten each other, they may try to defend their honor as a way to deny the other's primacy and distinguish the self. That assault might provoke its own counterassault from the shamed rival, equally concerned with asserting difference to regain the imperiled deference. The classic enactment of such duality in the South was the duel. Duelists faced off because they could not accept the similarity that Preston Brooks acknowledged when he averted a duel with Milledge Luke in 1849 by declaring, "I regard you as a man of honor and courage and of course equal to myself" (qtd. in Stowe 32). When the schema of carefully regulated differences broke down, and one man of honor confronted his intolerable double in another man of honor, they might choose the duel as a way to combat shame and to reestablish the social divisions that had been undermined. Resorting to violence in order to contend that each was indeed more of a gentleman, the doubles only became copies of each other all the more. They gave challenge for offense, acceptance for challenge, and, finally, blast for blast.

In the contest for honor, violence was the ultimate signifier. Indeed, for Girard, it is the signifier of ultimacy because it marks the realm where the sacred is set apart. To do violence, then, was honorable for the southerner because it was to raise a fist toward the transcendent signifier. Whether the historical precedent for such aggression can be traced to feudalism, Celtic values, or an ancient Indo-European ethic (Brearley 685–86; McWhiney 146–70; Wyatt-Brown 33–34), the dynamic was the same: violence was the means to honor, and honor was defended by violence. Men proved their worth through displays of bravado and bravery, and they protected that reputation from insult and outrage through whatever bloodshed was necessary. The more the aggrieved antagonists sought to imitate the cultural ideal and copy their equally resentful rivals, the more violence and honor became bloodied doubles of each other.

Although this furious pursuit of distinction pervaded the South, it made the region's westernmost hinterlands into a locale legendary for violence. Amid such a wilderness, as the prosperous Clement Musgrove muses in Welty's *The Robber Bridegroom,* "murder is as soundless as a spout of blood, as regular and rhythmic as sleep" (143). Cash viewed the cutthroat frontier as the preeminent cause of southern violence because it seemed a paradigmatic place for mimetic striving and strife. The pioneer's need to compete in order to survive and succeed enabled the industrious backcountry man to tame the wilderness, work ever more acres, and at last become the yeoman farmer and planter. When the aftermath of the Civil War brought a second frontier to the South, the same brutal self-assertion enabled a new master class to emerge once again out of the postbellum desolation. Finally, captains of industry and commerce opened up a third frontier where opportunity awaited—to be seized by those who grabbed for the main chance (Cash 192–93). In all of these hard-scrabble locales, opportunist met opportunist, and each was swift in using force to prevail. Frontier aggression was generated by the same clash of doubles, the same quest for degree that motivated duels. Whether on the field of honor or in the backcountry, violence was a means of asserting difference between those who were too much alike.

Such violence might have seemed especially necessary on the southern borderland because frontiers are characterized by a lack of the carefully ordered distinctions that Girard imagines culture as creating after its foundation in surrogate victimage. These differences are originally as simple as "before" and "after" the primal murder or "inside" and "outside" the community of bloodshed, but they later become more complex, structuring society according to denominations and ever more subtle gradations within these denominations. However, on the frontier many of those oppositions that organize culture have not yet been created or have begun to break down. Cash's frontier is a precultural or postcultural zone in the way that it dispenses with the forms and hierarchies that define society for Girard after generative violence. "And here was no aristocracy," Cash writes of the first frontier, "nor any fully established distinction save that eternal one between man and man" (8–9). In this fluid, starkly egalitarian world one fiercely self-assertive pioneer met an equal—and so, a possible challenge—in another fiercely self-assertive pioneer. "But the essence of the frontier—any frontier—is competition," Cash explains. "And on this frontier it was competition of a particularly dismaying order—a tooth-and-claw struggle, complicated by wildcat finance and speculation" (12). When such clashes were carried to the extreme, opponents on the early frontier might resort to bloodshed to restore a tenuous sense of order. But the social and economic leveling of the Civil War and the later competition in business and industry meant that a similar lack of status and structure might threaten whatever divisions were erected.

Although the frontier provided a psychological landscape for mimetic conflict, such violence was not inevitable there. Growing up in south Texas, on the border between the United States and Mexico, Gloria Anzaldúa discovered that the breakdown and commingling of differences so typical of frontiers might lead to exploitation and violence or to the liberating possibilities of living in multiple worlds. As she writes in *Borderlands / La Frontera:*

> *Cuando vives en la frontera*
> people walk through you, the wind steals your voice
> you're a *burra, buey,* scapegoat,
> forerunner of a new race,
> half and half—both woman and man, neither—
> a new gender. (216)

If this zone of ambivalence can lead to being treated like a brute, like a donkey or an ox or even like that ultimate beast of burden, the surrogate victim, it can also make possible the creative resolution of divisions, the confluence that Anzaldúa hails as "*La conciencia de la mestiza*" (99). Violence resulted on the southern frontier only when dwellers in the borderland were uncomfortable with its tentativeness and instability, only when they needed to redefine such liminality through asserting distinctions.

When the need for such demarcation incited the struggles, brawls, and rough justice of the frontier, there was always the threat that the violence of mimesis would spread beyond any individual opponents and get reflected as the mimesis of violence. In this intermediate realm such runaway imitation might one day unsettle the cultural order. The frontier thus localized a destabilizing possibility that was feared throughout the South. Although duels tried to confine the spread of such desire to the original antagonists and restrict it even further by ritualizing the violence, private quarrels might rage beyond any of the cultural forms designed to contain them. Since the personal was elevated to the public in the Old South, a grievance between two gentlemen risked undermining an entire community. Small-scale strife, local resentments, and minor acts of retaliation had the potential to pool together and fuel further discord. The closeness of blood kindred in southern life meant that such mimetic desire might easily propagate itself at home and proliferate with the kind of rapidity that makes fire and disease into Girardian images for the spread of violence (*Violence* 29–31). Family members might rally to protect one of their own, and entire clans might oppose each other for generations (McWhiney 160–62). Twain recorded precisely such an ongoing circulation of reciprocal antagonism when the Grangerfords battled the Shepherdsons, their violent and honor-bound doubles, in *The Adventures of Huckleberry Finn*. Since frontier government often lacked the centralized control to enforce compliance with the law, such feuds bloodied the South between the Civil War and World War I. In southern Appalachia lingering rivalries between northern and southern partisans were intensified by political factionalism and the government's attempt to control the distribution of whiskey. In central Texas conflicts over race, land, politics, and the growing cattle industry exacerbated the same legacy from the Civil War (Montell 22; Brown 9–10, 251–60). The result: there were the dead, then more of the dead, and then still more. When Huck Finn was so sickened by the latest bloody round in the Grangerford-Shepherdson feud that he could not even relate all the details of the carnage, his silence told of how close a southern community might come to being engulfed and undone by violence.

VIOLENCE DISPLACED AND DENIED

Irascible gentlemen, scrappy frontiersmen, envious upstarts, overbearing slaveholders, discontented blacks, and anxious poor whites—all might foment or be mistaken for fomenting the kind of mimetic strife in the South that Girard regards as constantly challenging the ordered oppositions of culture. The solution to such violence is often violence itself. When a society is convulsed by discord, it may turn to collective persecution as a way of seeking stability around the object of its attack. At its most harmless, communal exclusion in the South might take the form of the charivari. Like Mardi Gras, like all forms of Bakhtin's carnival, the noisy serenade of the bride and groom on their wedding night reenacted the turmoil before surrogate victimage but in a folk ritual that kept the chaos from escaping its good-natured boundaries. Such festivals of misrule came closer to revealing the violence at their origins when they became a crowd's way of punishing those who had violated cultural standards. Administering its own crude justice, a band of regulators might turn to caterwauling, dunking, whipping, branding, or tar-and-feathering to chastise those guilty of abolitionism, drunkenness, sexual offenses, or crimes that the courts seemed to have punished too lightly. Sometimes vigilantes repeated the expulsion of the scapegoat from Leviticus in a rather literal fashion and drove the victim, like the tarred-and-feathered Duke and King in *Huckleberry Finn*, from town on a rail (Wyatt-Brown 440–53). Such ostracism temporarily united a disintegrating community, for its members directed their enmity toward a common enemy rather than toward each other.

Behind and beyond these exclusions was a more fundamental and systematic form of victimization. It was what provided the precedent for the lynching of Norris Bendy, what Jefferson identified as the very basis for violent modeling in the South—slavery. Unlike the primal victimization that founded culture, slavery was not a single inaugurating murder but an ongoing sacrificial institution in the South. Girard argues that sacrifice developed in culture as a ritualized repetition of the original victimization. Just as a disintegrating community on the verge of chaos once displaced its violence onto a single member, it later sought to preserve the hard-won peace by returning to that generative moment and reenacting the slaughter. In the earliest sacrifices a human was killed in place of the surrogate victim. However, as culture worked to restrict violence even further, an animal was killed in place of the human victim. Scapegoating shifted this sacrifice from the distancing reenactment of ritual to the immediate workings of life in society. Girard claims that communities in times of crisis may repeat the founding mechanism of culture and eliminate one of their own who is perceived as other. The surrogate victim must be similar enough to the community that as surrogate it can bear all the violence that members would direct at each other, yet it must be different enough that as victim it can bear this violence away without generating new reprisals (*Violence* 269–73). Africans and African Americans provided the South with all the candidates it needed for surrogate victimage. Slaves might live so closely to the white world that they were not just the field hands and domestic servants but confidantes, nursemaids, consorts, or half-siblings in the master's family. Yet they also represented a monstrous alterity in the lives of their white captors and owners, who engaged in a psychological form of scapegoating to justify the socioeconomic one. Masters created this radical otherness by projecting onto slaves everything that they rejected in themselves. So, they considered the intellects of their kitchen help and cotton pickers more dulled, their culture more primitive, and their bodies more animal-like than those of their owners (Matthews, *Religion* 171). Whites constructed a negative double in their imagination that could be eliminated in the plantation world outside it.

Slavery made African Americans live out a substitute for the murder that befell the surrogate victim. Indeed, since slaves were used as victims in primitive religions (Girard, *Violence* 270–71), the very practice of bondage might well have begun as a way to provide a ready supply of offerings for sacrifice. Slavery transferred the ritual murder from a single ceremonial minute to the entire course of a lifetime and thereby perpetuated what Orlando Patterson has rightly analyzed as "social death." It used not just physical assault—forced expatriation, whipping, stripping, torture, exclusion, and sexual exploitation—but cultural violence to execute its victims. Because masters controlled such symbolic activities as naming, dressing, speaking, and worshipping, they violated the very identities of slaves by severely limiting their self-interpretation in signs (Patterson, *Slavery and Social Death* 8–9). Just as the death of the innocent is always hidden, denied, or misrepresented by those responsible for the victimization, the violence of southern slavery was disguised by justifications that acquitted owners and accused those held in bondage. Apologists for the South concealed its violence by taking refuge in myths, the stories that cultures regularly tell, according to Girard, to disguise their founding act of victimization. They imagined pious and sentimental masters taking charge of those who were too childlike, weak willed, or benighted to care for themselves (Cash 81–83; Bruce 122). The mythographers of slavery buried victims in perverse and tender-hearted fictions that allowed the white order to flourish.

Slavery institutionalized such a definitive form of scapegoating that it might have seemed to have forestalled all the complications of imitative desire. It rendered the debased slave an object of non-desire, and it set aside violence as the sacred and exclusive preserve of the master class. However, this seemingly perfected form of victimization did not so much remove the snares of modeling as redefine them. Precisely because slaves were so devalued, masters were free to fashion them into the fantasized medium of their desire. Whites did not want to mimic a slave, to live as a slave lived or to have what a slave had, but they might desire to possess the slave of their imagination. Like Martin Colbert lusting for Nancy in the cherry tree in Cather's *Sapphira and the Slave Girl* or Scarlett O'Hara longing for Mammy at the end of Mitchell's *Gone with the Wind,* they might covet the black body as the mediator of erotic or infantile gratification. Masters also desired their slaves on an even more fundamental level. As Hegel understood, every lord's sense of identity and independence depends on the mediation of those who are disenfranchised and dependent. White masters needed black servants as their defining counterparts, as the hidden foundation of their aristocratic world. And just as desire bound master to slave, it also bound slave to master. The slave was supposed to desire *what* the master desired, but the denial of liberty and dignity might make the slave desire *as* the master desired— desire the same honor and power that the owners desired solely for themselves. Eugene Genovese recognizes precisely how this doubling of desire might lead to mimetic antagonism when he describes slavery as "the extreme form of the psychology of the oppressed." The disenfranchised "longs for acceptance by the other, perceived as the epitome of such superior qualities as beauty, goodness, virtue, and above all, power. But the inevitable inability of the lower classes, especially but not uniquely slave classes, to attain that acceptance generates disaffection, hatred, and violence" (597). The southern planter became an ideal and obstacle to those who were owned. The master-slave relationship thus radically redefined the model-disciple bond by playing out the claims and counterclaims of desire amid social and economic bondage.

Since violence may be not just the effect of mimesis but also its fiercely attractive cause, masters in the South always worried that slaves might carry out the consummate form of imitation. They might desire to become too much like their brutal overlords, resort to force, destroy all distinctions between owner and owned, and plunge society into something like the sacrificial crisis from which it once emerged. Although masters were horrified by the prospect of such a Dixie apocalypse, slave rebellions more often took place in the imaginations of uneasy whites than on the grounds of their plantations. Their fears of revolts were usually based on meager, specious evidence, as Wyatt-Brown argues, and fueled by social, political, and economic tensions. The result was that apprehensive owners displaced all of their anxieties onto the easily available black other and fantasized about outbreaks of rivalry in which slaves would not just copy but surpass the cruelty of their masters. In the ongoing cycle of imitative desire, the possibility of such violence provided the impetus for masters to justify further violence against their slaves. Troops might be mobilized, new supplies might be requested for the military, and the hysteria was frequently relieved by some climactic bloodshed that would later be given dubious legal sanction (Wyatt-Brown 406–25). Wyatt-Brown writes an almost Girardian analysis of the arrests, convictions, and executions that finally quelled the distraught community when he claims that the prosecution of alleged slave revolts was so compromised that it "must be seen as a religious more than a normal criminal process. By such means individual slaves, and sometimes whites affiliated with them, were made sacrifices to a sacred concept of white supremacy" (402–3). White reprisals for suspected black insurrections placed violence at the service of a racial cult that, like some primitive deity, demanded a blood offering. Such scapegoating suppressed any potential turmoil among whites as well as among blacks and fortified the status quo—at least until the cycle of instability, accusation, and retaliation began once again.

The victimization of slavery was so central to the South that it helped to support not just the plantation economy but the entire social order of the region. The culture of violence profited from the way that scapegoating allowed those who felt impotent and insignificant to find self-affirmation in the fact that someone else was even more devalued. Slavery thus upheld not just racism but sexism, economic inequality, and the class system in the South. It helped to keep the disenfranchised from rivalry with each other and with those more privileged because, as Olmsted observed, it made whites feel as if they were always superior to those who were in bondage (251; cf. Cash 39, 168). It minimized the differences based on wealth, gender, or social status that might lead to discontent and disturbances, for it united all ranks of society by polarizing them against the black other. Slavery thus replicated the way scapegoating founded all cultural order. Its exclusion of and violence toward a single victim established the signal difference in the South upon which other systems of difference were grounded.

After the Civil War slavery no longer provided the legalized victimization to structure southern society. The comfortable gradations and distinctions that had once governed relations between blacks and whites were officially undermined, if not actually eliminated. In particular, the African American male appeared less like the excluded other and more like an aspiring member to the once all-white world of power. The Freedmen's Bureau declared that the black man was the head of his household; by 1868 black men could vote, serve on juries, and hold public offices. Some even sought to gain a share of the land on which they worked, but most competed with whites for wage labor. Blacks were sometimes even preferred as farm help because landlords believed that the ex-slaves did more work, required less compensation, and were easier to manage than their white counterparts (Cason 20, Woodward 208). It seemed as if the former scapegoats could now realize the desires that were once the privilege of their masters.

White discomfort at the possibility of black doubles turned resentment into rage. The more African Americans gained in status, the more tenant farmers, sharecroppers, and mill workers who labored beside blacks feared anything that might further erode the dwindling differences between them. Miscegenation became the ultimate terror in such a destabilized society because it dissolved the prime distinction upon which white culture was based. It seemed like nothing but a sexualized form of violence. Displaced ever so slightly from their previous position in the social hierarchy, anxious whites in the postbellum South lived out a version of the shift from feudal to democratic society that Girard's *Deceit, Desire, and the Novel* (chapters 5 and 9) traces in nineteenth-century and early-twentieth-century continental fiction. Whereas the old order minimized conflict because its stratifications kept possible competitors apart, novelists like Stendhal and Proust showed how modern egalitarianism made such conflict more likely because citizens met on a more leveled field. In growing more like the white southerner under the law, the black man and woman came to be perceived as the would-be equal and rival. "Nigger, you think you're *white*, don't you?" the young Richard Wright was asked by a white co-worker in an optical factory, who was amazed that the African American youth wanted to learn about the trade of grinding lenses ("Ethics" 6). Confronted by what seemed like mimetic desire, the white South met threat with counterthreat. Girard claims that when sacrificial systems, like slavery, collapse, overt violence may actually increase because society no longer has a formalized way to displace its collective wrath (*Violence* 39–49). Since postbellum whites could not secure their position by relying on the old exclusion of slavery, they struck back against the would-be double as if in a reactionary mania to preserve whatever modicum of racial separation might yet be possible (Cash 168, 214–15). They sought to eliminate mimetic rivalry by legalized persecution. Jim Crow laws placated white laborers by defining the physical space of the African American more rigidly than even in the antebellum South

(Woodward, *Origins of the New South* 212). The rules about where blacks could eat, study, live, work, play, travel, and socialize once again founded cultural differences and discriminations by way of the ostracized victim. Like slavery beforehand, these restrictions kept in place not only blacks who were excluded but also lower-class whites who were newly satisfied that they were still a priv-ileged part of those who were included.

Although the scapegoating of slavery was replaced by the scapegoating of segregation, there was always the possibility that the surrogate form of communal killing might no longer displace the violence of the white community. Instead, the legislated oppression might devolve into actual murder. Resentful of the social and economic gains made by African Americans, whites made bloody victims out of those who seemingly aspired to the supremacy of their own incontestable position (Wyatt-Brown 453–54). Between 1889 and 1893 seven hundred victims were lynched in the South (Ayers 238), most of them blacks. James W. Messerschmidt identifies precisely the mimetic antagonism behind such lynchings when he writes that the most likely victim was the African American man who seemed to be "acting like a white man" ("Men Victimizing Men" 140), the upstart who dared to seek or even surpass the social, political, or economic status of the master race. Published just five years after Norris Bendy's death, Wright's *Uncle Tom's Children* portrayed the furious reprisals that African Americans might suffer for trespassing upon what the white world regarded as exclusively its own. When Norris Bendy allegedly struck Marvin Tollis, he might have seemed like just such a rivalrous double, turning imitation into violence and arrogating the power that the white world reserved for its own sacred use. The avengers who left Bendy's body at Old Sardis church reclaimed that fury for their own private cult. One account of a lynching glanced at how the mob partook of such holy violence by observing that "the wildest religious mania seizes the crowd, they surge to and fro, sing and raise the holy dance" (qtd. in Ayers 248). The ecstasy of the mob supports Orlando Patterson's claim that a number of these racial killings should be regarded as ritual murders. The holiday spirit of the lynching party, the brutality of the torture, the hush of the crowd at the time of death, the use of fire to torment, sanctify, and consume, and the feasting on the dead through the smell of charred flesh made the African American as much a sacrificial victim as any slave clubbed to death and then cannibalized by the pre-Columbian Tupinamba in Brazil (*Rituals of Blood* 185–202). Once again, the idol of the tribe—sacred violence—got its due.

Scapegoating might even transfer some of this divine mystique to the victim. Much as Girard notes that the communal outcast was celebrated as well as scorned, the African American accused of breaking the law might be assigned a similarly paradoxical status. The editor of the *Atlanta Constitution* feared that transgression already brought the offender a kind of divinity when he wrote in 1883, "The moment that a negro steals, robs, or commits some other crime, his person seems to become sacred in the eyes of his race, and he is harbored, protected and deified" (qtd. in Ayers 229). Indeed, the "bad black man" became a legendary figure in African American lore, for he had seized the bloody lordship that whites honored and reserved for themselves (Ayers 232–33). Since the postbellum culture of violence feared such imitation, it was determined to keep the sign of the transcendent under its own control. Yet if whites resorted to lynching to commandeer such brutal holiness for themselves alone, the effect was not always as unambiguous as the victimizers might have wished. In 1897 a spokeswoman for the Georgia Women's Federation worried that lynching might set the precedent for ongoing sacred violence, for "there is a glamour of martyrdom about it that makes of the criminal a hero to be patterned after by his kind" (qtd. in Ayers 248). Having been regarded as the cause of terrifying violence while alive, the surrogate victim became the magical restorer of order and meaning after death. The murderers found esprit de corps by gathering around its corpse. Sometimes they even saved the teeth and small bones of the slain as talismans or used the rope and larger bones to terrorize other African Americans into submission (Brearley 681).

Since violence and mimesis are Girardian doubles of each other, it was almost inevitable that one lynching would provide the model for other lynchings in the South. Twain understood how such mob justice proliferated. In "The United States of Lyncherdom" he described how even children know that "by a law of our make, communities as well as individuals are imitators, and that a much-talked-of lynching will infallibly produce other lynchings here and there and yonder, and that in time these will breed a mania, a fashion; a fashion which will spread wide and wider, year by year, covering state after state, as with an advancing disease" (586). In his vision of murder à la mode, Twain imagined the contagion of violent imitation that made the closing years of the nineteenth century, according to Edward Ayers, "the time of the most brutal mob violence in Southern, indeed American, history" (238). C. Vann Woodward reaches even further back in describing the South of the 1890s as "one of the most violent communities of comparable size in all Christendom" (159). Although most of the victims were African Americans, any who lived at the margins of the white community might be violated. In 1884 four Mormons were killed at Cane Creek, Tennessee, when a mob attacked a house where the Saints were holding Sunday morning services (Sessions 212–13). In 1891 eleven Italians were lynched at the parish prison after they had been acquitted of assassinating the New Orleans police chief (Nelli 62). In 1895 the Mexican Florentino Suaste, who was charged with murdering a rancher, was carried from his jail cell in Cotulla, hanged, and then shot repeatedly (De León 91). In 1915 Leo Frank, a northerner, an industrialist, and a Jew, was lynched outside Marietta, Georgia, for the murder of Mary Phagan (Dinnerstein 32). Catholics, whites who sympathized with blacks, union organizers branded as communists, and foreigners who supposedly would take away jobs and dilute bloodlines were all casualties of the way that the South defined itself against the other and then used violence to eliminate the detested difference (Cash 296–98).

Many southerners justified such lynching as exacting the retribution required by Old Testament morality (Ayers 247). They would have been appalled at Girard's contention that all lynchings are alike, "whether they take place in Palestine during the Roman Empire or in the American South after the Civil War" (Williams, "Anthropology of the Cross" 273–74). The execution of a rabble rouser outside Jerusalem nearly two thousand years ago would have seemed unrelated to stringing up the latest threat to southern culture. However, Girard believes that across countries and centuries the victim wears a similar face, much as Allen Tate implies in "The Swimmers." The speaker of that poem recalls how as a boy in 1911 Kentucky he heard a posse returning to town after it was too late to prevent the lynching of a black man. The band of a near-dozen were like the apostles who failed their teacher, "eleven same / Jesus-Christers unmembered and unmade, / Whose Corpse had died again in dirty shame" (*Collected Poems* 133). A body on a tree: from Calvary to Clinton, South Carolina, where Norris Bendy was left in the yard of Old Sardis church after being hanged, the primal scene of bloodshed has been staged again and again.

VIOLENCE DEIFIED

Why did that "Corpse" die so many shameful times? How can a region of the country that the narrator of Percy's *The Second Coming* calls "the most Christian part" of "the most Christian nation in the world" be so notorious for its violence? When Will Barrett drives down Church Street near the beginning of

Percy's novel, he glimpses from his car window a humorous assortment of signs pointing to the South's omnipresent Christendom:

> He passed the following churches, some on the left, some on the right: the Christian Church, Church of Christ, Church of God, Church of God in Christ, Church of Christ in God, Assembly of God, Bethel Baptist Church, Independent Presbyterian Church, United Methodist Church, and Immaculate Heart of Mary Roman Catholic Church.
>
> Two signs pointing down into the hollow read: African Methodist Episcopal Church, 4 blocks; Starlight Baptist Church, 8 blocks.
>
> One sign pointing up to a pine grove on the ridge read: St. John o' the Woods Episcopal Church, 6 blocks. (13)

Amid this wryly hypersectarian South, Will increasingly desires to imitate his father's suicide, as if no church could keep him from killing himself. This fictional son of Faulkner's Quentin Compson and surrogate for a depression-prone author whose own father had shot himself wants to make violence double back on itself and find its second in the sacred. The death-haunted Will tries to redefine the Parousia so that the Second Coming nearly becomes the culmination of a grandiose plan to victimize himself.

Will's desire to join violence and divinity is a perverse variation on the frequent failure of southern religion. Although the churches that Will notices should stand out as signs of contradiction in a century infatuated with death, southern Christianity often did little to oppose and sometimes much to promote the culture of victimization. Violence and religion have supported each other in the South because the region's Christianity was too much like Christendom at large: it never completely renounced the divine wrath that Girard views the Bible as exposing. In *Things Hidden since the Foundation of the World* Girard traces this demystification of the sacred, reinterpreting the psychological and anthropological insights of his earlier books by way of Jewish and Christian Scripture. He confronts a version of the problem that troubled Stark Young in *The Pavilion* when the novelist recalled living among some North Carolina hillfolk who read the Bible every day. Young wondered how the Hensons made sense of injunctions to offer the first-born animals to God, of David's complicity in the death of Bathsheba's husband, or of Jeremiah's prayer that his enemies be slaughtered like sheep. He concluded that they "must have gone through it all in a state of godly hypnotism; they must have read it spellbound and overlooked much of it; or they must have translated into some softness or oblivion of their own the brutal ruling of the Lord; they must rather have seen in the prophets the slowly developing conception of mercy and grace and fatherly love, and some final blessedness and wider application, of which in the outcome they were themselves so sweet and right a flowering" (176–77). Unlike the mesmerized Hensons, Girard does not overlook how traces of violence still hallow the biblical deity, but he would agree with Young's speculation about the way Scripture has revealed the God of nonviolence.[13] The founding stories of Judaism, like those of Cain and Abel, Esau and Jacob, or Joseph and his brothers, exposed the perils of violent reciprocity. Jewish law worked to eliminate such antagonism by stipulating prohibitions against what might lead to violence and penalties for those who violated others. And the prophets of Judaism denounced the preoccupation with sacrificial ritual, advocated for the rights of victims, and often found themselves, because of such protest and sympathy, the target of victimization.[14]

Girard views Jesus as culminating this long countertradition of decentering culture by disclosing its dedication to violence. Jesus modeled the most positive form of mimesis. The son re-presented the Father without ever positioning himself as the rival to God, without ever allowing desire to degenerate into envy and animosity. Instead, Jesus simply lived out his likeness to and harmony with divine love, and he invited his disciples to imitate his imitation. Jesus's teaching warned against mimetic antagonism, exposed the killings that have dominated history since Cain, exhorted followers to eschew violence, and advocated caring for the victim. Jesus's ministry to social and religious outcasts provided a model for how his followers should challenge the exclusiveness around which culture structures itself. Girard maintains that precisely because Jesus criticized the way that desire leads to violence and violence leads to a sacrificial cult, he became the victim of the very surrogate victimage mechanism that operates within the culture of killing. Jesus was caught in the familiar pattern of all against one: civil and religious authorities joined in desiring his death, crowds called for his execution, and close followers betrayed, denied, or abandoned him. The demythologizer of scapegoating was himself scapegoated.

Girard claims that the gospels took a radical stand by not sanctioning this violence. Unlike myths, which made the victim seem reprehensible and the murderers seem blameless, the gospels revealed the innocence of the slain and the collective guilt of his slayers. Although Jesus was accused of inciting violence, the gospels testified to how he preached the good tidings of nonviolence. Although Jesus was violated, the gospels recorded that he neither collaborated with his persecutors nor avenged himself with reciprocal violence. Rather, the gospels disclosed the murderous passion that masquerades as the sacred, for they showed how the Crucifixion resulted from human design, not from divine plan.[15] God was not simply a transcendent misnomer for the mimesis that was staged between rivalrous doubles, eventually displaced onto victims, and finally worshiped in cults. Girard proposes that in place of such deception, the cross revealed what was truly sacred. The son mediated a Father who loves rather than envies, forgives rather than retaliates, and invites nonviolent imitation rather than obstructs followers with his wrath.

Although a tradition that stretches from patristic literature to Karl Barth rightly emphasizes the nonviolence of God (Hunsinger 35), Jesus's revelation of the Father's love was too often forgotten by his followers. Girard maintains that historical Christianity never completely renounced the long-reigning cult of sacred violence. When Christians understood Jesus's death in sacrificial terms, they risked reinstating a furious godhead whose appetite for carnage was only appeased by the crucifixion of his son. When Christians longed for a world cleansed of their enemies, they looked forward to the triumph of this violent god, who would authorize a bloody campaign on earth. When Christians engaged in sectarian warfare, scapegoated the Jews, waged the Crusades, persecuted witches, and defended colonization as evangelization, they worshiped only their own rivalry and murders. Failing to imitate Jesus, Christians at times undermined the very revelation of Judaeo-Christianity and concealed their violence behind a religion that had been founded on nonviolence.

Some historians of the South have viewed the Christendom that Will Barrett sees everywhere proclaimed on Church Street as restraining the culture of violence. For example, Dickson Bruce argues that religion in the antebellum South controlled the passions that might have otherwise disturbed the order of the community (12–13). And Ted Ownby contends that evangelical culture in the postbellum South limited the rampant aggression in the culture of manhood. However, Christianity in the South did not always separate itself from the cult of victimization that Jesus critiqued. Edwin McNeill Poteat calls attention to a more disturbing side of the civilizing rule brought by religion when he notes that faith in the South "can, under violent stimulation, run all the way from personal hysterics to social madness, encompassing en route all the fine, sane, regulative, and elevating impulses of true religion" (251). As Will Barrett discovers in *The Second Coming*, southern religion, in part, was violent, and southern violence, to an extent, was religious.

The South demonstrated the legacy of sacred violence most clearly in the way it tended to reinforce rather than challenge the exclusions of white male society. Whereas the Puritan emphasis on moral obligation and communal life provided the impetus for religion in the North to question culture, the Anglicanism of early planters established a pattern for religion to corroborate culture. The governor of Virginia, for example, sought to rally his beleaguered settlement out of its crisis in 1610–11 by using martial law to impose the beliefs, rituals, and morality of the Church of England. Subsequent legislation throughout the seventeenth and eighteenth centuries promoted a state-sponsored religion as a way to advance social cohesion (Matthews, *Religion* 1–5). This church-state accord received no challenge even from an ethic that was quite contrary to the Bible's—the stoic strain in southern life. For a tight-lipped emphasis on dignity, as Walker Percy has argued, caused the stoic's moral code to be flawed by "its exclusively personal character and its consequent indifference to the social and political commonweal" (*Signposts* 332). Dwelling apart in a kingdom of inner virtue, the stoic was too removed from the world to appraise the accommodations between religion and culture. The result of these classical and Christian traditions was that church-state relations in the South were contradictory. Church and state were allied enough that Christians generally supported the cultural order; however, church and state were divorced enough that southerners viewed the church's concerns with the order of grace as distinct from the state's interests in the order of justice (Holifield 154). Hence, when churches did take positions concerning the everyday lives of their members, they typically upheld or never adequately undermined the status quo. If the mission of Christianity was to expose the culture of violence, southern Christianity failed because it was never sufficiently countercultural.

The evangelicalism that galvanized frontier believers in the Awakenings at first seemed as if it might disturb the rapprochement between southern religion and the culture of violence. If the First Great Awakening rejected the rationalism of Anglican churches, it also rejected the violence associated with the Anglican gentry. Baptists, for example, identified planters with hunts, duels, cockfights, and attacks on revivalist preachers, and they viewed themselves as called to radically different lives based on collaboration rather than competition (McLoughlin 92–93). Since evangelical churches emphasized that dignity depended not on the rank, wealth, and honor commonly connected with upper-class Episcopalians, they had the possibility of creating a faith that was free from the strife-filled pursuit of social distinction. To be worthy was to feel convicted of sin, to accept God's mercy and forgiveness in Jesus, and to live out sanctification by self-discipline and spreading the gospel. Such Baptist rituals as the holy kiss, love feast, and handshake of fellowship renounced the degrees of difference regarded as important in Anglican churches (Matthews, *Religion* 8–15, 26). Rather than practicing the exclusions of sacrificial cults, this more egalitarian religion seemed to rediscover the biblical spirit of inclusiveness by appealing to such outcasts as women, slaves, and members of the lower class. Evangelicalism offered all of these disenfranchised groups the affirmation, sense of community, and possibility for leadership normally denied them outside the church (Matthews, *Religion* 102–10, 192–99).

If evangelicalism never adequately realized the compassion for victims that its revolutionary origins might have promised, the reason was that it did not completely separate violence from the sacred. Sallie Lathrop of Alabama witnessed to this preference for a fierce lordship when she remembered how her father usually read the Old Testament every night: "The New Testament was too meek for him. Papa was a fighter" (qtd. in Ownby 105). Although Girard's work reveals the antisacrificial spirit of both testaments, the evangelical fondness for a supposedly militant Old Testament ignores this continuity in Scripture and champions a primitive God of wrath. Conversions to such a spirit-filled faith were founded on a violent theology. Sinners recognized that they were the proper victims of divine anger, but they accepted a substitute victim in the Jesus who bore their sufferings on the cross. Cash vividly evokes the ancient legacy of holy violence when he describes the religion of his prototypical frontier settlers as "a faith to draw men together in hordes, to terrify them with Apocalyptic rhetoric, to cast them into the pit, rescue them, and at last bring them shouting into the fold of Grace. A faith, not of liturgy and prayer book, but of primitive frenzy and blood sacrifice—often of fits and jerks and barks" (56). On the frontier, the evangelical God seemed like a transcendent version of the belligerent genius loci.[16] And when zeal for this lord turned into spiritual torpor, revivals were preached with a familiar fury. "American revivalism, with its endless Great Awakenings, is as recurrent a phenomenon as American violence," Harold Bloom writes. Speaking of the great August 1801 camp meeting in Kentucky, he claims, "Cane Ridge set the pattern of addiction in which Americans bear away the Kingdom of Heaven by violence" (*American Religion* 64).

Evangelicalism further confirmed the harmony between religion and the culture of violence by emphasizing the soul's private relationship with God rather than the Christian's responsibility for building the kingdom of God. Revivalist churches focused on the individual in the moment of conversion and in the life of sanctification that followed. When evangelicals imagined community, those bonds typically extended not to the world at large but to the fellow-saved, who provided models of good conduct and discipline to inspire everyone from the faithful to the faltering (Matthews, *Religion* 39–44). This dichotomy between the Christian and the world limited social activism on behalf of the victim, for evangelicals tended to be more preoccupied with their own spiritual welfare than with the physical well-being of the unconverted. The result was that, in Samuel Hill's formulation, southern Christianity came to emphasize ethos over ethics (3–7).[17] Southern revivalism never challenged society to profound and widespread reform because such alignment of the spiritual and political would "cut too deeply into the traditional fabric of the southern way of life. It threatened rather than consolidated communities; it promised violence when the function of religion was to curtail violence" (McLoughlin 136). Yet in seeking to "curtail violence," the upheaval that might come if churches undermined the social order, southern religion served as a bulwark for a culture founded on violence.

Southern churches fostered violence the most to the extent that they accepted the institutionalized sacrifice of slavery. Reynolds Price is blunt in criticizing white Protestant congregations as "the strongest pillars" of southern racism since the very moment captured Africans were first exiled to Jamestown (261). Religion and racism reinforced each other in the American South for the same reason that Christian churches, according to David Chidester, supported apartheid in South Africa (67–68). Since both whiteness and holiness may get defined around a sacred difference—an included group of the pure and an excluded group of the impure—the spiritual distinctions of the church member may easily become indistinguishable from the racial discriminations of the master class. Although southern Christians generally regarded slavery as an acceptable form of scapegoating, evangelicals at first questioned this collective persecution. Inspired by their belief in the confraternity of the saved and by the principles of the Revolution, southern preachers in the late eighteenth century spoke and wrote to condemn slavery. In 1784 Methodist ministers even pledged to excommunicate those who did not free their slaves in two years (Matthews, *Religion* 68–73). However, evangelicalism eventually compromised this biblical concern for the victim. It lamented the institution of slavery but did not denounce its sinfulness, and its reasons were both practical and fantastic. Some who were converted continued to own slaves. And most of the church members generally regarded such ownership as a necessary defense against the brutality of those who reputedly practiced cannibalism and human sacrifice in their native lands (Matthews, *Religion* 74–79, 171–77). Having projected their own violence onto slaves, whites accepted the bondage as a kind of oblation to keep such savagery from erupting at home. Southern evangelicals grew so comfortable with this violent alternative to violence that Methodists in 1844 and Baptists in 1845 divided from their northern counterparts over whether representative leaders—the Methodist bishop and Baptist missionary—could own slaves (Matthews, *Religion* 160–63; Eighmy 10–17).

To defend such victimization, southerners found specious biblical justification. They pointed to how the Ten Commandments did not condemn slavery but even seemed to accept it, and they cited how Paul sent the fugitive slave Onesimus back to his master (Matthews, *Religion* 158). Such interpretations ignored not just cultural context but the texts themselves. Paul, for example, insisted that Onesimus was not a slave but a brother and son (Philem. 1:10, 15–16) and developed in Galatians 4 a theology of adoption that metaphorically rejected slavery. Yet as even more farfetched explanations for slavery demonstrate, southerners were not looking to Scripture for guidance but for pretexts to sanction how a sacrificial cult had become a social institution. In the classic proof text, white Christians imagined blacks as the children of Cain or the accursed Canaan. According to Genesis 9, Noah was so angry after his son Ham beheld him naked that he cursed Ham's son Canaan, the mythical progenitor of the African peoples. "Black! He and his seed forever," Noah declares in "The First One," Zora Neale Hurston's dramatization of this story. "He shall serve his brothers and they shall rule over him" (85). Savvy to the deceptions of desire, Hurston's modern mystery play presents Ham as the scapegoat for his brothers' mimetic rivalry. Although Ham ultimately rejoices in his status as outcast, Hurston's subversive comedy could not be further from the earnestness with which white southerners read the sanctioned exclusion of blacks into this founding story. Genesis 9, as Thomas Virgil Peterson demonstrates, provided the central racial and political myth of the South, for it seemed to legitimatize and conjoin bondage and racism (123–38). Like all myths, according to Girard, it concealed how scapegoating makes culture possible. Just as Noah's curse attempted to reestablish order after the chaos of the Flood and the transgression of Ham, slavery founded a social and economic hierarchy by enacting this same sacred violence against Ham's supposed descendants in the South.

Although Christianity sometimes inspired masters to turn concern for the souls of slaves into better care for their bodies (Genovese 189–91), it did not advocate boldly enough for the black victim. Indeed, churches upheld such exploitation to the extent that they counseled accommodation, delayed all hope for a just world to the afterlife, and discouraged revolution (Genovese 283–84). Sometimes religion even perpetuated the victimization in its own ranks. White Christians might segregate slaves in churches that allowed mixed congregations, prohibit them completely from attending at worship, or restrict and monitor their services. Such discrimination made it clear that conversion affected a vertical change rather than a horizontal one; it left blacks saved but still enslaved. Much as evangelicals affirmed the worth of women yet insisted on wifely submission to husbands, they might support religious inclusiveness for slaves yet never question their basic belief in social exclusion.

Slavery profoundly challenged African Americans to come to terms with such sacred violence. Some found bondage an argument against God, and so they doubted or rejected the religion of those who oppressed them. Others joined violence and the sacred by believing that their owners would certainly be damned and by taking comfort in the biblical promise of apocalyptic vindication (Raboteau 290–93, 312–14). However, the triumph of African American Christianity was that even amid such victimization slaves refused to let religion become merely a tool for the oppressor or an anodyne for the oppressed. Blacks found new dignity and power through Christianity, for it provided the chance to assume positions of leadership as preachers, exhorters, and church overseers (Raboteau 152). They gained fresh hope, for churches held out the possibility of escape, amelioration, or heavenly reward. Finally, they recovered the biblical faith in behalf of the outcast that was often lost amid lordly white congregations. African American churches found a rare affirmation by identifying with the enslaved Hebrews in Egypt and with the persecuted Jews of the Exile. They took heart that the God of Judaeo-Christianity stood on the side of the victim. "God is no respecter of persons" (Acts 10:34) became one of the key texts of black religion, for it told how slave churches rejected the distinctions of race, class, and wealth that generated mimetic rivalry (Matthews, *Religion* 218–20). African Americans returned to the fundamental insight of the evangelical movement: they recognized that such invidious differences were as nothing to God, who valued all people apart from their standing in the social order. The testimony of an ex-slave that "the love of God is beyond understanding. It makes you love everybody" (qtd. in Genovese 255) witnesses to how black Christians might understand the antisacrificial message of the gospels more fully than did their white evangelizers.

As the issue of slavery intensified the South's conflict with the North, the regional cult of violence became more militant. Ministers viewed the war as a "baptism of blood" that would consecrate the South to its divine destiny. They ardently supported secession, served as chaplains, and preached revivals among the troops, especially as losses multiplied (Wilson 4–6). During the war God often seemed little more than the exaltation of sectional belligerence. Much as the Jehovah of the Union was invoked with wrathful imagery from Revelation, the Lord of Hosts in the South was imagined as leading Dixie into battle to smite the armies of the blue-shirted Antichrist (Wilson 63–65). Churches translated such grand analogies into very practical gestures in support of the war. To preserve the Promised Land, Baptist congregations, for example, sponsored days of prayer and fasting, sacrificed church bells so that they could be recast as cannons, and promoted the South's cause in church periodicals (Eighmy 24). Leonidas Polk, Episcopal bishop of Louisiana, even became a general and was killed in battle (Wilson 54–55).

After the supposedly Chosen People of the South were vanquished, the loss might have readily precipitated a crisis of faith. However, preachers justified the defeat in terms of the duality of sacred violence: whom God loved he punished. "Did He not suffer the first Chosen People to languish in captivity," chastened southerners might have wondered, "to bleed under the heel of Marduk and Ashur and Amon and Baal?" (Cash 132). Echoing Deuteronomic theology of the Old Testament, the Southern Baptist Convention claimed that the loss was a summons to repentance (Eighmy 25). Yet if postbellum ministers indicted the South for such sins of mimetic desire as greed and covetousness, offenses especially associated with a longing to imitate the mammonism of the North, they overlooked the victimization of slavery or, at best, lamented that owners had not properly provided for the bodies and souls of their servants (Wilson 68–69, 85–86). The South generally avoided more searching self-scrutiny in favor of trying to rally itself out of ruin by once again exploiting the paradox of the sacred. Since the region believed that the God who punished with violence would one day save his people with violence, it looked to a glorious future when the Lord would vindicate Dixie over the godless Yankees (Cash 132, Wilson 73–78). Until that deliverance came, the South would practice an aristocratic cult that looked to revive the venerable past. Bourbons sought to undo Reconstruction and restore Democratic-sponsored white supremacy in a campaign whose very name told how sacred violence pervaded southern culture. It was called "Redemption." And churchmen perpetuated this same bloody divinity by creating a theology, mythology, and set of rituals that Charles Reagan Wilson has chronicled as "the religion of the Lost Cause."

The postbellum cult of the antebellum South was founded on the deceptions of surrogate victimage. Appropriating the duality of the godhead, it portrayed the region as sacred in both its violence and its violation. Preachers created a Girardian myth that exalted bloodshed, exonerated the guilty, and obscured the true scapegoat. They glorified the war by depicting Confederate soldiers not just as the sons of Achilles, Arthur, and George Washington but as the successors to the Crusaders. Ministers praised the armies in gray as the epitome of moral and evangelical fervor, waging a holy war in behalf of faith, virtue, and freedom (Wilson 37–39). One such memorialist made the sacrificial mentality explicit when he compared the oblations of the wandering Israelites to the way devout Confederate soldiers offered God their souls when they might face death in battle the next day (Wilson 43). The generals were just as blessed. Clergymen repeatedly invoked Robert E. Lee as the saint of the Old South, Jefferson Davis as its near-martyr, and Stonewall Jackson as its warrior out of the Book of Judges (Wilson 48–52). 2 Timothy (2:3–4) might have portrayed the Christian as belonging to God's army, but the South after the war reimagined its army as belonging to God.

If the religion of the Lost Cause consecrated the violence of the South, it concealed the South's own victimization of African Americans by focusing on the South as a victim. Ministers imagined the North as a monster of chaos and carnage that ravaged the South, most heinously in Sherman's fiery march to the sea (Wilson 40). They sanctified the suffering homeland by comparing the Confederacy to such biblical victims as Isaac, Job, the three young men in the fiery furnace, and even Jesus (Wilson 44–45, 72). In particular, preachers described Lee as if he were the New Testament Man of Sorrows, and they remembered Davis, imprisoned in Fortress Monroe, as a scapegoat (Wilson 48–51). Building on this rhetoric, the South honored its victims of war through funeral statues, cemeteries, gravestones, and stained glass. By 1914 over one thousand monuments made material this cult of the dead (Wilson 29). All of these memorials marked the way that the religion of the Lost Cause, like all violent cults and cultures for Girard, was founded around a tomb. Since tombs commemorate but also conceal the dead, Girard claims that they make visible how societies try to keep invisible the violence in which they originated (*Things Hidden* 163–67). The funerary cult of the Civil War solemnized the valiant soldiers around whom the postwar culture of elegy and eulogy arose. However, this religion of whitewashed tombs, gleaming on the outside but inwardly full of ugliness (Matt. 23: 27), also hid the victimization that made it possible. It ignored the sufferings of slaves through remembering masters as paternal and saintly benefactors. It exacted new sacrifices through the lynchings that Orlando Patterson has described as rituals of atonement after the loss of the war (*Rituals of Blood* 215). And it covered the deceased champions of the Confederacy not just with earth but with a mystique of sentimental veneration. The South could thus be violent and victimized, the militant champion of a grand cause and the mournful celebrant of a cause that was lost.

While the religion of the Lost Cause enshrined the scapegoated South in a civil mythology, the South's institutionalized religion frequently abandoned the actual scapegoat. At its most shameful, postbellum Christianity collaborated with the victimization. Ministers did not merely join the Klan; they supported its racism from pulpit and platform, sometimes to the extent of letting their churches be used for Klan gatherings. The Klansmen, in turn, exploited the quasi-religious aspects of their terrorism. They commandeered the symbol of Christ the victim and set it ablaze with sacred violence to create their perverse ensign—the flaming cross. They relied on initiation rituals, liturgical white robes, conical or horned hats, and alleged magical powers to consecrate themselves with the ancient aura of the bloodthirsty divinity (Wyatt-Brown 454–58). Lynch mobs sometimes set fire to African American houses of worship and might choose churches, like Old Sardis, to serve as a hallowed background for collective killings (Patterson, *Rituals of Blood* 204–5). Donald G. Matthews has articulated how a violent theology of expiation provided the rationale behind such outrages ("Southern Rite"). If God demanded the death of his only son to atone for the sins of the world, then Christians might seem to have sanction for seeking such retributive justice from all who violated the law, from all who transgressed the coded distinctions for race, gender, and power. After all, as Gwendolyn Brooks recognizes in "The Chicago Defender Sends a Man to Little Rock," "The loveliest lynchee was our Lord" (89). Hang the Son of God on a cross, and any hanging becomes justifiable.

Southern Christians also betrayed the victim through less bloody sins. Their churches never allowed the social gospel movement to become as widespread or influential in their homeland as it was in the North (Roland 126–29; Hill 126–31). From the 1890s to the 1930s this form of Christianity in the streets dominated much of Protestantism, and churches rediscovered their role to proclaim a religion of the outcast. Such progressive faith sought to apply biblical ethics to problems associated with urbanization and industrialization. It put the victim at the center of its campaigns to promote workers' rights, to reform prisons, and to improve schools and health care (Eighmy 63). Southern churches were not indifferent to the social gospel, yet they devoted much of their activism to passing laws that enforced private morals (supporting prohibition, preserving the Sabbath, opposing gambling) rather than public morality. Most typical of this negligence was that churches did not oppose racism vigorously enough and were largely guilty of what Walker Percy has called "the Great Southern Sin of Silence" (*Signposts* 329), the omission common to all who conceal and tolerate scapegoating. When churches did raise their voices, they generally spoke out at the level of denominational leadership or association rather than in the pulpit or through the actions of individual church members (Bailey 43, 136–51); they proposed few specific plans that challenged the social and economic exploitation (Eighmy 95–104, 113). Since southern Christianity sought to promote interior righteousness rather than to right social injustices, it tended to avoid risky positions against sacred violence.

This lengthy tradition of fusing violence and religion found classic reformulation during the Southern Renascence in the work of John Crowe Ransom and Allen Tate. Ransom was disturbed that the tropes of sacred violence had been lost to what the title of his 1930 book called a "God without thunder." Like Girard, he recognized that Christianity worked to demystify the lord of awful vengeance, and like Girard, he connected the disappearance of that deity with the emergence of science. Ransom argued that Christianity deprived the Lord of his mystery when it turned Jesus into the Logos, "the Reason which governs the universe so far as the universe is amenable to science" (154). The result of this rationalization was that God became a kind of cosmic engineer, and humans were empowered to discover the principles behind creation for the betterment of humanity. But whereas Girard exposes the heavenly fulminations as the smokescreen for human violence, Ransom elegized the passing of this savage divinity and called for an alternative to the comprehensible and benevolent deity created by modern science and humanism. In its place, he honored his own supreme fiction, a Supreme Being imagined out of nostalgia for a mythical— read "violent"—past. Ransom's Jupiter Tonans ruled by whimsy rather than by design, brought evil as well as good according to no explicable plan, and desired the sheer wastefulness of sacrifice (27–52). Under such a reconsecration of violence, Ransom envisioned the South as living out the agrarian model that he found in the early chapters of Genesis—a humble, pastoral idyll, free of technology and history, utterly deluded about the human origins of the divinity that thunders.

Although Tate began as a disciple of Ransom, he developed a more complex position about religion and violence than his mentor's fondness for the trappings of a sacrificial cult. In "Remarks on the Southern Religion," his contribution to *I'll Take My Stand* (1930), he followed Ransom's example in criticizing the modern spirit of abstraction and in positing religion as the very opposite of such obsession with patterns and categories. Since Tate viewed his region and its religion as reaffirming each other in their cult of the concrete, he regarded both as being challenged by the prevailing spirit of science. Beleaguered by such threats, Tate wondered at the end of his essay, "How may the Southerner take hold of his Tradition?" "The answer is," Tate wrote in a clarion one-sentence paragraph, "by violence" (174). The southerner must take a radically reactionary stand "to re-establish a private, self-contained, and essentially spiritual life" (175). Although Tate hoped that his agrarianism might lead to such a goal, he conceded that any political solution is "so unrealistic and pretentious that [the southerner] cannot believe in it" (175). And he ended his essay with the recognition that it "remains to be seen" whether such a revolution would ever take place.

Whereas Ransom wrote *God without Thunder* with the confidence of a zealot, Tate complicates and qualifies his "Remarks on the Southern Religion" because he keeps meeting his own negative double on its pages. Tate the political theorist faces off with Tate the spiritual seeker, who shared the South's "true conviction that the ends of man require more for their realization than politics" (174). The Tate who discusses religion from the first words of his essay confronts the Tate who admits "any discussion of religion is a piece of violence, a betrayal of the religious essence undertaken for its own good, or for the good of those who live by it" (156). Tate was attracted to violence as a programmatic assault against the incursions of the modern world. He hoped that it might restore what was southern, what was religious—the two were virtually the same at their best—whatever resisted abstraction through being holistic, particular, sensate, or symbolic. Yet although Ransom would have agreed with his pupil's rejection of scientific transcendence, Tate could not commit himself to violence with the same certitude that made his one-time model embrace neoprimitivism. And although Tate was twenty years away from entering the Catholic Church, even in 1930 he shared none of Ransom's fondness for the bloody godhead of old. Fictional southerners often seem as if they have taken Tate's essay to heart; however, they have attempted to seize their Tradition without any of Tate's hesitation or politicized understanding of violence. In their immense desire for an idealized South, they have usually created a furious consecration of the self and left only victims in their wake.

DEMYSTIFYING VIOLENCE IN MODERN SOUTHERN FICTION

What Girard hailed as Faulkner's truth-telling about victimization is not limited to such novels as *Absalom, Absalom!, As I Lay Dying, Intruder in the Dust,* and *Light in August* but can be found in a whole tradition of works that manifest how desire, violence, and divinity have become intertwined—and sometimes interchangeable—in the South. This fiction does not just enact the culture of violence, observing its manners, chronicling its rituals, depicting its social hierarchies. Rather, it performs the countercultural task of exposing the desire that the South has made sacred. Such a complex awareness places twentieth-century southern fiction in a tradition that extends far beyond its period or place. Girard contends that whereas the romance records a world of mimetic desire, the tradition of the novel from Cervantes to Stendhal, Flaubert, Dostoevsky, and Proust has worked to reveal the perils of the model-disciple relationship. Romances reflect lives driven by imitation and frustrated by rivalry, but they do so from the inside without ever reflecting upon the portrayals. Novels are more cognizant of mimesis, for they do not simply copy desire and its deceits but critique them.[18]

The novels of the Old South and Lost Cause tend to be romances, for they create a dream world out of concealing the workings of mimetic desire. In the fictitious South that stretches from John Pendleton Kennedy to Thomas Nelson Page, *Don Quixote* has been both rewritten and unwritten. Whereas Girard regards Cervantes's work as a novel par excellence because it exposes the folly of chivalric imitation, of reading reality by literature, southern romance assumes that the courtly culture of Scott's *Ivanhoe* has been rightly and rightfully copied on the plantation. It endorses rather than uncovers mimetic desire. Since such fiction idealizes what Cervantes actually indicts, it provides a literary equivalent for what a speechmaker after the Civil War extolled as his region's "irrational devotion to lost causes which we call Quixotism; that infinite sympathy with failure; that tolerance of dreamers and visionaries" (qtd. in McWhiney and Jamieson 173). Written to perpetuate, defend, or recall the old order, romances offer quixotic models of desire for readers in need of a fantasy of the South. In such literature of apologia and nostalgia, duels are noble contests rather than rituals of rivalry, the southern belle is an original rather than an imitation, and slavery is a sentimentalized form of fatherly solicitude rather than a pretense for brutal victimization. Most importantly, the religion of romance upholds culture by concealing and consecrating the violence rather than criticizing it. Romances retell the myths of primitive and ancient religions but relocate the communal exclusion and cultural delusion downhome in the South.

If a whole school of nineteenth-century southern literature never separates itself from the portrayal of mimetic desire in order to question this furious reciprocity, a countertradition distinguished itself by revealing the dark side of Girardian interdividuality. For example, Poe depicts the self's feverish rivalry with the double, its reduction of women to bodies and then to corpses because they were no more than mediators of transcendent desire, and its destructive quest for the absolute through violence. Twain returns to what Girard regards as the very impetus of the novel by recovering the spirit of Cervantes in *Huckleberry Finn*. His antiromance ridicules Tom's increasingly dangerous imitations of the chivalric ideal, exposes how mimetic antagonism led to the violence between the Grangerfords and Shepherdsons, Boggs and Sherburn, as well as the Duke and the King, and discloses Jim's slavery as the victimization that society likes to keep secret. George Washington Cable in *The Grandissimes* and Charles W. Chesnutt in *The Conjure Woman* further undermine the plantation novel that Twain loathed by revealing the racial violence at its center. Kate Chopin in *Bayou Folk* and *A Night in Acadie* explores how oppression based on race is parallel to and sometimes entwined with exclusions based on gender. Whereas southern romances hide the victim to celebrate a mythic old order, these Girardian novels refuse to conspire with the culture of violence.

Fiction writers of the modern South make central this focus on the snares of mimesis, the pervasiveness of violence, and the misrepresentation of the sacred. Far from being entranced by the imitative desire of the Scott-inspired romances, they look askance at such infatuation, much like Tom More in Percy's *The Thanatos Syndrome* sadly and sardonically recalling "Sir Walter sending all these English-Americans to war against the Yankees as if they were the Catholic knights in *Ivanhoe* gone off to fight the infidel" (181). Exploring this novelistic critique of desire provides another way of understanding—and expanding—some of the frequently cited theories about the development of modern southern fiction. Allen Tate has explained the Southern Renascence as a "shift from melodramatic rhetoric to the dialectic of tragedy" (*Collected Essays* 568), and Lewis Simpson has reformulated this thesis by proposing that the Renascence arose from realizing "the dialectical quarrel between the truth of history and the deceptions of gnosis" (82). Girard's work might suggest that the Renascence resulted from taking a more critical perspective on the turmoil caused by mimesis. As the South moved further away from romance and closer to the novel, it enacted Tate's change from mythopoeic oratory to introspective analysis as well as Simpson's struggle between fantasy/forgetfulness and memory. Whereas the southern romance disseminates propaganda for a lovely realm outside time, suppressing critical self-reflection in favor of self-justification and self-delusion, the novel scrutinizes this ahistorical desire and exposes how the myth is founded on scapegoating in quotidian history.

If modern southern fiction reveals the victimization in and behind culture, focusing on the outcast may help to redress the marginalization that several recent critics have faulted in traditional accounts of southern literature. Mab Segrest in *My Mama's Dead Squirrel* (1985) criticizes the Agrarian-Fugitive-New Critical tradition of Ransom and Tate because it reinforced a racist and classist society by promoting an art detached from life and devoted to the past. In opposition, she outlines a suppressed tradition of lesbian writing that has more in common with slave narratives than with the dominant literature of white male masters (100–145). In *Inventing Southern Literature* (1998) Michael Kreyling tells of suddenly wondering how the southern literature that he had been teaching could "accommodate the murder and secret burial of Civil Rights activists, or a thousand other nonloving acts" that the Agrarian-based industry of southern literary studies typically excluded (xii). Richard Gray in *Southern Aberrations* (2000) detects another kind of omission when he observes how a canon based on Tate's definition of the Southern Renascence has overlooked women writers, proletariat writers, politically liberal writers, and writers of color (96–109). And in *Dirt and Desire* (2000) Patricia Yaeger faults southern writers and scholars for focusing too much on community, the past, a white patriarchy, and an epic understanding of race (34). Instead, she traces a history of southern women's writing in which the landscape is filled with throwaway bodies and the lives of its characters are marked by persistent misrecognitions.

Because these re-readings from the margins focus on what has been expelled from the literature of the South, they invite attention to the workings of the surrogate victimage mechanism in modern southern fiction. If a myth for Girard is the story of victimization from the self-justifying viewpoint of the victimizer, the canon and criticism of southern literature have at times been as mythical as the legend of Oedipus. They have taken the form of stories constructed by a powerful elite to justify eliminating, silencing, or forgetting what does not fit into the scholar's particular system. Yet if southern literature "has long been marked by its project of imposing boundaries and exclusions," as Susan Donaldson notes, it "has also been marked by the slippages, disruptions, and battles in literary texts inevitably resulting from the imposition of those boundaries" (493). Girard's theories suggest that southern fiction is powerfully realizing its goal when it focuses attention on all such rifts and expulsions. Reading his early *Deceit, Desire, and the Novel* by way of the later *The Scapegoat* makes clear the ultimate demystification of the novel. It exposes not just the hidden workings of desire but the founding violence to which desire may lead. Whereas this victimization dominates such narratives as myths, romances, and even literary canons precisely because they do not acknowledge it, the scapegoating loses its power when texts turn back upon themselves and confront the bloodshed at their source. Southern literature has been adept at uncovering such sites of violence and occlusion that have recently troubled some of its most perceptive critics. It locates the makeshift grave, digs up the buried body, and lifts into daylight the corpse.

In criticizing the violence of southern culture, southern fiction contains a warning for its critics. Since mimetic rivalry can rage among academics as much as between adversaries on the field of honor, each new interpretation of southern literature should be careful that it does not replace one set of exclusions with another. The root of "criticism" takes the task of "making judgments" back to its meaning in "cutting" or "separating." What a mimetic reading of southern literature teaches critics is that every "cut" is selective and leaves a portion overlooked. Hence, readers who would be on the cutting edge must take care that judgments—no matter how incisive—do not pretend to be comprehensive when they are actually based on severing some part of southern literature and creating a reading of what is left without it. And they must try to include, no matter how canonical or noncanonical, what their arguments most often drive them to exclude in the name of their well-wrought interpretation.

How do twentieth-century writers of the South tell a story that resists being told? How is a counternarrative written when desire is hidden by deceit, violence is dissimulated as the sacred, and victims get dumped in improvised graves? The desire to expose the scapegoating mechanism has provoked modern southern novelists to develop an aesthetic that rejects the idealization and obfuscation of romance. So, they do not write "novels of violence" in the sense that W. M. Frohock titled his study of such American fiction. Frohock imagined that the heroes of novels by Dos Passos, Hemingway, and Steinbeck as well as Caldwell, Faulkner, and Warren fulfilled themselves when they were virtually forced to resort to violence (6–10). Yet as much as the rivals, assailants, and murderers in modern southern fiction might like to justify their violence, the novels in which they wreak their havoc are hardly so fatalistic. Modern southern fiction astutely recognizes how desire, not destiny, may drive doubles to violence, how violence may culminate in victimization, and how victimization conceals a furious desire for the sacred. Louise Gossett began to formulate the artistic principles behind such a critique when she claimed in *Violence in Recent Southern Fiction* (1965) that contemporary authors wrote violence by distorting language, wrenching it toward extravagant expression, syntactic complexity, metaphor, symbol, dialect, and lyricism (199–200). However, southern writers go beyond such purely linguistic resources in making violence underwrite their fiction. They instinctively sense the truth of Girard's claim that "no matter how diligently language attempts to catch hold of it, the reality of the sacrificial crisis invariably slips through its grasp" (*Violence* 64). Language depends on systems of differences, yet violence causes these very structures to break down. Southern fiction "catches hold" of this elusive process of dissolution through the way it transforms and even deforms not just language but all fictional conventions.

The aesthetics of modern southern fiction mimics the violence that it exposes. The novel and short story get misshapen and reshaped much like what happens to art during what Victor Turner has called "liminal periods." Turner describes the creations from such critical times as tending toward the "grotesque because they are arrayed in terms of possible or fantasied rather than experienced combinations—thus a monster disguise may combine human, animal, and vegetable features in an 'unnatural' way, while the same features may be differently, but equally 'unnaturally' combined in a painting or described in a tale. In other words, in liminality people 'play' with the elements of the familiar and defamiliarize them. Novelty emerges from unprecedented combinations of familiar elements" (27). Turner claims that when artists create in this marginal zone, they rely on shock, surprise, satire, parody, burlesque, lampoon, and the blending of pop, high, and underground cultures (40, 41). Influenced by Turner, Girard has noted that the same kind of mutations are produced during the sacrificial crisis when violence breaks down differences. Since traditional patterns of representation have been undermined, peculiar variations may take shape during this fluid and uncertain era.

Modern southern novelists often cultivate the technique of the unusual and unfamiliar that Turner and Girard find typical of this unstable borderland.[19] They fashion a liminal art for the in-between time when violence disturbs and distorts the work of culture. These writers intensify action toward extremes to show how violence increasingly drives antagonists beyond the regular boundaries and into this transgressive zone. They create images that compel and repel to mimic the way violence draws eyes to look even as it drives them to look away. They tend toward what is shocking and surprising as a means of duplicating the sheer onslaught of violence on its victims. They make the body a site of anguish and assault to register how violence wounds no somatic abstraction but the palpable flesh. They conceive of characters in terms of doubling and opposition to trace how violence arises from mimetic rivalry. They employ the grotesque to reflect how violence disfigures the familiar and conjoins the contradictory. They expose the warped body to reverse the way violence is frequently disavowed and disguised. They rely on satire, burlesque, and parody to convey how violence inverts and subverts the established order. And they blend different strata of culture to portray how violence overrides the distinctions that once kept such levels separate. Walker Percy identifies the fierce impulse behind such aesthetics when he claims that during times of crisis "the greatest service a novelist can do his fellow man is to follow General Patton's injunction: Attack, attack, attack. Attack the fake in the name of the real" (*Signposts* 161). The techniques of modern southern fiction repudiate the denials, evasions, concealment, and mythology of romance so that readers can see how "the name of the real" is the victim.

The chapters that follow explore how four southern writers have imagined the dynamics of desire, violence, and divinity in their fiction. Each looks especially closely at one stage in the process by which mimesis starts, spreads, upsets the social order, and is finally expelled by counterviolence. All show how modern southern fiction may disclose that cycle of violence rather than simply depict it. Chapter 2 examines how mimetic desire attracts models and disciples even as it ensnares them in conflict. Chapter 3 traces how the resentment and animosity caused by mimetic desire may lead to violence. Chapter 4 argues that such violence at its most extreme can be traced back to a primitive conception of the deity. And the final chapter considers how a society may get beyond such sacred violence when it renounces scapegoating.

Katherine Anne Porter's "Miranda" stories are discussed first because they place mimetic desire in historical context: they focus on a young girl growing out of the imitative Old South and into womanhood against the background of the more confusing New South. Miranda's family seeks to take hold of southern tradition by a cultivation of the past that hides the casualties of the old order—from the victimized family slaves and servants to the partly self-victimized Aunt Amy. Much like modern southern fiction itself, Miranda matures to the extent that she lives out the critical spirit of the novel rather than living in the deceptions of romance. Although Porter's "Miranda" stories are not as obviously violent as the novels of O'Connor, McCarthy, and Percy, their focus on imitative desire exposes the fiercely pitched duality that leads to victimization in the works of these later writers.

In O'Connor's *The Violent Bear It Away* the mimetic antagonism that Miranda glimpsed among her relatives reaches a crisis as a family battles for the soul of the South. Like some disciple of John Crowe Ransom, old Mason rejects the modernism of his nephew Rayber and worships a God of thunder. Yet if Mason attempts to seize this tradition by violence, Rayber's liberalism is even more savage than his uncle's neo-orthodoxy. The schoolteacher dreads the love that his uncle desires in spite of himself. Torn between Mason and Rayber, the young Francis Marion Tarwater finally participates in the scapegoating that Miranda merely feared during the nightmare of her illness in "Pale Horse, Pale Rider." Tarwater becomes a victimizer and then a victim, and only after painfully knowing his ruthless idol in the flesh does he finally come to reject sacred violence.

McCarthy's *Child of God* imagines what happens when violence does not stop with one individual victim but threatens to bear almost everything away. Lester Ballard incarnates the possibilities of a bloody godhead that fascinate Tarwater but that the youth eventually renounces. McCarthy's serial killer stages a gruesome parody of Tate's summons to seize tradition by violence. Displaced from his family farm, he creates a ghastly pastoral order by hiding corpses in the Tennessee hillside, as if to localize a private South entombed in himself, his own sorrowful lost cause. When Ballard can find no redemption in his cult of one, he finally becomes a citizen of the cultural order that he terrorized. However, McCarthy inscribes the relationship between murderer and reader so disturbingly into the novel that even after Ballard dies in its last pages, this child of god lingers as if he were a god-child to all of those in the culture of violence.

Ballard escapes being a victim of mob fury, but Percy's *The Thanatos Syndrome* envisions a future when such scapegoating is once again being used to revive a Dixie as romanticized as the old order that Porter's Miranda rejects. As Dr. Tom More investigates a plague of mimesis, he comes to discover the violence in and behind the most baleful forms of imitation. The mission of More,

Percy's fictional alter ego, is the mission of the novel: exposing the exclusions that underwrite culture, opposing the sacrifices that make nothing truly sacred. Together, Porter, O'Connor, McCarthy, and Percy offer a mimetic overview of the South and a prospectus for its future. They explore the role of desire in southern culture, examine the antagonism and violence that erupt as a result of rivalry, disclose the scapegoating that frequently resolves such strife, and consider the possibility of a nonviolent rejection of violence. If there is to be a genuinely new South, it will be founded only when the culture does not seek new ways for hanged bodies to be left in churchyards.

"GIVEN ONLY ME FOR MODEL"

Porter's "Miranda" Stories and the Dilemmas of Mimetic Desire

Katherine Anne Porter wrote so intimately of the mimesis behind the southern culture of violence because she herself was the mistress of desire. Porter spent a lifetime in trying to live up to the models of southern womanhood that she at the same time rejected in her life and demythicized in her fiction. In "Old Mortality" she itemized with rigorous exactitude the features of the lady beautiful that nineteenth-century southern culture bequeathed her: dark hair, imposing stature, fair and fine skin, graceful movements, skill as a dancer and rider, and a sociability that was never improper. "Beautiful teeth and hands, of course," Porter's narrator continues the emblazonment, "and over and above all this, some mysterious crown of enchantment that attracted and held the heart" (*Collected Stories* [*CS*] 176). Porter's desire to imitate this ideal seized her in childhood, inspired her to romanticize her family's past, made her always anxious about her appearance in person or in photos, and ultimately turned her into a model of the belle as grande dame. She possessed such striking looks and posed with such grand drama that pictures of her by haute couture photographer George Plath Lynes added their glamour to the pages of *Vogue* and *Town and Country*. Through such glossy celebrations of high style the writer became an image of desire in the intensely imitative world of fashion.[1] Porter took comfort in this kind of idealization. The author à la mode felt so besieged by shutterbugs at a conference in 1939 that she lamented to Lynes, "My poor little female vanity has suffered perhaps fatal shocks, except that I am always able to remember what *you* can do, given only me for model. It sustains me, darling" (*Letters* 171).

As Porter aged elegantly into her role as the doyenne of American letters, her silvery coiffure, elbow-length gloves, and stately evening gowns sought to hold the hearts of all who heard her read. When this bewitching impersonation faltered, Porter might appear as the slightly comic, slightly grotesque lady author that Flannery O'Connor recalled from Porter's visit to Georgia in 1958. O'Connor had heard that Porter read well in Macon. Writing out of the plainness that O'Connor made a stylistic and spiritual virtue, she recounted, "They say she had on a black halter type dress sans back & long black gloves which interfered with her turning the pages. After each story, she made a kind of curtsy, which someone described as 'wobbly.' She's about sixty-five" (*Habit* 276). O'Connor hosted Porter the next day at her farm outside Milledgeville and found her quite congenial, although the older writer was so fascinated by O'Connor's peacocks that in her desire to see all of the birds she "plowed all over the yard" with her spiky shoes.

If Porter cultivated her deepest imitative desires even into old age, she was always a disciple in spite of herself. As Janis P. Stout has argued, Porter sought to define herself by conventional notions of femininity even as she defied them as an artist and intellectual. She became a wife five times over, yet she asserted that a woman could find fulfillment without marriage. She detested being called a "feminist," but she early voiced her support for suffrage and regularly associated with women who disregarded traditional restrictions on sexuality, social position, and professional ambition (*Katherine Anne Porter* 170–95). Although Porter insisted that women should not be confined by superficial standards, she cultivated the belle's magical sine qua non to attract not just numerous husbands and lovers but an admiring public. In the world of letters, she liked to appear, Don Graham writes, as "a sort of Scarlett O'Hara who was also a literary genius" (59).

Porter wrote her ambivalence about enacting southern womanhood into her fiction about Miranda Rhea, her quasi-autobiographical counterpart.[2] In the short story sequence "The Old Order" as well as in her two short novels, "Old Mortality" and "Pale Horse, Pale Rider," Miranda searches for and struggles with models who might help her define her relationship to the problematic old order of the South. Since that regime, like all culture, sought to keep a much-feared chaos from destabilizing society, it upheld the distinctions of the white male hierarchy by regarding women as among the excluded others. They were what men were not—alluring, submissive, nurturing—but they were what supported and supplemented men by their very difference. Miranda is attracted by the cultural model that validated one gender by subordinating another, yet she increasingly questions the models that she makes her own as well as modeling itself.[3]

Reading Porter by way of Girard also provides an opportunity to read Girard by way of Porter. The "Miranda" stories offer a chance to test whether

Girard's work is flawed by sexism, as has sometimes been charged. Although Eve Kosofsky Sedgwick makes the Girardian triangle of model, disciple, and object fundamental to her analysis in *Between Men: English Literature and Male Homosocial Desire*, she claims that Girard writes as if the triangle of desire were abstracted from the historical complexities of power and gender (22–23). And Toril Moi objects that Girard generally avoids discussing works by or about women, understands mimetic desire as "masculine," and cannot accept the way Freud's Oedipal theory recognizes women as an independent object of desire. Girard has largely focused on works written by men, but his critiques of Dante's Francesca (*Double Business* 1–8), Shakespeare's Helena and Hermia (*Theater* 40–49), Flaubert's Madame Bovary (*Deceit* 8, 10, 62–64), and Stendhal's Mathilde (*Deceit* 142, 154–56) indicate that mimetic desire is not exclusively a problem for men. Discussing Porter's "Miranda" stories may help to expand on these readings by demonstrating that triangular desire is deeply implicated in the role playing and ranking of what is masculine and feminine.

Miranda lacks the usual first model for a young girl in the old order, for her mother died shortly after childbirth. However, unlike Shakespeare's motherless Miranda who remembers no woman's face (III.1), Porter's Miranda was raised in a family that provided numerous examples of her sex. In fact, these women vividly model the young Miranda's very dilemma with modeling. Each of them—Sophia Jane, Nannie, and Aunt Eliza in "The Old Order," Amy and Eva in "Old Mortality"—anticipates Miranda's struggle between imitating the ideals of the old order and striving to get beyond the risks of such mimesis. In "Pale Horse, Pale Rider" an adult Miranda tries to resist the lure of imitation amid the jingoistic conformity of World War I America, but she finally succumbs to being like everyone else among the living dead. Only in "The Grave," when Miranda is at her oldest in these stories, does she escape from desire and death by becoming, like Porter herself, an artificer of memory. "It is a victory over metaphysical desire," Girard asserts, "that transforms a romantic writer into a true novelist" (*Deceit* 307). Much as Porter exposes the dangers of the southern romance tradition, Miranda comes to reject the perils of mimesis and to live in the clear-eyed world of the novel.

Miranda draws her models from a virtual social history of womanhood in the South. Spanning the nineteenth and early twentieth centuries, the "Miranda" stories almost dramatize the changing possibilities for the southern lady that Anne Firor Scott has chronicled as the move "from pedestal to politics." Although the lady might have been idealized as a belle, like Aunt Amy and Cousin

Miranda Gay, or later revered as the wife and mother who tended the domestic shrine, she typically spent her day in a much less exalted realm. Miranda's industrious grandmother Sophia Jane would have found her prototype in the chatelaines who were responsible for spinning, weaving, sewing, cleaning, gardening, cooking, raising poultry, caring for the sick, supervising slaves like Nannie, minding the children, and giving birth every year or so. The Civil War, in which Sophia Jane's husband was wounded, helped to free women from their traditional domestic roles by creating opportunities to manage plantations, run soldiers' aid societies, nurse the wounded, and administer hospitals. In the postbellum years the sheer absence of men, the weakened patriarchal structure, and the need for widows and wives of the injured to support their families meant that many women continued to run farms and estates as did Miranda's redoubtable grandmother, who became the matriarch in a family of largely feckless men. However, after the war, women increasingly left the land and made a living as teachers, journalists, office clerks, and factory workers. If Sophia Jane scorned this "'new' woman who was beginning to run wild, asking for the vote, leaving her home and going out in the world to earn her own living" (CS 333), much like the independent wife of her youngest son, it was a sign of how the once-pioneering grandmother had already become outdated by the early twentieth century. Missionary societies, temperance unions, and women's clubs helped to reinforce women's confidence in themselves and taught them the skills in organization that were finally directed toward achieving the suffrage that the formidable Cousin Eva sought.

"Where did southern girls growing up in the twenties find a model?" Scott asks, in what amounts to the central question for the "Miranda" stories (226). Although many women still followed the traditional role of homemaker, others explored modern opportunities, like Great Aunt Eliza, the scientist of the Gay family, or they found their models in "businesswomen, political activists, teachers and social workers, librarians and newspaperwomen, lawyers and doctors" (226). In "Pale Horse, Pale Rider" Miranda writes for a Colorado newspaper; however, her ultimate model is the journalist who became her creator, the artist of memory and desire, Porter herself. Although Porter admitted to being educated by James, Joyce, Yeats, Eliot, and Pound (Collected Essays 40), she cautioned against precisely the kind of discipleship in art that so preoccupies Miranda in life: "If a young artist must choose a master to admire and emulate, that choice should be made according to his own needs from the widest possible field and after a varied experience of study. By then perhaps he shall have seen the

folly of choosing a master" (*Collected Essays* 452).[4] Porter might have been coun-
seling the fictionalized self that she created in so many of her stories, for, like her
creator struggling under the anxiety of influence, Miranda must confront the
dangerous imperative of mimesis.

Porter's fiction about Miranda and her models illustrates Girard's belief that
novels record their writers' own struggles with imitative desire. Indeed, Girard
contends that the death and rebirth of the novel's hero retell the same earlier
crisis in the author, for only after the novelist renounces mimetic desire does the
novel that reveals its workings become possible. At the end of the novel, the
"hero" reaches the same point from which she or he was created in the author's
own life. Hence, every novelistic conclusion "is always a memory," Girard claims,
what Proust called a "past recaptured" (*Deceit* 297). Girard's connection between mimesis and remembrance helps to formulate anew what Lewis Simpson
terms the southern aesthetic of memory (67–71). For Porter did not so much
live and write as relive and rewrite. As she explained, "This constant exercise of
memory seems to be the chief occupation of my mind, and all my experience
seems to be simply memory, with continuity, marginal notes, constant revision
and comparison of one thing with another" (*Collected Essays* 449). Indeed,
memory is so formative for Porter's fiction that her "Miranda" stories demonstrate precisely the fragmentation, disconnection, and achronological organization that Estelle Jelinek has claimed as distinguishing women's autobiography
(17). Porter foregrounds recollection by making it the very form and activity of
her fiction. Porter, her narrators, her fictional double Miranda, and Miranda's
family are always remembering, and what these memoirists are recalling and
forgetting and concealing is the dilemma of desire. If Girard is right that novels
originate in the writers' Proustian recapturing of things past, memory generates
Porter's fiction by its salutary power of revelation. It discovers and recovers what
"The Grave," Porter's climactic "Miranda" story, reveals as always waiting to be
uncovered—how mimesis is hidden by denial and deceit. It thereby empowers
the novelist to turn the autobiography of desire into the critique of fiction.

As Porter explores her own and Miranda's contradictory attitudes toward
models for womanhood, she makes this focus on gender a way of investigating
the pervasive consequences of imitation throughout southern life. If these short
stories and short novels have something of the range and resonance of the much
lengthier works by Stendhal and Proust that Girard discusses in *Deceit, Desire,
and the Novel,* the reason is that they seem aware of every direction to which desire may lead—attraction, obsession, frustration, deception, antagonism, vic-

timization, delusion. They pursue these permutations of desire at dances and duels, during hunts and holidays, inside circus tents and cemeteries, across youth and old age, from legends to revisionist histories, amid honor-bound gentlemen and coquettish ladies, in the lives of slaves and their masters, with southerners at home and southerners in exile, throughout the Old South, the changing South, and the New South. Remembering her own struggle with mimesis and rewriting it as Miranda's, Porter's fiction recalls and reassesses an entire culture of desire.

Although O'Connor, McCarthy, and Percy make the connection between desire and sacred violence more central to their work, Porter provides the historical foundation for their critiques because she chronicles the role of modeling as the South shifts from the traditional order to the twentieth century. Her focus on the perils of imitation reveals the conflict between doubles that may later lead to bloodshed. However, such antagonism rarely erupts in Porter's "Miranda" stories, for it is played out below the surface of southern society and limited by the conventions of the old order. The forms and formalities of an older South restrict violence through manners, rituals, and the privileges of race, class, and gender. Yet if culture is still largely efficacious in these stories, Porter sensed the violence that made it all work, and in an unpublished story that seemed designed to be part of her "Miranda" cycle, she contemplated what might lie at the foundation of this world.

The various titles on the pages of this story—"The Man in the Tree," "The Southern Story," "The Never-Ending Wrong"—witness to how it might have exposed the recurrent victimization at the heart of the old order.[5] The story centers on the grandson of Nannie Bunton, who has been lynched for supposedly attacking a white woman. Maria (also called "Miranda" on one page) Gay is so disturbed by the killing that she feels as if she might have been responsible for the murder and fears that one day she too might be murdered. Porter was never able to bring the various drafts and fragments of this story into a final form, perhaps because she was not yet ready to face the full implications of the hanged man. The consummate craftswoman was still too much the daughter of the Old South, still too limited by some of the racial prejudices that make her fictional surrogate feel so guilty. The explicit violence in this lynching story points by contrast to how covert violence is in the published "Miranda" stories. Instead of being shaken to her very foundation, Miranda beholds occasionally disquieting glimpses of a hidden violence in "The Old Order" and "Old Mortality." And even when worldwide war explodes in "Pale Horse, Pale Rider," Porter locates the violence not so much on the battlefield as deeply sublimated in Miranda's psyche.

MODELS OF DESIRE IN "THE OLD ORDER"

In titling her group of short stories about the young Miranda "The Old Order," Porter not only names the dominant model for Miranda's life but also calls attention to the very role of imitation. Order is intrinsically mimetic. Having been "imitated" from observation of the regular movements of the heavens, as Freud thought, it is "a kind of compulsion to repeat which, when a regulation has been laid down once and for all, decides when, where and how a thing shall be done, so that in every similar circumstance one is spared hesitation and indecision" (*Civilization* 40). If order depends on copying the sanctioned models, the old order in which Miranda is raised intensifies the compelling power of that imitation by conferring upon it the preeminence of the past. This long-established mimesis seeks to make Miranda a disciple by having her order her life according to traditional conceptions of gender, class, and race. However, Miranda repeatedly challenges that venerable regulation through her "hesitation and indecision"—through seeking new models or even no models for her new order.

Although "The Source" was actually the last of the "Miranda" stories to be written, Porter placed it first in "The Old Order" to emphasize the primacy of its central character in Miranda's life. Sophia Jane, "the Grandmother," commands discipleship. She is so magisterial in this founding story of the sequence that Miranda is not even mentioned by name in it. Rather, the young devotee is absorbed into the three anonymous children who accompany the old lady on her annual summer trips from her house in town to her farm. When the Grandmother arrives in the country, her black servant does not even notice that Sophia Jane brings along other family members in her retinue, for all, including Miranda, dwell in her unremarkable background. Sophia Jane dominates "The Source"; she ordains, she organizes, she originates. Above all else, she orders.

Since the Grandmother is the ultimate model for Miranda, she becomes a model of ultimacy. Sophia Jane so forms Miranda's world that she mediates the divinity that makes models so sublimely attractive to their disciples. She becomes what Girard calls "the god with the human face" (*Deceit* 61), for behind her countenance is the divinity as the founder of cultural institutions. If the sacred for Girard is at once a force for order and disorder, Sophia Jane is most obviously an avatar of its beneficent and creative side. The radical meaning of her first name links her with the female personification of divine wisdom in Proverbs 8, who accompanies God in the work of creation. Religious language hallows the summertime visit of this spirit of re-creation. When Sophia Jane arrives at her farm, she calls out "greetings in her feast-day voice"; after she has supervised the cleaning of the main house, the kitchen becomes "a place of heavenly order where it was tempting to linger" (*CS* 322, 324). The divine Grandmother embodies as well some traces of the sacred as a force for disorder. She stirs up rocks and twigs when she walks in the orchards; she causes a "frenzy" and "uproar" in the unkempt huts of the black farmworkers (323). However, even this commotion is ultimately productive, for, like the violence in any ritual, it restores the cultural order. Sophia Jane is so much a force for this order that there is even an order to her orderings. "The Source" describes not a single visit to her farm but what Jane Krause DeMouy describes as the yearly cycle of renewal in which a goddess descends to the earth (121). The Grandmother corrects what is amiss in the homes of her tenants and her own family, repairs the outlying farm buildings, then rides her aged horse, walks among the fruit trees, and finally returns to town, where she begins her work of renewal once again— all in just that order every year.

The Grandmother's ordering is most obviously focused on house and farm, yet it extends far beyond the surface of home economics. Like Wisdom in Proverbs 8, she instructs her wayward offspring in the right way to act. Sophia Jane provides the stability and structure lacking in the lives of her motherless and virtually fatherless grandchildren. The children appropriately love her as "the only reality to them in a world that seemed otherwise without fixed authority or refuge" (*CS* 324). Indeed, Sophia Jane demonstrates such genius for shaping and rearranging that she exemplifies the aesthetic ordering that Miranda will finally achieve in "The Grave." Sophia Jane is the source not just of the nameless, faceless grandchildren in "The Source" but of the entire old order.

Although the Grandmother is the grand motherly figure in the life of Miranda and her siblings, she illustrates how the model-disciple relationship can easily degenerate into bondage. Sophia Jane demonstrates little regard for the followers whose imitation enables her to be the origin. Rather, the plantation mistress brings the Old South's hierarchy of power into the emerging New South of Miranda's girlhood, for she behaves like "a tireless, just and efficient slave driver of every creature on the place" (*CS* 324). Sophia Jane rules by force and fear. Although this imperious white woman takes pleasure in returning to "the black, rich soft land and the human beings living on it" (*CS* 322), she overmasters blackness at every opportunity. She begins her expulsion of dirt right in the huts of her African American dependents and then oversees their labors as she re-orders the rest of the property. She governs these black workers with an old-fashioned noblesse oblige that ameliorates their problems but never eliminates the racial inequality behind their litany of complaints. She governs her dirty grandchildren with such rigidity that "they felt that Grandmother was tyrant [*sic*], and they wished to be free of her" (*CS* 324). The little slaves of the family resent Sophia Jane so passionately because she exerts a domination that goes beyond the privilege of her age, race, and class—the thralldom of mimetic desire (*Deceit* 109–12). As Miranda grows older, she increasingly discovers the subjugation of consciousness to the old order that the children feel even in this first story. The youngsters are ensnared in the double bind of mimetic desire, for they want to imitate the attractive order that their Grandmother imposes, yet they resist that very order because it seems so authoritarian.

"The Journey," the second story in the sequence, complicates "The Source" because it shows how Sophia Jane became the sublime model only after a lifetime of frustration with being a disciple. In displacing Sophia Jane as the origin, it reveals that the Grandmother herself is nothing but an imitation. This paradigm of southern womanhood typifies Judith Butler's contention that "the action of gender requires a performance that is *repeated.* This repetition is at once a reenactment and reexperiencing of a set of meanings already socially established; and it is the mundane and ritualized form of their legitimation." However, precisely because such imitation expresses no attribute or perduring essence but depends on continued reenactment of these social codes, it can at any time fail or be distorted (*Gender Trouble* 140, 141). Sophia Jane copied a set of manners by which the South stylized the female body, but she also sought to violate these cultural expectations and transcend the way gender was performed in the old order. As a belle, wife, and mother in Kentucky, widow in Louisiana, and grandmother in Texas, the pioneer woman was constantly divided between the compulsion of mimetic desire and the challenge of other forms of desire— erotic, maternal, and feminist—that undermined her southern femininity. Sophia Jane once again dominates this story, but Miranda emerges slightly from the margins of "The Journey" because she now appears by name. Although the young Miranda, like the rest of her siblings, is made uneasy by the Grandmother's archaic ways, the child does not realize that Sophia Jane anticipated her own ambivalent journey. The Grandmother is actually Miranda's ancestral double in struggling with the models of southern womanhood.

Before her marriage the youthful Sophia Jane had tried to internalize the ideal for a young lady in the South. She appeared "gay and sweet and decorous," and she had earned the attention of a "mysteriously attractive young man," her second cousin (CS 335, 334). Sophia Jane modeled herself so completely after a culture that located female identity in her "virtue" that she developed a nightmarish obsession with the chastity required of her gender. The young woman repeatedly woke in terror from dreams about losing her virginity because it defined "her sole claim to regard, consideration, even to existence" (CS 335). In the world of secondhand desire, to be Sophia Jane was to imitate an ideal of intactness by which society gave her worth. Yet the southern maiden yearned for what she most feared, the license for carnal desire forbidden her as a belle but readily excused in her dissolute male cousin. So, she took Stephen, who looked so much like her that they were confused for brother and sister, as her model for a life in the flesh. Sophia Jane romanticized the licentiousness of her body double and longed for "the delicious, the free, the wonderful, the mysterious and terrible life of men" (CS 335). The disciple of desire concealed such transgression of gender by miming allegiance to the expectations of her culture. Whenever her parents happened to interrupt her erotic fantasies, Sophia Jane mouthed specially memorized lines of noble verse or broke into a sad song to hide her illicit yearnings. Since she could not imitate the sexual freedom of males, she copied the sentimental propriety of well-behaved females, as if gender were just a role to be performed for her audience.

Sophia Jane finally lived up to traditional feminine expectations by becoming a wife and mother, but she did not always act or think like a disciple of the old order. Since the mistress of the plantation household was supposed to shun anything too fleshly, she at first became accustomed to suppressing her milk so that her children could be suckled by Nannie, her black surrogate. But when Nannie almost died of fever, Sophia Jane violated the conventions for a woman of her class and race. She imitated her African American servant and breastfed with absolute impartiality not only her own child but also Nannie's as well. The nursing mother found in such new intimacy a tender sensuality that she had missed in her own marriage, and so she provided such nurture for her next seven children. As a wife and mother, Sophia Jane deferred to the right of her husband and sons to make financial decisions. However, she always knew that she managed the estate and household economy more shrewdly, and she came to hate the men in her family who squandered her dowry and hard-won fortune. Sophia Jane recognized and sometimes challenged the inequities of the old order, but she never rebelled against it completely. Instead, she increasingly suppressed her reservations until she finally grew into the grand model of devotion to duty and obeisance to authority. If southernness is a kind of religion, as Edgar T. Thompson has proposed, in which "society is God" (46), Sophia Jane became the high priestess of its old order.

At the beginning of "The Fig Tree," Miranda reveals how much Sophia Jane has actually become her own model for a southern woman's ways of knowing. The Grandmother's old order lives by the rigid and absolute distinctions that typify how culture seeks to prevent the violent confusion that once led to surrogate victimage. Miranda has become so acculturated that she regularly practices being a disciple in its cult of clear and certain differences. Whenever she found an animal that was not moving "or looked somehow different from the live ones," she buried the creature with flowers and a headstone. "Everything dead had to be treated this way," the narrator observes in a voice that echoes the model for the obligation: "'This way and no other!' Grandmother always said when she was laying down the law about all kinds of things. 'It must be done *this* way, and no other!'" (*CS* 354). Miranda would like all of life and death to be as well-defined and demarcated. However, if she has internalized and imitated her grandmother's dictatorial voice, she also keeps noticing what disturbs this attractive orderliness—the evasive language of adults, the confusion that her father causes by calling Sophia Jane "Mama" and "Mammy," even the failure to make a distinction on the part of that maven of degree, Sophia Jane herself. Miranda finds it "strange that Grandmother did not seem to notice the difference" between the greenish white figs at Cedar Grove and the sweet black ones at home.

Amid such disturbing indifferentiation, death offers Miranda a consoling certainty. "Dead meant gone away forever," she resolves. When a caterpillar did not move after being poked, "it was a sure sign" that it was dead (*CS* 354). Miranda desires to be so definitive about death and fig trees, but she becomes frightened lest the two have become the scene of the worst confusion. Having buried a chick, which she thought was dead, under the fig tree in town, Miranda fears from the cries of "weep, weep, weep" that she may have been grievously wrong. Whereas the dead and hidden body forever grounds the Girardian culture of violence, the weeping girl risks being ungrounded by the possibly live creature that she has buried. Miranda's tears over her failure at the fig tree, sometimes identified with the forbidden tree of knowing good and evil in Genesis, are at once naive and profound. They turn the title image of the story from being a site of epistemic certainty into the place where such ways of knowing originate, the grave of the ambivalent victim.

Although Miranda imitates Sophia Jane in her obsession with preserving difference, she also chafes under the gendered differences that the old order seeks to impose upon her. When the young girl is being prepared for the long ride to Cedar Grove at the beginning of "The Fig Tree," she squirms as Nannie tries to force her hair into a sun bonnet that will protect her face from freckling. Miranda is not interested in conforming to the ideal of the fair lady, even if the dead chick, "naked and sunburned," warns her about the toll for flouting such a standard for loveliness, even if Nannie's wrinkled black face, looking "like a fig upside down with a white ruffled cap," demonstrates how the girl's privileged position depends upon her white skin (CS 355, 358). Rather than wearing the old order's version of fig leaves, the rebellious child dresses her kittens in the outfits and wigs of her dolls, as if to play out how she will definitely not grow up to be a lovely plaything. Hence, when Miranda arrives at Cedar Grove, where the large, soft figs grow, she turns away from the models for womanhood in the old order and finds an exemplar of how to live in the new world of science.

Just as Nathanael became an apostle after a clairvoyant Jesus told of how he had seen his follower sitting under a fig tree (John 1:43–51), Miranda becomes the disciple of Great-Aunt Eliza, a scientific visionary who helps the girl to understand the fruit of the title. Although Eliza is herself a mother, Miranda loses under her tutelage the nascent maternal instinct that once made a little girl love to feed and pet baby animals on the farm. The woman-to-be senses other possibilities than the maternity that she had been bred to desire. Instead of playing mother, Miranda constantly follows her new model about and gazes at her, especially when Eliza violates Sophia Jane's standards for decorum by dipping snuff. Eliza returns gaze for gaze. Indeed, she models a new way of looking that does not give a fig for the conventional concerns about female appearance. Unlike the thin and still-pretty grandmother, the great-in-size great aunt never looked like a beauty. Eliza lives not to be looked at but to look at the world through her microscope and telescope.

Whereas Jesus promised apocalyptic visions to Nathanael, Eliza actually reveals the heavens to her new disciple. The aunt shares a glimpse of the moon with Miranda, who promptly lives up to the astonishment in the radical origins of her name. She exclaims as much at the night sky as at the brave, new shift in paradigms that her instructor has revealed, "Oh, it's like another world!" (CS 361). As Miranda walks home from the chicken house observatory, she behaves just like the Girardian disciple that "imitates constantly, on its knees before the mediator" (*Deceit* 298). The follower treats her mentor and model with proper deference by walking behind her. And Miranda shows just how much she has become like her aunt by repeating Eliza's answers to her own question about whether the unseen worlds were like her own: "Nobody knows, nobody knows" (*CS* 361). Unlike the old order that thrives on idealized certainties, Eliza testifies to the scientific agnosticism of the modern age. She proffers her disciple the fruits of what she does know about this earth. Eliza explains that the lament of "weep, weep," which Miranda heard after burying the chick, was not its cry from the grave but merely the call of frogs from the fig tree warning of rain. Eliza's contemporary faith seems to bring a new order to the world of differences that Miranda fears may be dissolving.

Although the contrast between the conservative Sophia Jane and modern Eliza at first frames "The Fig Tree" as a tale about opposing models, Porter understands the parallel desires behind such apparent dissimilarities. Eliza is actually the very double of Sophia Jane in her differences.[6] Both of these elders reduce modeling to the arrogance and authoritarianism that make them so much alike. Miranda notes how the sisters were "two old women, who were proud of being grandmothers, who spoke to children always as if they knew best about everything and children knew nothing, and they told children all day long to come here, go there, do this, do not do that, and they were always right and children never were except when they did anything they were told right away without a word" (*CS* 359). Because Sophia Jane and Eliza understand imitation as obedience to their orders, the pair are as similar as the two apparently distinctive fig trees in the story. The black sweet figs of the tree in town seem different from the greenish white ones at Cedar Grove, but the country orchard is, in fact, "much like the one in town" (*CS* 361). Just as each grove echoes with the cry of the grave, each sister models radically incomplete ways of responding to mortality. As Miranda will discover more fully in "Old Mortality," her grandmother's old order idealizes and sentimentalizes death. The tenderhearted Miranda copies this way of mourning by wanting flowers and gravestones for every dead creature that she finds. Eliza's clinical realism demystifies mortality. In "her most scientific voice" (*CS* 361), the great-aunt explains away the injunction to weep as a misinterpretation of the natural world. However, she never reinterprets the imagined cry in terms of the grief that haunts Miranda throughout all of Porter's stories—sorrow for the victim. Neither sister can model for Miranda how to mourn without being maudlin.

Since Eliza and Sophia Jane assert equally masterful claims to their competing orders, they become sovereign rivals. The measure of their similarity is that both clash over the pettiest opportunities to affirm their primacy and superiority. Even before the Grandmother meets her sister, she complains that Eliza, who has arrived at Cedar Grove first, will set up her telescope, appropriate Sophia Jane's horse, and ruin it by her careless way of riding. At the farm, the partners in resentment continue being the same by being so different. When Sophia Jane sees her sister directing how her telescope should be positioned on top of the chicken house, she warns Eliza about climbing ladders in her old age. The caution becomes a challenge to one-upmanship: Eliza moves a step higher and reasons that if Sophia Jane can traipse around on her horse, she can mount a ladder: "I'm three years younger than you, and *at your time of life* that makes all the difference!" Both flaunt their differences, but Miranda recognizes how these old ladies "were bickering like two little girls at school" or were like her and her sister in the way they provoked each other with small squabbles and ongoing harassments (*CS* 358, 359). Leaving behind the sibling rivalry of old age to walk by herself, young Miranda wants to be the one who is truly different from these childish adults. Although the impressionable girl eventually drifts back to discipleship under Eliza, she has begun to glimpse how her dilemma involves not just choosing a comforting model but living out the ambivalence of desire.

In "The Circus" Miranda finds all of the complications of mimesis staged as a chaotic spectacle. The story begins by continuing to explore the models for southern womanhood, but the wildness of the carnival exacerbates Miranda's dilemma so that it rises to a screaming pitch in which mimesis itself is placed under the limelight. The progression illustrates how Porter understands gender in terms of the dynamics of desire that culture puts on stage. Southern femininity depends upon imitation, upon a performance that may be as calculated as any act under the big top, but that very imitation may conceal a private spectacle more lurid than the public ever recognizes. Because the South constructs womanhood as supportive of and submissive to the old order, Sophia Jane clearly senses how the disorder of the circus may endanger her granddaughter. The conservatrix has not wanted to let Miranda come to the show and only conceded to the entreaties of others because the entertainment was part of a family reunion. The gathering of relatives erects a virtual bulwark against the confusion that Sophia Jane fears, for they spread across a curved row of circus seats, as if the family circle could keep at least the circumference of the old order intact.

At first, mimesis makes that center seem to hold in the circus. Whereas Sophia Jane had sometimes seemed an oppressive model for the ancient regime in "The Source," Miranda sees a more attractive model for the old order in the spirited and stylish Miranda Gay. The narrator observes that "Miranda hoped to be exactly like her when she grew up" (CS 343). Like the ring later in "The Grave" or Amy in "Old Mortality," this cousin mediates the aesthetic conception of womanhood that, according to John Berger (46–47), makes every lady a thing to be surveyed and appreciated. The belle's perfume, silk skirts, black curly hair, and coltish eyes have appropriately turned her into the object of attention for two rival suitors. Miranda Rhea is bound by name, blood, and desire to Miranda Gay. As mimeticism circulates between and then beyond the doubles, the young disciple at the circus waves to the cousin whom she hopes to imitate, and the older model not only returns the greeting but also provides the example for her pair of gentlemanly attendants to respond in kind. All of these redoubled courtesies act out the way this society finds stability in the manners that pay elaborate respect to mutuality. No distinction is unrecognized lest the slightest disregard violate the social order by implying that one partner is superior to the other. However, in the four scenes that follow, Miranda is scandalized by coming face-to-face with how such reciprocity may degenerate into nothing but lust and bloodlust.

What these equally polite ladies and gentlemen do not know is that an attraction below the stands provides a leering commentary on the attractiveness of Miranda Gay above them. Underneath the old order lurks the even older disorder of mimetic desire. When the young Miranda "peeped down" beneath the rows of banked seats, "she was astonished to see odd-looking, roughly dressed little boys peeping up from the dust below" (CS 344). Their ogling coarsens the way that every disciple looks up to a model, for it perverts reverence and regard into mere voyeurism. In becoming like her cousin and model who receives the attention of two males, Miranda becomes a titillating circus sideshow for two licentious boys. They are less interested in the romance of the silk skirts that a belle like Miranda Gay wears than in a reductive glance at what lies hidden underneath all of that clothing. If Miranda lives up to her name and lives to be admired like Miranda Gay, she may be no more than the object for the lustful eyes of childish men.

Although Miranda is amazed by the boys' furtive obsession, the model of female sexuality cannot turn away, for she has become a passive disciple of these budding anatomists. The triangle of children is joined in the double mediation of desire. Miranda and the two young peekers engage in a reciprocity of looking that crudely copies the public display of genteel appreciation she has just witnessed: "She looked squarely into the eyes of one, who returned her a look so peculiar she gazed and gazed, trying to understand it. It was a bold grinning stare without any kind of friendliness in it." After the smirky spy beckons to his companion, "the second little boy caught her eye. This was too much" (CS 344). The young Miranda twice glimpses the degraded sexual underside of the old order that Eva will fiercely expose in "Old Mortality." She finally frees herself from the mutuality of this hypnotic gaze by turning to Dicey. The servant girl suggests Miranda's complicity by warning her against "throwin' yo' legs around that way" and reminding her that there are more than enough monkeys in the circus "widout you studyin dat kind" (CS 344). To redirect such "monkey-see-monkey-do" mimicry, Dicey models the proper behavior for a demure lady. She closes her knees and gathers her skirts around her.

When the circus begins, Miranda finds that the young voyeurs have only given her a preview of the coming pageant of desire and deceit. Although the Grandmother cannot later deny being entertained by the circus, she complains with ladylike propriety that some of the show was "to say the least, not particularly edifying to the young" (CS 347). Her objection is understandable, for the pandemonium of the circus abolishes degrees and differences, especially the gendered ones that keep Miranda sitting with such decorum. Miranda feels its shock—somewhere between ecstasy and abjection—acutely. Much as the protective Sophia Jane retreats to the background of this story, the sensitive Miranda emerges to provide its point of view. Miranda witnesses how at the circus a seeming lack of order challenges the old order.

Like the festival (Girard, *Violence* 119–23), the circus is a cultural re-creation of the sacrificial crisis. The show restages the collapse of differences that once led to scapegoating as if it were a blurring of the boundaries between the animal and human worlds. Miranda watches goats that dance, monkeys that wear vests and ride ponies, and a lion tamer that puts his head in the mouth of the beast. At the beginning of the story, Miranda knows in her flesh this breakdown of difference, for she is invaded by a carnival of violent sensations—furious music, searing lights, riotous laughter. This crisis drives Porter's language and images into excited extremes as she conveys the tumult of Miranda's inner life: "She jumped, quivered, thrilled blindly and almost forgot to breathe as sound and color and smell rushed together and poured through her skin and hair and beat in her head and hands and feet and pit of her stomach" (CS 344). Porter's polysyndeton levels all subordination in a headlong stream of coalescing sensations. Miranda's perceptions fuse; her thrashing and throbbing duplicate the excitement of the arena. There is no longer any distinction between the genteel Miranda and the prodigious circus, for she has internalized its uproar. The sensory profusion and confusion as well as the melding of subjective and objective worlds make vivid the chaos that Miranda feels in the deterioration of her model-disciple relationships with others—first with the boys who eye her while they hide below and then with the circus performer above her from whom she finally hides her eyes.

The daredevil on the high wire makes a vocation out of exploiting mimetic desire. The skeleton-faced performer stimulates the crowd's desire for violence by the way he clowns with his double on the tightrope—death. However, if the mob depends on the entertainer to provoke its longings, the entertainer depends on the mob to confer his very worth by the way it looks up to him. The audience roars its approbation "with savage delight, shrieks of dreadful laughter like devils in delicious torment," and the performer copies the signs of fierce pleasure by blowing to these grotesque followers "sneering kisses from his cruel mouth" (*CS* 345). Like the high-wire artist, his admirers below are in love with hatred for the other. This barely suppressed sadism makes the circus crowd resemble the ferocious spectators who become Porter's own models in "Saint Augustine and the Bullfight," her essayistic account of discovering how much she relished the deadly duel between man and beast that she witnessed in Mexico. Both hippodrome and stadium restage sacrifice as if it were a blood sport. The acrobat's dance with death realizes the threat that Girard senses behind all performance when he writes of how Salome defied the laws of gravity in executing her macabre choreography: "If the dancer does not control the desires, the public immediately turns on her, there is no one else to become the sacrificial victim. Like a lion-tamer, the master of ritual unleashes monsters that will devour him unless he remains in control through constantly renewed efforts" (*Scapegoat* 135). High above the crowd, the aerialist must balance between pleasing his thrill-crazed audience and scorning their fiendish hunger for his death. The circus is the arena where the violence of desire turns into the desire for violence.

What makes this drama of desire and deceit particularly horrifying for Miranda, the would-be belle, is that, with his whitened face, reddened lips, and flouncy costumes, the androgynous high-wire artist is a grimly clownish version of the southern lady. The actor/actress precariously straddles the boundaries between male and female. If drag typifies how all gender is imitative (Butler, *Gender Trouble* 137–38), the dolled-up entertainer consummates the way in which the circus has been a showplace for performing womanhood in the old order. The clown puts a parody of Miranda Gay under the big top. For, as Miranda Rhea learns more fully in "Old Mortality," every belle walks the same tightrope, where a faux pas can be a deadly false step in trying to allure and secure her beau. Every coquette conducts just such prolonged flirtation with her audience as she repeatedly pretends to slip and then to save herself, each stumble titillating onlookers with the prospect of her "death," each rescue denying gratification for the sake of some future tease. Whether at the circus or in society, there is nothing but the sheer craft of her well-timed dalliance to keep the performer of gender from becoming a victim of the old order.

Miranda is appalled at the would-be violence of the entertainment. She cannot be like the rest of the spectators, who vicariously participate in the clown's high-wire pratfalls yet remain distanced from the possible terror of his balancing act. The girl feels with and for the performer rather than simply at second hand. Having been "astonished" to see her own audience of voyeurs, "Miranda shrieked too, with real pain" at the figure who wears a "perpetual bitter grimace of pain, astonishment, not smiling" (*CS* 345, 344). The callow Miranda does not understand that the circus ritualizes rather than actually repeats the hurly-burly of the sacrificial crisis, and so she becomes upset when the clown's risky antics seem to imitate too closely the crowd's desire for a victim. Miranda hides her eyes, screams, cries, and is told to leave. Dicey once again helps to reestablish the old order by obeying the orders of Miranda's father to take his daughter home.

Although Miranda is sent away from the circus, as if the scapegoat at the climax of some communal upheaval, her exclusion brings no return to order. The circus plays out its cruelty at home, for it is not a single site but a cultural moment, the gaudy show of violence that the old order repeats and represses. When the other youngsters later return, they pretend to commiserate with Dicey and Miranda, but they actually feel only indifference for the servant and wicked glee over their frightened cousin. Miranda tries that night to remember the circus as the place of animal antics and human derring-do, in the same way her cousins delightedly recall it. However, after she falls asleep, she wakes up screaming from a nightmare about falling. No different from her bad day, her bad dream exposes the terror that underlies the romanticization of the old order. The nighttime vision doubles back upon the garishly lit scene at the circus as Miranda imagines "the bitter terrified face of the man in blowsy white falling to his death—ah, the cruel joke!" (*CS* 347). Miranda understands nothing as sophisticated as the Girardian origin of culture in victimization, but she does intuit that behind the pretty masquerade of Miranda Gay and the whole old order is the face of violence and death. Miranda ends "The Circus" by living in a perpetual circus, the spectacle of model-disciple relationships at a crisis in the old order.

When Porter recalls in "Noon Wine: The Sources" the role of violence in her own childhood, she might almost be glossing Miranda's disturbing memories of the circus. The writer remembers growing up in "a civilized society, and yet, with the underlying, perpetual ominous presence of violence; violence potential that broke through the smooth surface almost without warning, or maybe just without warning to children, who learned later to know the signs" (*Collected Essays* 472). Porter translates this same menacing possibility into her "Miranda" stories. They record a "civilized society," as in the romantic courtesies at the beginning of "The Circus," but they also register what lurks beneath the formalities of time past. Violence just seems to erupt in Porter's fiction as if some alien disturbance from deep below the personal or cultural order. However, because her fiction is seen through the eye of memory rather than purely from the untutored perspective of the child, the violence is actually carefully anticipated and understood. Written out of what has been "learned later," Porter's narratives record all of the premonitory "signs" in the desires and doublings of interdividuality.

"The Grave" culminates "The Old Order" and anticipates both "Old Mortality" and "Pale Horse, Pale Rider" by depicting how mimetic desire may lead beyond the violence that Miranda feared at the big top. It gravitates ultimately toward death. Like "The Circus," "The Grave" climaxes in a quietly stunning glimpse of how the old order thrives on hidden victims. However, the story lacks the superficial gaiety of Miranda's holiday entertainment and proceeds more somberly toward a scene of consummate gravity. Miranda discovers how the downward pull on flesh, especially strong on female flesh, inexorably ends under ground.

The casual prelude to that revelation foregrounds the role of mimesis and mortality that will together darken and deepen into the story's grave within a grave. As nine-year-old Miranda and her brother Paul take time from hunting to explore an abandoned family cemetery, they become increasingly similar. Both lean their rifles against the surrounding fence, gaze "into the pits all shaped alike," and feel the same mixture of delight in their adventure and dissatisfaction at the sheer ordinariness of what they view (*CS* 362). Both Miranda and Paul discover treasures in an old grave and then compete unsuccessfully in a guessing game to learn what the other has found. Although the brother and sister are at first gratified by their unexpected riches, their pleasure quickly degenerates into a double form of acquisitive mimesis, the desire that leads "two or more individuals to converge on one and the same object with a view to appropriating it" (Girard, *Things Hidden* 26). The narrator observes how "Miranda was smitten at sight of the ring and wished to have it. Paul seemed more impressed by the dove" (*CS* 363). Each views the other as the mediator who possesses the object of desire; each wants what the other has discovered. Miranda and Paul quarrel briefly in a childish version of the antagonism that such double mediation often causes, but their squabble never puts them in risk of the grave, and they ultimately exchange their finds. Although Paul seems to claim victory by telling his sister only after the trade that the forfeited dove is a coffin screw head, its uniqueness no longer matters to her. "Miranda glanced at it without covetousness" (*CS* 363).

If mimetic desire first causes the siblings' convergence and conflict, it quickly makes them want to explore their differences as brother and sister, male and female. The object of desire mediates a new desire beyond itself. Miranda and Paul want to imitate not each other but the gendered identities that their culture has invested in the cherished talismans. The shock for Miranda—and Porter's readers—comes from the way these tokens from the grave inevitably but unexpectedly lead male and female back to the grave. Paul wants the dove that Miranda has found because he associates the coffin screw head with the traditional male ideal of singular achievement. Crying "I'll bet nobody else in the world has one like this!" (*CS* 363), Paul gains supremacy from exclusive possession of the mimetic ideal that distinguishes him from all possible rivals. Since the children had been looking for doves and rabbits, the screw confirms Paul's status as master of the hunt. After obtaining the silver dove, the twelve year old lives up to the cultural model by a boyish display of his might: he shoots a rabbit with his rifle, skins her with his phallic Bowie knife, and delicately penetrates her flesh all the way to the animal's womb. The man-child acts out the way masculinity in the old order often finds its expression in violence, especially in the victimization of his gendered opposite. Paul, possessor of the screw, can send females to the grave.

Ignorant of such violation, Miranda fantasizes about being a woman of the old order. She values the gold ring carved with flowers and leaves because it mediates the conventional female concern for self-presentation. Miranda had been accustomed to spending the summer roughing it in overalls, shirt, and sandals that made her look like the double of her brother. She had virtually become his disciple on the traditionally male hunt, following his footsteps on the trail and copying his example in using a rifle. However, the shining gold ring on Miranda's grimy thumb makes her long to be a thing of beauty. The tomboy wants to leave the hunt so that she might bathe, scent herself with talcum, and sit beneath the trees in her loveliest dress. Like Sophia Jane in "The Source," she seeks to banish the dirt that challenges categories and disrupts patterns (see Douglas 36–40) in favor of an uncomplicated female purity. This desire to imitate the customary model for southern femininity evokes a desire for the entire culture that supports such an image of womanhood. Although the fortune of Miranda's family has declined after the death of her grandmother, the girl feels "vague stirrings of desire for luxury and a grand way of living which could not take precise form in her imagination but were founded on family legend of past wealth and leisure" (CS 365). The would-be grande dame daydreams herself into becoming a disciple of the old order, but as Miranda discovers throughout Porter's stories, such romanticization only hides the way to the grave.

Just as the ring that inspired Miranda's reverie about the old South was found in a cemetery plot at the beginning of the story, another treasure is found in another grave toward the end. Living up to her name, Miranda watches "admiringly" as her brother skins the rabbit and reveals the tiny animals in its womb (CS 366). Miranda beholds in the pregnant animal an image of her own nascent sense of womanhood. "She understood a little of the secret, formless intuitions in her own mind and body, which had been clearing up, taking form, so gradually and so steadily she had not realized that she was learning what she had to know" (CS 336–37). Yet Miranda's growth in female consciousness is accompanied by an anguish that her earlier discovery of buried treasure lacked. Touching one of the wet fetal animals, the frightened girl gets baptized into a blood knowledge of her burgeoning sexual identity in society. This wisdom, unconscious and ineffable, is not just biological but cultural. Whereas the ring evoked latent fantasies of how to appear as a lady, the slain rabbit with offspring initiates her into how the female body is interpreted in the old order.

Like the hunted rabbit whose blood she touches, Miranda's flesh is the site of the bloodshed and mystification associated with scapegoating. Girard proposes that hunting originated in the communal need to find substitutes for the scapegoat so that the peace originally achieved through the primal victimization could be preserved through ritually slaughtering animals (Things Hidden 72–73). This sacrificial origin shadows the children's search in "The Grave."

Whereas Miranda and her brother are accustomed to bickering and competition during the hunt, she lets Paul shoot the creature "without dispute" (*CS* 365). Having been reconciled by the rabbit, they kneel before the slain animal, according to Cleanth Brooks, as if it were "a kind of bloody sacrifice" (118). Miranda is seized by a particularly feminine form of the identification that hunters have long felt for their prey (Burkert 20–21). The rabbit's bone, flesh, and blood may be like Paul's, but its capacity to bear life is like Miranda's alone. If the gold ring conjures up lovely constructions of gender under the old order, the dead and pregnant rabbit embodies the link between mortality and sexuality deeply hidden in this culture. Up to this moment, Miranda has understood neither the violence of the graves where she played nor the biological facts of the farm where she was raised. The dead rabbit with its unborn offspring introduces the girl to both of these mysteries in terms of her own body and of each other. The old order of maleness sacrifices women by the way it mistreats and misconstrues their flesh. It puts such a premium on virginity that Sophia Jane was tormented by the dream of losing "her sole claim to regard, consideration, even to existence" (*CS* 335). However, after marriage it then values a woman's body according to her rabbitlike ability to reproduce. The culture expects females to bear so many children—Sophia Jane had eleven, Nannie bore thirteen—that women may die as a result of childbirth (like Miranda's mother), and their babies may die in being born. And as Miranda learns later in "Old Mortality," when a woman is not pregnant, the culture fears her menstrual blood as if it were the fluid of deadly pollution. The culture of violence constructs a woman's body in terms of the grave.

With the rabbit's blood on her hand—if not also on her hands—Miranda rejects the scapegoating of women by rejecting the pelt even though in the past she had enjoyed having one made into a fur coat for her doll. Miranda's wiser blood wants no vestige of a culture that dolls up the women it will later victimize by the constraints of gender. Yet this knowledge of the sacrificial order is so disturbing to a daughter of the traditional South that Miranda cannot live out its exposure. Even her brother knows that he has transgressed upon forbidden realms. Because Paul's killing and dissection of the pregnant rabbit have brought him in touch with the primal forces of eros and thanatos, he has violated the taboos that Girard traces to a fear that violence will erupt again and hurl society into another crisis. So, just as culture obscures scapegoating by denial and displacement, the siblings bury their revelation of the bloody destiny of the female body in layers and levels of secrecy. Paul hides the fetal rabbits in the mother, the mother in the stripped skin, and the whole "bloody heap" of flesh and skin by some bushes (*CS* 367). Having been repeatedly told by her brother not to tell about their discovery, Miranda hides the epiphany still further in silence and oblivion. The children of the oldest order of them all conceal the violence that always lies just below the surface of the South's old order.

Although Miranda and her various models may be ambivalent about the old order, none of these women escapes the cultural pressure to imitate its conventions or the dangers inherent in imitation itself. The only woman who overcomes the risks of mimetic desire is the one who does not have the cultural status to be taken as a model, the human victim in a childhood filled with animal victims—Nannie Gay. Toni Morrison's claim that the Africanist presence in white American literature has too often been marginalized (3–17) points the way to understanding how integral is Nannie to Porter's stories. Whereas Porter writes Nannie into a crucial role in the sequence, Miranda writes her off. The little white girl is too much a child of her culture to see how the former slave, servant, and friend of Sophia Jane eventually overcomes the confinement of the old order. In "The Last Leaf" Miranda and her siblings deem Nannie a happy member of the family, for they have been "brought up in an out-of-date sentimental way of thinking" (*CS* 349). Only when Maria is older does Miranda's sister see through the myth of the postbellum South and realize that all of the children have allowed Nannie to work too hard and too much for the family.

If the children do not appreciate Nannie's labors, they understand even less about the history that resulted in her domestic servitude. In "The Witness" the children view slavery as having occurred in a fairy-tale-like "once upon a time" and as having ended when slaves advanced their lot by becoming servants. They are surprised that the bent and stiff Uncle Jimbilly was born a slave, and they innocently imagine that he has overcome his years of bondage quite well. Although the threesome are growing up near the turn of the century, they seem to know nothing of Jim Crow laws and the kind of lynch mob that Porter imagined in her unpublished "The Man in the Tree" or that killed Norris Bendy just two years before "The Witness" was published. Uncle Jimbilly initiates them into the violence hidden by their sanguine naiveté. The youngsters fret over getting a tombstone carved as a witness to the grave of a pet jackrabbit, but when they come to the elderly African American for his handiwork, he testifies to how thousands of slaves were beaten and burned or left to die in the swamps after being tortured. Uncle Jimbilly rightly make his young audience squirm with guilt, for the possibility of ritual sacrifice darkens the storybook history that Miranda has been used to hearing. He casts this specter over Miranda's future as well. Alluding to some new version of the slave uprising so often feared by whites in the nineteenth century, Uncle Jimbilly intimates that the powerful should be vigilant against some unspecified and unexpected calamity.

Although Jimbilly's stories may be heightened by his penchant for melodrama and the tall tale, "The Witness" brings the voice of the victim into Miranda's childhood. The story thereby becomes Porter's way of witnessing. She eventually chose "The Source" as the first story in "The Old Order," but "The Witness"—originally called "Uncle Jimbilly" and joined with "The Last Leaf" as "Two Plantation Portraits"—was actually published first, as if Porter knew from the inception of the sequence the real hidden foundation of Sophia Jane's world. Whereas the children romanticize African Americans in the old order, Porter does not allow Nannie to become just a jolly mammy or a stoic saint. Far from turning the slave and servant into mere southern decor, Porter gives her such a central role in "The Old Order" that the African American woman becomes a kind of twin to Sophia Jane. Indeed, Porter imagines Nannie so fully that she portrays how race always colors the black woman's mimetic bond with her white counterpart. "The Old Order" virtually enacts Morrison's reclamation of the Africanist presence in American literature, for Nannie grows from being a shadowy double of Sophia Jane to becoming a self-possessed woman who is finally more free than her white mistress.

In "The Journey" Porter makes Sophia Jane and Nannie so similar that their resemblances might almost seem more important than their differences.[7] Both suffered from the "burdensome rule" (CS 327) imposed upon women in a culture crafted by men. As Sophia Jane and Nannie are wont to recall the past, the two old-timers review how a master-slave bond grew into a more benevolent model-disciple relationship and finally approached a kind of kinship.[8] Sophia Jane first saw her lifelong companion as a "little monkey" of a plaything (CS 330) after her father brought the dark girl with spindly arms home from the auction block. But five years later the white child indicated how ambiguous her relationship had become with her black counterpart when she made their names— Jane and Nannie both having roots in the Hebrew word for "grace"—and approximate ages converge. Sophia Jane Gay inscribed her slave's name as Nannie Gay in the family Bible and gave the little black girl her own year of birth. The young mistress obviously wrote out of the prerogatives of ownership when she presumed to redefine the identity of a companion who was her coeval but not her co-equal. However, Sophia Jane also penned a quasi-sisterhood with her

slave that shocked her elders, who resented the implications behind such famil-
iarity. As the pair grew up, they grew even more alike. Sophia Jane and the slave
girl slept, played, and worked together; "they fought on almost equal terms." The
white child felt that she was so much the master and mediator for her black play-
mate that she defended her disciple "fiercely against any discipline but her own"
(CS 333). At seventeen, they married within days of each other and became still
more symmetrical. As doubles, even competitors, Sophia Jane and Nannie "then
started their grim and terrible race of procreation" (CS 334), Sophia Jane bearing eleven to Nannie's thirteen children. Nannie nursed Sophia Jane's babies until Sophia Jane, in a reversal of roles, took Nannie for a model and nurtured her
own newborn.

Nannie becomes so much the likeness of Sophia Jane that she becomes her
accomplice in preserving the old order. When the Grandmother goes to the
country in "The Source," she leaves Nannie in charge of the house in town. In
"The Fig Tree" Nannie tries to keep Miranda's complexion unspotted by the sun,
threatening even to tie the girl's bonnet to her hair so that she is as free of freck-
les as any of the South's fair ladies. In "The Last Leaf" Sophia Jane's grandchildren realize how much work Nannie has done to keep their house in order "simply by seeing how, almost immediately after she went, everything slackened, lost
tone, went off edge" (CS 350). Sophia Jane and Nannie spend their old age as virtual soul mates in "The Journey," both observing family life from the sidelines,
both longing for the past, lamenting the present, and excusing the other's
offspring for the very faults they condemn in their own, both piecing together
coverlets and patchworking memory to memory by the subtle, private code of
their talk.

Although the resemblances between Sophia Jane and Nannie create a veteran camaraderie, they also expose the way the old order oppresses all women,
especially those who are black. Mistress and servant may seem like doubles of
each other, but Porter knows that the community of gender in the postbellum
South cannot elide the distinctions of race. Race transforms their mimesis into
what Girard recognizes as external mediation, the bond between model and disciple who come from two forever segregated worlds (Deceit 9). Sophia Jane and
Nannie never live on the same social level, and so they never come into the kind
of conflict that sets Sophia Jane against Eliza. They share a lifetime of similarities, yet they do not become similar enough to become rivals, for color keeps
these near-twins from ever feeling as if they were sisters in the skin. Having "no
ideas at all as to her place in the world," Nannie "all her life obeyed the author-

ity nearest to her" (*CS* 328). From childhood Sophia Jane has always been ready to authorize such deference and differences. When the young mistress wrote "black" after Nannie's name in the family Bible, she inscribed the color line that would forever divide them. Years later, when Nannie is grieved upon meeting her first owner, who remembers once selling a "strip of crowbait" for twenty dollars (*CS* 332), Sophia Jane neither sympathizes with her companion's pain nor criticizes the wealthy judge's callousness. Too preoccupied with worries about her own family, the white matriarch dismisses the insensitive remark as merely the product of a thoughtless man's intoxication. Sophia Jane neglects the way a judge hurts Nannie on earth for the same reason that she imagines herself as Nannie's "sponsor" before the ultimate judge in heaven (*CS* 337). Nannie lacks the inherent worth of a white woman of property.

Although in "The Journey" neither mistress nor servant can escape her bondage to the old order, Nannie achieves a form of liberation in "The Last Leaf." Miranda is not even mentioned in this story, for she is just one of the children who provide Porter's narrator with an occasionally naive point of view. However, much as in "The Source," the relegation of Miranda to the background allows Porter to concentrate on a woman of superhuman strength who, in modest ways, overcomes the limitations that the old order places on race and gender. When Nannie moves away from Sophia Jane's family to live across the creek in a cabin that a black family has recently left, she moves beyond the whiteness that has kept her from finding her place in the world. Nannie's face now looks "like an eyeless mask" (*CS* 349) because she has assumed a new form of mimesis. She no longer shadows Sophia Jane as her dark, unequal double but instead has grown into the image of her very own origins: "But she was no more the faithful old servant Nannie, a freed slave: she was an aged Bantu woman of independent means, sitting on the steps, breathing the free air" (*CS* 349). So, her head is wrapped in a blue bandanna rather than her domestic mob-cap, and her eyes are suffused with an unfamiliar chocolate color. Nannie's masquerade does not dramatize the monstrosity that makes Girard view masks as expressing the confused and distorted face of the sacrificial crisis (*Violence* 166–68); rather, her new yet ancient persona makes visible Nannie's harmonious appropriation of her tribal past. As in rites of possession, she has identified with the other so completely that imitation turns into incarnation (Oughourlian 98–144). Nannie has made her own what the old order can only regard as foreign, and so at her end she embodies her beginnings in a purely nonviolent act of mimesis.

Just as Nannie has freed herself from the old order's white world, she has also liberated herself from its economic and sexual rule by men. She rejects Uncle Jimbilly's suggestion that after years of separation they live together once again as husband and wife. "I don' aim to pass my las' days waitin on no man. . . . I've served my time, I've done my do, and dat's all," she explains (*CS* 351). Sophia Jane was never able to voice such powerful self-determination as a challenge to her weak husbands and wrong-headed sons. Since Nannie and Jimbilly no longer regard their children or their memories as shared with each other, to resume the marriage would be to endorse its purely economic origins in slavery. Whereas Uncle Jimbilly is a tired and beaten handyman, Nannie has redefined her socioeconomic identity. It no longer comes from breeding more hands to work but from the artful work of her hands as she crafts the patchwork and braided rugs that attract a wide clientele to her home industry. Ready to die at the very beginning of the story, Nannie has already undergone the transforming death to the old order and mimetic desire that Miranda lives out in the coda to "The Grave."

DESIRE AND DEATH IN "OLD MORTALITY"

In "Old Mortality" Porter makes the grave central to her most incisive and sustained critique of mimetic desire. Her short novel continues exploring the models of southern womanhood that she has examined in "The Source," "The Journey," "The Fig Tree," and "The Grave," but it complicates this feminist critique with the recognition (first seen in "The Circus") that the model-disciple relationship may inherently lead to its own inversions and perversities. Porter shows that if characters do not die to desire, as does Nannie, they die from desire, as do Amy, Gabriel, Miss Honey, and Eva. She places Miranda at the edge of the grave throughout "Old Mortality," virtually pushes her into it in "Pale Horse, Pale Rider," and finally depicts her emergence at the conclusion of the "Miranda" stories, the last paragraph of "The Grave."

Models are so important in "Old Mortality" that it almost seems as if Miranda cannot be Miranda without one. Some of her exemplars are so outlandish that they patently point beyond themselves to what they mediate. As a little girl, Miranda wants to be a violin-playing tightrope walker. Such a fantastic profession will endow her with the glitter of the big top that her cousins cheerfully report in "The Circus" and with the glamour of the concert stage that her elders bring home with them after hearing Paderewski. When Miranda becomes a student at the Convent of the Child Jesus in New Orleans, she finds a new way to gain such notoriety through her equally juvenile fantasy about living in a nunnery. She takes as her model not the dull lives of the sisters who care for her but the lurid depictions of convents that she read the summer before in the novels of anti-Catholic propagandists. Imagining herself a long-suffering heroine from one of these feverish tales, the would-be masochist envisions herself "immured" in the cloister and secretly watched by vigilant nuns while she sleeps (CS 193). As Girard explains, masochists desire not persecution but the very being of their models who exhibit a divine autonomy by persecuting others. Students of thrilling suffering regard their agony as proving the exalted status of their wicked mediators, for these gods can be approached only through utter self-abnegation (*Deceit* 176–84). In fantasizing about the convent as prison, Miranda attests to the absolute transcendence of the tormentors that she hopes to imitate. However, when she tells some of the sisters about her plan to become a nun, they recognize the pride in her "expressed ambition" and wisely discourage her vocation (CS 194). Miranda only desires the frisson of her gothic romances as a delightfully debased preparation for her self-glorification.

Since Miranda recognizes that the convent lacks the piquant melodrama promised by her romantic fiction, she finds another form of the religious call in aspiring to be a jockey like "her idol, the great Tod Sloan" (CS 196). The cult of the racetrack promises the glory that the drab nunnery lacks and that the old order confers upon only its most favored members. Realizing that she will never resemble such tall, lovely beauties as Aunt Amy or Cousin Isabel, Miranda hopes to imitate the small and skillful jockeys. She dreams of secretly training to ride and of then surprising her family by winning a great race. While at the track, in Part II, she resolves to copy some day the serenity that jockeys evince amid victory or defeat. However, Miranda abandons her plan to become a disciple of the raceway after the novice discovers how she has again romanticized the latest model for her life. When she observes her uncle's mare just after it has unexpectedly won first place, she witnesses the violence that fascinated her in the fictional tales of convent life, now made brutally real for the highly feminized Miss Lucy. The red that streams from the nose of this beauty of a horse sickens Miranda. Like her baptism into the culture of violence in "The Grave," it reveals what she learns yet more forcefully in confronting the family memories about her belle of an aunt. The reveries of mimetic desire often hide a toll in blood.

Although Miranda's fantasies typify the way all children try on various roles in their quests for maturity, the modeling reflects a particular desire common to the South of her childhood. The old order desires to imitate, and what it imitates is the desire for transcendence that it idolizes and memorializes in its fabled mediators. Miranda discovers the most captivating models for her mimetic desire in this southern culture of memory. Memory, as Jean-Michel Oughour-lian maintains, is the temporal form of mimesis that complements imitation as the spatial form (6). It is instilled by imitation, and it makes further imitation possible. Because Miranda's family is so fond of retelling its own stories, it is constantly engaged in such mimesis, and that mimesis is inseparable from the family's desire. Miranda's relatives desire the past that they remember yet remember the past that they desire. Their memory does not undermine the culture of violence so much as perpetuate its example. This family tradition nurtures in Miranda and Maria the desire to imitate the present by mimicking the glorified past.

On her own Miranda knows little desire for this past. She finds the photograph of the legendary Aunt Amy not romantic but merely archaic. She deems the old clothes and odd mementos that her grandmother ritually displays twice a year not precious but faded, foolish, and old-fashioned. However, Miranda and Maria "were drawn and held by the mysterious love of the living, who remembered and cherished these dead. . . . [T]heir living memory enchanted the little girls" (*CS* 176). Whereas the sisters consign the past as past to the unattractive realm of old mortality, they are entranced by the immortality of the past as still present, as re-presented in the beloved remembrances of the elders. Since young Miranda and Maria feel that the recollections of their grown-up relatives make their own memories extend far back before their births, their mediated desire is itself mediated by their schooling in the legends of the old order. Miranda's desire is thus the product of multiple displacements. She and Maria desire what their elders desire, and what these older models desire is what their idealized Amy desired—or at least what they desired her to have desired. Hence, Miranda "believed for quite a while that she would one day be like Aunt Amy, not as she appeared in the photograph, but as she was remembered by those who had seen her" (*CS* 177).

The Rhea sisters do not lack models closer in time, but these exemplars are at once formed by the paragons of the past and found inadequate by discriminating elders in the present. The models that fill Miranda with awe during her girlhood are themselves modeled on the family tradition of the lively and lovely southern beauty. Although Maria recognizes that she and her younger sister will never reach such revered status, the willful Miranda—small, skinny, and sun spotted—hopes that "by some miracle she would grow into a tall, cream-colored brunette, like cousin Isabel; she decided always to wear a trailing white satin gown" (*CS* 176–77). When Miranda watches dashing Cousin Isabel easily mount and master her horse, her "heart would close with such a keen dart of admiration, envy, vicarious pride it was almost painful." Even the more commonsensical Maria cries out with desire "to be grown up" when she beholds young cousin Amy glide through the hall in rustling white taffeta on her way to a dance (*CS* 177).

However, just as Miranda's nostalgic seniors prefer Jenny Lind to the contemporary Nellie Melba, they devalue current models for femininity in favor of the family nonpareil from the past. The arbiters of gender believe that Amy of yore displayed more skill and grace than any of her modern counterparts. They regard mortality as having elevated Miranda's aunt even further in the empyrean of family lore, for she lives forever in the supernal realm of external mediation, where she can be imitated but never rivaled (see Girard, *Deceit* 9). Remembered as the untimely victim of consumption, Amy benefits from the kind of exaltation that scapegoats often receive after their deaths. Her sentimentalized demise makes the unequaled Amy into the unchallengeable ideal. In the cult of family life, the dead beauty plays the same role as the lost cause in the southern civil religion—the vanished but hallowed center around which survivors and subsequent generations organize themselves in mythic memory.

If Amy is the model for all to remember, she is also the ultimate example of modeling. The custodians of the family past mediate Amy, but Amy mediates the way a culture's image of womanhood was formed by mimetic desire. "The desire to please is undoubtedly the ruling passion of the female heart," Thomas R. Dew, professor and later president of William and Mary College, opined in 1835. "Women are precisely what men make them, all over the world" (qtd. in Scott 67). Amy's idealization in Miranda's family is largely based on her success at imitating such patriarchal desires. More astute about the compulsions of mimesis than her younger sister, Maria realizes that Amy's brothers "remembered her tenderly as a sensible girl" (*CS* 183) because she flattered their gentlemanly sensibilities.[9] Before she left for a dance, Amy would ask her brothers for comments on her appearance and would then change her dress or hair until she satisfied their critiques. They validated her because she validated them. The model woman made herself conform so completely to the image expected by the male culture that she might even have tried to stop her menstruation before going to one of these soirees. As Miranda learns, young women once believed that men could detect their monthly periods merely by a look or a touch of their hands. If Cousin Eva is correct, Amy sought to avoid such shame by drinking a nostrum of lemon juice and salt. In denying her own womanhood Amy would have conspired with the menstrual taboos that Girard views as a cultural way of victimizing women. He speculates that such prohibitions originated in a fear of the violence associated with blood and always possible in sexuality. Since these bans hide a male desire to make women responsible for all forms of disorder (Girard, *Violence* 33–36), Amy's willingness to suppress her menstruation might have made her an accomplice in the culture of scapegoating.[10] She could become the supreme model for southern women because she was also the supreme disciple of the sexist old order.

Amy needed the approval of her brothers and the admiration of her suitors in order to live out the particular form of imitative desire that Girard has described as coquetry. What honor was to the public sphere, coquetry was to the romantic—a kind of secondhand self-regard. In this vicious circle of desire and disdain, the beloved and lover serve as models for and disciples of each other. The coquette thrives on deferred affection, yet she seeks the very glances that she denies because they alone validate her sense of self.[11] "The favor she finds in her own eyes," Girard claims, "is based exclusively on the favor with which she is regarded by Others" (*Deceit* 105). The coquette identifies in every gaze and compliment the image that she imitates, the desire that she doubles. Such a mistress of mimesis is the inverted counterpart of her admirers, for she mirrors their dependency as independence, their obsession for her as absolute indifference to them. The lovely narcissist desires according to a crowd of others so that what she really desires is herself. To provoke such desire, the coquette refuses it, and refusing it, she only provokes that desire all the more. Stimulated by such denial, each suitor redoubles his attentions because he detects in his lady "that divine autonomy of which he feels he has been deprived and which he burns to acquire" (*Deceit* 106). The coquette's apparently sublime self-sufficiency makes her the obstacle to and model of his desire.

The culture of the South fostered Amy in precisely such coquetry. Raised to be a belle, she was at once empowered and constrained by the flirtation expected of her gender. Shirley Abbott notes how southern women found in the ambivalence of the coquette a rare form of authority (104–15). Although the southern lady might be oppressed and repressed by a male culture, she could master men in the realm of romance, compelling the affection that she also seemed to forestall. However, coquetry also limited a woman to conventional roles that gratified male needs. Since mimetic desire tends to make its models seem as gods (*Deceit* 53–82), the belle might at first be adored by her beguiled followers. Such lavish devotion gave her the affirmation that every coquette needed from her minions, but it also compromised her humanity and risked nurturing egotism and self-indulgence. Hence, in the 1834 *Southern Literary Messenger* "H." reproved "the hundreds and thousands of the gay, simple, fluttering insects dignified with the names of fashionable belles,—born and reared in the lap of luxury,—reposing in moral and intellectual sloth, and quaffing the delicious but fatal passion of adulation." And in 1836 Caroline Lee Hentz confided to her diary her anxiety about when her own daughter, "that innocent being, would become elated by vanity & (sic) learn to feed on the world's applause." She hoped in prayer that her daughter would be "shielded from a too ardent love of admiration—by the aegis of moral rectitude" (qtd. in Foxe-Genovese 209, 273–74). Although such veneration was a heady affirmation of the coquette as master and model, it was only a stage toward becoming dependent on males as a wife and mother.

As a southern belle, Amy took pleasure in the combination of mimetic desire and strategic deceit that typifies the coquette. Eva understands the way her kinswoman craved the gazes of others, for she judged Amy to be not so much beautiful but extravagantly conspicuous: "She always got herself up to be looked at, and so people looked, of course. She rode too hard, and she danced too freely, and she talked too much, and you'd have to be blind, deaf and dumb not to notice her" (*CS* 215). Although Eva's censure of Amy's coquetry resounds with bitterness over her own failure to be a coquette, she understands how Amy courted the attention of onlookers through an almost reckless extremism. The flagrant belle assured herself of such notoriety after a legendary Mardi Gras ball. Dressed in the provocative costume of a shepherdess that enraged her father, Amy ignored the devoted Gabriel, danced with a flock of men, cried out Raymond's name with pleasure as soon as he approached, and finally stepped out for a moment with this rival beau. After Miranda's father shot at Raymond and then escaped into Mexico, the feverish Amy rode for three days to bid her honor-obsessed brother farewell at the border. She returned exhausted but exalted. Whereas the photograph of Miranda's mother from the Mardi Gras celebration shows "her lovely face without a trace of coquetry" (*CS* 184), Amy behaved with a defiant flamboyance that would deliberately get her noticed.

Although Amy thrived on the regard of others, she seemed to show those others little regard, and so she thrived all the more. Every belle knows that deceit only exacerbates desire. Amy cultivated the askesis, what Girard defines as an indifference to desire for the sake of desire, that makes the coquette always appear as if she might live half of the time in a convent (*Deceit* 153–75). Sophia Jane spoke precisely of such paradoxical asceticism when she observed that "young girls found a hundred ways to deny they wished to be married, and a thousand more to test their power over men" (*CS* 183). Amy had mastered this calculated evasiveness. She frequently refused to explain herself, often left questions unanswered, and used "a tone of voice, which made it impossible to discover what she meant by what she said. It was possible always that she might be serious" (*CS* 182). Such verbal passive-aggression, as Janis P. Stout rightly argues, provides many of Porter's women a way of "asserting self-will in the face of a powerful and threatening male hegemony" (*Strategies* 145). But if Amy's elusive speech was a feminist tactic, it could also make her seem maddeningly coy when she trifled with men's hearts. Amy twice broke engagements with suitors "for no reason" and laughed at the elders who "thought it very capricious of her not to return the devotion of such a handsome and romantic young man as Gabriel" (*CS* 181).

Amy's blunt denials of Gabriel's affection merely made him desire her with greater ardor. But the more that he attended to her, the less Amy wanted his tender esteem. Girard explains that, rather than feeling valued, the coquette eventually comes to devalue the doting lover, relegating him "to the realm of the banal, the insipid, and the sordid where dwell objects who *let themselves be possessed*" (*Deceit* 107n.). Amy voiced this wearied disgust as she complained to her mother, "I'm sick of this world. I don't like anything in it. It's so *dull*. . . . Gabriel is dull, Mother—he sulks. . . . I could see him sulking every time I passed. It spoils things" (*CS* 188). Since a romantic like Amy judges only the distant, only the difficult and indifferent, as truly desirable, she tired of the faithful Gabriel as if he were too perfect a disciple. He allowed Amy to do all the work of interposing the fetching obstacle. When Amy finally accepted Gabriel's marriage proposal, she paid tribute to her own inconstancy by seeming to reverse the roles of capricious beloved and smitten swain. The soubrette urged Gabriel to get married at once so they could spend Mardi Gras in New Orleans: "'You might change your mind,' said Amy. 'You know how fickle you are'" (*CS* 191). Amy mimicked Gabriel's role as the ever-loyal suitor and reimagined the devoted Gabriel as a dandy, the male double of her own role as a southern belle. Such consummate deceit denied her many years of flirtatious denial and transformed her long-suffering disciple into the mock-model of her own mimetic desire. By casting the lovesick Gabriel in the part of coquette, the masterly Amy made the very most of being a coquette.

"And if I am to be the heroine of this novel, why shouldn't I make the most of it?" Amy wondered after her scandalous Mardi Gras ball and adventure to Mexico (CS 189). Whereas Girard argues that heroism in novels from Cervantes to Proust results from rejecting mimetic desire, Amy lived up to her metafictional awareness by embracing imitation. Much as Don Quixote or Dante's Paolo and Francesca found their mimetic models through reading about Amadis of Gaul or Lancelot and Guinevere (Deceit 1–3; Double Business 1–8), Amy consummated a pattern that had already been written by her culture and would be written again by her family. She foresaw how communal memory would collaborate with the literary tradition in which she was raised to re-create her. As Kathryn Lee Seidel notes, the literature that young women of the Old South were encouraged to read "fostered the preoccupation with beauty and fantasy that typify the belle's attitudes" (81). Male novelists after the Civil War intensified this ideal by mythologizing the belle as the image of a lost southern Eden (Seidel 127). Since Amy recognized that her kinfolk would turn her life into a work of fiction, she was determined to engage in her own grand self-invention even if along familiar southern lines. Amy was a character in the making who decided that she would at least be her own co-author. And that double consciousness virtually made her claim a place in the tradition of literary belles extending from Bel Tracy in John Pendleton Kennedy's Swallow Barn (1832) to Scarlett O'Hara in Margaret Mitchell's Gone with the Wind, the number-one bestseller in 1937 when "Old Mortality" was published (Seidel 53). While the beguiling heroines of these novels contended with romance, marriage, and usually motherhood, they continually demonstrated the same combination of desire and denial that characterized Amy. If such fiction circumscribed female readers with its cultural expectations for women, it also gave Porter's belle literary license to carry to the utmost her role as heroine of her life's story.

After Amy succumbed to old mortality, her relatives completed the process of modeling her life on literature. Her legend seemed "such a story as one found in old books: unworldly books, but true" like the works of Dante, Spenser, Shakespeare, and Poe. Gabriel's epitaph for his wife finalized her fictional destiny by immortalizing her as "A singing angel, [who] forgets / The griefs of old mortality" (CS 178, 181). The tribute appropriately alludes to the author whose fiction provided a model for the family's memorialization of Amy and inspired such widespread mimetic desire in the Old South. Old Mortality, the title character of Sir Walter Scott's 1816 novel, recalled the past so vividly that he almost seemed the contemporary of those slaughtered Covenanters whose dilapidated gravestones he spent a lifetime in repairing. Likewise cherishing their dead, the Rheas inscribed Amy in family idylls, as if her story were another volume out of the immensely influential Scott. Her tale of old combined the chivalric view of gender and class in *Ivanhoe* with the melancholy regard for a vanished but idealized age in *Old Mortality*. But the modeling inspired by one of the nineteenth-century South's favorite authors had pernicious consequences for Amy as well as for her culture. "The damn war stretched / from *Ivanhoe* to *Old Mortality*," Sidney Lanier observes in Andrew Hudgins's *After the Lost War* (30). Twain made the indictment famous. In *Life on the Mississippi* he traced the Civil War to Scott's sovereignty over Dixie, for southerners took up arms as if they were chevaliers out of *Ivanhoe*. Indeed, most of Amy's family suffered from the "jejune romanticism of an absurd past" that Twain diagnosed as a symptom of "the Sir Walter disease" (*Life* 266).

The fictional malady contracted from the author of *Old Mortality* may well have contributed to Amy's untimely mortality. Amy died from the romanticism that Twain mocked: the South's desire to emulate Scott's novels through its aristocratic life and overinflated literature. More clearly than any of her contemporaries in the old order, Amy understood how mimetic desire leads to death. Although her mother wanted Amy to wear white for her wedding, the prescient bride chose a more somber silver-gray instead. "'I shall wear mourning if I like,' she said, 'it is *my* funeral, you know'" (*CS* 182). In six weeks Amy proved that she was dead right. Eva reports that Amy virtually courted death while suffering from tuberculosis so that she could live to the end as the quintessence of the lady beautiful. If plague is often used in literature, according to Girard, to dramatize the violent spread of mimetic desire (*Double Business* 136–54), then Amy's death from the dreaded disease of her age showed how a lifetime of modeling cultural expectations finally exhausted the flesh. Consumption was an especially appropriate agent of her mortality. As Susan Sontag has shown, the disease was viewed by nineteenth-century romantics as the body's way of revealing hidden desire. Indeed, it made the afflicted openly desirable because it disclosed their passion and intensified their physical attractiveness (45, 26–31). Suffering from consumption, Amy thus became the ultimate model. Eva understands the sad relationship between such all-consuming modeling and Amy's mortality when she recalls for Miranda how Amy used to give her advice about winning a husband. "Then she would laugh and fly away, and where did she fly to?" Eva answers her own question with a destiny right out of Girard: "To scandal and to death, nowhere else" (*CS* 211).

Being a disciple led Amy to her death as much as did being a model. Porter's belle cooperated with a culture that eroticized and aestheticized her illness so that she would die as a well-regarded beauty. Since the old order of the South esteemed Poe as "our greatest poet" (*CS* 178), Amy seems to have fashioned herself after the dying beloveds that spellbind the narrators of his elegiac verse. Amy did not allow herself to be taken to the hospital where she might have received the kind of medical attention that helped Eva when she twice almost died. Rather, wrapped in becoming shawls and surrounded by flowers, Amy entertained crowds of visitors at home, where she was careful always to sit up so that her hair might remain curled. She suffered hemorrhaging and then went out to ride or dance. She coughed up blood, but the tuberculosis was more effective than any cosmetic in making her complexion transparent and in giving a blush to her cheeks. Amy was not so much a pitiful victim of old mortality as of herself and of her culture—of her desire to imitate her imitation-crazed South. Amy lived so completely up to the ideal of the belle that she died a lovely casualty of mimetic desire. Hallowed by family legend, she lost her life once again after her death. She became the heroine of a Scott-inspired southern family romance but not the Girardian hero of Porter's novel.

What the family lore regarding Amy's life ignored was precisely this Girardian impulse in Amy. She continually sought to escape her scripted identity and to reject the culture of mimetic desire recorded in family fictions. The possibility of such insubordination is, for Judith Butler, always intrinsic to the imitation that enacts gender: "That there is a need for a repetition at all is a sign that identity is not self-identical. It requires to be instituted again and again, which is to say that it runs the risk of becoming *de*-instituted at every interval" ("Imitation and Gender Insubordination" 309). Amy capitalized on this need for constant instauration by introducing momentary deviations from the cultural model. She played the coquette, but she also continually violated the expectations of the old order, as if seeking some less conventional way of being a woman. When Gabriel complimented Amy on her long black hair, she horrified him by having it bobbed, and she would not change the style even to please her usual models, her brothers. She shocked her father by wearing the Mardi Gras costume that left too much of her bosom and legs exposed. Although coquetry was ultimately meant to attract a husband, Amy told the handsome Gabriel that she did not want to marry him and sent him away. Amy questioned the traditional models for southern womanhood most flagrantly in claiming that she would copy the example of the family spinster and be "a nice old maid like Eva Parrington" (*CS* 183).

Yet if Amy wanted to escape from the mimetic desire that defined her as a lady, her defiance of the ideal was always complicated by the essential ambiguity of the coquette. Deception and denial are fundamental strategies of the coquette. As the mistress of teasing indirection, she lives by the paradox that encouragement and discouragement must continually turn into each other. Hence, even when Amy might have been rejecting the southern model for femininity, she might have given the impression of reinforcing it because she seemed to be so coquettishly contrary. And even when Amy might have been acting most like the belle, she might have so exasperated onlookers with her audacity that they thought her more radical than she ever meant to be. When Amy's father was infuriated by her immodest costume for the ball, she pointed to a Dresden-china shepherdess on his mantelpiece that inspired it. In effect, Amy justified her impropriety by suggesting that she was merely embodying a culturally sanctioned image for her gender. Amy carried the ideal of southern womanhood to its extreme in her outrageous coquetry, but she never completely abandoned it. She was traditional and subversive, the exemplar of and rebel against mimetic desire.

Although Miranda's kinship with Amy through memory and desire forms the center of "Old Mortality," what makes this short novel so insightful is that over twenty-seven years and across a panorama of family life, it locates this mimesis in the context of an entire culture. The South thrives on the passion for imitation that Miranda sees in her hallowed aunt. The result of such doubling is that, like her storm-tossed Shakespearean namesake, Miranda lives amid a world always on the brink of mimetic conflict, what Girard in an essay on *The Tempest* calls "the tempest of human beings among themselves" (*Theater* 351). These gales of envious antagonism made Antonio seek to overthrow his brother Prospero as Duke of Milan before the play began. On Prospero's island they foment the contention between Sebastian and Alonso as well as the plot of the clownish Stephano and Trinculo against the lordly magician. In the worlds of Shakespeare's and Porter's Mirandas, the more that members of a society selfishly seek to imitate the same exclusive ideal, the more they become adversaries. Whereas Girard contends that Prospero abjures the "theater of envy" at the end of *The Tempest* (*Theater* 352), the insular and invidious society of "Old Mortality" proves by default that "The rarer action is / In virtue than in vengeance" (V.1.27–28). Porter's novel reveals the ferocious competition for place in the southern hierarchy where every man and woman may find an obstacle in every other gentleman and lady.

The men of the old order vie for the mimetic ideal of honor. Gabriel and his grandfather seemed to quarrel over horses, but the real prize behind their conflict was the public regard that gentlemen confer on each other. When Gabriel argued, "By God, I must have *something*. . . . You had racehorses, and made a good thing of them" (*CS* 181), his grandfather voiced the traditional objection of the Old South against gamesters by countering that he never relied on the track for his livelihood (Wyatt-Brown 346–50). Although both men viewed horses as an indispensable trapping of the chivalric life, they disagreed about how horsemanship might lead to honor. Gabriel found honor in turning his elder's example at the track into a way of distinguishing himself as a professional gambler; his grandfather found honor in racing as a noble sport for the wealthy rather than as a mere source of lucre. The clash between doubles was complicated by the fact that Gabriel as his grandfather's favorite was the presumed heir of a large share of his fortune. "By dispossessing himself," Girard writes about the motif of extravagant offers, "the donor makes the receiver another self" (*Scapegoat* 141). Grandfather and grandson, benefactor and beneficiary, quarreled because they were too much alike, and the mimetic conflict came to encompass the entire family. Gabriel's relatives envied his privileged place in the grandfather's affections because it was not their own. So, when the old man actually left his dear but troublesome grandson only one dollar in his will, the rest of the family rejoiced at Gabriel's ruin and made no effort at compensation for "this last-minute act of senile vengeance" (*CS* 191).

Since Amy was the epitome of the old order, it was almost inevitable that the mimetic opposition in this society would erupt into near-violence over her. She became the contested ideal that doubles would possess. At the Mardi Gras ball Gabriel, who had courted Amy for years, staked his claim for the scandalous shepherdess by imitating her choice of costume and dressing as an elegant swain. But Gabriel simply looked foolish, and Amy danced four times with the rival Raymond, a would-be Jean Lafitte. The masquerade was a time intrinsically charged with the possibility of violence because its beginnings, like those of the circus, can be traced back to the primal act of scapegoating. Its holiday license and costumed confusion all typify the way festivals recall and reenact the sacrificial crisis. But such merriment, Girard observes, can sometimes founder "in the sense that it has reverted to its violent origins. Instead of holding violence in check, the ceremonies inaugurate a new cycle of revenge" (*Violence* 125). After Amy stepped out for a moment with Raymond, she returned to precisely such a celebration that has broken out of its ritualized boundaries and regressed toward its origins in mimetic conflict. Although stories varied in explaining what happened during Amy's tête-à-tête, her interlude with Raymond made both of her beaux into models as obstacles. The amorous intruder desired the attention that Gabriel deemed his own, and the rejected paramour desired the attention that Raymond received in his place. The clash of suitors led to the proposal of the ultimate ritual for asserting honor among southern gentlemen. The duo would fight out their enmity and imitation in a duel. As mimetic antagonism spread, the doubling increased until actual violence was used to forestall what only loomed as potential violence. Harry became Gabriel's hotspurred twin. He shot at Raymond to avenge his sister's honor and to keep Gabriel himself from fighting a duel. Harry's assault could easily have provoked gentlemanly retaliation because it was considered "the lowest sort of manners" (CS 184), but the violence of further repetition was finally halted. Friends persuaded Raymond and Gabriel not to fight and Harry to escape from his "vindictive" (CS 188) opponent by fleeing to Mexico.

Although the mimesis at this legendary costume party finally played itself out without any fatalities, the world of "Old Mortality" remembers a far bloodier theatrics. Eva instructs her cousins that "no one, not even a good Southerner, could possibly approve of John Wilkes Booth's deed"; however, Miranda is enamored by the sheer panache of the cloaked performer who shot Lincoln and then jumped to the stage declaring, "Sic semper tyrannis" (CS 180). Eva's protest against seconding the assassination and Miranda's fascination with its melodrama indicate how the old order is allured by such violence. Booth dramatized how mimetic desire can find its end in murder, for the actor/assassin found a model and obstacle in both the brother he resented and the president he killed. Booth was widely thought to support the South—where he always found greater acclaim than in the North—out of jealousy toward his brother. Idolized in the North, the illustrious Edwin Booth cast the single ballot of his life for Lincoln. What might have intensified the sibling rivalry to a regicidal drama out of Shakespeare was the metaphysical desire that has joined so many celebrity assassins to their victims. As Joel Black explains, such killers seek an identity by claiming the aura of those they kill (181, 144). In taking Lincoln's life, Booth became the negative double of the president he shot. Miranda longs for a mediator who can bring to her house, at whatever remove, the kudos that Booth gained for his greatest role in history. Wishing to be part of the "fine story" of killing a president, she regrets that an elderly distant relative who had often seen Booth on stage had not been there "at his greatest moment. . . . it would have been so pleasant to have the assassination of Lincoln in the family" (*CS* 180).

The ladies of "Old Mortality" engage in the same fierce competition and conflict as do the gentlemen, but the restrictions of gender force them to express such animosity more covertly. In such a male-dominated order, the chief source of contention was provided by a woman's desire for whatever place was allowed her in the patriarchy. Eva explains to Miranda that parties and dances were nothing but fashionable marriage markets, where "a girl couldn't afford to miss out, there were always rivals waiting to cut the ground from under her. The rivalry— . . . you can't imagine what the rivalry was like. The way those girls treated each other—nothing was too mean, nothing too false" (*CS* 216). As the cynosure of the southern belles, Amy excited the envy of her admiring competitors. Although Amy could not be drawn into a quarrel, the contentious Eva reports, "She had enemies. If she knew, she pretended she didn't. If she cared, she never said" (*CS* 211). Amy acted in the very best tradition of the coquette by showing an apparent indifference to such animosity, and that disregard only made her seem more powerfully desirable. Mortality did not end this rivalry but only intensified it, for family memory preserved Amy's image as an unsurpassable ideal. Hence, Miss Honey and Cousin Eva continue to live out the resentment for the model who is beyond them and beyond the grave.

Although Miss Honey has been married to Gabriel for twenty-five years, she can never escape being a disappointing substitute for the more fetching Amy. Since Gabriel has not allowed his second wife to forget his first, Miss Honey disdains the rival that she cannot duplicate as well as the entire family that mediates Amy's memory. When Miranda and her family visit Gabriel in Part II, Miss Honey's eyes burn with such rage that she risks violating the tacit family understanding that glorifies and mystifies violence. "Family quarrels were sacred," Porter's narrator explains, "to be waged privately in fierce hissing whispers, low choked mutters and growls. If they did yell and stamp, it must be behind closed doors and windows" (*CS* 202). As if some highly refined legacy of the founding murder, manners kept the hostility that underlay the old order secretly and safely contained in a domestic sanctuary, where its very concealment let such fury reign as god. Miss Honey's pinched nostrils, trembling mouth, and uncomfortable silences threaten to trouble the family peace by disclosing and desacralizing household quarrels. Her antagonism disturbs Miranda, for it exposes supposedly sacred violence as entirely human. It is the wrathful envy of mimetic desire.

Eva Parrington seethes with the same hostility as does Miss Honey toward the model that eludes her. As cousins, Amy and Eva were bound together in the double mediation that made each the pattern of southern womanhood for the other. If Eva longed to be a coquette like Amy Rhea, Amy dreamed of being "a nice old maid like Eva Parrington" (*CS* 183). Amy's mimetic desire was apparently so much a part of family memory that a generation later Miranda remembers it when she meets Eva on the train to Gabriel's funeral. Amy's wish to remain single flouted all expectations for women in the Old South, for ladies were typically married in their early twenties (Foxe-Genovese 255). Although such a longing for spinsterhood might have been no more than a belle's provocative jest, the desire might also have concealed a deeper wisdom. Eva's feminist campaign might have demonstrated a constructive way for Amy to express her discontent as a belle. And Eva's courage in losing her teaching position and being imprisoned for the sake of women's rights might have exemplified precisely the kind of fortitude that the possibly suicidal Amy lacked.

However, while Amy was alive, she more often seemed the model for the charm and vitality that the drab Eva lacked. Amy cautioned her protégée not to talk to gentlemen about suffrage and not to recite Latin poetry but instead to dance in silence and to look out so that she might seem to have a more pronounced chin. Eva was attracted to the role as Amy's disciple. The failed socialite happily reminisces about going to dances with Miranda's handsome father and to holiday celebrations at the Grandmother's house "even if I wasn't a belle" (*CS* 208). Although Eva is delighted that Miranda recalls learning Latin years ago from her, what the acrimonious old lady really hopes Miranda will remember is her sapphire velvet dress with a train. It hardly matters to Eva that the formal attire was a remade cast-off from her mother and that its color never suited her: it was already the dress of secondhand desire, of a want-to-be belle.

Eva seems to have finally renounced the model provided by Amy. Since she was convinced that her receding chin kept her from ever having the beauty of Amy's breed, she became a teacher and feminist. Eva's vocation could not have made more explicit her rejection of the old order, for suffragists were viewed by many in the South as threatening the femininity of women and the privileged status of men (Scott 167–69). When she meets Miranda on the train in Part III, Eva helps her younger cousin discover the death hidden in the southern idolization of the lady. She exposes how Amy risked her delicate health to cultivate her image as a beauty. Eva's critique is motivated by more than obvious envy; it speaks for the way that writers of the Southern Renascence often indicted the belle for narcissism, masochism, and frustrated eroticism (Seidel 26). Maintaining that such unwholesome desires led to Amy's death, Eva inspires Miranda to imagine "a long procession of living corpses, festering women stepping gaily towards the charnel house, their corruption concealed under laces and flowers, their dead faces lifted smiling" (*CS* 216). The dreamy Miranda needs to hear such demystification. However, she rightly judges this vision of the Grand Guignol behind the graciousness of the lady to be as romantic as her family's fanciful redactions of its past. Despite her denunciation, Eva is a true daughter of the traditional South. Just as the Rheas idealize beauty, the unlovely Eva absolutizes corruption.

Eva's kinship with the past goes beyond this coincidence of opposites to a frustrated longing to imitate the old order. Although Eva demythologizes the model for southern femininity, she has actually internalized the ideal of Amy as the standard against which she fiercely measures her own deformity. Eva painfully recalls for Miranda how throughout her girlhood, her family called good-humored but hurtful attention to her imperfect chin. Eva's obsession with her own physical defects and fervor in exposing Amy's character flaws result from desiring what she cannot imitate. She is so filled with fury at the model who became her lifelong obstacle that she pours her bile into the escalating violence of her rhetoric. As Eva progresses from the "ferocious sarcasm" (*CS* 206) at the beginning of her conversation with Miranda to the apoplectic renunciation of the family as an institution at its end, she bares her teeth, stabs her finger, makes her eyes gleam with a "light like daggers" (*CS* 212), and finally shakes her doubled-up fists at Miranda. Eva passionately hates what she loves too much. As Amy's would-be double and embittered rival, she appropriately shares a similarly grievous fate. Although only in her early fifties, Eva "looked so withered and tired, so famished and sunken in the cheeks, so *old,* somehow" (*CS* 208) because she has spent her life in rancor and resentment. In both women, mimetic desire virtually consumes the flesh: Eva's exhausted old age is the counterpart of Amy's too-early mortality.

Although Eva never escapes the romanticism of her family, her zealous exposure of the cult of Amy helps Miranda reject the most obvious forms of mimetic desire. Miranda needs such a model because she has already begun to follow her legendary aunt's perilous example. Just as Amy courted the approval of her brother, Miranda has sought to satisfy her father's demanding standards for personal appearance. And just as the Amy of family myth rather impulsively married the disinherited Gabriel, Miranda has pursued an equally reckless romance. In absconding from her convent school to marry a man of no great financial promise, Miranda seems to have lived up to Eva's verdict on her father's branch of the family as having "no more practical sense than so many children. Everything for love" (*CS* 213). But the eighteen year old has already grown disillusioned with such amorous folly. Less than a year after the elopement Miranda finds the marriage "very unreal" and unconnected with her future. Indeed, she might have been headed toward the same mortality that ended Amy's impetuous wedlock. Miranda's marriage oppresses her with "an immense weariness as if it were an illness that she might one day hope to recover from" (*CS* 212, 213). The heartsick wife has risked joining the grotesque parade of southern ladies conjured up by Eva's critique of Amy's sex-obsessed rivals.

Eva's diatribe against the old order reinforces Miranda's desire to recover from her romantic malady. She even considers imitating her cousin despite her fear of becoming the very image of her wearied elder: "Oh, must I ever be like that?" (*CS* 208). After Eva relates how she was dismissed from her teaching position and jailed because of her political activism, Miranda deems the cause "heroic and worth suffering for" (*CS* 210). The disciple is drawn to a feminism so sublime that it requires ennobling sacrifice. Such a crusade promises the glorious tribulation that the young masochist had once sought in her perfervid fictions of convent life. Like Miranda's other ambition of becoming an airplane pilot, a career as a suffragist in 1912 would at once fulfill her increasingly countercultural desires and gratify her appetite for vainglory. The schoolgirlish infatuation wanes, however, when Miranda realizes that her formidable cousin would leave in her wake no opportunity for triumph. Miranda confronts the dilemma of Girardian rivalry, for Eva is the model as obstacle.

Since Eva undercuts not only the model of beauty that Miranda might have inherited but also the kind of modern antimodel that the feminist's own life might have provided, Miranda appears ready at the end of "Old Mortality" to follow the heroic course that Girard finds typical of novelistic conclusions: the renunciation of a lifetime of mimetic desire (*Deceit* 290–314). Whereas she had once desired the past as glorified in family myth, Miranda repudiates both her relatives and their southern romanticism. At the train station and on the ride home for Gabriel's funeral, her conservative father and radical cousin let their conflicts dissolve in a community of memory and mortality. Miranda does not share in the surprising way that her apparently rivalrous elders become doubles of each other. Instead, she decides to free herself from her own and her husband's family. And she intends to forget "not the past but the legend of the past, other people's memory of the past, at which she had spent her life peering in wonder like a child at a magic-lantern show" (*CS* 221). As Miranda professes her hatred of love and resolves not even to remember her father and cousin, she comes close to realizing in her own life Eva's wish that the "whole hideous institution" of the family "should be wiped from the face of the earth" (*CS* 217). Rather than imitating or rivaling such models, Miranda is determined to pursue a defiantly independent search for existential self-definition. She will seize hold of her own life and discover her own particular form of truth. Miranda will be mistress of her own desire.

Miranda rejects mimesis under one form only to accept it under another. Aspiring to autonomy, she deludes herself about the very origins of her desire. Porter's prose on the last pages of the novel is complicated with so many questions, contradictions, and qualifications that Miranda's new-found maturity is always undercut by her continuing naiveté. Despite her disavowals Miranda still desires according to what her family desires. Although she physically distances herself from the camaraderie of the past enjoyed by her father and Eva, she yearns for the solidarity that they share. "Where are my own people and my own time?" she wonders. "She resented, slowly and deeply and in profound silence, the presence of those aliens who lectured and admonished her, who loved her with bitterness and denied her the right to look at the world with her own eyes" (*CS* 219). The liberating promise of Miranda's question is undermined by her animosity toward the kindred who must be included in "her" people and toward the past which inescapably forms part of her "time." And Miranda's own embittered love for the estranged others fills her with the hatred and jealousy that Girard views as a typical result of internal mediation. Much like Eva, Miranda does not realize that she secretly desires to imitate what she seemingly denounces.

Although Miranda resolves, "I won't have false hopes, I won't be romantic about myself" (*CS* 221), she is supremely romantic in her resolution to embark on a solitary quest for selfhood.[12] "Romantics and symbolists want a transfiguring desire that is completely spontaneous; they do not want to hear any talk about the Other," Girard contends. "They turn away from the dark side of desire, claiming it is unrelated to their lovely poetic dream and denying that it is its price" (*Deceit* 39–40). Thinking herself most the original, Miranda is actually most the disciple of such a belief in subjective desire. When she forsakes family legend for the private truth of her own experience, she is the child of a romantic tradition that extends at the very least from her South's cherished Poe to her own family. As the narrator explains, Miranda does not know that her very question about what to make of her future results from the fact that "all her earliest training" had taught her that life was to be crafted and "directed towards a definite end" (*CS* 220). Miranda embraces the teleology of her family so ardently that she makes its emphasis on self-fashioning even more extreme by seizing her life "in a fury of jealous possessiveness" (*CS* 220). Porter's romantic thereby reveals the lie behind her claims to lonely individualism, for her envy and greed indirectly recognize the Other that she wholeheartedly seeks to exclude. Imagining that she has overcome mimetic desire, Miranda still finds her models and her rivals in the old order. She ends "Old Mortality" "in her hopefulness, her ignorance" (*CS* 221) because she does not know that her defiant self-assertion is flawed by self-deception.

RIDING TOWARD DEATH IN "PALE HORSE, PALE RIDER" AND WRITING BEYOND "THE GRAVE"

"Pale Horse, Pale Rider" begins almost as if a continuation of Miranda's attempt to escape from imitating the old order six years earlier in "Old Mortality." The twenty-four-year-old Miranda has left her family and the entire South to work as a journalist in Denver. Although in the opening pages she dreams of waking in the house of her childhood, the fugitive has no desire to return to the entanglements of family life. Rather, Miranda rejects the past because it is too old and too mortal. The house has provided space for the living and dying of too many ancestors whose "storied dust" never settles (*CS* 269). And whereas those elderly relatives welcomed death's horseman, the young Miranda chooses Graylie rather than Sophia Jane's Fiddler to race the pale rider in her dream. Miranda hopes to evade old mortality and pursue a new immortality, a life freed from the fatal modeling of the past. However, her flight is in vain, for the future is only a more deadly version of the old order.

The apocalyptic horseman of the title races across the world of the novel through the twofold violence of World War I, which took fifteen million lives, and the influenza epidemic of 1918, which claimed over twenty-one million victims (Crosby 171, 206–7).[13] Whether in the South or away from the South, Miranda lives in a culture of violence that makes war and plague—indeed, the plague of war—a global form of the same dire mimesis that she discovered in the old order. There are more victims, and they are more visible in "Pale Horse, Pale Rider" than in any other "Miranda" story, as if her world were being carried away by a sacrificial crisis that it simply cannot restrain. Since Porter relates

Miranda's race against these twin forms of death entirely from her limited point of view, this public catastrophe gets personalized and internalized as psychic disaster.[14] Falling into the grave at last, Miranda reaches her nadir because at the end she does not even know that desire has ridden her to death.

World War I provides the appropriate background for "Pale Horse, Pale Rider" because the clash between Allied and Central Powers raised to international levels the conflictual desire that Miranda has discovered in the old order. "We see the same indignation, the same theatrical gestures, on both sides," Girard writes of the mimetic desire that fueled the Great War. "The speeches are all the same: to make them admirable or atrocious, depending on the listener, all that is necessary is to reverse the proper names. Germans and French slavishly copy each other" (*Deceit* 225). The chauvinism that Miranda hears trumpeted throughout the novel results from such rivalry. "It is a negative sentiment based on hatred," Girard explains, "that is to say, on the secret adoration of the Other. . . . The chauvinist hates a powerful, belligerent, and well-disciplined Germany because he himself is dreaming of war, power, and discipline" (*Deceit* 205). Miranda detects such an egotistical rationale when she notices how the combat in Europe has origins in American self-interest. Unlike some southern ministers who favored the war as an attack on German materialism (Wilson 171), Miranda despises a greed that is much more local. She denounces the mercantile motives for the war when she hears a bond salesman claim that it is directed toward more noble ends. "Coal, oil, iron, gold, international finance, why don't you tell us about them, you little liar?" she wonders (*CS* 293). In such high-flown sales pitches as much as in everyday banter, Miranda hears the language of the primitive sacred in which "violence is venerated insofar as it offers men what little peace they can ever expect" (Girard, *Violence* 258). Indeed, the novel resounds with President Wilson's famous description of the Great War as the means to peace. With questionable confidence Adam asserts that "there won't be any more wars, don't you read the newspapers? . . . We're going to mop 'em up this time, and they're going to stay mopped, and this is going to be all" (*CS* 281). The bond salesman echoes the same triumphalism but without the irony when he intones "the war, the *war,* the WAR to end WAR, war for Democracy, for humanity, a safe world forever and ever" (*CS* 293).

The influenza epidemic brings the violence of war to the home front. Reminding Miranda of a medieval plague, the devastating disease increases the military casualties, closes the moribund theaters that Miranda regularly attends as a newspaper critic, and fills the streets with funerals by day and ambulances by night. From *Oedipus Tyrannos* to Camus' *The Plague,* as Girard notes, pestilence has served as a metaphor for the infection of mimetic antagonism (*Double Business* 136–54). In "Pale Horse, Pale Rider" the war in which over 116,000 Americans were killed and the influenza outbreak in which 675,000 Americans died are so closely related that these twin scourges almost seem like a single catastrophe. As Janis Stout notes, Porter "developed the atmosphere of epidemic into a metaphor for spiritual illness associated with the nation's aggressively patriotic entry into the war" (*Katherine Anne Porter* 29). Miranda believes that her headache started with the war. Her colleagues at the newspaper speculate that the flu epidemic began after a German vessel secretly sprayed an infectious cloud over Boston. The plague may be nothing but germ warfare. Although influenza was actually spread by crowded army camps, by soldiers traveling across the country, and by sailors going to and from Europe (Crosby 39, 53, 56), it is convenient for patriots not even to consider the American military's own role in fostering home-front fatalities and to blame the Germans. Such an etiology conceals what Girard proposes as "the principle behind all 'foreign' wars": conflicts abroad serve as ways of displacing the violence that might otherwise erupt in conflicts at home. Domestic unrest gets stifled as the country adopts "a form of violence that can be openly endorsed and fervently acted upon by all" (*Violence* 249, 280). It is not surprising that nativists and businessmen in 1917 America often turned to flag waving on behalf of the war, because such displays of national pride could be used to suppress dissent among immigrants and laborers (Kennedy 62–75). In Porter's short novel, the conflict with Germany might not have caused the illness so much as the contagion of mimetic rivalry might have caused the conflict with Germany.

Throughout "Pale Horse, Pale Rider" Miranda struggles to live in this land infected with war fever. Having seemed to renounce the South of family legend in favor of contemporary Denver, Miranda devotes most of her energy to repudiating not the claims of the past but the dominant model in 1918 America, the patriotic ideal. She is surrounded by Americans who outdo themselves to be home-front nationalists. They sew, ration cream and sugar, sing patriotic songs, and buy bonds. Desire to imitate this ideal makes her colleague Chuck swagger with soldierly bravado even though he has been rejected by the military for health reasons, and it makes Towney, another co-worker, effusive about volunteering for Hut Service even though she was earlier hysterical about being intimidated into supporting the war effort. The same mimetic desire turns nonentities into the ominous Lusk Committeemen. Full of "fussy pride and vainglory," these goonish agents "had a stale air of borrowed importance which apparently they had got from the same source" (*CS* 274, 271). Their secondhand superiority comes from rank imitation, from so completely living up to the national ideal that they try to bully Miranda into imitating them by buying a Liberty Bond. Miranda notices that the aging, paunchy Liberty Bond salesman who makes his pitch before the third act at the theater has likewise found a missing self-sufficiency through chauvinistic mimicry. It is appropriate that Miranda is a theater critic because she discerns how in wartime America everyone is a performer, each aspiring to play the part of hyper-patriot best.[15]

The red-white-and-blue mimeticism wields such power that Miranda tries to impersonate the all-American disciple. She writes columns urging young women to knit and roll bandages, and she even considers buying a war bond despite having to scrimp on her salary of eighteen dollars a week. She joins the crowd of society ladies who visit army hospitals with candy, cigarettes, and forced cheerfulness. However, if Miranda cannot completely resist the compulsion of such mass mimesis, she questions the model for the citizen warrior. When she sees a hospitalized soldier glaring bitterly during her visit of charity, she feels as if she has turned a corner and met her own skeptical double. The do-gooder resolves never to come to the hospital again. At the theater Miranda reflects on the war mania that seems to have gripped everyone but her: "we are speechless animals letting ourselves be destroyed, and why? Does anybody here believe the things we say to each other?" (*CS* 291).

Miranda can expose the chauvinism of 1918 so readily because it is only a grander version of the high-sounding but violent cult of honor that she has known from her youth in the South. Like the old order, the new order requires members to follow rigidly defined conventions or face ostracism as a traitor. Miranda notices how fear of seeming disloyal and suspicion of others' loyalty have made the community that might have formed around the war effort degenerate into mere conformity. Citizens say only what is safe, only what is the same cliché. Their language is typically as sentimental as the romantic rhetoric of Miranda's ancestors. Miranda hears its emotional manipulation most clearly when at the theater the speech of the bond pitchman is reduced to a decontextualized compendium of flag-waving tropes: "These vile Huns—glorious Belleau Wood—our keyword is Sacrifice—Martyred Belgium—give till it hurts—our noble boys Over There—Big Berthas—the death of civilization—the Boche—" (*CS* 293). Such liberal pieties simply invert the conservatism of the old order to create a cause as transcendent for doughboys as the South once was for Confederate soldiers. Although the South's enthusiastic support of the Great War affirmed that it was once again a member in good standing of the United States, it also revived the lost cause of the old order. Indeed, if Miranda returned home, she might have heard southern preachers championing the war as a chance for the sons of Dixie to prove their virtue and once again marshal in the name of freedom (Wilson 171–73). Like the old-time daughters of Dixie, the women left behind by World War I were supposed to defend civilization by sacrifice—giving up sugar, serving in the Red Cross, and dancing at military socials. Such offerings to the patriotic cause reinforce the same patriarchy that limited the possibilities for women in Amy's South. While the war abroad bonds men ever more closely together as they confront death, the war on the home front patronizes the wives, sisters, and daughters of these soldiers. Miranda recognizes that relief work only busies the women who were "running wild with the men away" so that they can keep "their little minds out of mischief" (*CS* 290). Having been relegated to the post of theater critic as one of the "routine female jobs" appropriate to her (*CS* 275), Miranda knows how such works of home-front charity perpetuate the sexism that Cousin Eva opposed.

Miranda's romance with Adam seems like a way of rejecting the jingoistic models of the present. Although Second Lieutenant Barclay virtually glows in his uniform as if he were the soldier par excellence, he can also undercut his too naive belief in the noble American cause. Together, Miranda and Adam adopt a style of ironic deprecation or self-mocking exaggeration that challenges the rah-rah rhetoric of the war at home. Their speech may sound as if it is copying the model for patriotic oratory, but it subverts the usual hyperbole with a shrug, an almost-laugh, or a self-conscious set of quotation marks. Like grim copies of the comics that Miranda reviews at the vaudeville theater, the pair answer each other in kind and call forth reciprocal responses. When Miranda laments that war can maim the mind and heart worse than it can harm the body, Adam objects with a mixture of sentimentality and sangfroid that "if anything happens to the poor old human frame, why, it's just out of luck, that's all." His double in understatement knows her cue: "'Oh, yes,' mimicked Miranda. 'It's just out of luck, that's all'" (*CS* 294). Speaking out of their own romance, Adam and Miranda stylize the war out of being overromanticized.

Although the dialogue between Adam and Miranda is free of the stereotypical phrases that corrupt so much speech in wartime America, even this anti-model has its own model in home-front culture. Adam and Miranda imitate not just each other but an entire parlance of insouciant disaffection. Porter's narrator regularly calls attention to how familiar and frequent is this talk. When Miranda denounces the bond salesman at the theater as "just another nasty old man who would like to see the young ones killed," she speaks with her generation in speaking against its predecessors: "The young people were talking like that about the business by then. They felt they were seeing pretty clearly through that game" (CS 294). The problem with copying such antiwar irreverence is that it can easily lose its fresh responsiveness and become a stony, self-protective pose. Much as Miranda was kept from expressing the anticipatory grief that disturbed her in "The Fig Tree," she is now prevented from speaking the sadness that haunts her romance with Adam throughout "Pale Horse, Pale Rider." Miranda has feared doom from her opening dream, yet she cannot let herself be like the sorrowful young woman that she "envied" (CS 296) at the dance hall for being able to weep openly with her beloved. Since Miranda cannot mourn with Adam, she can only mourn for Adam, mourn him as another lost cause, mourn him after the model of her sentimental family past.

Miranda is still so entranced by the central narrative of the old order that her wartime love for Adam Barclay repeats the melancholy romance that captivated her as a girl. Appearing as innocent as his unfallen namesake, as golden as the sun god, Adam is the glorified male counterpart of the much-admired Amy. Although brazenly modern in his love of autos and engineering, the fellow Texan is so much the old-time gentleman that Miranda imagines he would carry her across a puddle. And Lieutenant Barclay is so much the son of the southern military tradition that he has his army uniform tailored to perfection. Like Amy, Adam is a down-home idol overshadowed by doom. Just as Amy pursued beauty unto death, Adam risks his life for honor because he could not look himself in the face if he did not go to war. After Adam dies of influenza, Miranda comes close to imitating the past that she had so passionately renounced: she turns Adam into a dead and beloved ideal like Amy.

Miranda exalts Adam in life and in death because, just as Amy is the model of desire for the old order, Adam is the pattern for Miranda's mimesis. Lover and beloved pursue a psychic likeness. As Thomas Walsh notes, the similarities between the pair—age, vanity, Texas background, temperament—suggest that Adam is not so much an independent character as a projection of Miranda's needs. He embodies the immortality that she wants but also the death that she fears and seeks (186). Adam is the model and obstacle, the nexus of attraction and frustration for his heartfelt disciple. Miranda aspires to imitate him because he is only the imitation of her own desires; however, she also needs to deny him, even sacrifice him, because she wants to be free of the death wish that has pursued her since the beginning of the novel. Adam is the pale rider of Miranda's dreams as well as the Miranda-like hope to outrun old mortality.

At the climax of "Pale Horse, Pale Rider," Miranda is overtaken by the sinister horseman. Sickened by the war, she becomes a casualty of the influenza that galloped through her nightmare and swept across the home front. And as she loses the contest with mortality, she succumbs to the baleful effects of mimetic desire. In a feverish sequence marked by surreal images, jarring contrasts, and abrupt transitions, Porter dramatizes a phantasmagoria of interdividuality gone awry that recalls Miranda's terrifying visions in "The Circus." In this private place of strife, Miranda duplicates the way communities in crisis turn to scapegoating. She internalizes the social dynamic that ends in expulsion so that it becomes a psychic struggle to rid herself of the other. While Adam and a German doctor care for Miranda during her delirium, she engages in fantasies of such febrile desire that victim and victimizer keep metamorphosing into each other.

Miranda's dream about Adam as scapegoat gives ritual meaning to the interpretation that she has been developing throughout her romance. He consummates a long line of victims—the chick in "The Fig Tree," the rabbit in "The Grave," the clown in "The Circus," the slaves in "The Witness," and Amy in "Old Mortality"—that challenge Miranda to mourn. Indeed, she earlier views Adam as the surrogate who bears the violence of war for others. Miranda shares with Adam her sacrificial understanding of his role when she tells him of her scorn for the elderly cowards who deliver patriotic declamations but themselves do not fight: "they know they're safe; it's you they are sending instead" (CS 294). Adam goes without protest, like the Suffering Servant who "is brought as a lamb to the slaughter, and as a sheep before her shearers is dumb, so he openeth not his mouth" (Isa. 53:7). Miranda echoes this biblical description when she concludes, "No, there was no resentment or revolt in him. Pure, she thought, all the way through, flawless, complete, as the sacrificial lamb must be" (CS 295).[16] Like all scapegoats, Adam stands out by reason of his difference. If "physical monstrosity and moral monstrosity merge" in the extraordinary figure of the scapegoat (Girard, Scapegoat 33–34), Adam is grotesque in his freedom from what disturbs most mortals in the death-obsessed "Miranda" stories. He has the "monstrous uniqueness" of never having had a memorable pain (CS 280), as if he were as immortal as his prelapsarian namesake. Adam matches this bodily well-being with an inner perfection, for he lacks any antagonism toward the chauvinists who remain at home. Unlike Miranda, who detests the bond peddler, Adam views the salesman with a forbearance that comes from pride in his own strength. His very lack of resentment makes him an especially fitting candidate to save the resentful Miranda. However, Miranda does not want a surrogate victim so much as a chance to continue the beloved doubling of their romance. Right before the onset of her illness, Adam and Miranda dance together in absolute symmetry, his hand tightening on her waist as her hand tightened on his shoulder, both silent, both speaking in smiles. Sharing such reciprocity before the prospect of a common doom, Miranda wonders to herself, "why can we not save each other?" (*CS* 296).

That private question becomes the text of Miranda's dream about scapegoating. Having fallen victim to influenza, she imagines Adam repeatedly being felled by arrows that pierce his heart but then rising unhurt "in a perpetual death and resurrection" (*CS* 305). If the darts come from Cupid's quiver and Mars's arsenal, these shafts of love and war also have a history of association with the scapegoat. Before her dream Miranda may have evoked that tradition when she playfully recalled the prayers from her Catholic childhood. Part of her religious heritage would have been the arrow-strewn image of St. Sebastian, who during the Middle Ages was thought to have the power of saving the faithful during times of plague by becoming the target of the illness (Girard, *Scapegoat* 60–61). And since Miranda is no parochial Christian, she even boasts of knowing an invocation to Apollo, the god famed for sending arrows of the plague and for curing pestilence. Miranda transfers all of these violent and sacred associations to the stricken Adam so that he becomes the cursed but redeeming scapegoat. Indeed, after Miranda finally recovers from her delusions on the day that the war ends, it seems as if Adam has taken upon himself the infirmities of the world. She learns that her beloved has become the victim of the influenza he probably contracted while caring for her; yet Miranda has survived, and peace has replaced worldwide conflict. The logic of violence suggests that Adam has died so that all might live.

During the nightmare of her illness, Miranda wants to prevent precisely such salutary victimization. She had earlier joked with Adam about her being a home-front "martyr" (*CS* 281). Now shot by love's arrows, she seeks to take the place of Adam, to be the substitute victim for the substitute victim. At its best, Miranda's willingness to lay down her life for her friend reflects the continuing reciprocity of their generous loves. However, Miranda turns self-sacrifice into self-centeredness and emulation into envy. She hurls herself "angrily and self-ishly" before the volley of arrows in her dream, "crying, No, no, like a child cheated in a game, It's my turn now, why must you always be the one to die?" (CS 305). Just as the girl Miranda once longed for the afflictions of convent life, the young woman wants to suffer for the most unholy reasons. Miranda engages in a juvenile competition for place by transforming the rivalry that may lead to scapegoating into a rivalry about who will be the scapegoat. Her commitment to violence is folly. After Miranda places her body before Adam's, the arrows pierce her heart and then kill her beloved. However, Miranda still survives as his fond and foolish victimizer. When a briefly lucid Miranda tells Adam about this vision of tormented self-seeking, she recasts the scene in a less incriminating form. She relates a fantasy in which the two of them have become live valentine hearts carved on a tree and transfixed by an arrow. Although Miranda's revision may partially be caused by the sheer elusiveness of dreams, her bowdlerized version glosses over too much that is telling. She not only follows what Girard regards as the very human tendency to conceal scapegoating but also hides her own mimetic rivalry with Adam. Miranda's romanticized nightmare does not reveal how she has killed the attractive model for her death wish and her desire to escape death.

As Miranda's illness plays out the crisis between self and other in the world of her body and psyche, the afflicted turns from trying to save Adam to persecuting the doctor who is trying to save her. Throughout the novel Miranda has rejected the inflammatory rhetoric of wartime America that envisions "'innocent babes hoisted on Boche bayonets'" (CS 293). Nevertheless, the patriotic model is so compelling that she actually internalizes its most ferocious language. When Miranda lies dying, she imagines her physician, who has a German name, committing precisely such infant atrocities and then throwing the slaughtered child along with some poison into a well on her father's farm. As the virulence of her war fever breaks out in the violence of her own speech, Miranda howls about her doctor that "Hildesheim is a Boche, a spy, a Hun, kill him, kill him before he kills you" (CS 309). Her version of the pollution of the waters in Revelation 8:10–11 recalls the speculation that the Germans might have caused the current epidemic. However, her claim reveals more about the contagion of mimesis than about the enemy's strategies for contaminating the home front. Miranda converts the doctor who rescues her from her rooming house and who cares for her in the hospital into a scapegoat, for she has been poisoned by the very cultural desire that she sought not to imitate. Sickened by mimetic antagonism, the victim of influenza becomes the double of the wartime victimizer she denounces. Miranda's xenophobia is particularly bloodthirsty because the demo-

nized Hildesheim threatens her father's farm, the homeplace that this ambivalent daughter of the South has left but feels compelled to defend. Although her
savage jingoism is the raving of an ill mind, in April 1918 a mob of five hundred
near St. Louis actually carried out something like Miranda's wish: they lynched
a young man because he had been born in Germany (Kennedy 68).

Miranda lives out her death as if it were a rite of passage beyond such violent duality. Rituals of transition, according to Girard, reenact the crisis and ensuing calm of surrogate victimage, for they stage a descent into and then an as-
cent out of violence (*Violence* 280–86). Porter localizes each stage of Miranda's
crossing from old mortality to life everlasting. After passing through "the landscape of disaster"—a malevolent jungle, hostile wood, terrifying fog, and endless abyss—she finds that death frees her from inclination and imitation (*CS*
309). Reduced to a fiery crystallization of being, she feels all ideas and questions,
"all ties of blood and the desires of the heart," dissolving until she becomes completely independent, "not susceptible to any appeal or inducement" (*CS* 310).
Miranda enjoys heaven as a transcendence of mimetic desire. She joins a familiar and welcoming circle of "pure identities," where each is "alone but not solitary; Miranda, alone too, questioning nothing, desiring nothing, in the quietude
of her ecstasy" (*CS* 311). Miranda is neither model nor disciple but sublimely
herself in the company of others.

When Miranda awakens in the hospital from this ecstasy of identity, her
death and resurrection might seem to repeat the pattern that Girard identifies
in the great European novels of desire: the rejection of mimesis and the discovery of rebirth. However, Porter's romantic immediately rededicates herself precisely to such imitation. Miranda follows her family's example of mythicizing a
lost order, as Robert Brinkmeyer has observed, for she longs to behold once
again her vision of heavenly bliss, and she denigrates the moribund world to
which she returns (*Katherine Anne Porter's Artistic Development* 177). Miranda
is so filled with desire for her vanished beatitude that she survives the everyday
ordeal of muted colors and blunted shapes only by resorting to continued
mimesis. At first, the theater critic adopts a self-conscious theatricality by ordering make-up and a silver walking stick. She wants to play the part of a woman
who is not so much a resurrected body as a resuscitated cadaver. Her deadly
bondage to mimetic desire is voiced in an internal dialogue that burlesques the
relationship between the biblical lord of life and the friend he raised from the
dead: "Lazarus, come forth. Not unless you bring me my top hat and stick. Stay
where you are then, you snob. Not at all. I'm coming forth" (*CS* 316). Just as Je-

sus summons Lazarus from the tomb as a sign that he is the ultimate model of the resurrection, the hospital staff and Miranda's cronies from the newspaper call her forth to be alive like them. But Miranda views her return from the dead as a return to the dead, to the dullness of diurnal living. And if she is to reenter such a pale world, she will come forth not as a passive corpse summoned from the grave but as a rivalrous contender for lordship who walks out on her own terms. Miranda will not just copy her well-wishers; she will outdo them as the most well-appointed of zombies. She will return to the bedimmed world in a costume of such high style that it surpasses any other mode of self-presentation. However, Miranda will be only mimicking mimetic desire. Her grand performance will conceal her scorn for the lackluster life on this side of the grave. "Still, no one need pity this corpse if we look properly to the art of the thing," the actress assures herself after a check in the mirror (*CS* 316). No belle from Aunt Amy's generation ever combined more desire with more deceit than does this revivified poseur. Freshened by the cold cream and apricot powder that she orders, Miranda will live as a thing of art, an embalmed beauty who escapes the pity that might come to the convalescent by feeling only pity for a world that does not know it is moribund.

Miranda rediviva lacks the defiant strength to sustain the kind of postmodern showmanship that empowers Plath's Lady Lazarus. Even before leaving the hospital, the patient imitates the everyday values of the colleagues who visit her when she mouths the blithe assumptions about living that they want her to echo. Miranda "smiled and told them how gay and what a pleasant surprise it was to find herself alive. For it will not do to betray the conspiracy and tamper with the courage of the living; there is nothing better than to be alive, everyone has agreed on that; it is past argument, and who attempts to deny it is justly outlawed" (*CS* 315). Miranda cannot endure being ostracized by those who are naive and sanguine but dead. As she prepares to leave the hospital, she foresees a time when she will imitate her comforters without even being aware of her imitation. Whereas the title character of O'Neill's 1928 *Lazarus Laughed,* the only figure in the pageant who does not wear a mask, returns to criticize life as death and to celebrate death as an entry into life, the disguised Miranda will simply act like one of the play's chorus. Wearing a death mask, she will seem devoid of spirit and fearful of mortality. The model disciple will visit others who have escaped from death "and help them dress and tell them how lucky they are, and how lucky I am still to have them" (*CS* 317). Miranda's cheerful consolations to those recovering will repeat the same truisms that now seem so suffused with sadness to her. However, the traumatized Miranda will no longer appreciate how all of her encouragements are only grand acting amid the grayish actuality.

Before Miranda allows her life to lapse into such mimetic desire, she briefly considers what seems a more desirable form of mimesis. Rather than wanting to be like the others who are secretly dead, she turns to wanting the likeness of the only Other for her, the idolized but all-too-mortal Adam. Miranda seeks to be not the one raised from the dead but the one who raises the dead. Having learned that her beloved has died of influenza, she succeeds in wishing his ghost into haunting her hospital room. Her fantasy is a highly private way of dabbling in the spiritualism that provided comfort for many of those bereft by World War I. The wonder-working Miranda creates a mimesis of her own desire. Although she may at first seem like the kind of magician that tutored her namesake in *The Tempest,* Miranda is not so much the master of mysteries as the self-deceived slave. Jean-Michel Oughourlian explains that the sorcerer gains power by exploiting the interdividual relationship so that he or she suggests what the bewitched imitates (28–29). In summoning Adam's ghost, Miranda becomes both the enchanting model and enchanted disciple. She falls victim to auto-suggestion and evokes the revenant as "the last intolerable cheat of her heart . . . the unpardonable lie of her bitter desire" (*CS* 317).

So desirous is Miranda that she seeks to go beyond merely sensing Adam's presence to actually seeing his form. She uses the power of volition that conjurors often exert over their subjects and tries to hypnotize herself further into beholding the specter of Adam (Oughourlian 45). Miranda wants to intensify illusion so that it becomes delusion. "If I could call you up from the grave I would, she said, if I could see your ghost I would say, I believe . . . 'I believe,' she said aloud. 'Oh, let me see you once more'" (*CS* 317). Although Miranda's equation of seeing and believing makes her sound like Thomas, the doubting disciple, she really longs to be the godlike model who brings Adam-Jesus back to life. Miranda is bewitched by her own mimetic desire. Porter creates fiction out of the way her imagination orders her memories, but Miranda makes fantasy out of the way her desire disorders her memories. When the past for which Miranda grieves becomes indistinguishable from the future for which she yearns, there is only the single moment of hallucination, of memory as desire, that spellbinds her.[17]

Miranda escapes the delirium of her own magic by the struggle and expulsion that Oughourlian finds typical of disenchantment. Such countermagic derives its power from surrogate victimage, for the disenchanter identifies the sorcerer responsible for the spell and then presides over the actual or symbolic violence that drives the malefactor away (54–59). Miranda's prayer for Adam's spirit to appear ends all possibility of such an apparition. The spirit of Adam is "struck away by the sudden violence of her rising and speaking aloud" (*CS* 317), as if the sheer force of Miranda's movement and outcry breaks her fascination with Adam's shade by violating the stillness and silence conducive to her self-enchantment. Miranda's catharsis repeats the primal act of scapegoating; it releases her from her dangerous reveries by exorcising Adam's ghost. Miranda wisely turns away from her wishful fantasies, but she turns toward a bleak prospect, "the dead cold light of tomorrow" (*CS* 317). When Miranda leaves the hospital to become like everyone else, the pale rider seems to have caught up with her once again. Driven by mimetic desire, Miranda succumbs to the deathly conformity that she always detested.

Girard claims that the end of a novel is the past recaptured because it recounts the author's own victory over mimetic desire (*Deceit* 296–97). However, the somber close of "Pale Horse, Pale Rider" points to the distance between Miranda and her creator in 1918. The short novel was inspired by Porter's own quasi-death in the influenza epidemic at the end of World War I. At its conclusion Miranda does not gain the critical detachment and panoramic comprehension that Girard finds necessary if she is to write her own story, yet Porter, having herself skirted death in 1918, was moving precisely toward such an art of memory. If Porter's biographers are correct in arguing that Adam was probably inspired by a mere acquaintance rather than a beloved soldier (Givner, *A Life* 127–29; Stout, *Katherine Anne Porter* 28), the embellished accounts of her savior that Porter gave interviewers reflect a lifelong desire to create a romantic myth about herself. "Pale Horse, Pale Rider" might be one more attempt to live out this desire in a story rather than in the fictions that she sometimes shared with journalists as if they were facts. Less legendary, however, is Porter's claim that her confrontation with mortality helped to shape her life's work. The nearly fatal illness "simply divided my life, cut across it like that," Porter declared. "So that everything before that was just getting ready, and after that I was in some strange way altered, ready" to become a writer (Givner, ed., *Conversations* 85).

Although Porter might easily have exaggerated the crisis of her vocation, her biographers have noticed signs of a transformation beginning in her. Givner detects how after her illness Porter started to hold the silly and sentimental plays that she reviewed to more demanding standards (*A Life* 132–35), and Stout observes that Porter soon afterwards went to New York in pursuit of her ambition to become an artist (*Katherine Anne Porter* 33). Porter's bout with influenza may have taught her the truth of Walter Benjamin's observation that "death is the sanction of everything that the storyteller can tell" (*Illuminations* 94), as if encountering mortality provided her with the vantage point for the retrospective ordering of her fiction. And the war, the violent double of the epidemic in "Pale Horse, Pale Rider," may have further encouraged Porter's talent for remembering as re-vision. If the Southern Renascence, according to Tate, resulted from the South's entering the modern world by way of World War I even as it took "a backward glance" at the old order, Porter gained after 1918 the viewpoint that enabled her and her contemporaries to write "a literature conscious of the past in the present" (Tate, *Collected Essays* 292). However, Miranda does not discover in her race with the pale rider the authority or the awareness of history that could have turned the journalist into her author. Instead, Porter's fictional counterpart imitates her colleagues at the newspaper in denying death and forgetting the past. Miranda returns to a grim, gray life where she will daily face deadlines as she writes herself into the grave.

Only at the end of "The Grave," the finale to Porter's "Miranda" stories that takes place nearly five years after "Pale Horse, Pale Rider," does new life emerge out of a Girardian death to mimetic desire. If the story proper dramatizes Girard's claim that "the ultimate meaning of desire is death," its one-paragraph coda enacts the corollary that "death is not the novel's ultimate meaning" (*Deceit* 290). As a nine year old at the beginning of "The Grave," Miranda climbed into and then out of the pit that once held her grandfather's bones. As an adult nearly twenty years later at the end of the story, she escapes from her own grave—not from the mortality that is as old as humanity itself but from the sinister horseman that once claimed her as one of the living dead. The means of her deliverance is an imaginative act of recollection, which startles her out of her lifelessness and shows her the future by way of the past. While Miranda walks through a market street in a foreign country, which resembles the Mexico where Porter sojourned at a similar age, she finds that the sight of rabbit-shaped confections and the mixed smells of drooping flowers and meat for sale coalesce to call up a likeness from her youth. What makes the market stalls open into the grave of her childhood is that Miranda exercises her mimetic faculty, the "gift of seeing resemblances" that Benjamin views as "nothing other than a rudiment of the powerful compulsion in former times to become and behave like something else" (*Reflections* 333). The candy on display resembles a rabbit, and the rabbit recalls the slain creature that shocked her into awareness when she was nine. Miranda beholds anew the carnal complexities of twenty years past, the sad-sweet flesh that lives and dies. Her clear-eyed reenvisioning lacks the romanticization and deception used by the old order to conceal the workings of desire. Rather, Miranda sees by what Eudora Welty identifies as Porter's own mode of vision, "the dispassionate eye of time" (*Eye* 38): "as if she looked through a frame upon a scene that had not stirred nor changed since the moment it happened, the episode of that far-off day leaped from its burial place before her mind's eye" (*CS* 367). The fusion of sight and insight culminates the progression through which Miranda has matured in Porter's fiction—from being virtually unseen to being a passive onlooker and then to being an active observer. Finally, she becomes a visionary, whose glimpse of the most trivial imitation—a candied rabbit—leads to a different form of re-presentation—the composition of the past. Miranda recalls what has been interred deep within the grave of her own self and recovers it as if a framed work of art.

Although the vision of the dead rabbit terrifies Miranda again, it leads to a contrasting memory from the same day, now seen with unprecedented and radiant clarity. She beholds her brother Paul, "whose childhood face she had forgotten, standing again in the blazing sunshine, again twelve years old, a pleased sober smile in his eyes, turning the silver dove over and over in his hands" (*CS* 368). Whereas at the end of "Pale Horse, Pale Rider" Miranda tries to raise up a ghost out of the sheer power of her mimetic desire, at the end of "The Grave" Miranda witnesses recollection as if it were resurrection. The young woman comes back to life through reconnecting with a revitalizing past. Miranda regains in lucid memory the treasure that she had years ago traded, but now she has lost the covetousness that first inspired the exchange. The dove becomes for her not the sign of manly violence but of artistic creation.[18] Paul's fingering of the well-crafted object repeats how Miranda years ago handled the silver bird with such connoisseurship. Like Uncle Jimbilly who carves or Sophia Jane and Nannie who piece together "a carefully disordered patchwork" (*CS* 326), Miranda must find her handiwork in making, especially the making of meaning through the ordering of memory, through turning over and turning back to the past. When Miranda pairs these separate and dissimilar memories of the grave so that they can interpret each other, she performs what Porter herself described as the integrating work of the artist—"to take these handfuls of confusion and disparate things, things that seem to be irreconcilable, and put them together in a frame to give them some kind of shape and meaning" (Givner, ed., *Conversations* 88). The beginning of Porter's fiction is the kind of creative remembering that Miranda achieves at the end of "The Grave."

"In my end is my beginning," Porter's own gravestone inscription that she copied from the motto of Mary Stuart, describes how "The Grave" concludes the "Miranda" stories by circling back to what the first of them might call "The Source." The last page of Porter's cycle offers a fictional representation of what makes such fictions at all possible according to Girard: "The title of hero of a novel must be reserved for the character who triumphs over metaphysical desire in a tragic conclusion and thus becomes *capable of writing the novel*. The hero and his creator are separated throughout the novel but come together in the conclusion. . . . The aesthetic triumph of the author is one with the joy of the hero who has renounced desire. Therefore the conclusion is always a memory" (*Deceit* 296–97). Although Porter in her public life may have never gotten beyond her desire to be a model of the lady beautiful, her own confrontation with mortality and her understanding of mimesis enabled her to work toward such a triumph in her imagination. In "The Grave" Porter uncovers and recovers the very origins of her artistry in Miranda's rediscovery of a treasured scene from two decades ago. Rather than wanting to imitate the past like a disciple of the old order, Miranda orders it by a discipline akin to the artist's. Miranda's remembering of her past "as if she looked through a frame" (*CS* 367) finds its double in Porter's aesthetic that arranges what is diverse and chaotic "in a frame to give them some kind of meaning" (Givner, ed., *Conversations* 88). Miranda finds what would be the source of Porter's fiction, of her mimesis, in memory, not desire.

"LIKE A BOULDER BLOCKING YOUR PATH"

O'Connor's Skandalon in *The Violent Bear It Away*

In the imitation-obsessed South that is the background of Porter's "Miranda" stories, the result of not living up to the cultural model may be scandal. Like Eva's feminism and Miss Honey's rage, Amy's rebelliousness seemed shocking because it challenged the example for female discipleship in the old order. After the coquette returned from her wild ride to see her brother escape across the Mexican border, "the scandal, Maria and Miranda gathered, had been pretty terrible." While Amy took to her bed, the rest of the family sat tensely "in the twilight of scandal" (*CS* 189). Although Amy's fever might have been a belle's self-protective ploy, it might also have been symptomatic of how this daughter of the old order bore in her flesh the burden of the resentment and indignation that prostrated her. Yet Amy continued to be attracted to scandal even as it hastened her death. Eva recalls how Amy would give her advice about winning a husband: "Then she would laugh and fly away, and where did she fly to?" Eva answers her own question with a destination almost predictable by Girard's work: "To scandal and to death, nowhere else" (*CS* 211). Indeed, Eva intimates that Amy's sudden marriage to Gabriel and her death six weeks later were both attempts to avoid another scandal.

The old order's fascination with scandal indicates that even in this highly mannered society such offensiveness was more complicated than merely involving an embarrassing violation of social norms. As Girard understands, it always contains a hidden element of desire and its opposite: "Even in its accepted modern meaning, which converts scandal into a mere matter of representation, the notion of the scandalous cannot be defined univocally. Scandal always implies a mutual reinforcement between desire and indignation through a process of *feedback* in the interplay of mimetic interferences. The scandalous would not be scandalous if it did not form an irresistible and impossible example, offering itself for imitation, as both model and anti-model at the same time" (*Things*

Hidden 426). Girard redefines *scandal* in terms of the compulsions of mimesis. It results not from an individual's outrageous actions but from the interaction of master and disciple, the complex and contradictory action-reaction of inter-dividuality. It is not just Amy who is a source of scandal; it is also found in the enticement and opposition operating between Eva and Amy, Amy and Miss Honey, and Miranda and the entire old order.

FROM SCANDAL TO SKANDALON

Girard draws upon a biblical precedent for understanding the spellbinding but self-defeating desire for mimesis that underlies traditional notions of scandal. He returns the term *scandal* to its ancient source in the skandalon. On the basis of passages in the Old and New Testaments, Girard argues that the biblical skandalon, or stumbling stone, is the double bind of mimetic desire. It "is the model exerting its special form of temptation, causing attraction to the extent that it is an obstacle and forming an obstacle to the extent that it can attract" (*Things Hidden* 416). The skandalon thrusts itself forth as if reifying all that seemed inviting and invidious between counterparts of desire. The disciple may stumble over this stone if the model wants to retain exclusive possession of the ideal rather than mediating it to another. Yet even as the model seems like the only barrier between the self and its goal, the admired other also increases desire precisely by impeding its fulfillment. And the more the disciple grows to be like the model, the more the threatened model may oppose the disciple as the rival-image of desire and stumble as well. When scandal gets reflected in this mirror, model and disciple come to resemble each other all the more because each keeps confronting the enticing snare of the other as adversary. Whereas Porter's old order understands scandal primarily in terms of shame and shock, Girard recognizes that the sine qua non of the skandalon is the way that doubles cannot escape the fascinating frustration and frustrating fascination with each other.

Girard sees the scandal of the model-disciple relationship as clearly embodied in the disciple of disciples, the biblical Peter. Although Peter's name is meant to designate the "rock" upon which Jesus builds his community of disciples, it might just as appropriately signify his role as the divisive stumbling block. Immediately after Jesus affirms Peter as the foundation for his church, the apostle rebukes Jesus for announcing his passion, death, and resurrection. Jesus, in turn, rebukes Peter for trying to make him fall: "thou art a [skandalon] unto me: for thou savorest not the things that be of God, but those that be of men" (Matt. 16:23). Peter is a scandal to Jesus because he offers an attractive antimodel for the messiah, which has nothing to do with undergoing the suffering that Jesus has just foretold. He and his ungodly kind do not desire Jesus to reveal the nonviolent love of the Father and the scapegoat mechanism that founds "the things that be . . . of men." Rather, they desire him to be the powerful prince of this world "so that they can become godlike according to the logic of violence" (*Things Hidden* 419). Jesus rejects the age-old temptation. Offering an entirely new model of discipleship, he invites his disciples to follow him by being willing to lose their lives in order to gain them (Matt. 16:24–26).

Since Peter desires prestige at any cost, he aspires to be the first of those followers, and the result is that he sets himself up again for scandal. When Jesus announces at the Last Supper that he will die and rise from the dead, Peter boasts of the discipleship that he desires: "Though all men shall be [scandalized] because of thee, yet will I never be [scandalized]" (Matt. 26:33). Jesus answers that the supposedly stalwart Peter will be guilty of a triple betrayal. "To imagine oneself immune to scandal," as Peter does according to Girard, "is to claim the self-sufficiency of the god of violence and so to expose oneself to imminent disaster" (*Things Hidden* 419). That night the follower who protests that he will never be offended by Jesus is actually so offended by the prospect of following his master unto death that he stumbles three times. By his triple denial Peter imitates the crowd's victimization of Jesus so that he can escape being likewise victimized (*Scapegoat* 154). If you want the kingdom of this world, Peter implies again and again, remember that the nonviolent do not bear it away.

The kingdom of God has no room for such scandal and strife. Girard sees the biblical rejection of such snares as receiving early codification in Leviticus 19:14 (*Things Hidden* 420). Jews are enjoined not to put any stumbling blocks before the blind as one of a series of commands that seek to forestall violence from breaking out in society. The epitome of these mandates is to love one's neighbor as one's very self. Jesus repeats this precept, extends such love especially to one's enemies, and warns about the scandalous duality that gets in the way of such charity. He cautions against the judgment that brings a counter-judgment, against noticing the mote in a brother's eye but not the beam in one's own (Matt. 7:1–5). Such fault finding risks entrapping each partner in an unending circle of rivalrous obsession with the other (*Things Hidden* 427). Paul likewise advises the Christians in Rome, "Let us not therefore judge one another any more: but judge this rather, that no man put a stumbling block or an occasion to fall in his brother's way" (Rom. 14:13). And the first Letter of John affirms, "He that loveth his brother abideth in the light, and there is none occasion of stumbling in him" (2:10).

Whereas scandal in Porter's old order results from a failure in imitating the cultural expectations, the skandalon arises between model and disciple when imitation becomes so successful that it provokes rancor and resentment. Porter depicts how mimetic rivalry trips up many of the opposing doubles in the "Miranda" stories. However, except during her feverish dream about victimization in "Pale Horse, Pale Rider," the stumbling stone never really threatens to make Miranda fall or to drive her to violence.[1] In *The Violent Bear It Away* the cultural hour is later than in the "Miranda" stories. O'Connor is careful to set her novel in 1952, for it locates her stumblers against a specific background of national and international violence. Richard Giannone has rightly noted how during Tarwater's short life of fourteen years, from 1938 to 1952, "the powerful nations committed themselves to turning the planet into a charnel house" through the Holocaust, World War II, Hiroshima, and the Korean Conflict (*Flannery O'Connor, Hermit Novelist* 148). Although O'Connor never mentions such cataclysms in *The Violent Bear It Away,* they inevitably bear down upon the strife in her novel. O'Connor recognized that no story could ever be separated from history. She believed that "the serious fiction writer always writes about the whole world, no matter how limited his particular scene. For him, the bomb that was dropped on Hiroshima affects life on the Oconee River, and there's not anything he can do about it" (*Mystery* 77). Powderhead, the Tarwater family property that provides the scene for the beginning and ending of the novel, is a powder keg of aggression, a world in miniature waiting to explode. Tarwater's racism there suggests how two years before *Brown v. Board of Education* (1954) the South was still pursuing its own local forms of the victimization that was being carried out in the global arena. Set in the inaugural year of the Eisenhower era, O'Connor's portrayal of how the skandalon is idolized in a corner of Tennessee lays bare the mechanism behind the horrors of the century.

In *The Violent Bear It Away* O'Connor places this skandalon at the very center of her novel.[2] The violent nephews and uncles of her family tale struggle with it, hurl themselves at it, gash themselves upon it, and fight to get beyond it. "It" is immense and immovable, for it is the fascinating and offensive god of the novel, the sacred reflection of the discord that adversaries perpetuate even as they try to overcome it. O'Connor's models and disciples encounter this stumbling stone so frequently that the whole novel seems a prolonged obstacle course. In this scandal-laden story there is nowhere to turn away from one impediment except toward another obstruction, yet there is no hindrance without its perverse enticement to keep on returning to it.

Everything rises against and in front of O'Connor's characters—barriers that are as much physical as figurative—and what gets in the way of her violent wayfarers the most is other violent wayfarers. Blocked from entering his sister's house, Mason shouts his gospel of sin and salvation outside it until he is finally taken captive and confined to an asylum for four years. After being released and going to live with his nephew Rayber, the angry old man feels his tongue lying like a stone in his mouth when he reads a critical article that the schoolteacher has written about him. Years later Mason stands before the door of Rayber's house, "his heavy shoulders hunched as if he were going to crash through it" so that he can baptize Rayber's son (141). The perpetually frustrated prophet finally entrusts this mission to his great-nephew, but on the day of Mason's death Tarwater renounces the commission in order to struggle with the stone before the cave that hides the old moonshiner's cache of whiskey. A stranger encourages the teen to drink by describing the overbearing Mason as "the stone before your door and the Lord has rolled it away" (150). Tarwater travels to Rayber's to find such deliverance from Mason, but after banging on his uncle's closed door with the knocker, his fist, and his foot, he enters only to find his path in the hallway blocked by Bishop, Rayber's developmentally disabled son. Tarwater becomes obsessed with the child that he loathes but that he feels compelled to baptize, and Rayber becomes obsessed with Tarwater.

When Rayber and Tarwater first meet, the uncle does not notice how his nephew's face has become so stony that "it was a fortress wall to keep his thoughts from being exposed" (177). Like Tarwater, Rayber cannot get beyond the skandalon. While pursuing his nephew as the country boy explores the city by night, Rayber wanders down alleyways and stumbles on a garbage can that mysteriously rises in his path. The schoolteacher later imagines that his real obstacle is Tarwater and feels liberated after dreaming that his opponent has finally left him. Rayber tries to overcome the youth's "oppressive presence" by turning him into an abstraction, but "every now and then the boy's actual face would lodge in the path of a plan" (229). Rayber makes vivid the compelling impasse felt throughout the novel when he describes Tarwater's mandate from Mason to baptize Bishop as an "order lodged in your head like a boulder blocking your path" and lectures his disciple that he must "understand what it is that blocks you" (237).

The Violent Bear It Away positions the skandalon as the "it" that O'Connor's violent characters cannot bear away. Although O'Connor believed that her novel failed to clarify the biblical meaning of its title (*Habit* 382), her focus on the skandalon suggests that the work resonates with the critique of violence in

Jewish and Christian scriptures. She quoted the signal text from Matthew 11:12 at the beginning of her novel: "From the days of John the Baptist until now, the kingdom of heaven suffereth violence, and the violent bear it away." Especially when read out of context, the passage that provided O'Connor with her title and epigraph might seem to affirm a kingdom of sacred violence. However, the gospel verse actually undermines such a bloody realm.³ Jesus appropriately cites the days of the Baptist as one reference point for this reign of violence, for John's arrest and murder result from the mimetic desire that finally leads to the "now" of its imminent end, the victimization of Jesus himself. As Girard demonstrates in *The Scapegoat* (125–48), the beheading of John climaxes a dance in which the mimeticism of art spreads the desire for violence from Herodias to Salome and then from the scandalized child to Herod and his guests. The collective murder of the Baptist points ahead to the scapegoating of the innocent and nonviolent Jesus. In fact, in the verses immediately before and after O'Connor's citation from Matthew, Jesus rejects the envy and animosity that foster such violence. Jesus does not view John as a rival but praises the Baptist as the greatest "born of women" and then identifies his kinsman with the returning Elijah, the master prophet of O'Connor's novel. Unlike Jesus, the competitors in *The Violent Bear It Away* too often view each other as nothing but obstacles to seizing the foremost position in their own version of heaven. Jesus displaces such pride of place and even revises his own estimation of the Baptist by claiming, "he that is least in the kingdom of heaven is greater" than John (Matt. 11:11). Jesus turns the obsession with rank against itself, for such hateful competition may culminate in the violence that has reigned from Israel to Powderhead, from "all the prophets and the law [that] prophesied until John" to the children of the prophets in *The Violent Bear It Away* (Matt. 11:13). On this rock of offense, the scandal of rivalrous discipleship, Mason, Rayber, and Tarwater dash not their feet but their heads and their hearts.

TO OUT-ELIJAH ELIJAH: TARWATER VS. MASON

Amid the backcountry sanctuary of a Tennessee farm, eighty-four-year-old Mason has raised fourteen-year-old Tarwater to be his disciple. The aged prophet openly acknowledged this mimetic bond when he "compared their situation to that of Elijah and Elisha" (147), perhaps the most famous model-disciple relationship in the Old Testament.⁴ The book of Kings records how Elijah chose Elisha as his follower and how the disciple ministered faithfully to his master. And when Elijah was finally transported to heaven by a fiery chariot, Elisha received the mantle of his model and the double portion of his master's spirit that he had sought. In the tradition of Elijah, Mason intends that Tarwater will be "trained by a prophet for prophesy (*sic*)" (133).

Since the message of the prophet is countercultural, the elder has created at Powderhead what Jon Lance Bacon describes as a refuge from the conformity of cold-war America (98–100, 136). The country at midcentury is so opposed to the threat of difference that it conceives of education as a process to enforce collective imitation of all-American ideals. Tarwater knows that if he attended the kind of school where Rayber teaches, he would only be "one among many, indistinguishable from the herd" (134). Running a hard-scrabble home school for prophets, Mason tries to educate his disciple in a form of imitation entirely unlike the public school mass homogeneity that he scorns. The veteran prophet at his best wants Tarwater to be a disciple not of himself but of the loving God he tries to enflesh by his *imitatio Christi*. Mason shows this love by providing sustenance for the hungry soul, heart, and body of his young follower. The old man has baptized his heir, rescued him from the bloodless abstraction of Rayber, and nurtured him on the food that even the rebellious teenager remembers with fond satisfaction. Although Mason is dead from the first paragraph of the novel, the way that Tarwater's frequent and vivid memories of his great-uncle keep bearing away the narrative present in part 1 gives fictional form to how unforgettably the model of solicitude has begun the spiritual formation of his disciple.

The problem with Mason's faith is that it stumbles on the skandalon. Living as if in a perpetual state of antagonism, Mason finds virtually everyone he encounters an obstacle to his grand prophetic vocation. However, he keeps flinging himself against these rivals and allowing his foes to provoke him into ever escalating anger. For example, after an attorney tells Mason that he cannot keep the infidel Rayber from inheriting his farm, the master of Powderhead and his lawyer rail at each other in angry imitation, both hitting the desk between them with their fists. Yet even as the counselor tries to disengage himself from the quarrel, Mason's dudgeon rises higher and higher until his voice is a barely audible shriek of exasperation. The law is one of culture's fundamental ways to contain and restrain violence, but it merely goads Mason into further fury.

Throughout such tantrums, Mason's ill-temper is never abstracted but always worked out in his flesh or on the flesh of another. When Tarwater suggests that he might not follow his great-uncle's instructions to bury his body and mark his grave with a cross, the scandalized believer roars, hisses, hollers, slams his fist on his coffin, and finally grabs the boy by the straps of his pants to glare into his insolent face. Even memory perpetuates the old-timer's enmity by driving him to reenact unforgotten indignation. The irate uncle merely has to remember Rayber's charge that Mason called himself to the prophetic life, and he shakes Tarwater by his braces as a kind of surrogate victim for the real target of his rage. Mason and Rayber are so bound by mimetic rivalry that sometimes the old man, "imitating the schoolteacher's voice" (157), would repeat with exaggerated silliness his nephew's most provocative claim: Rayber once asserted that he helped his sister take a lover as a way to increase her self-esteem. Mason's parody seeks to appropriate yet overcome Rayber, to mimic and mock him, in sound and speech. Yet if Mason is spurred to new heights of hysteria by his pimp of a nephew, he is also frustrated by such brazen immorality. Facing Rayber, Mason confronts what sharpens his sense of his prophetic mission like a whetstone yet obstructs it like a monolith, the stumbling stone that he cannot spurn or surpass, the skandalon.

Mason's fiercest attempt to get beyond this enticing impediment took place years ago when he resorted to actual violence against his arch-obstacle. After Mason kidnapped Tarwater to save the infant from Rayber and for God, his nephew tried to retake custody of the child at Powderhead. The gun-wielding defender of the faith rebuffed the attempt by wounding Rayber in the leg. However, in an instant Mason showed how much his holy wrath was really personal pique. Outraged by "the nephew's expression of outraged righteousness" after the shooting, Mason climaxed the face-off by shooting again, this time nipping the ear of his rival for Tarwater's discipleship. In *The Stumbling Block,* a book O'Connor once recommended to a friend (*Habit* 263), François Mauriac might almost be speaking for her rifle-toting evangelist when he laments, "What scandalizes me in the unbelieving is their dismissal of even a hypothesis, their security in negation . . . . I am scandalized that they never ask themselves: 'But if it were true nevertheless?'" (6–7). Although some of Mason's outbursts might be explained away as a technique for reaching hardened hearts, even the old man knows that the gunshot blasts cannot easily be excused. Sometimes when he would retell the violent story to Tarwater, "as if he did not want to think of it, he would speed over the part where he shot the nephew and race on" (128). Mason's hasty narration betrays his deep guilt at acting as if Rayber were one of the modern prophets of Baal whom this latter-day Elijah had to vanquish (1 Kings 18:20–40). The two shots are nothing more than one more round in the reciprocal antagonism between two models warring for mastery over each other and a potential disciple.

The prophet who rages preaches a religion of rage. Mason's fury at others gives earthly expression to the fury of the Other that he adores. In fusing violence and the sacred, the old man comes from a long line in the South. The backwoods preacher is the descendant of the frontier religious tradition that Cash describes as having demanded a "passionate, whimsical tyrant, to be trembled before, but whose favor was the sweeter for that. A personal God, a God for the individualist, a God whose representatives were not silken priests but preachers risen from the people themselves" (56). Mason the moonshiner is also the voice of the revivalism that has continually called the South back to such a stormy deity. Sensing their religious tradition to be at bay in the contemporary world, southerners have often returned to "the older religiousness of dreams and drunkenness" (Weaver 95). After the Civil War the South cultivated the Lost Cause through a recommitment to the bedrock teachings and values of its religious past. And after World War I the South defended itself against the liberalism of the North through a biblical fundamentalism that opposed evolution, drastically limited the social gospel, and scrutinized the orthodoxy of college faculty (Cash 130–33, Bailey 44–71). Now after World War II, Mason rebuffs the modernism of his family's atheism and immorality through preaching an angry God of imminent destruction.

Yet Old Mason speaks out of a tradition older than even any in the South. The great-uncle illustrates Girard's contention that much of historical Christianity has misinterpreted the antisacrificial revelation of the gospels and perpetuated a mythic understanding of the godhead. Mason's error has its precedent in the biblical prophets who serve as his models. These messengers opposed the religion of violence by criticizing the sacrificial cult and affirming a life based on nonviolent love. In Isaiah's Songs of the Suffering Servant, Girard hears one of the clearest revelations of the scapegoat mechanism, for the laments record the persecution of an entirely innocent victim and attribute his death to purely human forces. However, Girard argues that the prophets never completely renounced the vengeful God who would purify the world of its wickedness and deliver the chosen to their glorious destiny (*Things Hidden* 157–58, 200). The model prophet for O'Connor's novel, in particular, demonstrates this ambiguity. When Elijah condemned the seizure of Naboth's vineyard by the covetous Jezebel and Ahab, the man of God criticized a startling example of how mimetic desire may lead to murder. But Elijah also believed that he saw God at work in violence. When the servant of Yahweh defeated the prophets of Baal in a sacrificial competition on Mt. Carmel, he turned his enemies into a bloody offering by ordering all 450 of them to be slaughtered. Fleeing their patroness Jezebel, Elijah retreated to Mount Horeb, where he expected God's theophany in the violence of wind, earthquake, and fire. The prophet of divine tumult was disappointed. Elijah discovered that God speaks not with such terror but with what he heard in the quiet aftermath, "a still small voice" (1 Kings 19:12).

O'Connor's Tennessee Elijah lives out this ambivalent legacy from the prophets. Although Mason loves the world profoundly, he calls down destruction on the part of it that always keeps getting in his way. God has rejected the old man's violent eschatology from his youth when Mason beheld a kind of anti-apocalypse as quietly corrective as Elijah's encounter on Mt. Horeb. O'Connor's prophet had been warning the city about its doom for rejecting salvation in Christ, but he preached only his own choler in predicting the worldwide vision of a bloody sunburst. The natural and supernatural order silently rebuked his noisy tidings of imminent disorder. The sun "rose every morning, calm and contained in itself, as if not only the world, but the Lord Himself had failed to hear the prophet's message" (126). Having missed God's announcement in the dailiest of events, Mason finds it delivered again deep within himself. The egotism behind Mason's apocalyptic predictions gets fiery chastisement in an apocalypse of the ego. One morning when it seems as if God has finally listened to the word of the lordly Mason, a heavenly finger blazes forth from the sun. It scorches not the earth but Mason's heart; "the destruction he had been waiting for had fallen in his own brain and his own body" (126). Mason feels his revelation as a violent rejection of his violence. Although cast in his favorite images of flaming judgment, it actually internalizes the eschaton and indicts his godlike anger. The accusation tenderizes Mason's flinty heart, for after the catastrophe he "had learned enough to hate the destruction that had to come and not all that was going to be destroyed" (126). Mason undergoes such conversion several more times throughout his prophetic vocation, but never again after he saved Tarwater by kidnapping him from Rayber's house. Although the old man's rage while he raised the boy suggests that he may continually need such redirection, his aura of sacred violence is precisely what inspires Tarwater to imitate him.

If Mason desires to make Tarwater his disciple, Tarwater desires to take Mason as his model. O'Connor's narrator observes that the youth regularly followed all of his great-uncle's customs, even to always wearing his gray hat except when in bed. Tarwater is most attracted to Mason's calling when the old man returns from having "thrashed out his peace with the Lord" in the woods. Hallowed by the divine conflict and chaos, Mason "would look the way the boy thought a prophet ought to look. He would look as if he had been wrestling a wildcat," as if he had just beheld the great winged and wheeling creatures from chapter 1 in Ezekiel (127). Indeed, Tarwater expected this very vision when his great-uncle died, as if the young disciple might witness a fierce and fiery commissioning for his own role as prophet. Tarwater wants to imitate Mason's rage as a means to the sacred. Although the youth stubbornly clings to his hat, violence is actually the prophetic mantle in which this adolescent Elisha wraps himself as he seeks to storm his way into the kingdom of heaven.

Tarwater's desire to be a prophet of God's ferocity brings him into conflict with the furious uncle who provides the model for such mimesis.[5] The disciple trips upon the same skandalon that rose in the path of the biblical Elisha. Either the follower of Elijah who received a double share of his master's spirit was driven by envious duality, or the followers of Elisha, who preserved the anecdotes about their master, recorded their own rivalrous desires in 2 Kings. For in too many of the stories in the Elisha cycle, the disciple is portrayed as an even more awesome wonderworker than his master. Tarwater feels the same competition with Mason and the same need to surpass his mentor in a religion of self-promoting razzle-dazzle. Elisha does not just multiply oil and raise the dead son of a generous woman as did Elijah. The thaumaturge performs more astonishing versions of his predecessor's signature miracles, and he also brings about a whole series of unique marvels that exalt him even further, such as renewing the waters of a spring, bringing destruction on children who mock him, curing a leper, and making an ax that has fallen into the Jordan float. To read 2 Kings after 1 Kings is to see one prophet contending, by way of story, with his double.

O'Connor's Elisha clearly intends to be no second to his great-uncle Elijah. The would-be prophet keeps implying that the self-declared prophet is not prophet enough. The impetuous Tarwater chides his dilatory relative with not acting decisively enough to get young Bishop baptized. Tarwater "wanted to see the old man in action, wanted him to kidnap the child" and provoke Rayber into once again attempting a rescue. When Mason and his ward visit the city for the first time in Tarwater's life, the upstart taunts the veteran man of God for not living up to his vocation by denouncing all the sinful citizens. "Elijah would think a heap of you," he jeers (139). For Tarwater, to be a prophet is not to speak the divine word but to burn with the divine wrath. And so the scandalized disciple scorns Mason's commission to pour some water over a dim-wit's head as a second-rate mission for a prophet like himself who will act and speak more boldly than his failed model ever dared. Although Mason believes in a sometimes furious God, Tarwater wants to become a god of fury.

Even more fiercely than Porter's stage-struck Miranda, Tarwater seeks what Homer terms "kudos," the glory of the demigod that comes from victory in competition. "Man can enjoy this condition only fleetingly," Girard writes, "and *always at the expense of other men.* To be a god is to possess kudos forever, to remain forever a master, unchallenged and unchallengeable" (*Violence* 152). Anticipating some grandiose destiny, Tarwater boasts to Mason that God "don't mean for me to finish up your leavings. He has other things in mind for me" (128). The braggart immediately recalls more attractive models, biblical figures like Moses, Joshua, and Daniel, who achieved kudos by overturning the natural order. Tarwater may seem like an antiprophet in rejecting Mason's charge, but he actually speaks from the same corrupted tradition of prophecy that consecrates wrath for his great-uncle. Driven by mimetic desire to violence, Tarwater would out-Elijah Elijah.

Just as Tarwater dismisses Mason's ire as too tepid, he regards his relative's love as too threatening. The insolent youth has not realized that "it is a sign of maturity not to be scandalized," as O'Connor wrote to Ted Spivey, "and to try to find explanations in charity" (*Habit* 346). Charity explains much of Mason's solicitude for his great-nephew. But since Tarwater is attracted to the scandal of discipleship, the aspiring champion finds little obvious appeal in the nonviolent heart of his great-uncle's faith. When the apocalyptic fire leaves Mason's eye and he speaks of "the sweat and stink of the cross" (128), rebirth through baptism, and the heavenly banquet, Tarwater is a heedless pupil. Such truths testify to the victim rather than the victimizer, to renewal rather than repeating the violence that has been done from the foundation of the world, to communion rather than the rivalrous doubleness of the skandalon. Tarwater scorns a nonviolent conception of the sacred, yet he is summoned by these very mysteries. The apostate intuits their underlying truth through Mason's constant concern for him, a providence that was never concealed even by his elder's angry apocalypticism. After Mason's death Tarwater is troubled by a hunger that he cannot satisfy because it is a yearning for the kind of affectionate nurturing that the old man once tendered him. Despite rejecting his great-uncle's mandate, the youth obscurely desires to baptize Bishop because he knows that the sacrament will signify the child's initiation into this loving life of God. Tarwater is Mason's disciple in spite of himself. "Every day . . . you remind me more of the old man," Rayber later tells his nephew. "You're just like him. You have his future before you" (227).

Tarwater feels the claim of this destiny so passionately that he tries to reject it by torching the house at Powderhead that he mistakenly thinks contains Mason's dead body. The arsonist unwittingly hallows Mason with the sacred violence that the youth himself sought, for the flames seem to bear Great-Uncle Elijah away in a burning chariot. Tarwater flees the fiery transmission, travels to the city, and assaults Rayber's door. He hopes that he can escape the most reprehensible form of mimesis—imitating Mason's desire to baptize Bishop—by embracing a far more gratifying form of modeling—imitating the desire of Bishop's father to desacralize the world. However, he trips once again on the familiar obstacle of mimetic desire. Late in the novel at the Cherokee Lodge, Rayber finds two stones in the pants that Tarwater discards before he plunges into the lake. The rocks manifest the skandalon of violent duality on which Tarwater and Rayber continually stumble.

ALWAYS THE STUMBLING BLOCK: TARWATER VS. RAYBER

"Rayber, of course, was always the stumbling block," O'Connor wrote to John Hawkes in 1959 after she reviewed the proofs of *The Violent Bear It Away.* Creating Rayber consumed most of the seven years that she worked on the novel. Indeed, after O'Connor heard Porter confess that it had taken her twenty-seven years to write *Ship of Fools,* she had nightmares over working on her second novel and hoped that it would not take her as long (*Habit* 279–80). As early as New Year's Day in 1956, O'Connor faced the artistic obstacle in creating *The Violent Bear It Away* when she wrote to Betty Hester, the anonymous "A" of her letters, "My novel is at an impasse. In fact it has been at one for as long as I can remember" (*Habit* 127). While O'Connor wrote and rewrote, she labored to make Rayber seem less evil so that he would not be a caricature and so that he would seem worthy of Mason's efforts to save him. Some readers have viewed O'Connor the novelist as being tripped up by her cartoonish schoolteacher; Harold Bloom, for example, dismisses Rayber as an "aesthetic disaster" ("Introduction" 2). However, such criticism overlooks how the father's poignant affection for his son complicates what might otherwise seem like a comic book characterization. The teacher might appear less of an artistic obstacle if understood exactly as O'Connor described him, a "stumbling block"—a skandalon for O'Connor and in O'Connor's novel.

Rayber the intellectual challenged O'Connor as both novelist and believer.

Although a writer of formidable intelligence, she recognized the limitations of the human mind, and she believed that the flesh was a means rather than an impediment to holiness. Indeed, O'Connor scorned Rayber's sublime abstraction so completely that her ire created a fictional obstacle. She found that her normal artistry in voice failed her in depicting Rayber, yet the stonewalled novelist strangely sensed her kinship with this character who could not hear well when she admitted to not having "the ear for him" (*Habit* 352, 353). O'Connor's frustration with the man of mind only increased her fascination with him, especially because she was writing into Rayber a believer's testing of unbelief. Although O'Connor opposed reading an author's psyche by way of her stories, she believed that an artist must invest a part of herself in any character with whom she sympathizes (*Habit* 170, 105). If, as Robert Brinkmeyer suggests, O'Connor's "dialogic interplay" with her characters made them "on one level refracted doubles of herself" (*Art and Vision* 134), Rayber was such a stumbling block because O'Connor was contending with her mimetic counterpart. She might have loathed her atheist schoolteacher, but he was a part of the self that a writer sounds "to reach those underground springs that give life to his work" (*Mystery* 50). O'Connor seemed to recognize this disturbing connection when she wrote to John Hawkes about her two novels, "There are some of us who have to pay for our faith every step of the way and who have to work out dramatically what it would be like without it and if being without it would be ultimately possible or not" (*Habit* 349–50). Rayber enabled O'Connor to translate into fiction her potential falterings on her way toward God. In stumbling over Rayber, O'Connor was feeling what it was like to be blocked by the kind of negative double that continually captivates all of her models and disciples in *The Violent Bear It Away*.

Tarwater desires to imitate Rayber because he believes the schoolteacher lives out the radically liberal education necessary to oppose Mason's pernicious religious indoctrination. The modernist Rayber espouses the scientism, materialism, and rationalism that southern Christianity spent the first half of the twentieth century in rejecting. Even before coming to stay at Rayber's house, Tarwater sounds like one of the schoolmaster's students; "I ain't bothering with trifles," the scornful youth objects to Mason's request that a cross be placed over his grave (132). When Tarwater threatens to call Rayber to oversee the disposition of the old man's body, the prophet rages that Rayber would cremate him. Tarwater eventually imitates his new model's desire for dealing with dead prophets. The would-be disciple announces the mimesis in the first words he shouts to Rayber: "My great-uncle is dead and burnt, just like you would have burnt him yourself!" (175).

Rayber longs to have a disciple perhaps just as much as Tarwater has longed to have a model. He has been scandalized that Bishop's limited intellectual abilities have kept the boy from living up to the model for perfect sonship. Since Rayber desires nothing more than to be desired, he decides to adopt Tarwater in his head so that his new son will embody his cerebral ideal. When his prospective pupil comes to Rayber's house, the pedagogue "gaze[s] through the actual insignificant boy before him to an image of him that he held fully developed in his mind" (177). Rayber fathers Tarwater in mimesis, conceiving the ideal that he wants his future disciple to reproduce, propagating the very self-image that Tarwater desires. Flesh has even prepared the way for this imitation, for the two are already doubles in body. On coming to his uncle's house, Tarwater finds Rayber's face "so familiar to him that he might have seen it every day of his life" (175). That night Rayber gazes at his sleeping nephew and decides that Tarwater looks as if he could be his own son.

As Rayber tries to turn his kin into his own kind, the double in and of his mind, the two engage in what Girard terms "the mimesis of apprenticeship," the education in cultural standards that comes through modeling and imitation (*Things Hidden* 290). Whereas Mason raised Tarwater to be a prophet, Rayber teaches him to be, like himself, a man of the modern world. The schoolmaster turns their early days together into an extended field trip in urban studies and provides lots of observational learning activities, all designed to make his protégé a respectable citizen of the secular city. Girard claims that education, especially with its exams to be "passed," transfers rites of passage to the school system, where students undergo the death and rebirth that originate in surrogate victimage (*I See Satan* 90–91). O'Connor's schoolmaster uses all of these educational excursions with Tarwater to initiate his pupil into the gospel of Rayber: humans can save themselves by their own intelligence.

Rayber imagines that he models for Tarwater how to escape from his mimetic bondage to Mason. The uncle sees in Tarwater's current discipleship at fourteen the double of his own that began at age seven when he suddenly felt Mason's "mad fish-colored eyes" staring at him (224). The old prophet used to recall the four days that followed at Powderhead as an idyll of imitation. According to Mason, Rayber responded to his summons with the readiness of the disciples whom Jesus called to be fishers of men and women. Having rescued

Rayber from a materialistic father and an alcoholic mother, Mason initiated him into the Christian faith as well as the country pleasures of fishing, plowing, and walking in the woods. However, Rayber remembers the discipleship as a tale of hypnotic domination. "It was the eyes that got me," he maintains to Tarwater. "Children may be attracted to mad eyes. A grown person could have resisted" (224). Jean-Michel Oughourlian has argued that hypnotism creates an intensification of the model-disciple relationship, causing the subject to imitate the desire of the mediator (qtd. in *Things Hidden* 320). Children are especially susceptible to hypnosis because of their "aptitude for good mimesis, peaceful mimesis—for taking a model who is not at the same time an obstacle" (qtd. in *Things Hidden* 322). Rayber regards his mimesis of the Svengali-like Mason in terms of just such mesmerism. The ensuing "six or seven years of unreality" as the old man's disciple were the mere entrancement of a helpless youth until he at last was able to overcome "his own childhood's seduction" and escape "the spell" as an adolescent (199).

Although Rayber lives so that he will never be spellbound again, the ex-disciple repeatedly defines himself in terms of his ever-captivating model. When Mason came to his home to baptize Bishop, Rayber rebuffed him with scandalous force, "a kind of subdued intensity, a passion equal and opposite to the old man's" (143). That identity amid antithesis means that if Mason favored baptism, Rayber opposed it "'just as a matter of principle, nothing else'" (143). Or that if Mason poured the sacramental water on Tarwater's infant head, his contrary double would repeat the rite and derisively baptize the child's bottom as well as his top. Imitating Mason even as he inverts him, Rayber cannot get beyond the negative symmetry of the model and disciple who have become rivals for mastery.

Rayber is ready to continue this rivalry by teaching Tarwater how to reject the fanaticism of Mason's faith, the violence of the old man's God, and the violation of Christian discipleship. The seemingly dispassionate schoolteacher has formed his own belief out of mimetic opposition to the militant prophet. Rayber has sought to avoid Mason's extremes by creating his own. Seeing himself "divided in two—a violent and a rational self" (207), the teacher has decided to repress his rage and live by the ways of reason. Rayber carries to its humanistic conclusion the secularization of God that Ransom mourned in *God without Thunder,* for he believes not in a rational deity but in rationalism. In trying to make Tarwater his enlightened disciple, Rayber rivals his old master. If Mason tends to set aside violence as the sacred, Rayber sets aside the sacred as a rational way of rejecting violence. So, he desacralizes. The rite of Christian initiation is no more than a matter of words and water, all hunger is only a desire of the stomach, and death is merely an event in nature. In place of these cardinal beliefs, Rayber propounds to Tarwater a secular creed that seems based on promoting nonviolence. He believes in humanity rather than Mason's raging divinity, in science rather than the deceptions of mythic thought, and in stoicism rather than emotional upheaval. However, Rayber does not realize that he is actually more violent and less rational than he thinks. He has not only glorified and rationalized violence but also made the rational into a new form of violence.

Rayber believes that he has rejected sacred violence in favor of humanity, yet he allows the fury that Girard considers the human engine behind primitive religion to consume his body, mind, and will. When Rayber charges Mason, "You infected me with your idiot hopes, your foolish violence," he rightly describes how he imitates his uncle's bad temper (166). Rayber shouts, curses, hisses, and croaks his way throughout the novel. He hurls his wife across the room when she suggests that Bishop be institutionalized, tries to drown his son at the beach, and finally acquiesces in the boy's murder at the Cherokee Lodge. When Rayber is not actually doing violence, he often lives on the verge of doing violence. He wants to fling his hearing aid against the wall when Tarwater inquires about it, plans to roar at Tarwater to leave the chapel where Lucette Carmody preaches, and would like to swing his chair in the faces of the teenagers who look at Bishop as if he were a freak of creation. Rayber ultimately believes in the divinity of violence that he imagines himself as forswearing.

Indeed, Rayber's unacknowledged deity is more terrible than Mason's wrathful Lord because it hides behind the appearance of being humane. As Rayber listens to the young and lame Lucette Carmody fiercely proclaim the gospel in a tabernacle that has attracted Tarwater, he is moved to pity "all exploited children"—Lucette exploited by parents who commercialize the sacred, himself and Tarwater exploited by Mason, even Bishop "exploited by the very fact he was alive" (203). When the little evangelist recounts Herod's slaughter of the innocents, Rayber longs to rescue their modern counterparts, to move "like an avenging angel through the world, gathering up all the children that the Lord, not Herod, had slain" (204). Rayber's anger at a God who is guilty of infanticide makes him desire to be a counter God, but his spirit of vengeance is really no different from the brutal lord that he condemns. Although Rayber imagines that he feels for the victim, he is actually the most unfeeling of victimizers. His pity for the suffering young is compromised by a rationalized sentimentality that would allow him to slay his own child. If Bishop is exploited merely by being alive, then the maudlin father is justified in wanting to murder his son. Like Herod, Rayber can have the child who has become an obstacle killed; moreover, he can sanction it as a work of mercy.

Rayber's intellect allows him the illusion that he has repudiated something as archaic and unsavory as victimization. "I don't believe in senseless sacrifice," he tells Tarwater in explaining why years ago he did not save his infant nephew from the gun-wielding Mason (187). Rayber does not realize that all sacrifice is senseless in its service to the idols of violence. Indeed, he has not so much re-jected sacred killing as merely redefined it by staging the murder in his own mind. The high priest sacrifices all who come before him, for he converts a hu-man being into what Mason terms "a piece of information inside his head" (133). Rayber finds in form some alternative to the babel that occasionally blares through his hearing aid, a mental order that he distills out of the disorder of noise. Such abstract knowledge enables Rayber to achieve cybernetic equilib-rium. He escapes what Michel Serres hears as the "furiously raging ocean" of background sounds that disrupt the transmission of messages (77). But Rayber can only maintain the stasis, the reception without static, that he substitutes for Mason's frenzy by creating this information through a violent act of cognition.

The origin and model for this detached reflection is an ancient slaughter. Gi-rard regards symbolic thought as a faculty that developed during the calm fol-lowing the primordial murder (*Violence* 235–36). Once a single victim had been substituted for the community in conflict, the principle of re-presentation al-lowed a ritualized scapegoat to be substituted for the victim, and finally an an-imal offering to be substituted for the scapegoat. The sacrificial stand-in estab-lished the very principle of symbolization. Rayber uses his mind to culminate this series of cultic displacements. In a bloodless slaughter he turns a person into a bit of data, leaving his victim as disembodied and dispirited as a heartless idea. Rayber translates Mason, for example, into an obsessive whose "fixation" about a divine call reflects his own "insecurity" (134), and he makes Tarwater into a compulsive who cannot overcome his desire to baptize. If, as Allen Tate warns, "abstraction is the death of religion no less than the death of anything else" (*Col-lected Essays* 156), Rayber professes a faith that is as dead as the world his mind empties and intellectualizes.

Bishop is Rayber's ultimate sacrifice. Having reduced the child to no more than "an x signifying the general hideousness of fate" (192), the sacerdote en-courages Tarwater's killing of his son as if it were no more than the elimination of a bad idea. Such abstraction, as Serres argues, reaches its ideal form by excluding all that is empirical and particular. It eliminates noise for the sake of a purified realm of information (69–70). Pursuing such gnosis, Rayber once tried to put his mind to the service of Molech by drowning young Bishop. His motive was perfectly cerebral, for the inarticulate child, who repeatedly bellows in the novel, seems like nothing but noise, nothing but the jamming in Rayber's sublime world of information science. The child sacrifice would keep Rayber free from being borne away by the "runaway" that information theorists view as destabilizing cognitive order. No longer would the intellectual engineer have to worry about the paroxysms of love for the child who runs away with his heart. Bishop's death would only be a necessary negative feedback, the correction that helps a system preserve its state of equilibrium (Girard, *Things Hidden* 292). Despite such rationalization, Rayber was kept from this terrible stumble, for he failed at the beach to impose pure form on the intractable flux that besieges his mental realm. However, he models for Tarwater an appealing and appalling destiny in hoping to turn Bishop's slaughter into just one more piece of information. Rayber casts the first stone, which is always the most difficult to throw because there is no model (Girard, *I See Satan* 56–57). Tarwater follows and hurls the second. Whereas the youth imitates Mason's desire in wanting to baptize Bishop, he comes to mimic Rayber's desire in wanting to kill Bishop. The way to become the violent god that attracted Tarwater in his great-uncle's faith is to follow his murderous and self-deifying uncle.

Despite the complementary need of Tarwater and Rayber to learn and to lead, the model-disciple relationship is disastrous. Tarwater might walk with Rayber through the city that has become his classroom, but the disciple of O'Connor's Elijah "wore his isolation like a mantle, wrapped it around himself as if it were a garment signifying the elect" (190). As a former student of the caring Mason, Tarwater knows that Rayber's cult of the mind is not worth imitating. The youth continually rejects his uncle's efforts to intellectualize him with the same disdain for heartless analysts that old Mason taught him. Yet because Tarwater also rejects his great-uncle's prophetic vocation, he also remains enthralled with and to Rayber. The ambivalence creates for Tarwater and Rayber a school for scandal in which the model-disciple relationship continually degenerates into mutual rivalry.

Although O'Connor edited from the final version of the novel the way earlier drafts exposed fraternal organizations like the Ku Klux Klan (Prown 132–33), she did not eliminate her critique of the power-hungry masculinity behind such brotherhoods. In the virtually all-male world of *The Violent Bear It Away,* uncles and nephews translate family life into a struggle for mastery. Even before Tarwater met his uncle, the nephew resolved to kill Rayber if he ever asserted his rightful claim to Powderhead. Once Rayber and Tarwater become teacher and student, the traditional roles do not resolve the opposition but intensify the imitation and the antagonism. Rayber and Tarwater, Tarwater and Rayber, grow so much to resemble each other that any apparent mark of difference is just a momentary pause on the whirligig of mimesis. Uncle and nephew act out the ever-shifting inversions of this double mediation during their walks in the city. Although Tarwater the student is properly Rayber's follower, the pupil always stays slightly in advance of his teacher and tour guide, as if he were, in fact, the master. One night Rayber actually becomes Tarwater's follower when he trails the youth to the tabernacle where Lucette Carmody preaches. Back in his bed, Rayber rewalks in his sleep the same surreal way of the double. He dreams that "he chased Tarwater through an interminable alley that twisted suddenly back on itself and reversed the roles of pursuer and pursued" (207). Master becomes disciple, disciple becomes master, and the transpositions end in the violence that is often used to resolve the fluctuations of mimetic strife: Tarwater strikes Rayber in the head and disappears. Scandal bears him away.

The mimetic conflict among Tarwater, Mason, and Rayber provides the source of O'Connor's violent humor. Girard observes that both tragedy and comedy stage the clash between opposites and doubles. But whereas tragedy tends to respect the independence of the individual during this contest, comedy depicts how that sovereignty is lost amid the repetition of structural patterns (*Double Business* 124–25). In the typical scene of comedy, "an individual is trying to assert upon his environment what he takes to be his own rule. We laugh when this pretension is suddenly and spectacularly shattered. Impersonal forces are taking over" (126). The butt of comedy is less an individual than the casualty of some law of physics or psychology. Much as a person who slips on a banana peel is funny precisely to the extent that gravity gains the upper hand, O'Connor's bumblers provoke laughter from a more terrible kind of gravity— from the way they tumble over their mimetic antagonism. They ridicule and revile their counterparts even as they are unaware that they are executing the gravest kind of pratfall. The stumbler who lands on the ground cannot deny the fall; the very pretense to being upright is undermined by sprawled arms and legs. But O'Connor's buffoons are even funnier than such slapstick victims because they flounder over each other even as they steadfastly maintain their moral rectitude. In their desire to overthrow the other, they ignore how they have already been overthrown.

O'Connor's readers may laugh at the spectacle of so many knockdown collisions because they are kept distant from the conflict by her narrator and by the reassuring knowledge that they live outside the book. However, O'Connor's comedy typifies the way the traditional detachment between onlooker and fool is, according to Girard, really illusory. Readers laugh because of and despite the fact that Rayber and Tarwater and Mason are too much like themselves. O'Connor's three stooges enact the very mimetic conflict that readers reenact. "As I laugh," Girard explains, "I mimic and repeat the whole process I have been watching, both the attempt to establish mastery and its failure, both the dizzy feeling of superiority and the loss of balance that comes with the dizziness, the disintegration of self-control that is always creeping upon us in the wild reactions and uncontrolled convulsions of laughter itself" (*Double Business* 128–29).

Like the skandalon that bewilders O'Connor's characters, her comedy entices and threatens readers. It enables bystanders at first to feel superior, for they have—presumably—mastered the desire that causes such strife between her fictional models and disciples. Readers laugh because her antagonists have fallen over themselves, while they are still standing. However, in that very assertion of superiority, readers duplicate O'Connor's contentious pairs and so send themselves tumbling as well. Just as comedy can always unseat spectators with paroxysms of laughter, O'Connor's novel has the disturbing power to bear readers away. It can lay bare their pretenses of being so upstanding by showing how they are really like those who have fallen down. Uncomfortable with this revelation, readers may want to separate themselves from such laughter. They may hope that the goats of O'Connor's unsettling humor will be the surrogates to bear their responsibility away. Then, when the novel is finished, they may return, convinced of their innocence, to the familiar peace that is once again established by sacrifice. Only if readers understand that O'Connor sends up the entire scapegoating mechanism will they recognize that to escape from being the victim of her novel's laughter is to end the victimization of others.

STUMBLING OVER THE LOGOS OF VIOLENCE

Tarwater and Rayber are so far from sidestepping the skandalon and so intent on getting each other's goat that they provide one of the novel's chief sources of comedy. They speak their foolish rivalry through language that is violent at heart. Their rhetoric of scandal typifies what Girard calls the Logos of Heracli-

tus rather than the Logos of John. Girard argues that from Heraclitus to Heidegger, Western thought has tended to view the Logos, the central organizing
principle of the world, in terms of the power to dominate and enforce. Heidegger maintains that the Greek Logos "brings together entities that are *opposites,
and it does not do so without violence*" (*Things Hidden* 265). This violence is the
Girardian sacred, which keeps opponents from resorting to ever greater violence
because such rage has been set aside as transcendent. James Alison helps to explain this logos of violence when he calls the exclusion of the victim "*a linguistic construction of human reality* over against the expelled one" that is nothing
more than a "violent lie" (103). The central principle by which the first community defines itself is a radical act of delimiting that is then denied or disguised.
The logic of murder and the methodology of deception install the logos of violence as the cornerstone of culture.

Girard maintains that the Logos of John breaks decisively with this philosophical tradition. In the prologue to the fourth gospel, the Word is not the perpetrator of violence but the victim and the revelation of the victimage mechanism. The Logos is that which was not comprehended by the darkness, not
known by the world, and not received by its own people (John 1:4–5, 10–11). Although continually rejected, the Johannine Word never stops speaking itself as
love. "The Word of the Father, which is identical with the Father, consists in
telling mankind what the Father is," Girard writes, "so that people may be able
to imitate him: 'Love your enemies, pray for your persecutors; so shall you be
sons of your Father'" (*Things Hidden* 269). Whereas the logos of violence oppresses and suppresses, the Logos of the gospel expresses the way to live out the
image of a loving God.

Since Rayber and Tarwater are enemies of this Johannine Logos, they artic-
ulate a counterword and stumble over each other through the violence of their
language. Leaving no stone unturned, each relentlessly attacks in the other what
he fears in himself—some lingering allegiance to Mason's example—and each
argues that he has more completely renounced that discipleship than his counterpart in apostasy. Teacher and student do not so much engage in the dialogue
that Paulo Freire's *Pedagogy of the Oppressed* considers the hallmark of a liberating education as enrage themselves with repeated inquisitions and indict-
ments. If Rayber asks questions only to provoke his disciple or to assert his
power, Tarwater knows how to respond forcefully in kind. He prides himself on
his ability to stonewall, "each time he was questioned, raising his uncle's fury
until it was observable under his skin in patches of pink and white" (220). The

logos of violence makes the words of each into weapons. At every moment one model-disciple unsays what the other disciple-model has just been saying and then resorts to some countersaying of his own, always seeking to undercut and overwhelm his adversary. Neither achieves any victory, for the end of every sentence is just the prelude to its being undone and unspoken by a rival polemicist. The total effect of their incessant doublings and denials, their predictable parallelisms and tit-for-tat antitheses, is that amid all the words with which Tarwater and Rayber stone each other, only one word is being repeated, the word of rivalry, the skandalon.

Tarwater and Rayber keep tripping up themselves and each other on this adversarial language from their first day to their last night together. The youth's opening words to his uncle cast the first stone. When Tarwater claims that in burning Mason he did Rayber's work for him, the boastful student testifies to how he has not just lived up to his would-be mentor's ideals but surpassed his uncle's actual achievement. Rayber is a master at using language for the same kind of lapidation. Although O'Connor claimed not to have an ear for her schoolteacher (*Habit* 353), she unfailingly heard his voice in the contrapuntal rhetoric of his ongoing duet with Tarwater. Rayber's response to this young upstart expresses nothing so much as their doubleness and diametric opposition. He repeats his nephew's news about Mason but adds a question mark— "Dead?"—which conveys not only his shock but also his suspicion that the youth might be deceiving him (175). "Dead" may not really mean "dead" when diction constantly contains the possibility of its own contradiction. In other words, Tarwater's and Rayber's speech is always "in the other's words," always words against the other even as they use the words of the other.

Rayber's desire to be a model keeps him from challenging his new disciple much further on that first day. So, his language is initially filled with affirmations of how he will turn Tarwater into a model young man. But as Rayber's fervor wanes in the face of Tarwater's increasing belligerence, the uncle more frequently speaks the hostile repetitions and inversions that he first voiced in wondering "Dead?" When Tarwater reiterates on the next day that he has completed Rayber's work for him, the uncle interprets the gibe as proof that the guilty adolescent remains subjugated to Mason. Rayber thus turns his disciple's claim to be the real master into evidence of how much the youth still desires the dead model he supposedly rejects. The strategy is typical of how every word between Tarwater and Rayber generates its own antiword, implied in what is said by one and expressed with truculent pleasure by the other. The uncle solicitously offers himself not just as a substitute for the great-uncle but for the teenager's dead father. When a paternal Rayber tenders "You have a father" to the boy he renames "Frankie," Francis Marion Tarwater rages against such adoption: "'I ain't ast for no father,' he said and the sentence struck like a whip across his uncle's face. 'I ain't ast for no father,' he repeated" (188).

The narrator's stinging image for the orphan's renunciation visualizes how Tarwater and Rayber continually use language to verbalize their mimetic antagonism. They converse only to assert that each is the converse of the other, constantly echoing and inverting what the other has said. Tarwater's rejection of Rayber as father thus repeats his uncle's name for the proffered new relationship but only to deny such fatherhood and then to repeat the disavowal. And after affirming "I'm out of the womb of a whore. I was born in a wreck," he negates Rayber's new name for his most unfilial disciple: "And my name ain't Frankie. I go by Tarwater" (188). Whereas the Johannine Logos represents the Father as a model for others, Tarwater is an anti-Logos, who denies that he re-presents the would-be father in word and in example. The reprobate son does not hear how he actually imitates and incarnates the very way his spiritual sire has disowned the Logos of love. Tarwater is the word of violence become flesh. When Rayber answers the only-begotten child of his language, he voices the denial that their always unresolved disputation almost makes predictable: "Your mother was not a whore. . . . That's just some rot he's taught you" (188). The repudiated father figure restates Tarwater's proudly defiant name for his mother only to renounce it as one of Mason's lies.

Mason is the triangulation point in all of the conversations between Tarwater and Rayber. He is what Serres terms the "third man," the interference that partners in conversation always seek to exclude in order to enjoy successful communication. Like Rayber and Tarwater, such interlocutors are not really different but constantly changing roles, becoming source or receiver in turn just as model might become disciple, or disciple, model. Like Rayber and Tarwater, such interlocutors are not so much opposed to each other as to the demonized Other that disturbs their dialectical collaboration. The meddlesome Mason is "the prosopopeia of noise" (Serres 67) in the dialogues between Tarwater and Rayber. Tarwater proclaims his independence from the prophet by turning "whore," one of Mason's favorite terms of abomination, into a reason for bragging about his birth parent. Rayber matches his claim by rejecting the literal truth of the epithet for his sister and Tarwater's unmarried mother as more of Mason's misinformation. What is constantly being charged and countercharged in all of Rayber's and Tarwater's debates is who is less of a disciple of the old man, who is more of a model of antidiscipleship. Precisely because both want to vaunt their freedom from Mason, the duo bind themselves, in fury and fascination, to him and to each other all the more.

The sparring between Tarwater and Rayber makes each seem the winner of a verbal superiority that lasts only as long as it takes his warring opponent to claim kudos with his own triumphant reply. This logos of violence is O'Connor's masterly equivalent of the stichomythia used in the Greek tragedy that she enjoyed (*Habit* 68, 378), the dialogic thrust and counterthrust that duplicates the way opponents match blow for blow as they duel. Girard explains how such warfare seeks a permanent victory in words but achieves only fleeting supremacy: "The recipient of the blow is thrown momentarily off balance and needs time to pull himself together, to prepare a suitable reply. During this interval his adversary may well believe that the decisive blow has indeed been struck. Victory—or rather, the act of violence that permits no response—thus oscillates between the combatants, without either managing to lay final claim to it" (*Violence* 151). As O'Connor's mutual antagonists constantly echo, invert, and subvert each other in language, they turn dialogue into an attack on the Logos that Mason at his best knew as love.

Since neither Tarwater nor Rayber ever wins this linguistic contest, they become increasingly violent rivals over who can be more violent. By the time they reach the Cherokee Lodge at the novel's climax, their duality has reached its starkest and most pointed terms. Rayber takes Tarwater to the lakeside retreat as a prelude to a cathartic trip that he plans to Powderhead, which is only thirty miles away. Believing in a crude psychology of therapeutic violence, he hopes that such a return to the home place will be the shock therapy necessary to free Tarwater from his obsession with Mason. But Rayber finally decides to forgo such psychodrama in favor of a direct verbal confrontation. The schoolteacher signals the candor of this discourse by announcing at his last supper with Tarwater, "I want to talk straight to you." His message, as always, stumbles upon the tenacious Mason: "The old man still has you in his grip. Don't think he hasn't" (236). Rayber is so obsessed with the model-obstacle that even when he heightens his assertion into asseveration he cannot get beyond the skandalon. He words his repeated opposition to Tarwater in the purest verbal formulation of their contest as negative doubles—the double negative, "Don't think he hasn't." As wily as his namesake the Revolutionary War general dubbed the Swamp Fox, Francis Marion Tarwater marshals his forces for a strategic attack: "'It's you the seed fell in,' he said. 'It ain't a thing you can do about it'" (236). The youth makes a typically rigid contrast between the two by comparing his uncle to the poor ground where the seed was deeply buried and himself to a more resistant terrain. "'With me,' he said proudly, 'it fell on rock and the wind carried it away'" (236). The stony Tarwater knows that the word of God finds no haven amid scandalous soil.

Rayber trumps Tarwater's bid to be the baddest by countering his counterclaim. The violence of his language matches the force with which he seizes the table as if about to shove it into his rival's chest: "Goddam you! . . . It fell in us both alike. The difference is that I know it's in me and I keep it under control. I weed it out but you're too blind to know it's in you" (236). For a single sentence Rayber lets all the differences that these doubles have perilously set in each other's way collapse into a statement of the similarity that the quibblers endlessly deny: for good and for bad, they are both disciples of Mason. But then the die-hard structuralist resorts to the old language of binary opposition that allows him to restore some degree of distinction to his side. Rayber answers Tarwater's reference to the parable of the sower with a reference from the parable of the wheat and the tares that immediately follows it in Matthew's gospel. Point / counterpoint: the would-be exterminator inverts the possible heavenly harvest of Tarwater's biblical analogy so that it becomes a proliferation of weeds that has to be extirpated. After the stymied youth says nothing, Rayber resumes his confrontational language and shortly names the skandalon that none of O'Connor's violent seekers can bear away: "The old man told you to baptize Bishop. You have that order lodged in your head like a boulder blocking your path" (237).

Rayber tries to help Tarwater get beyond this stumbling stone by offering his nephew the sharpest of choices. The mentor challenges his blocked disciple either to perform the empty act of baptizing Bishop right then or to preside over his own secular baptism through committing himself to the powers of human intelligence. The pointed alternatives dramatize how Tarwater is impeded by the skandalon of mimetic desire. He is too much the disciple of Mason to consider baptism as insignificant and too much the rival of Mason to complete the ritual at last. Likewise, he is too much the disciple of Rayber to administer the sacrament and too much the rival of Rayber to accept a triumph that his opponent sanctions. Protesting his difference from Rayber, Tarwater speaks the very identity that he abjures, "It's nothing about me like you" (238). The more that Tarwater and Rayber repudiate each other in language, the more they resemble each other, and so they only strive to renounce each other all the more. They circle round and round the skandalon of mimetic rivalry but can never get beyond its massive and mutual frustration.

THE SPIRIT OF SCANDAL

Mason, Tarwater, and Rayber provoke such scandal in *The Violent Bear It Away* that O'Connor gives their contention a voice and a body as if it seemed to live apart from them. The spirit of their strife takes the form of the stranger who tempts and taunts Tarwater throughout the novel. The scornful seducer has ancient origins. Girard claims that in the gospels Satan is the source of scandal because he constantly places himself in the way as an attractive obstacle for imitation (*Things Hidden* 418–19). During the temptation in the desert, Satan tries to get Jesus to stumble by offering the kingdom and the power and the glory of the world if only his prospective disciple will fall down to worship him. Such idolatry, as Ezekiel recognized long ago (Ezek. 14:3–7), is the ultimate scandal because it turns the stumbling stone into a god (*Things Hidden* 421). Jesus rebukes the demon of scandal in the desert just as he later chastises Peter when the apostle repeats the temptation in a different form. After Peter tries to dissuade his master from his suffering and death, Jesus cries, "Get thee behind me, Satan: thou art [a skandalon] unto me" (Matt. 16:23). Peter is satanic because he is scandalous. He implicitly offers Jesus an enticing model of the godhead based on earthly standards rather than on the divine rejection of violence. Jesus puts behind him such devils in his own life, according to Girard, and through such exorcisms as the expulsion of the demons at Gerasa, he puts them out of wherever the kingdom of God takes hold in the lives of his followers (*Scapegoat* 165–83).

The stranger in *The Violent Bear It Away* is the demonic embodiment of all the scandal that draws together and divides Mason, Tarwater, and Rayber. The interloper denies, of course, that the devil exists because nonbelief in the genius of skandalon is the best way to hide a boulder in Tarwater's path. However, the stranger's denial expresses a fundamental truth of corrupted interdividuality: Satan's sole being depends on doubleness. He does not exist by himself so much as between rivalrous others (Girard, *I See Satan* 42). O'Connor thus appropriately locates her satan in the center of Tarwater's conflicted family circle. For O'Connor's narrator even to call this comrade a "stranger" is really a misnomer (130). Far from being alien and unknown, he is Tarwater's twin, the deceitful image of the desire that calls Tarwater to hateful imitation. Like Satan in the gospels, the youth's unfamiliar companion sets up appealing models to follow that are actually obstacles.

Since Tarwater's nemesis is mimesis in its most unholy form, his bosom buddy creates these models for imitation by imitation. His dissimulation consists of at once simulating and subverting the model by making it into an opposite. Once again demonstrating her mastery of voice, O'Connor makes the stranger speak in a tradition of doubletalk that extends from Milton's Satan to Porter's Hatch in "Noon Wine." The consummate dissembler is first heard in the unusual voice with which Tarwater chides Mason immediately after his death, "Just hold your horses. I already told you I would do it right" (129). Although the reassuring words still belong to an obedient disciple, their surliness and colloquial allusion to the chariot that might have carried away this latter-day Elijah hardly sound as if they were uttered by a very devoted Elisha. The stranger speaks out of both sides of his mouth, for he is the very principle of conflicting duality. "Bury him first and get it over with," the odd and unpleasant voice counsels as it repeats the command of Tarwater's model but makes the interment of the massive Mason seem an obstacle to be overcome—just one more skandalon (130).

The stranger convinces Tarwater to become his double by such double-voiced discourse that seems to lead the youth along familiar directions but actually leads him toward scandal. "I ain't denying the old man was a good one, his new friend said, but like you said: you can't be any poorer than dead" (144). The amiable enemy gives Mason a backhanded affirmation yet seconds Tarwater's own words as a way to undercut his old model. As the speech of the youth and his new confidant elide into each other, so too do their positions about dealing with Mason's remains. Surely it will not matter to this poor dead man if his body is buried or burned. "Ten foot now, remember," the stranger reminds Tarwater after he has dug only two feet of the grave (148). He repeats Mason's sole charge to his disciple yet twists the stipulation with a laugh so that the deceased prophet seems selfish to have imposed such a burden on his young survivor. Sinuous and insinuating, the demonic rhetorician does his most sinister work not by attacking Mason directly but by speaking from within the Mason-Tarwater relationship to destroy the model-disciple bond. Although this unknown voice claims that Mason was just a stone before Tarwater's door that God has begun to roll away, the trickster shows how much he is actually that stumbling stone of mimetic desire by imitating the very evangelical oratory that Mason himself might have used. "You got to finish up yourself but He's done the main part.

Praise Him" (150), the stranger rejoices even as he offers Tarwater the romantic freedom from others that attracted Porter's Miranda at the end of "Old Mortality." Satan wins a new disciple by sounding scandalously like the old master.

As the stranger subtly works to estrange Tarwater from his former model in Mason, he more blatantly offers him an antimodel for his imitation. This new model is rational enough to know that the old man was possibly crazy and worldly enough to reject belief in the Resurrection, baptism, and Judgment Day. Tarwater seems to find this infernal exemplar in Rayber, who in the city sections of the novel takes over the stranger's voice as tempter to Tarwater. But since this satan is the very avatar of mimetic rivalry, he does not find peace in simply replacing one master with another. Rather, the scandalizer tries to make the new model into another obstacle and incites Tarwater to rival Mason's rival. When the stranger reminds Tarwater that Rayber actually owns Powderhead, the would-be master of the family land threatens to murder his uncle if he dares to trespass. The supreme instigator later flatters Tarwater that the youth is actually more intelligent than the schoolteacher because Rayber needed his parents to show him Mason's insanity, but Tarwater has discovered his kinsman's madness all by himself. As the satan, literally "the accuser," the stranger inspires the way Tarwater and Rayber blame and defame their opposite in chapters 3 through 9, for all of their verbal wrangling amounts to incessantly bringing up charge and countercharge against their guilty double. The stranger's own words of denial and dissension make clear that the logos of violence, which uncle and nephew repeat, ultimately comes from his own crooked mouth. The relatives and rivals speak with this same voice of iniquity as they try to prove their mastery and prosecute their opponent as a model manqué. Tarwater and Rayber do not realize that they are satans to each other.

The mutual antagonism between Tarwater and Rayber is the quintessence of the stranger. O'Connor deftly manages this devilish figure, turning him from a strange voice in Tarwater's head to an actual stranger, then to a friend, and finally to an adversary, so that he becomes not just the self nor the other but the self and the other in the reciprocity of their imitation and opposition. Girard's interdividual psychology does not dismiss the appearance of such a double as the fantasy of a mind gone mad but regards this kind of specter as making visible the basic identity and mutuality that haunt warring counterparts. The double embodies how all those competing to be singular are really copies of each other, repeating the same rivalry in a different form (*Things Hidden* 299–305). As the satanic master of duplicity, the stranger is not just Tarwater's double but the very animus of invidious duality. His life breath is the desire that makes rivals resemble each other the more they deny their similarity and vaunt their superiority. The stranger is the devilish inspiration behind conflicting doubles, leading all who stumble into jealousy and violence to become doubles of himself.

Since Satan is the lord of baleful mimesis, he can be more than just double. In *The Violent Bear It Away* he is legion. The stranger as diablo is the double endlessly redoubled—or, like the number of returning demons rolled into one to which Rayber compares Mason, repeated at least sevenfold (Matt. 12:45). The stranger is the force that attracts and antagonizes the trio of family rivals—Tarwater, Mason, and Rayber. The stranger is also the face behind the quartet of would-be masters who try to ensnare Tarwater in exploitative model-disciple relationships. He is T. Fawcett Meeks, who wants to make the young hitchhiker an apprentice in his gospel of commerce so that the salesman can profit from the hick's hard work. He is the sinister but oddly familiar sage on the park bench who counsels, "Be like me, young fellow . . . don't let no jackasses tell you what to do," and looks at his prospective follower with a "malevolent promise of unwanted friendship" (222). He is the violent truck driver with a twisted nose who gives Tarwater a ride so that his passenger can talk his sleepy master into staying awake. Finally, he is the violet-eyed pedophile who takes fullest advantage of mimetic desire by making discipleship culminate in rape. Seen so often, the stranger casts a hallucinatory aura over *The Violent Bear It Away* so that everywhere there is mimicked and mirrored his two-faced look.

O'Connor's novel has been steadily moving toward just such a violent blurring of distinctions. The complicated family history of its apostles and apostates elides the obvious divisions among all of these relatives. Tarwater and Rayber duplicate each other as nephews; Mason and Rayber double each other as uncles. The frequent parallels between the generations—the recurrent baptisms, kidnappings, discipleships—further confuse one member of the family with another.[6] The doubling gets fictional form in so many repeated words, images, and actions that Frederick Asals argues, "déjà vu is one of the basic structural principles of the novel" (*Flannery O'Connor* 170). Although *The Violent Bear It Away* is powered by the irreconcilable opposition among Tarwater, Rayber, and Mason, the effect of so much polarity is ultimately to dissolve differences and lose individuality in a hateful interdividuality. By the time that Tarwater and Rayber arrive at the Cherokee Lodge, this undifferentiation has spread so far that it reaches from the primal chaos of an eventually deadly pond to the teenage dancers that trouble Rayber at the inn. "The girls could be distinguished from the boys only by their tight skirts and bare legs; their faces and heads were alike" (235). Girard recognizes such widespread sameness as the sacrificial crisis and maintains that societies in such disarray resort to scapegoating as a way of restoring the missing degrees of separation. The violent must bear someone away.

SCANDALIZING ONE OF THE LITTLE ONES

The casualty in *The Violent Bear It Away* is Bishop. Tarwater and Rayber form a small-scale version of the community in crisis that turns to surrogate victimage to reestablish order. Rather than killing each other, they unite to kill a substitute as a way of achieving personal peace. Girard observes that although scandal initially appears to generate unending opposition, at later stages the stumbling stones dissolve into each other, absorb and overpower each other, until finally one alone remains as the captivating center of contention (*I See Satan* 23). Tarwater and Rayber trip over each other throughout the novel, but Bishop is more of an impediment to them both than either one of them is to the other. So, all of their scandals converge upon and merge into the burden of Bishop. Killing Bishop will enable Tarwater to free himself from both his rivals. Tarwater will prove that he has forever rejected Mason's command to baptize the child and that he has not simply imitated the violent Rayber but outdone him once more. Letting Bishop be killed will enable Rayber to be freed at last from the child that threatens his hardened heart as well as from the young rival-disciple who "would never leave as long as Bishop was around" (240). For the good of Tarwater and Rayber, Bishop must die.

Tarwater seeks to eliminate this stumbling stone by relying upon the fascinating power of the skandalon. Having repeatedly heard how Mason's eyes bewitched the young Rayber into following him, Tarwater attempts to use the same kind of hypnotism to make Bishop into his compliant disciple. Although Tarwater usually avoids looking into Bishop's eyes, at the Cherokee Lodge the would-be master stares into their center so that he can ensnare the child in this trance of slavish imitation. In their room Bishop watches Tarwater "as if he were mesmerized by the steel-like glint that came from the boy's eyes and was directed into his own" (227). Tarwater later captivates Bishop with the same attentive rapture as he leads the child to the boat, where the cousins are "held still in some magnetic field of attraction" (240). Tarwater's triumph will be to reverse Jesus's warning about causing children to stumble, "But whoso shall [scandalize] one of these little ones which believe in me, it were better for him that a millstone were hanged about his neck, and that he were drowned in the depth of the sea" (Matt. 18:6). The scandalizer will give the punishment for the offensive model to the offended disciple. He will drown Bishop after trying to tie the skandalon around his neck.

As a youngster whose intelligence has been blocked at the level of a five year old, Bishop is particularly liable to the spellbinding effects of the skandalon. "The child's confident act of imitation," Girard writes, "always runs the risk of coming up against the desires of adults, in which case his models will be transformed into fascinating obstacles. . . . The adult who scandalizes the child runs the risk of imprisoning him forever within the increasingly narrow circle of the model and the mimetic obstacle, the process of mutual destruction we have so often described" (*Things Hidden* 417). Bishop shows this susceptibility to mimetic desire when he gets caught up in the "furious stern concentration" of the adolescents who dance at the Cherokee Lodge, becoming so "entranced" by their movements that he screams when the music stops and the dancers sit down (235). Music is "the quintessence, the vibration of mimetic desire," as Jean-Michel Oughourlian explains, because listeners copy it through their physical and psychological responses (115). They duplicate the repetitions of its melody and rhythm in the gestures of dance, and they form images and memories out of suggestive likenesses to its sounds. Having seen how Bishop is spellbound by the choreography of desire, Rayber foresees how Tarwater plans to exploit the child's sensitivity to scandal. The father imagines that his young opponent will make Bishop respond to "his command like a faithful dog. Instead of avoiding him, he planned to control him, to show who was master" (239). When Rayber decides that he alone will rule his son, he becomes Tarwater's adversary once again and turns Bishop into nothing more than a prize for competing rivals.

If Tarwater and Rayber seek to scandalize Bishop, Bishop seems a skandalon to Tarwater and Rayber. Both take umbrage at being unable to master the child who is as defenseless as he is compelling. Tarwater is attracted to Bishop because he recognizes that the cousin whose face resembles Mason's is the old man reborn in the spirit. Bishop bears the love of the great-uncle without any of its violent distortions. At the Cherokee Lodge the older cousin follows the younger "so directly that he might have been attached to him by a tow-line" (216). Tarwater stands "bewitched" in front of the child, who just sits down on the steps and sticks out his feet for his shoes to be tied (217). Despite his anger the teen cannot avoid obliging such heartfelt neediness. Yet Tarwater resents Bishop because the youth is outraged by giving and receiving such love. So, the little boy constantly appears as a physical obstacle in Tarwater's spiritual path. When Tarwater first glimpses Bishop at Rayber's house, the child only has to stand behind an almost shut door to incite his cousin's wrath. The fourteen-year-old rival cries out his lordly precedence, "Before you was here, *I* was here" (142). When Tarwater later returns to his uncle's, he suddenly notices his smiling cousin creeping toward him with outstretched hand. Tarwater strikes the tender threat away and repeatedly flinches from Bishop's touch throughout the novel. If Bishop stands or sits or walks somewhere, that place becomes for Tarwater "a dangerous hole in space that he must keep away from at all costs" (191).

Rayber likewise stumbles over being drawn toward and away from Bishop. Although O'Connor worried about creating a cartoon intellectual, Rayber is saved from being just an egghead by his shocking love for his son. Tarwater's repudiation of his cousin makes Rayber's ceaseless small attentions to Bishop seem even more spectacularly poignant. The youth intuits the truth of the Rayber-Bishop relationship when he envisions them as "inseparably joined" (178), for they are not just father and son but twins of the heart. At his best Rayber seems to share in his double's capacity for abounding love. He realizes that if Bishop did not provide a focus for his devotion, he might have to imitate Bishop even more closely and lavish his affections on everything that was not Bishop. "Then the whole world would become his idiot child" (230). As Rayber strokes Bishop's ear, orders Bishop's favorite food in a restaurant, or worries about Bishop's wet shoes, the daddy becomes a disciple of his unstinting son.

"Rayber's love for Bishop," O'Connor confesses, "is the purest love I have ever dealt with. It is because of its terrifying purity that Rayber has to destroy it" (*Habit* 379). Rayber resists Bishop precisely because the child summons the parent to accept his extravagant fondness and to give so limitlessly of himself. Although Rayber would like to live undisturbed in his egotism, he has to be careful that he does not look at a stick or a stone too long lest he be overwhelmed with a love so vast and profound that it unseats his reason and embraces the cosmos. So, like Tarwater, he chooses the stumbling stone rather than the stone to be contemplated and cherished. Scandalizing children, Girard writes, "is directly opposed to the process of opening up, of welcoming others, which is life-giving" (*Things Hidden* 417). Precisely this kind of acceptance is what Jesus enjoins right before his warning about causing children to stumble: "And whoso shall receive one such little child in my name receiveth me" (Matt. 18:5). Child Bishop challenges Rayber and Tarwater to be too much like himself rather than like each other. Closing their hearts to such imitation, the doubles reject the one model who could teach them the most sublime form of cordiality.[7]

Although O'Connor might easily have sentimentalized the generous Bishop by portraying him as a simpleminded victim in a world of scandalmongers, she refuses to yield to Rayber's bathos about exploited children. Bishop is not immune from scandal but in danger of scandalizing and being scandalized by others. However, he does not stumble over the model-disciple relationship because love frees him from the calculus of recrimination and resentment. If Bishop imitates, he does it with innocence and without envy; if he inspires imitation, he does it with his tender vulnerability and without fear of being displaced. When the little boy enters Tarwater's room shortly after the youth comes to live with Rayber, Bishop carries a wastebasket with a stone in it. The enigmatic moment is a virtual icon of how scandal does not bear him away but he bears the skandalon away.

Unlike the rest of the scandalmongers in O'Connor's novel, Bishop does not vie, covet, condemn, or violate. Although the child is occasionally given to fury, he shows none of the rancor of his hard-hearted family. When Rayber tries to drown Bishop, his face "under the water was wrathfully contorted, twisted by some primeval rage to save itself" (208). Likewise, Bishop howls, "his face red and hideously distorted," after Rayber keeps him from splashing in the pool where Tarwater seems about to baptize him (211). Bishop's anger results not from the frustration of rivalry but from an instinctive passion for the life that his father seeks to deny by drowning him and by preventing him from receiving the sacrament. Whereas the other members of his family tend to confront everyone and everything as an obstacle to be opposed, Bishop views all before him without antagonism. He lives by the Johannine Logos of love rather than the logos of violence. So, he reaches out rather than rejects and resists—to sit in Tarwater's lap, to hang onto Rayber's leg, to stare in fascination at any stick or scrap in the street, to splash in a park fountain before a stone lion. The statue of this beast, which suddenly seems to appear in the path of Tarwater and Rayber, looms as another skandalon for the competing prophets. The carved animal might be the very image of what 1 Peter (5:8) warns against—"your adversary the devil, [who] as a roaring lion, walketh about, seeking whom he may devour"—for the uncle and nephew play out one more scene of rivalry around it. However, there is no danger to Bishop in this den, for he welcomes and is welcomed by the stony mystery at the very center of the park. Bishop delights in the water, and the sunlight, "rest[ing] like a hand on the child's white head," delights in Bishop (221).

This indiscriminate love and lack of animosity make Bishop the one who, for O'Connor, bears Christ most fully in *The Violent Bear It Away* rather than the one who is borne away by violence. When O'Connor described her South as "Christ-haunted" (*Mystery* 44), she named how it cannot forget the figure who lived out the prophetic critique of the culture of violence. Jesus in O'Connor's fiction is not the fierce lord of the apocalypse that Mason desired nor the sentimentalized comforter that many of O'Connor's early pious readers desired. Rather, he embodies the way around the skandalon—from its origin in interpersonal relationships to its perpetuation in social institutions.

Girard's work suggests that Jesus might be a model for all of O'Connor's would-be disciples because he demonstrates the perfect discipleship. Jesus does not engage in rivalry with the Father. Rather, the Son embodies the love and nonviolence of God so completely that he is "the only person to achieve humanity in its perfect form, and so to be one with the deity" (*Things Hidden* 216). Jesus does not claim his relationship with the Father as an exclusive achievement or seek to provoke rivalry among those who would imitate him. Rather, the Son invites his disciples to end their squabbles about their status in the kingdom of this world and to become sons and daughters in the kingdom of heaven. Immediately before Jesus warns his listeners about scandalizing children, his followers come to him with a question that indicates how they have been confounded by the same mutual opposition that trips up doubles in O'Connor's novel. Jesus answers the scandal-laden question about who is the greatest in the kingdom of heaven by overturning all of their anxious worries about power and position. Calling a child into their midst, Jesus cites the little one as the greatest because the youngster does not seek the pride of place that makes rivals stumble (Matt. 18:1–5).

Bishop is that child in *The Violent Bear It Away*. Rather than striving for mastery, as do Rayber and Tarwater, he is the casualty of their strife. Bishop becomes the stone rejected by the bumbling builders, precisely the role of Jesus in Girard's reading of the Passion narratives. However, Bishop is a stumbling block only in the sense that Paul names the cross a skandalon (1 Cor. 1:23), only in the sense that O'Connor herself professes to believe in the God "who confounds the senses and the sensibilities, one known early on as a stumbling block" (*Mystery* 161). What is genuinely holy always scandalizes those devoted to sacred violence because it has rejected the skandalon. "Violence is unable to bear the presence of a being that owes it nothing," Girard writes, "that pays it no homage and threatens its kingship in the only way possible" (*Things Hidden* 209). And so, Bishop has to be eliminated just as Jesus had to be executed. Girard views Jesus as the most innocent and nonviolent of scapegoats, who is killed because his message of generous inclusion challenges the culture of victimization (*Things Hidden* 205–15). Jesus is just one more grotesque, as Patricia Yaeger understands that familiar category from southern literature—the irruption of a force that challenges the political order and has to be expelled because of its apparent monstrosity (4–7, 25–27). Bishop of limited intelligence and unlimited love is Jesus's counterpart in *The Violent Bear It Away;* he is the scapegoat as grotesque. Tarwater and Rayber hope that by killing this child they will end their mimetic rivalry and eliminate the rush of affection that constantly undermines their obdurate hearts. And they will finally get rid of the third man who has confounded all of their dialogues—old noisy Mason, whose face and grace Bishop bears after him in the novel. Although Rayber and Tarwater imagine that they are removing the stumbling stone from their path, they are actually foundering on the skandalon.

O'Connor's narrator emphasizes the collusion of Tarwater and Rayber in killing Bishop by relating the murder from both of their guilty perspectives. In his room at the Cherokee Lodge, the father hears the outcries that accompany his son's drowning as they are magnified by his hearing aid. However, Rayber steels himself against crying out in kind, for he wants at last to stifle the noise— to drown out the son—that has disrupted his abstract world of information. His silent acquiescence in the murder makes him as culpable as Tarwater: "What had happened was as plain to him as if he had been in the water with the boy and the two of them together had taken the child and held him under until he ceased to struggle" (242). From afar—a physical space as much as an emotional posture—the godless Rayber presides over the killing of Bishop, much as kings and commoners once brought their children to the Valley of Hinnom outside Jerusalem to become burnt offerings to the sacred. The Greek name for this site became the byword for hell (Schwager 89–91). Gehenna is the scandalous locale where little ones were led to violence, and Gehenna in Tennessee is the abyss of the Cherokee Lodge, where Rayber lapses into sublime indifference as his son is slaughtered.

On the lake Tarwater likewise seeks transcendent peace through violence. Nothing should resolve all of the competing claims on his heart more decisively than drowning Bishop, as Rayber once tried, rather than baptizing him as Mason commanded. Drowning inverts the first of the sacraments by bringing a return to the watery chaos out of which creation emerges in Genesis 1 as a series of differentiations. The Christian ceremony of initiation ultimately moves away from primordial disorder. "Baptismal rites clearly represent submersion in undifferentiation, from which something better differentiated then emerges," Girard writes in describing how initiation ceremonies repeat the paradigm of surrogate victimage; "it might happen that an initiate drowns but it is never in order to drown that one submits to baptism" (*Things Hidden* 29). Tarwater seeks to violate the sacrament by staging a literal version of the ritual drowning. Immersion will end in the pure undifferentiation of death.

Once again Tarwater hears the familiar voice of the stranger, and it urges the would-be disciple to drown Bishop. The fearful, the angry, and the hateful may decide upon violence, according to criminologist Lonnie Athens, if they find it justified by their phantom companions: the internalized attitudes of family members, mentors, and gangs who virtually accompany the perpetrator to the scene of the crime (see Rhodes 81–84). The moment of violence is thus mimetic, for it enacts the advice and example that haunt the victimizer from out of the past. The stranger in the boat is just such a ghostly interlocutor. Speaking for Tarwater's family history—from the violence that hides behind Mason's conception of the sacred to the sacred that Rayber worships in his violence—the satanic stranger intimates the violence to be imitated: "It's only one dimwit you have to drown" (251), and he seconds the murder in his double's mind. Satan is "a murderer from the beginning" (John 8:44) because he represents the principle of founding violence. All other killers mimic his crime, the slaughter to eliminate mimetic rivalry (Girard, *Things Hidden* 161–63). On the lake, Tarwater follows his terrible suit. Yet if the serene Bishop resembles the patient lamb led to slaughter in Isaiah (53:7), his slayer does not perfect a new sacrament of holy violence. Instead, the youth only proves how much he imitates the contradictory desires of both his hated models: Tarwater baptizes Bishop even as he drowns him.

STUMBLING BEYOND SCANDAL

The stumble does not bring a happy fall. The logic of violence dictates that mimetic rivalry should find its climax in a salutary act of scapegoating. Indeed, if *The Violent Bear It Away* were a myth or romance, it might conclude with uncle and nephew reconciled by the death of young Bishop. However, O'Connor imagines an ending beyond the traditional last pages in the southern culture of violence, for she exposes the attempts by Rayber and Tarwater to find a new order through victimization. The scandalizers discover no communal restoration, no unity, and no peace. Rather, each participant goes his own way, and each is borne away by the violence of Bishop's murder.

Rayber virtually kills himself in allowing Bishop to be killed. Since Bishop models the love that his father would deny, Rayber discovers that without his heartfelt child he is without a feeling heart. Even when the father forces himself to remember that tomorrow the pond will be dragged for his son's body, he cannot rouse himself from this fatal anesthesia. The imminent search seems so remote "in his mind that it might already have happened, a long time ago" (243). By Girard's reckoning, it did. The effort to raise the body participates in the revelation that Girard views as the mission of the Resurrection and of the entire Bible, "bringing to light all the victims buried by mankind—not in the interests of death but in the interests of life" (*Things Hidden* 235). The indifferent Rayber senses in tomorrow's search for his son a promise that the dead will indeed be raised and that the immemorial process of victimization will begin to be revealed. However, Rayber himself is moribund because he cannot feel the agony of a victimizer who stands judged by such a disclosure. By petrifying himself to the murder of his son, the father has committed the ultimate act of self-violence. Rayber finally collapses in his room at the Cherokee Lodge because the skandalon has become his own heart of stone.

Tarwater stumbles headlong toward similar disaster. After he kills Bishop, the teenager imagines that he himself has passed through an initiation ceremony. Since the violence of such a rite reenacts how surrogate victimage leads to a new social order, Tarwater appropriates the drowning as his own baptism into a violent maturity. He wants to mythicize murder, to tell himself a counterstory to O'Connor's exposure of victimization, to reinterpret Bishop's death as the occasion for his rebirth. "It was as no boy that he returned" to Powderhead but as a man "tried in the fire of his refusal" (254). As if having achieved the same tranquility that Rayber desired after the scapegoating, the man-boy "envisioned the calm and detached person" who would discard any of Mason's burnt bones that he found amid the ruins of the family house (255). Yet Tarwater cannot find such personal regeneration through violence. Just as Rayber remembers how the pond will be dragged, Tarwater keeps finding that his victimization will not remain shrouded in the kind of secrecy that Girard views as essential for perpetuating scapegoating. When a sleepy truck driver gives Tarwater a ride in exchange for talking him into staying awake, the murderer blabs his crime to the first person he meets after committing it. Continuing his journey toward Powderhead by foot, the thirsty youth stops to buy a drink and feels exposed before the woman "with a granite-like face" who runs the crossroads store (257).

The adamantine storekeeper is another stumbling block for Tarwater. She both attracts and impedes her customer because she reveals his scandal. Although the shop woman had made no gesture toward Tarwater, "he could feel her eyes reeling him in" from afar, as if he had now become the kind of victim that he earlier sought to mesmerize (257). Once Tarwater crosses the highway to her side, this mighty woman crosses him by blocking the doorway to the store. She fronts him with her massive presence and confronts him with a still more monumental charge. The figure with a "stony face," who looks as if she easily might have wings tucked behind her, folds her arms with a "judgment fixed from the foundations of time." She accuses him of shamefully failing to bury his dead uncle, but her charge that Tarwater "scorns the Resurrection and the Life" (257) applies as much to his drowning of Bishop. This magisterial angel knows that the scoffer is guilty of the most ancient wrongs. Although Mason used to luxuriate in conversation with the enduring storekeeper, Tarwater always found her as much of an obstacle as the gravel that he kicked while restlessly waiting for his great-uncle. Now when he again wants to put under foot this stony impediment and vanquish her with an apologia for his offenses, Tarwater can only scream an obscenity at the barrier in his path. The adolescent hopes at least to scandalize this rock of a woman by his experiment with forbidden language. However, he fails. The messenger of judgment does not respond with mimetic outrage and rise to the indignation that the profanity was meant to provoke. The storekeeper remains sublimely unmoved, and Tarwater only scandalizes himself. The mouthy fourteen year old keeps hearing the expletive being repeated in his own shocked mind, as if the echo were a verbal double of how the skandalon fascinates the youth but keeps him from ever going beyond it. When Tarwater meets a final stranger who offers him a ride, he finds this logos of violence becoming incarnate in the profanation of his own flesh.

The rape of Tarwater consummates the hateful mutuality of the novel. O'Connor makes the assault so climactic by making it recapitulate all of the scandalous model-disciple relationships in Tarwater's family. Wearing a lavender shirt and driving a lavender and cream car, Tarwater's latest stranger is the double of the violet-eyed tempter who has bedeviled him since Mason's death. Satan returns to assert his mastery over the boy who consented to become his prey by killing

Bishop. Since the arch-fiend lives only as the murderous desire between models and disciples, he assaults his pet by a surrogate victimizer. Tarwater's long seduction in mimetic desire leads to being waylaid by a sexual predator who takes him for a ride. Although Tarwater proclaims to him, "Nobody tells me what to do," the driver entraps Tarwater by getting the youth to do exactly what he tells him (259). The devious model inspires this imitation by scandalizing Tarwater, by offering the country boy an enticing obstacle over which he falters. The stranger prompts Tarwater to desire the strange-tasting cigarettes and alcohol by suggesting that they may be undesirable to such a callow fellow. The rube really does not want to smoke, but he accepts the infernal offer after the tempter makes it more alluring by evoking the mystique of what is taboo, "You don't get one of this kind every day, but maybe you ain't had much experience smoking." The devil's disciple immediately imitates his mentor to perfection by hanging the cigarette in the corner of his mouth. Tarwater accepts the whiskey from the lord of the flies after the conman tantalizes him with an even stronger prohibition: "If there's flies on you, you can't drink it" (259). Recalling all of Mason's cautions about deadly liquor and riding with strangers only makes the naif swallow it more avidly. Much as Tarwater sought to hypnotize Bishop, and the stranger in the boat sought to hold Tarwater spellbound with his devouring eyes, this sophisticated slicker seeks to take possession of Tarwater's desires by luring the backcountry kid into a trance of intoxication. Desiring what is forbidden because it is forbidden, the stoned Tarwater stumbles and falls into the snare of a pedophile.

The violent duality of O'Connor's novel makes Tarwater the victim and the victimizer in the rape. As a victim, Tarwater is a casualty of mimesis gone terribly awry. Although the adolescent becomes a disciple of the stranger's violent desires, the mimetic bond is so protean that Tarwater is also his assailant's much-cherished model. The etiology of child molestation is complex, but one way of understanding its origin is as a scandal of mimetic desire. Several theorists have proposed that such abuse is the attempt of the victimizer to seize the idealized childhood of the envied victim.[8] O'Connor suggests the connection between pedophilia and a perverted model-disciple relationship by having the rape be accompanied by a small-scale crime of acquisitive mimesis. The stranger possesses Tarwater's flesh and then takes possession of the teenager's phallic talisman, the corkscrew bottle opener that he earlier admired. Just as Bishop's body is sent to the bottom of a pond, the youth is left in the woods after being abused for almost an hour. Tarwater is one of those violated bodies that, according to Girard, have been hidden since the foundation of the world.

If Tarwater is a scandalized child like Bishop, he is also the scandalizer. The menacing driver is not really a stranger at all; the assailant looks so familiar because he is Tarwater's own rapacious double. Sitting in the stranger's car, "Tarwater could see a pale reflection of himself, eyeing him darkly from the window" (259). The image in the glass is Tarwater's, but it is also the malign face of mirror imaging itself, the satanic spirit of inverted and invidious duality that has been intimate with Tarwater from Mason's death to Bishop's murder. Having allowed this double to possess his soul when he did violence to Bishop, the fourteen year old finds that his consort now returns to possess his flesh in erotic violation. Since Tarwater rejected his cousin's love and nonviolence, he has nothing left in his life but the hatred and violence that get embodied in his hardhearted rapist. The sexual abuse is the counterpart and consequence of killing Bishop. Francis Marion Tarwater is ravished only by Francis Marion Tarwater himself.

After the rape Tarwater renounces the kingdom of mimetic desire and sacred violence. "It is the violation in the woods," O'Connor wrote, "that brings home to Tarwater the real nature of his rejection" (*Habit* 368), and she claimed elsewhere that Tarwater's meeting with the strange driver was the necessary prelude to his final vision of divine communion (*Mystery* 117). These interpretations of the culminating violence in *The Violent Bear It Away* are consistent with a larger tendency in O'Connor to view her characters as coming to God by way of the most outrageous opposition and antagonism. She explained, "In my stories a reader will find that the devil accomplishes a good deal of groundwork that seems to be necessary before grace is effective" (*Mystery* 117). O'Connor's fictional practice and her comments in essays and letters suggest that grace is violent. She objected to Betty Hester that "this notion that grace is healing omits the fact that before it heals, it cuts with the sword Christ said he came to bring" (*Habit* 411). Conversely, she implied that violence may be closely allied with grace. O'Connor declared, "I have found that violence is strangely capable of returning my characters to reality and preparing them to accept their moment of grace. Their heads are so hard that almost nothing else will do the work" (*Mystery* 112; cf. *Habit* 373). Writing in 1962 to Roslyn Barnes, who was attending a missionary training program in Mexico, O'Connor related this "school for sanctity" to the title of her second novel: "This is surely what it means to bear away the kingdom of heaven with violence: the violence is directed inward" (*Habit* 486). Such comments help to explain why readers of O'Connor have frequently maintained that violence can be salvific in her fiction.[9]

This consecration of violence raises a major obstacle in interpreting O'Connor, for it risks turning the God of these stories and O'Connor herself into brutal divinities. O'Connor may easily seem to believe in the very sacred violence that Girard views Christianity as demythologizing. Sarah Gordon observes that the deity in O'Connor's fiction often resembles the conventional Old Testament lord who chastises rather than the New Testament Jesus who heralds new life (168–70). And André Bleikasten argues that O'Connor's faith in a divine aggressor was part of the "heresy" of her unorthodox fiction (66–67).[10] Since O'Connor is the creator of her fictional country, she can easily seem like a god who enjoys the calamities that she inflicts in the world of her imagination. Louise Westling views O'Connor as punishing many of the angry daughters in her stories who are her fictional doubles (174). Josephine Hendin suggests that O'Connor's "religion provided a legitimate sanction for violent and destructive impulses, impulses which became acceptable when they were called righteous and directed at the 'godless'" (16). O'Connor herself "grew to celebrate the liberating power of destruction" (42).[11]

O'Connor's relation to sacred violence becomes even more problematic because she believed that the violence in her art might bring not just her characters but her readers to revelation.[12] Faced with the need to make the abnormalities of the modern world seem misshapen to readers who might view them as normal, O'Connor wrote that the Christian novelist "may well be forced to take ever more violent means to get his vision across to this hostile audience" (*Mystery* 33–34; see also 185). Through shocking reversals, sensational events, and grotesque characters, O'Connor hoped to bear readers away so that they might recognize the mystery to which they were usually opposed or indifferent. The rape of Tarwater just when he seems about to get away with murder typifies the fictional ambush that O'Connor described to Betty Hester: "You can't clobber any reader while he is looking. You divert his attention, then you clobber him, and he never knows what hit him" (*Habit* 202). The surprise attacks of O'Connor's artistry suggest that she is like the biblical prophets who reject violence as the sacred but never completely renounce the need for occasionally sharp corrections by the ultimate Author (Girard, *Things Hidden* 157–58). The lineage is appropriate to her own view of herself as a prophetic novelist, the kind who finds her vocation in "seeing near things with their extensions of meaning and thus of seeing far things close up" (*Mystery* 44). From this perspective, O'Connor resorts to fictional violence as a means of opening her readers' eyes to such prophetic vision.

Does O'Connor's violence ever bear her away? Her rhetoric of assault imagines a kind of scandalous relationship with her audience, for it risks turning the reader into a rival whom the masterly novelist must drub into faithful discipleship. She recognized the possible lure of such coercion in an early letter to Betty Hester. Responding to her friend's accusation that she was a fascist, O'Connor countered that "the Church is a mystical body which cannot, does not, believe in the use of force (in the sense of forcing conscience, denying the rights of conscience, etc.). . . . I in principle do not believe in the use of force, but I might well find myself using it, in which case I would have to convict myself of sin" (*Habit* 99). If O'Connor wrote a gospel of violence, then she would truly be, as John Hawkes famously claimed, of the devil's party. Although O'Connor's fiction generally works to reveal rather than conceal sacred violence, she occasionally romanticized such force in some of the comments already cited. They suggest how much O'Connor felt the lure of violence. It became her enticing obstacle, her always-inviting devil, her skandalon.

The potential danger of O'Connor's violent artistry is that it may alienate the very readers that she seeks to attract. For example, O'Connor wanted *The Violent Bear It Away* to be "rebarbative" (*Habit* 321), but she imagined that reviewers would react to it as the citizens of the sleeping city would probably respond to Tarwater at the end of the novel. "I expect this one to be pounced on and torn limb from limb," she wrote Betty Hester in 1959, and she later envisioned her prophet's fate: "The children of God I daresay will dispatch him pretty quick" (*Habit* 342). O'Connor feared that her novel, like its main character, would be victimized by a hostile audience and suffer one of the classic fates of the scapegoat—being dismembered. The response to a writer's violence may always be a reader's violence so that the work becomes an obstacle instead of helping to remove the stumbling stone.

O'Connor's ultimate fear was that her fiction might become the skandalon itself. "[As to] scandalizing the 'little ones,'" she wrote in 1956 to the editor of the Catholic newspaper where she frequently reviewed books, "When I first began to write I was much worried about this thing of scandalizing people, as I fancied that what I wrote was highly inflammatory" (*Habit* 142). To hear O'Connor return to the same issue in "Catholic Novelists and Their Readers" is to sense how she struggled with this artistic and spiritual obstacle. She recognized the "pious argument" that a novelist will "be read by all sorts of people who don't understand what he is doing and are therefore scandalized by it . . . . It is very possible that what is vision and truth to the writer is temptation and sin to the reader." Recalling Jesus's condemnation in Matthew 18:6, she added, "There is every danger that in writing what he sees, the novelist will be corrupting some 'little one,' and better a millstone were tied around his neck" (*Mystery* 187). O'Connor faced the possibility that her writing might provoke mimesis to the very extent that its sensationalism was caused by exposing mimesis. In particular, the violent extremes of her own fiction might not inspire the outrage that resulted in self-reflection, as O'Connor hoped, but the imitation that resulted precisely from being so outré. O'Connor's stories might become attractive for what seemed their obvious impediments—the ugliness, meanness, and fierceness of her fictional world.

Everything from O'Connor's views on violence in fiction to some of her critics' more violent depictions of O'Connor may seem to scandalize a Girardian reading of *The Violent Bear It Away*. If the novel that seems to expose violence as demonic actually deifies it, then a mimetic interpretation stumbles on O'Connor's skandalon. However, far from perpetuating the sacrificial understanding of Christianity in her fiction, O'Connor's work is sacrificed when it is read as celebrating sacred violence. Although O'Connor is undoubtedly fascinated by violence, to imagine her as wholeheartedly worshiping a god of rage risks confounding chronology with causality in her fiction. O'Connor's characters may turn to God after receiving some blow to body and soul, and so, the fury may often seem a heaven-sent corrective. Yet if such violation is consecrated, it only creates a stumbling block to appreciating how O'Connor's fiction works to expose the human origin of the idolized skandalon. O'Connor reveals how violence results not from the sacred but from the way reciprocal antagonists reject nonviolence in pursuit of a false understanding of the sacred. Bishop dies because of the scandalous rivalry among Tarwater, Rayber, and Mason. And Tarwater is raped because he has glorified such violence from the very beginning of the novel. Those who reject the kingdom of God, Girard contends, choose to allow violence to escalate until they create their own apocalypse (*Things Hidden* 203). Tarwater, not God, bears himself away.[13]

Just as violence in O'Connor's fiction is not caused by God, it does not necessarily have the effect of directing the victim to the God of Judeo-Christianity. Tarwater *can* do other than accept his holy mission after his violation in the woods. The mimetic basis of violence suggests that the most immediate response to violence is more violence, not a reorientation toward a nonviolent God. Indeed, Tarwater is so scandalized by the rape that he sets fire to the scene of his assault. If O'Connor's characters receive grace, it is not through being borne away by violence but in their responding to violence. Grace cannot be forced upon a recipient by assault, for as O'Connor recognized, it is offered as a moment that can always be accepted or refused (*Mystery* 118). Tarwater rejects violence not because he is violated but because he feels that violence as not sacred, not graced, not the embrace of God. Perhaps O'Connor came closest to explaining how violence is related to the kingdom of heaven when she regarded such fury not as inherently salvific but as providing an opportunity to clarify what is most fundamental to the self: "Violence is a force which can be used for good or evil, and among other things taken by it is the kingdom of heaven. But regardless of what can be taken by it, the man in the violent situation reveals those qualities least dispensable in his personality, those qualities which are all he will have to take into eternity with him" (*Mystery* 113–14). Having felt in his own flesh the agony of victimization, the victimizer of Bishop turns his heart instead to the God of nonviolence.

Like Tarwater, O'Connor's readers are challenged by her fictional violence to reveal "those qualities least dispensable" in their personalities. For despite her reservations about scandalizing readers, O'Connor did not flinch from revealing the destructive consequences of mimetic desire. Indeed, she recognized that her scruples—literally, small, sharp stones—might become impediments themselves. Obsession with the stumbling block could ultimately turn the author into nothing more than a rock: "What leads the writer to his salvation may lead the reader into sin, and the Catholic writer who looks at this possibility directly looks the Medusa in the face and is turned to stone" (*Mystery* 148–49). O'Connor understood that if she took absolute responsibility for the reader, she might be scandalized by the skandalon itself and become petrified from ever writing again. Rather than facing the ultimate writer's block, O'Connor produced art more audacious than her scruples might have allowed, art that likewise confronted her readers to get beyond their own stumbling blocks. "The fact is that in order not to be scandalized," O'Connor declared, "one has to have a whole view of things, which not many of us have" (*Habit* 143).

Precisely because O'Connor uses fictional violence so regularly to offer the possibilities of a more comprehensive vision, her attempts to move beyond such a fierce aesthetic, like Tarwater's similar rejection of bloody fury late in the novel, are sometimes less noticed. Toward the end of her life, O'Connor worried about repeating herself in fiction, sensed that she had "exhausted [her] potentiality," and foresaw that she needed to explore new areas of her "country" (*Habit* 468, 518). In 1960 the prophetic novelist glimpsed the clearest direction that her talent might take in imagining how the biblical prophet par excellence of her second novel challenged her as an artist. She observed how grace must be "violent" in her fiction "to compete with the kind of evil I can make concrete," but she then considered a different source of inspiration for her art: "At the same time, I keep seeing Elias (*sic*) in that cave, waiting to hear the voice of the Lord in the thunder and lightning and wind, and only hearing it finally in the gentle breeze, and I feel I'll have to be able to do that sooner or later, or anyway keep trying" (*Habit* 373). O'Connor, in fact, had been experimenting with such gentleness all along. Although her striking artistry often seems to take its cue from the mighty theophany that Elijah expects before the cave, there is in O'Connor another fictional strategy which celebrates the ordinary over the outsized, the quiet over the violent, the poignant over the piercing, the subdued and subliminal over the shocking. This O'Connor whispers rather than screams, touches rather than clobbers, writes with a Logos of love rather than the word of violence.[14]

The aesthetic of Elijah's gentle breeze explains why O'Connor finds in the world not just remarkable grotesqueness but an unremarkable goodness that points to God. In *The Violent Bear It Away* this godliness takes flesh in the tender-hearted Bishop, pours forth from the fountain and the sun while Rayber and Tarwater contend with each other in the park, and threatens to make every stick or stone that uncle and nephew stare at too long a sign of grace rather than a skandalon. This muted artistry leads O'Connor to avoid graphic excess in presenting the violence of Bishop's murder or Tarwater's rape. Bishop's death is actually related two times—from both Rayber's and Tarwater's perspective. Each time, O'Connor surrounds the noise of the drowning with a strange lack of sound and recounts it with the utmost in fictional reticence. Struggling to be still and stone-deaf, Rayber hears the death of his son as a bellowing that subsides into silence. Tarwater later remembers the murder in a dream that makes him cry out again the words of baptism while he rides in a silent truck cab. O'Connor's presentation of Tarwater's rape gains its power not from the gothic image of the child molester as a vampire stealing away after slaking his thirst but from far less sensational effects—the casual, deadpan way that the stranger ensnares his disciple in mimetic desire and the utter hush of the assault itself. The virtually "silent" woods, "drugged" air, and occasional "silent floating bird" enact the narrator's silence in describing the rape (261). And after the stranger has abandoned his sprawled and naked victim in the woods, O'Connor's wordless eloquence makes visual the space of silence by allowing a single blank line of text to intervene before Tarwater awakens. At such understated moments it is O'Connor's nonviolence that bears readers away.

When the cry of the recovering Tarwater cuts through the empty interval on the page, it sounds the way he returns to his prophetic mission with nothing like Elijah's whisper of wind. Rather, the victim imitates the violence that he has borne on his own body. Tarwater immediately sets fire to the place where he was molested as if to purify the polluted ground. Then hours later when the youth approaches Powderhead by way of an obstacle-laden path in the woods, he begins a conflagration to expel the stranger who once again seeks to befriend his disciple. The tempter, "a warm sweet body of air encircling" Tarwater, tries to repeat the seduction of the pedophile by urging Mason's self-proclaimed heir to take the family land for both of them (264). However, the ex-disciple at last does not just see double but sees envious doubling as the enemy. As Tarwater separates himself by a wall of fire from the insidious trespasser and second self, "he saw that his adversary would soon be consumed in a roaring blaze" (264). For the first time in the novel, Tarwater understands the stranger by his rightful name and turns in revulsion against the mimetic antagonism that has possessed him. As Tarwater consigns the demon to its own inferno, the youth makes violence the devil's own adversary and exorcizes the rivalry of the model as obstacle.

Although Tarwater's purgation always risks consuming him in his own incendiarism, in the gratifying pain of his ferocious indignation, the penitent averts a destructive self-righteousness by finally getting beyond raging at how he has been outraged. When Tarwater arrives at the scorched remains of his old house, he senses that some mystery abides there amid the rubble. However, the would-be master of Powderhead does not assert his ownership with the murderous threats that he once planned to use if Rayber ever tried to arrogate the contested family property. Tarwater forgoes such mimetic rivalry, knowing that this land has a different lord, and pays awed attention to a peace beyond his understanding. The pervasive stillness of the homestead, the softness of nightfall, and Tarwater's own reverent silence testify that here resides the sacred as the holy spirit of nonviolence. This God does not need to compete for place but makes a dwelling place amid the humble and the homely, among torched chimneys and a solitary privy, and in the loving kindness of Buford Munson.

When Tarwater first spies a black man seated on a mule next to the outhouse, it seems as if the figure might be another skandalon. "The mule was not moving; the two might have been made out of rock" (265). Tarwater starts toward the stony pair with the ambivalence that has complicated all of his model-disciple relationships, "raising his fist in a gesture that was half-greeting and half-threat" (265). Tarwater had seen Buford's own hand as nothing but threatening at the beginning of the novel when the drunken youth rebuked Mason's friend, "Nigger, . . . take your hand off me" (151). Tarwater's derogatory epithet bespoke the way his racism resulted from mimetic rivalry. Buford seemed an adversary to the faithless white boy because the pious black man challenged Tarwater not to violate Mason in death. Buford understood that to bury the old man rather than to burn him and to mark the resting place with a cross was to have faith that Mason's destiny was not to be consumed by violence. So, he performed all of the funeral rites that Mason's kin scorned. When Tarwater recognizes this witness to Jesus at the end of the novel, he overcomes the old impulse to view him as an antagonist. He waves to Buford and hopes to go home with him to eat. And when Munson chastises the youth for not burying Mason, Tarwater does not answer his critic, who has actually dug the grave, with the violent opposition that has plagued his last week. Instead, he opens his hands "as if he were dropping something he had been clutching all his life" and remains silent before Buford's deserved rebukes (266). Such self-discipline exemplifies what O'Connor understood her title from Matthew 11 as implying in "the violence of love, of giving more than the law demands" (*Habit* 382). Love is violent only if violence is redefined as the struggle to master one's mimetic desire, especially for the sake of the other, rather than the struggle to overcome the other. Tarwater's renunciation of violent desire is imaged in the way he seems to drop the tightly clenched possession of a lifetime. The unburdened youth is now prepared to take his place among those who hunger for what is genuinely sacred.

Tarwater's vision of Jesus's feeding the multitudes celebrates the triumph over mimetic desire as a messianic banquet. In reflecting on the miraculous multiplication of food in the gospels, Julia Kristeva wonders whether the story may not "show how petty excessive fixation on *one* object of need can be, that object becoming the *single,* obsessive goal of existence" (*Powers of Horror* 118). Guests at O'Connor's divine repast have transcended such monomania. They do not compete for place but share food and love, and there is more than enough for everyone. Since this feast in the vision, unlike the culture at large, includes all who genuinely desire it, Tarwater notices Mason there as the old man leans forward to be fed. Freed from the stumbling block of mimetic desire, Mason is at last ready to live up to the profession of his name and build on the stone that was once rejected but that has now become the cornerstone of the kingdom of heaven (1 Peter 2:7). As Mason's spiritual son begins his labors, Tarwater has overcome his enmity toward his former model by realizing that his own yearning for food is the same as his hardworking great uncle's. It is the same as that of centuries of people "whose lives were chosen to sustain it, who would wander in the world, strangers from that violent country where the silence is never broken except to shout the truth" (266–67).[15] Tarwater's communion sacramentalizes his entry into the age-old community of outsiders who hunger for and are nurtured by the good news of love and nonviolence. As one of these aliens and evangelizers, Tarwater will disrupt the silence to proclaim the truth about the culture of violence.

There is nothing romantic about Tarwater's new calling. O'Connor leaves little doubt that the youth's countercultural role as God's spokesperson will make him a target for the opprobrium that Mason knew as the fate of the prophet. Tarwater will fall prey to collective violence.[16] Since his vision of the heavenly banquet makes him feel a tide of hunger "building from the blood of Abel to his own, rising and engulfing him" (267), Tarwater clearly stands in the line of the first scapegoat. Girard views the story of Cain and Abel, like that of Romulus and Remus, as epitomizing the way culture has its genesis in violence. Such myths remember the mimetic antagonism of an entire society as if it were a single conflict between two brothers; when this legendary strife ends in murder, the victor founds the city out of the peace made possible by violence (*Things Hidden* 38–39). What is distinctive about the biblical narrative of the primal murder is that the sacred is allied with the victim rather than with the victimizer. God hears the blood of Abel crying out from the ground and declares that the soil that Cain once tilled will now be barren for him. Displaced from the fields, the first murderer builds the first city and names it after his son Enoch.

Jesus provides the basis for understanding Tarwater's lineage as scapegoat and messenger, for he includes Abel's death as among "the blood of all the prophets, which was shed from the foundation of the world" (Luke 11:50). In becoming a prophet Tarwater will probably become like the primordial victim in the Bible and be rejected in the "dark city" (267), the dwelling place of Cain's children. Tarwater is especially likely to be murdered because he bears a message about the very opposite of such violence: "GO WARN THE CHILDREN OF GOD OF THE TERRIBLE SPEED OF MERCY" (267). This clemency comes with awesome swiftness to a slumbering world because its arrival makes urgent a decisive response. O'Connor's ending does not mitigate the possibly grim implications of Tarwater's message or vocation. Those who continue to dedicate their lives to the kingdom of violence will violate Tarwater and bring their own violence upon themselves. But it raises the hope that those who awaken to be merciful will be blessed with mercy in a kingdom beyond scandal. As O'Connor's prophet heads toward the dark city to deliver these tidings, he has finally stepped around the boulder that has been blocking his path.

McCarthy's Enfant Terrible

Incarnating Sacred Violence in *Child of God*

When Francis Marion Tarwater sets out toward the sleeping city at the end of O'Connor's *The Violent Bear It Away,* the fourteen year old has earned the right to be named among those folk who will hear his urgent news about the advent of mercy. He, too, is one of the "children of God" (267). Although the numerous wayward and willful youths in O'Connor's fiction demonstrate that she had no delusions about the innocence of the young, children and God have a special affinity for each other in her second novel. At its beginning, Tarwater is attracted to the preaching of the child evangelist Lucette Carmody, who wonders about the infant born in Bethlehem, "Is this the Word of God, this blue-cold child?" (203). However, when Tarwater later drowns the inarticulate Bishop, he seeks to silence the Logos embodied in the novel's child of God. In O'Connor's fiction the sacred dwells not in the sophistry of violence but in the unvoiced word of love, not in Tarwater's murderous desire but in Bishop's gentle vulnerability. Only after the child killer undergoes child abuse does he come to renounce such victimization and become a manchild of God at fourteen.

The title of Cormac McCarthy's *Child of God* radically redefines the meaning of the biblical phrase that ends O'Connor's novel.[1] If Lester Ballard is described in the novel's opening pages as a "child of God much like yourself perhaps" (4), the twenty-seven year old seems like neither the Deity's son nor the reader's double. Carrying his totemic rifle with him virtually everywhere since he earned enough money for it as a child, Ballard does not belong among those peacemakers hallowed as "children of God" in the Beatitudes (Matt. 5:9). Arrogating the right to reorder the world through such violence, he lacks the humility of the little ones promised the heavenly kingdom by a God of children (Matt. 19:14). Such biblical references form the necessary intertext for *The Violent Bear It Away,* but they serve more as a kind of antitext for *Child of God.* They define what being a "child of God" does not mean for the ruthless Lester Ballard.

THE SACRED SONSHIP OF LESTER BALLARD

Rather than being the heir to O'Connor's Judeo-Christian tradition, McCarthy's title character is a child of sacred violence.[2] His birth is an aberration of the process by which the skandalon that attracted and obstructed generated the violence that saved and killed and then the sacred that blessed and cursed. Girard explains that since the sacred results from the apotheosis of violence, violence may erupt again if the sacred becomes too immanent. Like Dionysus in *The Bacchae* (Girard, *Violence* 126–42), the divinely begotten offspring of McCarthy's title unleashes the fury normally confined to the heavens or converted into culture. And we, the readers addressed at the beginning of the novel, may, like Pentheus, be scandalized to discover that he is our double. If violence confuses differences (*Violence* 49–51), the raging Ballard blurs the distinction that is the source of all other distinctions. He eliminates the difference "between genuine piety and the desire to claim divine status for oneself," between being a child of God in the biblical sense and being a brutal godling himself (*Violence* 135). Ballard is godlike precisely to the extent that he seems most ungodly. However, if Girard's work provides a context for understanding the religious tradition behind the mayhem in McCarthy's novel, it also makes clear that the title is actually a misnomer. Lester Ballard is less a child of God than of the human race, for he is created by its desire to hallow the self through violence.[3]

Although Ballard may be a descendant of primal conflict, his godhead displays a distinctively local coloring. He seems to have seized the tradition of sacred violence that lingered in southern religion and reshaped it into his own chilling faith. He is Tarwater without the cross. He is Cash's frontiersman with a radically privatized relation to the God of Thunder. He is a militantly regional version of what Harold Bloom describes as "the American religion," a gnostic view of the natural self as an offspring of the divinity.[4] Ballard's region may even have nurtured such a national faith, for Lewis Simpson has argued that the South was basically gnostic in seeking to create a sublime pastoral order outside history (76–82). Aspiring to institute just such an Eden, Ballard seeks to consummate the southern myth in himself and achieve "the solipsistic state existent under the secular dispensation dedicated to making the divine immanent" (Simpson 76).[5] The result is only a furious consecration of his own violence, for Ballard spreads the havoc that ruins gnostic idylls in the South from Poe's "The Fall of the House of Usher" to Percy's *The Thanatos Syndrome*.

Since Ballard is a child of God by the blood that he sheds, he dwells entirely apart from conventional religion in the novel. Indeed, southern Christianity is so devitalized in *Child of God* that it seems as if Ballard's cult of one has monopolized all of the passion that might have invigorated other forms of faith. The Southern Baptist theologian E. Y. Mullins, for example, could envision those reborn in Jesus as achieving a kind of "man-godhood, or theomorphism" (Bloom, *American Religion* 217), but the congregation at Six-mile Church, where Ballard attends a service, displays no signs of such divine affiliation. At this gathering the dynamism of O'Connor's evangelicals has been replaced by the automatism of rote worshipers. The rigidity makes a kind of spiritual sense in the culture of violence. "The sole purpose of ritual is to ensure total immobility, or failing that, a minimum of disturbance," Girard writes of the cult that developed in the wake of surrogate victimage. "If the door is opened to admit change, there is always the risk that violence and chaos will force an entry" (*Violence* 284). Such a challenge to ritual order may seem imminent when Ballard takes his place in a rear bench after the service at Six-mile has started. However, the church preserves its holy stasis. The congregation follows its usual custom of turning "like a cast of puppets" to stare at the slacker, as if mass mimesis were manipulating them into concerted postures against any intrusions and irruptions. Masterminded by such unanimity, the church folk have become precisely what Jean-Michel Oughourlian titles his study in Girardian psychology, "puppets of desire." After the marionettes, having turned back more slowly than usual, start to whisper about Ballard's arrival, the preacher conceals his need to pause for such a disturbance and politely drinks a glass of water. The worshipers have made a religion out of what Vereen Bell recognizes as the obsession in Sevier County to preserve an unassailable status quo (54–57). Just as such stolid folk keep the disaster of the flood or legends of local violence from overwhelming their routinely normal lives, these ladies and gentlemen have so refined the art of churchly decorum that they keep any threat of disorder at a comfortable remove.

Ballard rejects their overly anxious cult of form and conformity. The latecomer ignores the "biblical babbling" (31) of the preacher and reads the notices about church attendance and collections—tallies of further spiritual regimentation. He sniffles throughout the service, "but nobody expected he would stop if God himself looked back askance so no one looked" (32). Since even the deity cannot shame Ballard into proper behavior, the children of God imitate the divine impotence and simply ignore the irreverent interloper (Bartlett 7). Ballard is unbowed by the gods of church discipline. This votary of his own violent desire lives beyond human or divine censure, for he embodies the turmoil that threatens the entire religion of propriety. His alienation from traditional Christianity is finalized shortly before the end of the novel in a scene that stages one more version of its title. After Ballard glimpses a little boy staring into the night from the rear window of an illuminated church bus, he tries to remember where he had seen this face before: "it came to him that the boy looked like himself" (191). Far from enjoying the bright sanctuary of the church bus, McCarthy's adult of God lives in the bleak outer dark at which his young double peers.

Ballard travesties the way the boy on the church bus lives out what it means to be a child of God, for the murderer's violent godhead is inseparable from his chronically perverse childishness. If Ballard is the offspring of the ancient tradition of sacred violence, his furious divinity is only a glorified form of his own raging immaturity. The nouns of the title blur into each other to create a holy terror, a lord-almighty hellion, a cursed "son of a gun." Little Lester poses and dresses dolls—the corpses of his female victims—and then he copulates with them as if they were sex toys for the sovereign over life and death. Child Ballard clings to stuffed animals throughout much of the novel—a security blanket for an adult in regression who has been bereft of home and parents—yet the cuddly tiger and bears are also the puerile totems of his farouche heart, the country fair trophies of the marksmanship that he will turn to murder. Like a naughty toddler, Ballard trespasses upon the taboo territories of sex and violence, but the bad boy commits such atrocities that he is exalted to the realm of the archaic sacred. McCarthy's child of God thus completely perverts the longing for the biblical model of goodness that Girard recognizes in the young. "Nothing is more mimetic than the desire of a child," according to Girard, "and yet it is good. Jesus himself says it is good. Mimetic desire is also the desire for God" (Adams 25). Whereas Bishop in *The Violent Bear It Away* imitates the touching receptivity of the nonviolent sacred, Ballard copies the sacred violence to which mimetic desire may lead when it goes awry. As child of God, Ballard raises the narcissism of infants and the tantrums of two year olds to a sublimely heinous level where he acts out the ill-temper of a juvenile deity.

Although McCarthy's title invites readers to imagine the divine Ballard through the image of childhood, *Child of God* seems to write against that metaphor on a very fundamental level—that of narrative itself. It relates surprisingly little about Ballard's own early life. The reticence about Ballard's past is especially noticeable because the process of creating violent felons, as criminologist Lonnie Athens has argued, typically begins at an early age. The brutal adult has often been brutalized as a child. He or she might have suffered from actual or threatened violence, witnessed some family member being violated, and received coaching in violence from an authority figure (see Rhodes 112–24). The violent criminal, in other words, is the mimetic child of violence. Since McCarthy's narrators provide such limited details about Ballard's childhood, it is particularly significant that Lester undergoes just such trauma in one of the few chapters told about his youth. Having lost his mother when she abandoned the family, Ballard later lost his father when he committed suicide. "They say he never was right after his daddy killed hisself," one of the narrators comments (21). The nine or ten year old may well have grown up under the shadow of that parental violence, for almost twenty years later when the Ballard farm is auctioned, a rope still dangles from the loft in the barn.

The hanging made Ballard's father at once a victim, victimizer, and model for the sonship of holy victimization. Self, suicide, and the sacred, according to Girard, form three points of a perversely triangular desire. As young Miranda in Porter's "Old Mortality" demonstrates when she revels in gothic tales about the cruelties of convent life, the self may deliberately choose a remote, and even hostile, mediator. The more that the disciple feels rejected and humiliated by the model, the more it attributes infinite virtue to such a deservedly scornful master (Girard, *Deceit* 182). Only if the mediator thwarts the self, even threatens the self, sick with its own insufficiency and yearning for whatever it is not, does the ideal deserve idolizing. In such existential masochism the subject seeks not pain, as a linear understanding of desire might suggest, but the divinity that must belong, in the oblique world of triangular desire, to any model who makes worthless disciples bear such shame and suffering. The culmination of this metaphysical desire for what is apparently so undesirable may be suicide. The self pursues the thrilling torment of obstructed desire until it finally achieves the supremely enticing negation, the ultimate means of frustration and mediator of transcendence, death (*Deceit* 282–87). Self-violence beckons as if mortality might at last put the subject of such all-consuming desire into contact with the sacred. Rejected by his unattainable wife, Ballard's father hanged himself. Although McCarthy's narrators provide little more information to understand the suicide than this sequence of marital events, the stark chronology suggests how desire for the elusive ideal can culminate in one's ultimate destruction. Ballard's father may have prostrated himself so profoundly before his absent and adored wife that self-abasement climaxed in self-slaughter.

Lester is fathered by such sublime suicide. The shock of seeing a hanged man, any hanged man, is conveyed by a narrator who recalls how in 1899 he himself stood among the throng of spectators that gathered around the scaffold where two vigilantes would be executed: "I was thirteen year old but I remember it like it was yesterday. . . . Don't ever think hangin is quick and merciful. It ain't" (167). The discovery of a father's suicide must have bred an even more visceral response in his bereft son. Although the man who cut down Ballard's father seems disturbed even in remembering the corpse's bulging eyes and blackened tongue, the young Lester reacted with the silence and vigilance so characteristic of him: he stared blankly at the hanged body that he was the first to find. The boy "never was right" afterwards (21) because the suicide showed him the way from childhood to his later violent godhead. Lester found in his daddy's death the mimetic bond that Freud had long ago intuited but always subordinated to his cathectic understanding of desire. The Oedipal conflict is generated, according to Girard, not by libidinal impulses for the mother but by propensity toward the father as model and obstacle. The son aspires to be the double of the parent who signifies the way to imitate but blocks the path to its fulfillment (*Violence* 169–92).

Lester is the child of such paternal desire. The son of the suicidal Ballard is almost infantile in his sheer longings. He shivers. He thirsts. He hungers. He sleeps, dreaming of mountain streams, "with his mouth open like a dead man" (16)—one gaping yearning. Although Ballard is often shown hunting, buying provisions, building a fire, or searching for a home, such physical gratification only prepares him to live on the level of Girard's metaphysical desire. "Once his basic needs are satisfied (indeed, sometimes even before), man is subject to intense desires, though he may not know precisely for what," Girard writes. "The reason is that he desires *being,* something he himself lacks and which some other person seems to possess" (*Violence* 146). That other person for the childish Lester is his dead father. So close are son and sire in the underground of Lester's psyche that when Ballard hides out in a subterranean cave later in the novel, he poignantly imagines hearing the whistling which signaled to him as a boy that his father was returning home. The bloody course of Ballard's life is a kind of prolonged homecoming, a childish coming back to the father by becoming like the god who left him.

The father's death provided the son with a model for how the self may seek divine autonomy through violence. Ballard is so much a child of his father that after he loses the homeplace in an auction at the beginning of the novel, the sole scion of the family follows the bloody example of his elder. He tries to kill the paternal rival, the new owner who usurps the fatherland. Violence is Ballard's true patrimony. The son may even be haunted by a kind of hereditary death wish, a desire to sacrifice his life in order to rejoin the missing father. Later in the novel, after Ballard dreams of traveling to his death, he tries to assassinate Greer, the interloper on family property, but the attempt to defend his lost inheritance only results in Ballard's being wounded. Yet if the father's suicide left a legacy of bloodshed, it also undercut his actual example, for the death showed Lester that such imitation can end in the most degraded form of transcendence—a carcass suspended above the barn floor that fell to the ground as if the men Lester summoned were "cuttin down meat" (21). Lester's father thus became the model of butchery against whom the son had to define himself. Amid the shambles of childhood he learned the truth of Girard's claim that "one can commit suicide in order to become God but one cannot become God without renouncing suicide. In the face of death the desired omnipotence becomes one with extreme impotence" (*Deceit* 277). To solve the double bind of the parent's death, Ballard renounced the self-slaughter of the would-be deity but pursued the same sacred goal by directing his violence toward others. In effect, the son inverted the example of his father's masochistic suicide so that it became the model of the child's sadistic divinization (*Deceit* 185).

Ballard acted like just such a perverse overlord during one of the few other incidents recounted from his childhood—a game that ended in bloodshed. "A child's play is already triangular," Girard comments, "an imitation of adults" (*Deceit* 84). Children's games and contests re-present in stylized form far more dangerous kinds of grown-up rivalry that might end in violence (*Violence* 93, 311–12). They turn the mimetic antagonism that can destroy a society into the temporary pretense of two opposing teams, and they carefully restrain the conflict by rules and traditions of fair play. In a fragment from Lester's boyhood, one of the narrators recalls how the young Ballard returned the ritualized violence of sport back to the strife out of which it originated. Having lost a softball, Lester chose not the older schoolfellow who later narrates the scene but the younger Finney boy to retrieve it. And when the child would not comply with Ballard's request, the bully bloodied the nose of the uncooperative underling. Ballard was so brutally serious that he unleashed the ferocity normally restricted and redirected in child's play. The narrator and his friends rejected such violence by their boyishly confused sympathy for Ballard's young target: "I felt, I felt . . . I don't know what it was. We just felt real bad" (18). Throughout the entire novel Ballard never identifies with his victims so keenly, never feels even this awkward and inarticulate sorrow. The hearts of his childhood companions expose the child of God as, from his nonage, a little bruiser.

Since the divine Lester never grows beyond this infantile form of mimetic desire, he finds his virtual twin as an adult in the "idiot child" Billy (115). The hypertrophy of this "hugeheaded bald and slobbering primate" (77) makes literal the southern description of a youngster who is "not right in the head" as a "child of God" (Bell 68). The kid who consorts with roaches and spiders forces the narrator to put the very concept of child under question. Billy is so grotesque that when the robin that Ballard has given the boy as a pet eyes its new master, the bird is perplexed by the scarcely recognizable toddler: "It spied the . . . what? child? child, and veered off toward a corner" (77). Like O'Connor's Bishop, Billy has not followed the conventional course for maturation, but whereas Bishop is a true child of God, Ballard's little double is the child as god. When the girl who denies being Billy's mother warns Lester that the hellion will kill the pet robin, Ballard grins his murderous kinship with the tyke: "It's hisn to kill if he wants to" (77). The savage urchin chews off the legs of the fluttering bird, for, like some ravenous deity who can only be appeased by sacrifice, he has an appetite for violence. Ballard understands the motive for such mutilation. Explaining, "He wanted it to where it couldn't run off" (79), the divine Lester will murder to gain such infantile control over the life that is as elusive as the parents who deserted him in childhood.

Bereft of father and mother like Billy, Ballard is kin to the abject child that Julia Kristeva describes in *Powers of Horror:* "What he has swallowed up instead of maternal love is an emptiness, or rather a maternal hatred without a word for the words of the father; that is what he tries to cleanse himself of, tirelessly. What solace does he come upon within such loathing? Perhaps a father, existing but unsettled, loving but unsteady, merely an apparition but an apparition that remains. Without him the holy brat would probably have no sense of the sacred . . ." (6). McCarthy's "holy brat" fills the emotional void left by the missing mother and ghostly father with a murderous passion. He copies the father's violent "sense of the sacred" and eventually wreaks his "maternal hatred" on every woman he victimizes.

KILLING AND COPULATING A WAY TO HEAVEN

Ballard lives out his juvenile godhead through conjoining two fundamental challenges of maturity—sexuality and mortality. Miranda began to intuit a link between the two in "The Grave," and Tarwater felt their horrid union when he became the victim of the vampirelike abuser. Ballard exploits the intimacy between what convulses the body in ecstasy and in agony so that their conjunction becomes the basis for his divinization. Like some violent voluptuary in the religion of Georges Bataille (63–70), Ballard makes trespassing into these prohibited realms the very sign of his transcendence. Although Girard demystifies the fury that Bataille adores, both agree that taboos develop to restrain violence (Bataille 41–42). These restrictions make possible what Bataille recognizes as the world of work and what Girard understands as the work of culture. Both also agree that taboos not only obstruct but entice, delimiting regions that are feared and desired (Bataille 37). However, Bataille, unlike Girard, celebrates violating such interdictions as a kind of religious act (74). If taboos circumscribe sacred territory, transgression enables the devotee to stray into the illicit kingdom of God. Bataille encounters the prohibited domain most forcefully in death and eroticism, the two areas that define Ballard's violent life. Since both allow the isolated self to recover a lost continuity of being for which it yearns, Bataille imagines profaning one's way toward such mysticism by deliberately exceeding the limits of the workaday world. Venturing beyond the efficiency, utility, and productivity of mere labor, he revels in the waste and disequilibrium of sex and death (61–62).

Ballard seems like a member in this cult of the extreme. McCarthy's child of God feels free to violate primal taboos against murder and eroticism because he wants to leave behind the numbingly ordinary world of Sevier County and live in the forbidden zone of the violence that is called sacred. Yet as Ballard's desire for violence keeps eliding into the violence of his sexual desire, he sins his way into a heaven of frenzied excess that surpasses even Bataille's audacious fantasies. The violent *do* bear it away: if "it" is the kingdom of sacred violence, only those willing to go beyond the limits of Girard's culture or Bataille's world of work gain the royal realm of broken bodies and shed blood.

Having grown up with the example of his father's violent transcendence, Ballard finds new models of male desire through furtively watching the couples who make love in their cars at mountain hideaways. The boy who once just gazed and gazed at the dangling corpse of his parent has become the man who does nothing at first but stare and stare at the lovers' intertwined flesh. The spectacle of passion provides the abandoned son with a substitute version of the primal scene. His study is particularly instructive because Ballard is the child of a culture that defines a beleaguered manhood by its liquor and lusts. In jail he later claims that all of his trouble has been "caused by whiskey or women or both," but the boast seems less of a personal apologia than a repetition of a swaggering saw about expected machismo: "He'd often heard men say as much" (53). The couple whom Ballard observes models the way to live out this southern masculinity, for he beholds in them all of what he desires. Having turned the all-seeing eye of God into the kind of voyeurism that made Miranda the object of little boys' looks in "The Circus," the grown-up child carries such spying beyond youthful curiosity to actual imitation of his mediator. "In the birth of desire, the third person is always present," Girard observes (*Deceit* 21). Or as Bataille writes, more specifically, about the mimetic power of sexual activity, "In human affairs example is catching. A man enters the dance because the dance makes him dance" (115). While Ballard eyes the pair of lovers, he completes a triangle of erotic and mimetic desires, finding his stimulating exemplar in the youth whose lovemaking sets the car to rocking. A radio DJ heightens the aura of secondhand sexuality by commenting "with mindless chatter on the seduction in the rear seat" (19). Unlike the peeping Ballard, the "dark incubus" Bobby enfleshes there an ecstatic fullness, which his beloved affirms through the extremes that speech uses for the ambivalence of sacred violence, prayer and profanity. "O Bobby, O god," the girl cries, "O shit" (20). Ballard's voyeurism enables him to copy the sexual potency of the godhead. While the disciple looks hard at the lovers by the Frog Mountain turnaround, he gets caught up in the backseat liaison and becomes a body double. As a mockingbird sings, stops, and then starts again its musical imitation, Ballard engages in his own form of mockery, a kind of intercourse by proxy. The aroused onlooker mimics his model's orgasm and ejaculates on the car fender.

All of Ballard's sexuality seems equally once-removed. He stares at the underwear of one of the dump keeper's daughters and proposes owing her the twelve and a half cents that she would charge to see half of her bosom. He watches the woman sleeping in her nightgown at the Frog Mountain turnaround and then robs her of her scanty dress. He asks the girl who may be Billy's mother to show him her breasts. Such voyeurism and fetishism act out the paradox of mimetic desire. They objectify the beloved so that, like the skandalon, she entices even as she impedes; indeed, she entices because she impedes, for the object of desire becomes more desirable the more that it is denied. Whereas the traditional southern belle obtained power through her coyness, Ballard coarsens his ladies into nothing but teases. They excite his covetous gaze, but looking and longing also take the place of the direct and mutual expression of sexual desire that he witnesses between the Frog Mountain couples. Such vicarious eroticism always seems to distance and defer actual lovemaking by interposing some mediator between the disciple and the life of the flesh. Ballard knows only surrogates for the more immediate sexuality that he desires.

Ballard's sadism enables him to go beyond this stand-in and second-rate carnality. Girard views sadism as caused by displaced desire rather a lust for autonomous power. Sadists persecute because they long for the very being of their victims, who mediate what seems like divinity and who seem, in fact, to have been persecuting the tormentor. Although sadism may express itself in the eroticism of bondage and torture, it transcends the sexual realm, for its violence may erupt during any mimetic conflict (*Deceit* 185–87). As disciple of the body, Ballard has been frustrated by the mere existence of the young men and women who have been his models and obstacles. Sadism enables McCarthy's voyeur to act upon the violence of his desire. Having been tormented by simply watching his models, Ballard becomes the scourge of mountain road trysts. The once-passive observer transforms his male ideals into opponents that must be eliminated and his female objects of desire into victims that must be possessed.

Ballard has not known such masculine rivalry in the past. Since his father was rendered transcendent by suicide, this foremost model was never close enough to cause any antagonism with his worshipful son. Yet the young men whom Ballard watches at lovemaking readily become his mimetic adversaries because they share the same universe of desire (Girard, *Deceit* 9). Hence, after Bobby has provided the erotic example that Ballard can only copy in lonely pleasure, the libidinous onlooker tries to reassert his superiority through racial degradation. "It's a nigger . . . A nigger," Ballard whispers about the "dark incubus that humped in a dream of slaverous lust" (20). Precisely because Ballard wants to be so much like Bobby, he can only vent his animosity toward the ideal that he has not yet equaled. The young lover, in turn, resents the intrusion of Ballard's face at the car window and thereby comes to resemble his envious rival. When Bobby cries "you son of a bitch" at the "misplaced and loveless simian shape" that scurries away in the dark (20), he sounds like the violent and profane Lester Ballard that he has bested.

Ballard triumphs over Bobby's successors by an atrocious imitation. After the voyeur discovers that another pair of lovers whom he has spied copulating at the Frog Mountain turnaround are actually dead, he finds the pattern for coupling sexuality and mortality. The disciple of desire rolls the man to the floor of the car and—with pants similarly lowered—takes his model's place over the girl. As the dead man watches with open eyes and aroused flesh, Ballard becomes his second and his superior in the topsy-turvy world of mimetic rivalry, and the defeated model assumes Ballard's former role as voyeur. Ballard's desire intensifies from envious imitation to actual displacement in a deathly ménage à trois until it finally climaxes in a way that Bataille might have anticipated. In *Erotism* Bataille speculates that the violence associated with a corpse may tempt an onlooker to mimesis, to murder (47). When Ballard catches another couple in the intimacy of their pickup truck, he shoots the young man in a ferocious display of machismo toward the male world that has been his ideal and impediment.

The murder begins a killing spree in which Ballard eliminates every obstacle to desire. Ballard's violence confers upon him the sovereignty that he has been elsewhere denied in the cosmic order. As he passes felled trees and massive rocks, he notices the tumult in nature and the resulting need for new trails. "Given charge," the narrator says, "Ballard would have made things more orderly in the woods and in men's souls" (136). Through his bloodshed Ballard seizes command not of the natural or spiritual worlds but of the human rage that is exalted to divine status. Each of his murders disorders the world in order to reorder it as a dominion according to his own desires. Killing his way toward heaven, Ballard makes the kingdom of God into a kingdom of violence.

Ballard does not even allow his own childhood double to stand in the way of his rampaging divinity. Indeed, he cannot be hindered by any such scruple, for as Tarwater proved in killing Bishop, humans project their violence onto the sacred with such ultimacy that to be a god is to consume even a child as victim. After Ballard assassinates the young woman in Billy's house who has rejected his sexual advances, he turns to destroying the terrifying child as well. Lester and his "little brother" are connected by a circuitry of destructive desire, as if each took his violent cues from the other. For both, to "want" is to want ruin. Just as Billy received permission to destroy his pet bird from Ballard, the manchild gets his plan to destroy the house from imagining how the boychild might easily have set it ablaze. While Ballard earlier warmed himself at the stove that is fenced with chicken wire and anchored to the floor, he conjectured, "I bet he could push this over if he wanted to" (116). Ballard's speculation about the obstructed object of violent desire kindles his own desire in kind. Having murdered the girl, another object of forbidden desire, the fire starter accomplishes what the childproofing of the stove was designed to frustrate in Billy. The resulting conflagration does not at all terrify the child, for he has earlier modeled Ballard's own incendiary passions. As Ballard leaves the house with the body of his latest female victim, he looks back at the urchin who looks at him, "berryeyed filthy and frightless among the painted flames" (120). Whereas Bishop howls as he is being drowned because he is no child of violence, Billy at last lives in his own fierce element, the realm where desire rages and spreads like fire. McCarthy's child of God sacrifices his double as a burnt offering to sacred violence.

Repeating his crimes, multiplying the corpses, Ballard copies his own bloody example and begets himself again and again as a child of violence. He is imitation run amok, the ultimate conjunction of murder and mimesis—the serial killer. Although seven of his victims' bodies are finally discovered, not all of his murders are actually recounted in the novel, and not all of the corpses of the recounted murders are ever found. The tally of victims is fittingly inexact, for each body is just an emptied and generic "one more," an insignificant addition to the spoils of mimetic desire. Girard claims that even when the self achieves the object of its desire, it may be disappointed at not being ultimately fulfilled and transformed. The self then pursues ever new goals and becomes even more disillusioned when they provide such little gratification (*Deceit* 88–89). Ballard adds killing to killing to killing, but each victim does not satisfy the need for violence so much as perpetuate it. What Ballard ultimately desires is not the physical—the bodies that he makes his own through murder—but the metaphysical, the very being of the mediators that escapes him even as he idolizes it. The child desires to be "of" his gods.

Sex offers Ballard another way to this divinity. If arrogating sacred violence enables Ballard to act out his mimetic rivalry with men, it also provides the means to gratify his displaced desire for women. Much as Billy hobbles the bird to keep it with him, Ballard resorts to murder to make the elusive object of desire exclusively his, eternally available, forever unable to escape in the way that his mother abandoned her husband and young son. Ballard takes women's lives so that he may ultimately take their bodies. He can thus be at once lordly and fleshly, still dwelling in his divine autonomy but at last drawing near to the palpable beloved. The body of the beloved forms part of the triangle of sexual desire, according to Girard, whose other points are the beloved and the lover (*Deceit* 105). However, Ballard the lover does not desire the beloved, for he is unwilling to risk the necessary vulnerability of self-exposure. Nor does he even desire the living body of the beloved, for the vital flesh is only a threat to his almighty masculinity and an obstacle to the childish pleasures of solitary sexuality. What Ballard really desires is the ersatz gratification that preserves his power and distances him from any personal encounter. Whereas Stendhal's Julien in *The Red and the Black* would like to kiss Mathilde without her being aware of it, and Proust's narrator enjoys Albertine only when she is asleep, Ballard discovers the ultimate means by which the "lover need no longer fear that he may reveal to his beloved the humiliating spectacle of his own desire" (*Deceit* 160). He reduces women beyond corporeality to mere corpses.[6]

Discussing the serial killer's obsession with corpses, Mark Seltzer claims that for such murderers "*lifelikeness* . . . substitutes for the imperfection and threat of living life itself" (20).[7] Ballard creates precisely such a simulacrum through his female mannequins. After he buys a red dress for the first of his dead women, brushes her hair, and applies lipstick, he places her in various positions and then goes outside his shack to view her through the window. Ballard makes this doll his model female, a dummy who does not share, respond, demand, or challenge. In valuing the likeness of a woman over a woman herself, he loses sexual desire in mimetic desire; he seeks erotic fulfillment not with a person but with a gussied-up pretense of femininity. Whereas the Girardian subject imitates the desires of the model, Ballard desires nothing but the kind of store-window model that he poses and makes subject to his own desires. He does not so much simulate sexual intercourse as make love to mimesis.

Ballard's murderous misogyny makes literal the vision of the beflowered and belaced southern woman as a decomposing corpse that Miranda imagined in "Old Mortality." Indeed, this lady killer almost seems like a disciple of the writer that Miranda's family regarded as "our greatest poet," "our" unequivocally meaning that "he was Southern" (*Collected Stories* 178).[8] In poetry and fiction Poe pursued a passion for female flesh that went beyond even death. His narrators might hover over the bed of a lady's dormition ("The Sleeper"), lie down by the side of a lovely dead bride ("Annabel Lee"), extract the teeth from an alive but interred beloved ("Berenice"), or find a first wife possessing the corpse of her successor ("Ligeia"), as if the stilled body could mediate some participation in the life of the idealized woman herself. Andrea Dworkin denounces this fatal tendency to turn women into things of beauty when she claims that "women are sacrificed to male desire—including aesthetic desire, art for art's sake—with less concern than the early Hebrews had for their Yom Kippur goats." She believes such scapegoating through art "is sophisticated hating and produces sophisticated defenses of hate, as long as the hate is pretty, formally pretty" (29).

Miranda rejects the way her family romanticizes a woman to death, but Ballard is a child of this old order. Having inherited these cultural constructions of gender, he then reconstructs the traditions by warping them even further with his sexual violence.[9] Ballard's voyeurism caricatures the stereotypical image of the southern woman as standing sublimely on a pedestal, and his victimization travesties the alternative to such glorification that imagined her as merely a figure of flesh whom death makes even more desirable. McCarthy's Tennesseean carries the deadly aestheticism of Miranda's South to its decadent extreme. Ballard idolizes a woman as a statue upon which he gazes, or he desecrates her as a corpse that he rapes.

Ballard's necrophilia sexualizes the violence of mortality. Bataille views eroticism as causing "a violation bordering on death, bordering on murder" and writes that the Marquis de Sade viewed murder as "a pinnacle of erotic excitement" (17, 18). Ballard conjoins and transgresses upon these equally forbidden realms. He acts out the comparison between sacrifice and intercourse that Bataille merely dares to imagine: "The lover strips the beloved of her identity no less than the blood-stained priest his human or animal victim. The woman in the hands of her assailant is despoiled of her being" (90). Ballard's coupling with the dead is the conjunction of violence with violence. Death is typically the ultimate assault to the flesh, for it causes carefully delineated physiological structures to lose their differentiation until they achieve the final indistinction of dust. As Ballard hoists a victim into his attic or hauls his harem of cadavers across the countryside, *Child of God* never overlooks the sheer onslaught that death makes upon the flesh. Rather, stripping the beloved corpse of the ravishing romanticization cherished by Porter's old order, the novel cultivates the physics of mortality. It records the body's wooden rigor, downward drag, burdensome weight, and—in the Grand Guignol of the epilogue—dissolution and putrefaction. To prevent the spread of such violence, Girard writes, the living "quarantine death, creating a *cordon sanitaire* all around it. Above all, they have recourse to funeral rites, which (like all other rites) are dedicated to the purgation and expulsion of maleficent violence" (*Violence* 255). Ballard flouts the system of differences that culture constructs against the contagion of death, for he turns mortality into the very realm for carnality. After he has already broached the boundaries of the flesh through murder, the transgressor makes one final incursion with the weapon of his own rapacious body. Necrophilia is the only form of intercourse left by sacred violence. What else can a destructive god love but a stone-cold corpse?

The answer in *Child of God* is as obvious as the skandalon: stone itself. Much as Tarwater tripped on the stumbling stone of mimetic desire, Ballard makes rock into the ideal that impedes, the obstacle that he adores. He seeks a haven below the earth, as if having pursued violent transcendency to such heights, he can finally live only amid the depths of his own degradation. In the subterranean caves that he increasingly haunts, Ballard finds the locus for the desire that has drawn him from one dead weight to another, from his father's lifeless body to his consorts' inert flesh. McCarthy's underground man typifies those who seek self-divinization, according to Girard, by courting the ultimate idol and obstruction, the negation of self in inanimate matter: "That end is found in the mineral world, the world of a death which the absence of all movement, of all quivering, has made complete and definitive. The horrible fascination ends in the density of lead, the impenetrable immobility of granite" (*Deceit* 287). Stone scandalizes. It attracts the would-be god because it models the superhuman through the nonhuman, yet it blocks the devotee by its sheer stasis, tonnage, and magnitude. To be like stone is to cancel one's humanity. Ballard makes rock into his element of choice because he would petrify himself into the semblance of the alien and indifferent godhead.

Ballard finds stone so alluring that he gathers his victims into this same process of underground sanctification. Just as he incarnates the maleficent face of sacred violence in his murder and necrophilia, he also embodies its beneficent side through his cult of the dead. In the very "bowels of the mountain," inside "a tall and bellshaped cavern," Ballard creates a mortuary, where "on ledges or pallets of stone . . . dead people lay like saints" (135). Ballard's shrine seeks to exalt his victims beyond the violence of their death so they gain the otherworldliness of the sacred. Much as ancient people viewed the whitened bones of the dead as a sign that the skeletons had transcended the agony before death and the corruption after it (Bataille 46–47, 56), Ballard regards the corpses of his victims as hallowed after having suffered his fury. He builds a chapel out of a charnel house, constructs the sacred out of his own violence. Yet despite his attempt to turn his murders into a means of canonizing his victims, the crypt serves a far less transcendent purpose. Like the underground tombs to which Jesus compares the Pharisees (Luke 11:44), it hides the violence that flourishes in Ballard's sacrificial order. Beneath the mountain, behind the stone, there lies the victim.

SACRIFICIAL CRISIS IN SEVIER COUNTY

Although Ballard is the avatar of sacred violence in *Child of God*, his mayhem is not an isolated aberration in a culture that otherwise works effectively to manage strife. Rather, it is part of a more widespread crisis in Sevier County. The narrators record so much violence—flood, rape, incest, assault, hanging, stoning, vigilantism—that the whole world of the novel seems convulsed with confusion. The sacrificial mechanisms that developed after surrogate victimage to keep such brutality from happening again no longer hold animosity in check. Laws, taboos, manners, and festivals do not limit the conflicts between opposites and equals but provide new opportunities for outrage. And so, violence not only bursts out in a murderer like Ballard but also collapses all the distinctions that structure nature and society. The culture that once emerged out of bloodshed seems to be returning to its genesis in chaos.

This mass undifferentiation overruns the landscape in *Child of God*. Humans violate the natural order by tossing beer cans amid roadside grass, littering the bushes by a dump with refuse, and leaving a truck to corrode deep in a quarry. The green world reclaims what humans have set apart: weeds overgrow Lester's outhouse, and honeysuckle overtakes the rusting truck. Nature even seems to disregard its own distinctions. In the winter, snow grays the sky and land so that the ever watchful Ballard can see nothing outlined clearly. In the spring, three days of rain pour down primeval chaos by flooding the creek, overflowing the fields, and lifting jetsam high into the trees. Bottles, boards, and fruit float together in the waters, as if all antediluvian differences had been liquidated. The sheriff makes clear the biblical precedent for this confusion when he asks whether his deputy has seen a bearded old man building an enormous boat. The violent deluge only intensifies the deluge of violence. After the sheriff rows down the street to the hardware store, he inquires about the guns that have been stolen amid the disorder of the flood. He hears the typical response of archaic religion to such calamity: the violence has its source in the sacred. The hardware store owner wonders whether "there are just some places the good lord didn't intend folks to live in" (162), and an old woman is reported to have attributed the inundation to divine punishment for sin.

Ballard intuits the antagonism at the heart of McCarthy's tempestuous world. As he watches two hawks couple, grappling with each other as if in battle, the naif understands the violence, if not the sex, that impels the encounter: "He did not know how hawks mated but he knew that all things fought" (169). This universal tooth-and-nail struggle risks absorbing Ballard's reign of terror into a bleak naturalism out of Robinson Jeffers or, nearer to Tennessee, Robert Penn Warren in one of his grimmer moods. Yet what keeps *Child of God* from such neoromanticism is that the novel so firmly grounds its violence in human affairs—not just in Lester Ballard but in many of the folk in Sevier County. In his rivalry, resentment, and wrath Ballard is not a freak of malign nature but kith and kin to so many other like-minded men and women in the novel. The mimetic antagonism in *Child of God* does not reflect the fundamental disorder of the universe so much as the landscape of confusion localizes the breakdown of interdividual relationships in east Tennessee.

All of the novel's children of God contribute to this pervasive violence. After some of the mountain folk have been discussing Ballard's rascal of a grandfather, one claims for Lester a unique place in the family: "You can trace em back to Adam if you want and goddamn if he didn't outstrip em all" (81). However, a later speaker rephrases this same image so that Ballard seems much less singular in his ill will. The sheriff's deputy asks the elderly Mr. Wade if people were meaner in his youth than they are now, and the townsman answers, "I think people are the same from the day God first made one" (168). If there is a kind of original perverseness that dates back to Genesis, Sevier County has a lengthy history of dealing with the errant children of Adam and Eve. When a woman at the post office complains, "I never knew such a place for meanness," the sheriff counters, "It used to be worse" (164). Recalling the vigilantes that scourged the countryside of his boyhood, Wade rejects the possibility that the gangs brought even a crude justice: "No, those were sorry people all the way around, ever man jack a three hundred and sixty degree son of a bitch, which my daddy said meant they was a son of a bitch any way you looked at em" (165). More recent evidence of the rampant meanness adorns the walls of the post office. After being released from jail, Ballard stares at the posters of criminals as if glimpsing his future written on their skin: "Their tattoos. Legends of dead loves inscribed on perishable flesh. A prevalence of blue panthers" (55).

This general mean-heartedness provides the background for Ballard's rampage from the first pages of the novel when he is expelled from his paradisal homeplace in a festive auction. The musicians who "came like a caravan of carnival folk" in the novel's opening words establish the holiday mood for the lemonade sales and silver-dollar giveaways that follow (3). Girard traces such feasts of disorder, which Bakhtin views as carnivalizing literature, to commemorations of the violence that once preceded scapegoating. On these gala occasions the community restages the primal crisis through deliberately breaking down the differences that structure society. Celebrants engage in excessive eating, irreverent speech, and illicit conduct. They wear outré costumes, risk games of chance, and invert hierarchies so that fools reign as kings and parents obey their children. However, such revels normally confine the confusion by their stylized presentation and implicit laws about lawlessness so that it never really disrupts the community (*Violence* 119–23). The carnival at the beginning of

Child of God violates these ritual boundaries. It becomes a "holiday-gone-wrong" in which, instead "of holding violence in check, the ceremonies inaugurate a new cycle of revenge" (*Violence* 125). The reason for the breakdown is that the morning's main attraction borders on a rite of exclusion. Ballard is being forced to leave his family farm. The inheritance links this son of the soil to the tradition of folk rooted in land and kinship that fellow Tennesseean Andrew Lytle famously celebrated in "The Hind Tit," his contribution to *I'll Take My Stand.* At the beginning of McCarthy's novel, Ballard disturbs the celebration by taking *his* stand against forfeiting the family land. His tenacity prompts the violence that finally leaves the carnival in ruins.

The county-mandated auction of Ballard's land is conducted by CB, who presides, like a carnival barker, over the sale. He models the economy of desire that will erupt in mimetic possessiveness and undermine the merrymaking. Celebrating property rather than the old-time agrarian virtue of land, CB incites the crowd's desire to bid by inviting them to copy his own prosperous example. The auctioneer claims that real estate has brought him wealth and explains that he would try to buy these very premises if he had not already invested all of his money in other holdings. The master of ceremonies meets his rival in desire when the rifle-toting Ballard breaks up the holiday devoted to arrogating his homestead. "Saxon and Celtic bloods," the narrator observes, as if to explain why Ballard moves "with a constrained truculence" at the barn door while the carnival begins (4). Yet if Ballard has inherited what Grady McWhiney in *Cracker Culture* views as the violent legacy of the South's ancient forebears, that bloody desire originates in mimetic desire. "L.B." becomes CB's double and opponent because Lester Ballard's pride of place depends on his pride in place. What the auctioneer views as merely real estate to be sold, Ballard claims as his family's estate to be kept at all costs. Although Ballard's potential to reduce the carnival to violence is suggested by the way that the musicians look like porcelain figures "from an old country fair shooting gallery" (8), Ballard becomes the actual victim. When the dispossessed owner threatens CB, Buster busts Ballard in the head with an ax, and the property is sold to John Greer. Exiled from the seemingly edenic home, the butt of the communal celebration assumes his identity as county outcast with a vengeance. Ballard preys on Sevier's sons and daughters and finally tries to kill Greer, the trespasser who displaced him from his childhood home and replaced him as lord of the land.

This carnival in ruins initiates the many rounds of violence and counterviolence that take place amid ruins and at carnivals throughout the novel. Carnivals aestheticize and ritualize violence so that it becomes transformed into a gaudy and playful celebration. At the fair Ballard "fishes" by dipping a net to catch creatures of gold plastic, and he "hunts" by shooting at targets to win stuffed animals. However, in *Child of God* the virtual violence of such amusements always hovers upon reverting to actual mayhem. Ballard spits in the tank of goldfish where he had been trying to win a prize and sneers at the woman who rightly accused him of cheating, "You a busynosed old whore, ain't ye?" (63). After having clashed with players and pitchmen at the fair, the gamester joins a crowd "watching into the dark for some midnight contest to begin." While the sky explodes with the fire of sacred violence, two men huddle over their crates of rockets "like assassins or bridgeblowers" (65). The anonymous narrators place the potential menace of this revelry in its rightful context by recalling other casualties of the midway. At one fair a vengeful mob wanted to tar and feather the fraudulent sponsor of a shooting contest. At another, an ape in a boxing contest became so enraged after its human opponent delivered the first blow that the animal almost tore off the man's jaw. McCarthy's unstable carnivals seem not just to recall the violence of primordial conflict but to be poised upon reenacting it.

If a carnival ever completely transgresses the borders of its performance, it degenerates into nothing but ruins, into nothing but the dump run by Reubel, Ballard's partner in drinking bootleg whiskey. Suzanne Hatty objects that the media's fascination with Ballard's real-life kin—the serial killers and sexual predators of the late twentieth century—deflects attention away from violence in families and focuses it instead on monstrous others who seem entirely removed from the ordinary world (60–68). *Child of God* does not overlook such domestic strife in favor of the rampage of the more sensationalized Ballard. It uses a dissipated family out of the pages of Erskine Caldwell to embody the most ungodly ways of being a child and parent. Much as the violent Lester lives out his own perversely imitative sonship, the nine daughters of the junkman copy the reckless desire of the father who "spawned" them (26). Reubel cannot understand why his brood is so wild, for "their grandmother was the biggest woman for churchgoin you ever seen" (38). Her descendants are no grandchildren of God. Rather, Reubel's daughters are the children of rubble, for he fosters the undifferentiation of the rubbish heap.

The dump localizes the confusion of the mimetic desire and mutual antagonism that hold together and drive apart the family. Reubel named his stray children from terms that he chanced upon in a medical dictionary salvaged from his garbage pile. It might have seemed that such monikers as Urethra, Cerebella, and Hernia Sue would have at least brought the differentiation of language to Reubel's nondescript progeny. But since none of these idiosyncratic tags is attached to any particular daughter in the novel, they all dissolve into each other, becoming as indistinguishable for the reader as they are for their father, who cannot even tell which of his offspring is the eldest. Sharing the same sire and the same gender, the sisters live as if all distinctions have been thrown away in their random, refuse-filled lives. They stay at home but are virtual cast-offs, a sorority of junk. They simply blend into the jumble of ruins as they sit idly on chairs or crates rescued from the detritus—amorphous and virtually anonymous pieces of poor white trash. Like the dump's cats that dawdle in the sun, the litter of nine imitates the yard's lack of discrimination. They cat around, mating promiscuously with nameless country boys, whose cars all seem cobbled together out of the spare parts that litter the waste land. The generic lusts of these copycat felines make no difference between one horny paramour in his ramshackle vehicle and the next, as if their physiological labels entitled the flesh and blood of the trash man to be nothing more than flesh and blood. Their arbitrary and impulsive couplings embody the dissolution caused by violence, and this dissolute conduct, in turn, only spawns more violence in their equally remiss father.

Just as the daughters imitate their ill-defined father, the father also mimics his undisciplined children. Discovering two figures copulating in the woods, Reubel silently watches their mating, like the voyeuristic Ballard, until he at last recognizes one of his own breeding. Then, the dump keeper displaces his rival and beats his child with a stick. "Like father, like daughter" becomes a lascivious formula for how mimesis climaxes in violence. Reubel is so inflamed by desire like his daughter's that he sexually assaults his own flesh. Replacing her partner's body with his own, he ends the rape in coitus interruptus only when his daughter answers "no" to his query, "Did he dump a load in you?" (28). The trash man turns his daughter into a dump by spilling his seed on her thigh. In the oppressively inbred world that mimesis has made out of family life, the dump keeper's eroticism copies his own failure to discriminate that he witnesses being copied in his sexually indiscriminate daughter.

The violence of the incestuous rape is the violence of the dump itself—the disintegration of all distinctions, the intermixture of identities, the commingling of what should be kept apart. Such lack of differentiation between parent and child violates one of the fundamental taboos designed to keep the outbreak of primal violence from ever being repeated. Girard suggests that the rules of exogamy developed to preserve harmony in the society formed after surrogate victimage. Culture prohibited sexual relationships between men and women who came from the same specified group, for if such desire were allowed, it might easily lead to the mimetic rivalry that would destabilize the community. Brother might fight father or brother for sister or mother (*Violence* 193–222). Whereas Bataille views the incest taboo as an exuberant and generous renunciation of the violence in sexuality (217–20), Girard considers it a prophylaxis against violence. In committing this primal transgression the dump keeper acts with the same sacred fury as does Lester Ballard: he assaults difference itself. It is hardly surprising that Reubel's family eventually collapses, for it is founded on violence and undermined from within.

The rampant violence in Sevier County indicates how its culture has not developed a way to live comfortably with the sacred. Girard describes the dilemma when he explains, "The absolute can be likened to fire: too near and one gets burned, too far away and one gets nothing. Between these two extremes is a zone where one is warmed and heartened by the welcome light" (*Violence* 269). Whereas the godly congregation at Six-mile Church seems coolly detached from such vitalizing transcendence, the rest of the characters seem consumed by its ferocious immanence. The only one who lives in the hospitable zone that Girard describes is the novel's actual worker in flames. The blacksmith whom Ballard visits to have his ax repaired typifies the way civilization may benefit by keeping the divine burning at an appropriately pious remove. Metal workers embody the dichotomy of the primitive godhead, according to Girard, because they forge utensils that can be used not only for defense and domestic economy but also for violence within the community (*Violence* 260–61). Genesis understands the destructive potential of such a trade when it makes the first worker in metals a descendant of the first murderer (4:22). Filled with reverence for the sheer power behind his profession, the smith in *Child of God* bases his vocation on constructive violence. He harnesses fire to work on such implements of culture as the autos and farm machinery that clutter his workshop with their parts. And he tries to model for Ballard the way such flames may be used to perfect a Hemingwayesque ritual of craft.

The smith's elaborate instructions to Ballard about how to dress an ax might seem a gratuitous diversion in the novel were it not for the way they offer a very practical disquisition on how culture develops to constrain and redirect violence. The master artisan uses his demonstration to provide an object lesson for Ballard, as if his customer were a would-be disciple interested in learning how to discipline violence. The blacksmith pounds strength into the ax blade but warns against applying his hammer to the edges. He cools the steel in water but cautions that it must be done slowly so that the metal does not crack. He encourages the ever-vigilant Ballard to watch the fire and criticizes careless workers who "leave the tool they're heatin to perdition but the proper thing is to fetch her out the minute she shows the color of grace" (72). The smith forges this technology into a theology of sacred violence. He knows that fire can be infernal as well as refining, that the power reserved for the deity can be destructive when abused and uncontrolled, and that tempering steel models an entire temperament toward sacred violence. Despite such tutelage, the intemperate Ballard ignores his mentor's example. When at the end of his lesson the blacksmith asks Lester if he "could do it now from watchin," the oblivious onlooker shows how he has not learned anything from this pattern for the religious life by replying, "Do what" (74).

Whereas the smith uses violence to become a child of Vulcan, his inattentive student misuses it to become a child of Cain. After Ballard cuts stumps and fenceposts with his newly sharpened ax, he stokes an extravagant blaze in the hearth of his squatter's cabin. It lays waste the house that very night. The fire starter never intended such ruin, but his sheer excess typifies the violent prodigality that Bataille praises as divine, the "desire to consume, to annihilate, to make a bonfire of our resources" (185). Although Ballard may seem like a hillcountry Prometheus who steals the fiery power of the gods' wrath and then scorches the earth with his rage, he is a child of sacred violence much like everyone else in the novel, except the smith whom he ignores. Common family origins bind Ballard by ties of blood to the rest of Sevier County, but they do not legitimatize, relativize, or sentimentalize Ballard's bloodshed. *Child of God* is too toughminded to let the outrages of others provide any kind of apology for Ballard. Rather, the proliferation of violence marks the intensity of the sacrificial crisis in McCarthy's Tennessee. The antagonism that might be confined to petty jealousies or duels in Porter's postbellum order and that reached a murderous climax in O'Connor's post–World War II South seems to make an entire community catch fire.

READING AND SCAPEGOATING LESTER BALLARD

Child of God does not allow readers to remain completely aloof from the violence that overwhelms its world. Instead, the novel implicates its audience in the central issues of the text by challenging members to define themselves in relation to the sacred. It keeps bringing readers toward and then distancing them from its infantile deity, as if realizing Girard's comment on the fiery absolute: "too near and one gets burned, too far away and one gets nothing" (*Violence* 269). McCarthy creates a necessary fictional detachment from the violence through eliciting readers' horrified rejection of Ballard's crimes and through presenting Ballard with a cool objectivity. However, his novel recognizes that if readers are "too far away," they will get "nothing" because Ballard will simply become a monster who can be expelled without sympathy or scruples. Hence, it keeps insisting that readers draw near to Ballard and recognize this potential outcast as one of their own.

Although the opening pages describe the title character as a "child of God much like yourself perhaps" (4), readers may recoil at the comparison. Ballard's sacred violence subverts any conventional meaning of the title with which readers might identify. His assaults, murders, misogyny, incendiarism, and necrophilia should unsettle readers, for his thanatocracy parodies the whole world of the living. If culture is founded out of violence, Ballard crafts a mock-model of it based on his own murders. He creates a community out of the slain bodies who share his hermitage, a theater out of the tableaux vivants that he stages with the dead, an economy out of selling his victims' possessions, and a cult out of entombing corpses. Perhaps outrage at such ghastliness is more difficult recently because, as the avenging narrator of Walker Percy's *Lancelot* remarks, "the only emotion people feel nowadays is interest or the lack of it" (21). However, when readers allow themselves to get beyond mere curiosity or indifference, their shock is salutary, for it resists the numbness that so deadens Ballard. Some in McCarthy's audience may even become so scandalized that the violence becomes a stumbling stone. After admiring McCarthy's skill in *Child of God*, Walter Sullivan, for example, calls the novel "an affront to decency on every level" and "a portent of the barbarism that even now begins to engulf the world" (71, 72). Mark Royden Winchell likewise appreciates McCarthy's craft but deems the novel "calculated to produce revulsion on nearly every page" (300).

If such moral horror makes readers withdraw from Ballard, the frequently objective point of view used by McCarthy's third-person narrator only intensifies that detachment. Ballard is all eye, and the novel uses a narrative perspective that Andrew Bartlett aptly calls "voyeuristic" (4–5) to turn readers into onlookers as well. *Child of God* tends to record all of this staring and spying with few comments from the narrator and without depiction of Ballard's consciousness. The effect of such spareness and secrecy is to duplicate in fiction the way that murderers often report feeling dead inside (Gilligan 33). McCarthy makes Ballard seem devoid of an interior life, as if he were so immersed in his own violence that he hardly had room for the thoughtful discrimination that Girard considers the cultural legacy of scapegoating. Because it resolves the crisis of a society at odds with itself, surrogate victimage leads to the calm stability in which distinctions may at last be discovered amid a formerly confused world (*Violence* 235). Ballard does not live in that post-sacrificial calm but in the kind of ongoing chaos that can be heard in his occasional speech. Whereas the mutual attack and counterattack of Tarwater and Rayber verbalize some degree of forensic detachment from their violence, the largely silent and solitary Ballard is too close to the sacred, too remote from the system of differences that might structure subjectivity or culture, to utter any argument or insight. Hence, when he does speak, his language is shot through with threats, curses, commands, profanities, and denunciations. McCarthy's child of God is the word of violence become flesh.

Whereas understanding Ballard's motives or knowing him from within might help readers to identify with Ballard, *Child of God* keeps him an inscrutable primitive, who always wanders and murders at a fictional remove. Instead of portraying such inner life, the novel seeks to make the tumult of its outer world seen and felt. It emphasizes what is corporal and kinetic, the flesh in motion that will become the body in conflict. McCarthy's prose in *Child of God* is not as grave and elaborate as in others of his baroque novels, as if the chastened approach to language were an attempt to achieve a verbal congruence with his elemental world and his laconic title character. However, the rawboned sentences focus the power of McCarthy's exact diction so that it magnifies and intensifies the chaos and carnage to create a harrowing hyperreality. The novel partakes of the very physicality of violence—not merely in the patently southern gothic scenes of murder, necrophilia, and decomposition, but in the less sensational moments of purely external action. When Ballard cleans out the hovel that will be his new house, rummages through a car where lovers lie dead, or crawls amid his cave, he is so devoid of introspection and self-consciousness that he becomes simply a body opposed to the world, an antagonist by his very exertion against the obstacle of the moment. Eluding explanation, ranging beyond human ken, Ballard seems to gather around himself the mystery of the godhead.

Although the violence of reading *Child of God* is first felt in the shock that separates Ballard and the reader, an even more surprising form of fictional assault is the way that the novel works to undermine precisely this fundamental difference. McCarthy does not allow readers to take high-toned refuge in con-demning a miscreant who is so obviously unrelated to them. Rather, he suggests an unexpected kinship by inscribing a triangle in the very way that the novel is narrated. From the beginning, the narration makes the sacred epithet of the ti-tle into the third point of a delta that joins Ballard and the readers. He is a "child of God much like yourself perhaps" (4). McCarthy invites the novel's lecteurs not to be hypocrites by denying their likeness to Ballard and dares them to say instead, with Eliot in the *Waste Land*, "mon semblable,—mon frère!" (Eliot 39).

Readers may shudder at such a heinous family resemblance. Much as O'Con-nor's violence may alienate some who view her or her God as too fierce, McCar-thy's analogy between Ballard and the reader may simply cause others to disown this wild child as too monstrous to be their brother. Yet such readers deny their blood-relation at their own peril. Only if they can claim Ballard as one of their own can they begin to recognize the burden of mimetic antagonism that they must bear instead of casting it upon their surrogate in McCarthy's novel. Indeed, readers' aversion may be part of the way that McCarthy's grotesque hu-mor operates to enforce identification. "*We* don't practice incest or necrophilia or commit random murders," Wade Hall verbalizes readers' likely denials of such blood ties, but he then wonders, "Do we?" (51). The unqualified assertion of difference ambushes confident protesters with a disturbing suspicion of sim-ilarity, with a self-doubt almost too terrible to be faced.

Even if readers decide that Ballard is not "much like" themselves in such ob-vious ways, they may discover other reasons for identifying with him. Bataille suggests one way of understanding this disturbing likeness when he writes how the hero in fiction is an imaginative substitute for the reader: "Without too much personal discomfort we experience the feeling of losing or of being in danger that somebody else's adventures supply. If we had infinite moral re-sources we should like to live like this ourselves. Which of us has not dreamed of himself as the hero of a book? Prudence—or cowardice—is stronger than this wish, but if we think of our deepest desires which frailty alone forbids us to realise, the stories we read so eagerly will show us their nature" (87). Bataille views literature as offering the thrill of vicarious transgression. As "religion's heir" (87), it enables violence and sexuality to be staged and savored without any real risk. If the novel offers such secondhand adventure, Ballard might be the reader's double, whose violation of taboos provides the *jouissance* that the less audacious dare not seek outside the text.[10]

Although Ballard's connection to readers may arise from the pleasures of surrogate sinfulness, it need not depend on such perverse titillation. A less extraordinary similarity might be found in the shared pathos of being human. Vereen Bell appreciates the bond between Ballard and the reader when he describes McCarthy's grotesque as "a berserk version of fundamental aspects of ourselves—of our fear of time, our programmed infatuation with death, our loneliness, our threatening appetites, our narcissistic isolation from the world and the reality of other people" (55). Anatole Broyard likewise feels himself drawn to Ballard when he writes that "his crimes originated in a reaching for love. . . . I cared about Ballard and very nearly forgave him his sins because the author seduced me into feeling that he was someone I knew very well" (281). What is remarkable about such empathy is that it is felt at all for a figure who could easily be just a homicidal imp, a grotesque playboy, a hobgoblin of the inner dark. Continually playing with the doubleness between Ballard and the reader, *Child of God* incorporates this lonely and desperate exile into the human race even as it dares readers to see their own images in this collector of corpses.

If the initial simile suggests how Ballard and the book's audience may resemble each other, the narrator stresses not just similarity but desire the next time that the reader is addressed. When Ballard tries to ford a creek as swollen with violence as the whole horrid world of the novel, its turbulence threatens to engulf him in the very ferocity that he embodies. The narrator accosts the audience so that it joins the furious wayfarer in a hypothetical kinship of desire. "See him," the narrator beckons. "You could say that he's sustained by his fellow men, like you. Has peopled the shore with them calling to him. A race that gives suck to the maimed and the crazed, that wants their wrong blood in its history and will have it" (156). The startling shift into the second person co-opts readers into uneasy complicity with their frenzied relative. In the ever-alternating cycle of mimetic desire, Lester Ballard is at once the model and disciple, sire and suckling, and the readers become both the children and the parents of the godly Ballard. Like Reubel at his dump, Ballard provides the pattern to be imitated and duplicated. The raging lord proves how violence begets violence, for he mythically propagates himself in a tribe that mimics his own desire for disorder. The child of God has fathered and fomented an entire lineage of sacred violence. Ballard's offspring crave the very fury that has spawned them, honoring their father in their desire for all that is flawed and distorted by violence. The clan of this perverse Adam, in turn, nourishes their ancestor's desire by providing sustenance for his own unrelenting resistance. Ballard's descendants bear up their forebear and nurture all those like themselves, all those like their father—home-

less, maddened, wounded, and ravenous with desire. Out of violent consan-
guinity, they second his struggle; we want and will him to succeed. Hence, the
narrator claims, "His wrath seemed to buoy him up" (156), for there is ultimately
no difference between the fierce generations imagined on shore, who are the
counterparts of the readers, and the furor that the patriarch ceaselessly generates in the roiling water. Ballard lives by the very violence that he has engen-
dered.

Since the readers' own warped desires are the patrimony of Lester Ballard,
the father thereby creates the possibility of his own destruction. "He could not
swim, but how would you drown him?" the narrator asks in amazement and accusation. Precisely because the children of violence can only be violent, Ballard's
progeny—readers included—metamorphose from his doubles into his victimizers: "But they want this man's life. He has heard them in the night seeking him
with lanterns and cries of execration" (156). Their bloodthirsty pursuit culminates the victimization of Ballard—abandoned by his mother, orphaned by his
father, expelled by local authorities from the family homeplace, wrongly arrested for rape, then kneed in the groin and kicked in the head by his accuser.
The narrator comments that Ballard looks so guiltless when asleep that "you
might have said he was half right who thought himself so grievous a case against
the gods" (189), as if Ballard were a Job-like innocent who has been persecuted
by the deity.[11] Having become a victimizer, Ballard now finds himself a victim
once again, victim of his own offspring who clamor for his life. His murderous sons and daughters seem to act out Kenneth Burke's claim that the relationship between the mob and the scapegoat resembles that of child to parent.
Both victimizers and victim are bound by a "consubstantiality" that allows the
quasi-youths, the bearers of an insufferable burden, to transfer their onus to
some other member of the family, the "bad" father, who can then be expelled
(39). Ballard's violent children turn to patricide as a way of scapegoating their
similarly violent daddy.

The ferocious mob of family gathers into one murderous desire the tendency
to collective violence throughout the entire novel—the taunting and stoning of
an elderly hermit who lived in a cave and wore leaves for clothes, the vigilante
justice of the White Caps, the mimetic counterterrorism of the Blue Bells, the
legendary hanging of Tipton and Winn that half of Sevier County turned into
a New Year celebration, the execution of Nigger John for decapitating a man
with a pocketknife. The crowd of avengers hunts Ballard against the wider background of communal persecution in the South, from its mildest forms of social

ostracism to the mania of its lynch law and legalized lynchings. This dynamic of expulsion seems so pervasive in the novel that Ballard has even witnessed how the animal world, according to Girard, can provide images for the "transpositions of the collective murder" ("Generative Scapegoating" 86). The brutish mountain man has heard shrieking foxhounds crash through his window one night as they raced after their prey, and he has watched a pack of demonic dogs chase, encircle, and devastate a boar. Described as if a ballet in which the participants "tilt and swirl," "pinwheel and pirouette" (69), the choreography of the kill makes such victimization the kind of Eliotic ritual in which "the boarhound and the boar / Pursue their pattern as before" (Eliot 119). The clamorous posse that pursues Ballard repeats this timeless ceremony as it drives its quarry and surrogate across a landscape that might date from the very recent foundation of the world. The final chapter of the novel mentions that Ballard dies in 1965; however, the lack of specific time cues throughout much of the novel and the prehistoric terrain against which the vagrant scuttles make McCarthy's latter-day caveman seem to live in a primordial era when human sacrifice might be readily practiced.

 Child of God appears to rush toward a climactic act of communal killing. Since Ballard's violence makes him at once extraordinary yet exemplary in the violent world of the novel, he seems like a fit candidate for the ambivalent role of surrogate victim.[12] Such a scapegoat, Girard explains, must be at once unique but representative, the fiend who can be killed with impunity and the fellow member who attracts unto himself all the conflictual mimesis that must be purged from society (Violence 39). The first-person narrators have been steadily preparing Ballard to be viewed as such an outcast from their midst. They keep recalling him as some freakish figure out of mountain lore without ever understanding him fully. One admits that he never really liked Ballard even though Lester "never did nothin to me"; another suggests that Ballard was just not right in the head, and a third views the local oddity as the worst of his family line (18, 21–22, 81). By the end of the novel, Ballard has become so monstrous that he is hardly recognizable as human. Instead, he is described as a "gothic doll in illfit clothes," a "crazed mountain troll," a "part-time ghoul" (140, 152, 174). Yet if Ballard is demonized in the simplistic way that crowds favor to rationalize their persecution, he is strangely one of their own. Wearing the hair, garments, and make-up of a woman whom he has slain, Ballard brings together victim and victimizer, female and male, the dead and the living. In a novel whose locale is so circumscribed, Ballard is always the child of Sevier County. Onto this monster and double can be projected all of the community's murderous lusts so that he becomes their surrogate and savior. The delusion is almost too enticing to discredit: order and peace will be restored once Lester Ballard is killed.

McCarthy's narrator implies that readers join with the brigade that seeks to execute Ballard: "He could not swim, but how would you drown him?" (156). In envisioning this joint victimization, *Child of God* raises the possibility that reading it may itself be a surrogate for surrogate victimage—an act of collective violence in which the "you" addressed by the narrator imaginatively consent to driving out Lester Ballard from the world of the novel and from the world of their own selves. Out of outrage we, his children, want to expel the bogeyman Ballard, who terrifies us because of his revolting difference but who terrifies us even more because of his disquieting similarity. Such grotesques fascinate and horrify, Elizabeth Grosz suggests, because they reassure us that we belong to the category of the supposedly normal; however, they also embody the monstrous otherness "that must be ejected or abjected from self-image to make the bounded, category-obeying self possible" (65). It may seem that we have to lynch or drown Ballard just so that we can close the book on him, killing the author of our desires, keeping him safely within its confines and out of our lives, just so that we do not risk becoming deformed, depraved, and destabilized ourselves.[13]

McCarthy's novel thus violently recoils from its own glorified violence only to imagine more violence. It appears that Lester Ballard's murders will culminate in the murder of Lester Ballard. If, as Bataille suggests, "a sacrifice is a novel, a story, illustrated in a bloody fashion" (87), *Child of God* makes fiction almost re-present a sacrifice. Its world overflowing with brutality, McCarthy's novel moves toward repeating the kind of slaughter that originally set aside the violent as the sacred. While Ballard convalesces after losing an arm from trying to kill Greer, the manhunt that he earlier heard in the mountains at night actually tracks him down to his hospital room. The rogue enforcers might be his kin in bloodshed, for Ballard's own grandfather participated in such frontier justice; so did his great uncle, who was eventually hanged in Hattiesburg. When the self-appointed lawmen kidnap Ballard and threaten to kill him if he does not reveal where he has buried his victims, the child of lynchers seems poised to become a casualty of the family and regional tradition for vigilantism. Like his father, Ballard would find his violent end in a rope. However, the bond between the murderer and his would-be executioners goes beyond the local heritage of vengeance, for it grows out of an even deeper desire than any purely southern tradition. Since Ballard's lawlessness is copied and countered by the mob's pursuit of lynch law, the child of God and his children of violence are all caught up in the mimetic fury that cannot forestall its own replication: bloodshed at the beginning, and bloodshed for the end.

FROM CHILD OF GOD TO CHILD OF CULTURE

Although *Child of God* seems as if it is going to culminate in yet one more episode of collective violence, it actually moves toward a less bloodthirsty conclusion. The novel does not become what Girard calls a "persecution text" by adopting the viewpoint of the lynch mob and justifying group murder (*Things Hidden* 126–30). Rather, *Child of God* turns away from the surrogate victimage mechanism by cultivating the detached reflection and the cultural restraints that Girard views as the legacy of scapegoating. The old sacrificial institutions, although challenged and undermined by communal crisis, still rule in Ballard's world, and the novel ends safely within their confines. To accommodate the scourge of Sevier County to this official order, *Child of God* deepens Ballard's humanity toward the end so that he becomes a figure to be pitied rather than just a monster to be slaughtered, and it subjects Ballard to the humane violence of civilization rather than to the atrocities outside it.

As Ballard changes from victimizer to potential victim of the lynch mob, he gains an insight into his destiny that was once precluded by his complete immersion in violence. Ballard had been abused and attacked earlier in the novel, and he reacted with rage to losing his farm or being accused of rape. However, having pursued this fury to its divine end, he begins responding to the antagonism he has begotten in a new way: he reacts with mournful introspection rather than reciprocal aggression. The normally ruthless murderer actually cries after observing "the diminutive progress of all things in the valley" (170), for his own life seems to be hastening in a direction entirely opposite to the procession of trees that leaf and fields that get plowed. Ballard ponders that fateful course in a dream whose images of transience and transition illustrate how time and space are diminishing for him. As a mule carries Ballard through the woods on a day unsurpassed in its loveliness, the traveler grieves because he will never again pass by the translucent leaves that brush his face. However, he is determined to continue the passage until his transit ends in death. The dream reflects how the god who has ruled over an underworld of the dead is resigning himself to being mortal. But that serenely stoic fatalism darkens into a more horrifying naturalism after Ballard escapes from the lynch mob that has come to his hospital room and he hides in a cave. He imagines his body so stripped by time that mice spawn their young "in the lobed caverns where his brains had been. His bones polished clean as eggshells, centipedes sleeping in their marrowed flutes, his ribs curling slender and whitely like a bone flower in the dark stone bowl" (189). Ballard beholds in his own death the duality of sacred violence that he once visited upon his victims—the outrageous rapacity of corruption and the transcendent gracefulness of skeletal purity.

Ballard refuses to submit to such brutality. Bataille might rhapsodize that "death will proclaim my return to seething life" (57), but Ballard flees the relentless working of nature's refinery by seeking a way out of his subterranean haunts. Instead of the purgative violence of inevitable dissolution that he foresees underneath the earth, Ballard chooses the more civilized form of violence that awaits him above ground. The child of God who in the cave wished for "some brute midwife to spald him from his rocky keep" (189) emerges from his chthonian womb covered with red mud as if he were new born. If "the heavens wore a different look that Ballard did not trust" (190), the unfamiliar night sky shows that the bloodied infant is no longer guided by the cold celestial blaze of the stars with which he felt such kinship throughout the novel. Appropriating such transcendent fire can only lead to the kind of inferno that consumed baby Billy and destroyed Ballard's cabin. Rather, the child of the heavens is born from the earth to the earth, whose landscape seems gentler now than at any other time in the novel. Although signs of the flood's violence can still be seen in the littered woods, Ballard turns away from the mountains that have defined his savagery and walks to town on a fine night that is scented with honeysuckle. Before he returns to the hospital at dawn, roosters cry out as if sensing "a relief in the obscurity of night . . . . Perhaps some freshness in the air" (191).

Ballard's rebirth after escaping death at the hands of the lynch mob and living underground for several days is not the renunciation of desire that Tarwater finally achieves in *The Violent Bear It Away.* And it is more like Miranda's return to a living death sentence at the end of "Pale Horse, Pale Rider" than her recovery through memory at the end of "The Grave." Ballard is harried into surrendering to the cultural order that he flouted because outside its requirements and protections there is only the frontier justice of the vigilantes or the cleansing ferocity of nature. When Ballard returns to the hospital and the sheriff's custody, declaring, "I'm supposed to be here" (192), he seems to arrive at a compromise between his arrogant sense of self-entitlement and his need to obey community dictates. Having searched for a place where he was "supposed to be" since his dispossession at the beginning of the novel, the vagabond finds a makeshift home where personal desire converges with societal obligation. Ballard defers to the very institutions that originate in violence yet defend society's members from violence.

In accepting this role as a child of culture, Ballard becomes a victim of the violence mediated by law and medicine. The legal system puts an end to the ceaseless quest for retaliation that drives victims to become victimizers and causes a spiral which may eventually reduce a society to chaos. It halts this proliferation of mimetic violence through decreeing a carefully measured public punishment and through having it executed by a sovereign power that is beyond revenge (Girard, *Violence* 15–16). In *Child of God* the grandly titled high sheriff of Sevier County represents how the state has taken sacred violence out of the cycle of communal reprisals that often bloodied the South and taken such fury into its carefully delimited bailiwick. Pursuing McCarthy's title character throughout the novel and appearing with ever greater frequency as it moves toward a close, Sheriff Fate is Ballard's appositely named destiny. The officer seeks to end the vicious reign of the child of God, as if he were one of those champions of order and justice that emerge as a counterforce to many of Shakespeare's self-destructive tyrants. Much like Richmond and Richard III or Macduff and Macbeth, McCarthy's lawman and outlaw are set against each other as mimetic antagonists. Both are aloof, imperious, and implacable. And both may share an even more shadowy resemblance, as Ballard suggests when Fate orders the loitering mountain man to go home: "You kindly got henhouse ways yourself" (56). The elusive criminal even enacts a violent parody of the county agent who pursues him. Playing the part of a moral policeman, Ballard shines his flashlight on a couple embracing in a pickup truck, asks for the driver's license, and accuses, "You was fixin to screw, wasn't ye?" (150). Ballard then executes his own law by shooting the young man in the neck and the young woman in the head. Fate stands on the opposite side of such private and random executions. Whereas the murderer unleashes violence over the Tennessee wilderness, the marshal from the town embodies the culture that seeks to curtail such bloodshed.

After Ballard submits to his fate in the criminal justice system, he is expelled from the community, yet in a way that keeps him relatively safe. If the banishment recalls the lot of the surrogate victim, such exile actually protects Ballard the victimizer as much as it saves the townspeople from his mayhem. Ballard is spared the vengeance of the lynch mob, and since the courts recognize Ballard as insane, he also escapes any formal indictment that might lead to his execution. Instead, the law ostracizes Ballard by confining him to the state hospital at Knoxville, and psychiatry further ostracizes him by locking him in a cage. The patient as much as the prisoner benefits from an ancient legacy. As Percy explores in *The Thanatos Syndrome,* medicine is founded on the principle of surrogate victimage. It uses violence to expel impurities as a way of restoring health to the body rather than to the body politic (Girard, *Violence* 286–90). Ballard's expulsion to a hospital cell crudely seeks to promote such communal well-being through therapeutic violence. Whereas the raging god once roamed over hills and caves as he terrorized the community, he is now more drastically restricted than any wayward child that has been confined to a playpen. After death Ballard suffers a scientific version of the sparagmos that often befell primitive and mythic casualties of collective violence (Girard, *Violence* 131–32): his body is dissected by students at the state medical school in Memphis.

Although Ballard's fate may resemble the dismemberment of Pentheus in *The Bacchae,* the rituals surrounding his death give it an order that is lacking from the king's frenzied victimization. The discipline of medicine keeps the severing and slicing from becoming a gratuitous hacking of the flesh, for it transforms the violence inflicted on the cadaver into a way of educating a new generation of healers. Custom and religion recognize that such physical assault never deprives the dead of an intrinsic dignity. A proper regard for the flesh necessitates that the remains be taken to a cemetery, even if the deposition outside the city and "with others of his kind" suggests some final exclusion (194); a pious respect for the spirit requires that the burial be solemnized by a simple funeral. The violence that overtakes Ballard in death is not unlimited but is changed and constrained by culture. Apart from such mediations of the social order in *Child of God,* there is only the raw violence of nature. When the seven corpses in Ballard's underground mausoleum are accidentally discovered in the last chapter, the restful positions in which he had placed the bodies have been violated by mold, fungus, and decay. The high sheriff hauls the slain out of the cryptlike caves in a process that seems to treat the dragged and dangled flesh almost as unceremoniously as did Ballard. However, the official works to take charge of violence so that it loses its ultimacy. The dead do not become the hidden foundation of a new communal order but are unearthed and exposed. The victimization is brought to light.

The interment of Lester Ballard and the disinterment of his victims' bodies bring a rightful finality to the last pages of *Child of God,* but McCarthy's novel undermines such comfortable closure. The future physicians who inspect Ballard's entrails glimpse a prophecy of possibly greater ruin; "like those haruspices of old [they] perhaps saw monsters worse to come in their configurations" (194). And when the jeep carrying the seven bodies from Ballard's underground shrine sets off in the last paragraph of the novel, a glimmer of that potential violence quickens the predatory nighthawks which "[rise] from the dust in the road before them with wild wings and eyes red as jewels in the headlights" (197). Despite the seemliness of its resolution, *Child of God* does not rest securely in the decisive expulsion of Lester Ballard and the reestablishment of a humane and halcyon order. Rather, it recognizes that the violence embodied in McCarthy's enfant terrible can always erupt in some new Girardian deity run amok. After all, he is "a child of God much like yourself perhaps."[14]

NO MORE FOR AZAZEL

Victimizing the Sign and Signifying the Victim
in Percy's *The Thanatos Syndrome*

When the lynch mob nearly hangs Lester Ballard in McCarthy's *Child of God,*
the novel seems poised to repeat the way that a community in crisis often resolves its strife by killing one of its own. Such violence is a familiar remedy in
southern fiction. In "Pale Horse, Pale Rider" Miranda fears that Adam will be
sacrificed to the greed and animosity that drive America's participation in World
War I. In *The Violent Bear It Away* the rivalrous Tarwater and Rayber try to end
their mimetic conflict through the murder of the innocent Bishop. If southern
culture has long sought to hide or deny the expulsions that make it possible,
southern fiction has regularly brought such exclusions to light. It points to the
outcast, calls attention to the buried body, and inquires about the unmarked
grave. In *The Thanatos Syndrome* Walker Percy makes scapegoating so central
that from the Old South to the New, it comes to form the hidden foundation of
its sunshiny but enslaved world.[1] Dr. Tom More, the narrator of the novel, must
undertake an exposé similar to Girard's own work. He must reveal how the role
of violence in creating culture has been disguised or denied.

Percy's final novel carries scapegoating back to the biblical ritual that has
provided the name for communal victimization. In Leviticus 16 two goats are
used during the annual ceremonies for the Day of Atonement. One is taken to
the innermost part of the temple and sacrificed to Yahweh as an offering for sin.
The other is brought before the high priest, symbolically laden with the sins of
the community, and then sent out to the wilderness as a means of bearing the
violence away. The beast carries its burden of iniquity to the enigmatically
named Azazel. Modern commentators typically view Azazel as a demon who
dwells in the desert. In the book of Enoch and in Midrash he is a corrupt angel
who tempts humans into the kind of licentiousness that More finds rampant in
The Thanatos Syndrome. However, the Vulgate, following the Septuagint, provided a different understanding by rendering the passage about the goat's being

sent to Azazel (literally, "removed") as *caper emissarius*. William Tindale's 1530 translation of the Bible conveyed the same idea when it brought the phrase into English as the "goote on which the lotte fell to scape" or "scape-goote." The King James Bible continued the tradition, but the 1884 Revised Version of the English Bible abandoned it in favor of using the proper name of the demon. Still other translators have viewed Azazel as referring to the precipice from which the scapegoat was hurled to its death. Escaping consistent interpretation, the term *Azazel* comes to comprehend the entire process of scapegoating—victimizer, victim, and place of victimization (Jacobson 168–71; Faley 77–78; *Compact OED*).

In *The Thanatos Syndrome* Azazel is the sign for a sacrificial mechanism that has become so commonplace it is a virtual convention. A convention indeed: More learns by chance the ancient name for such scapegoating when he asks John Van Dorn, the bridge champion and apostle of sexual liberation, about a term that his card-playing wife has been mumbling the night before in bed. More heard her say "Azalea" and interpreted it as some new erotic invitation, but Van Dorn tells him that the proposition was actually the name for a bidding strategy in bridge. It is the Azazel convention. Whether in foreplay or card play, the term carries the residue of the ancient ritual for the Day of Atonement, and that trace helps to prepare More for how the victim in *The Thanatos Syndrome* is the sign that cannot be eliminated.

Van Dorn explains the Azazel convention to More. It is named "After the fallen angel. . . . It means you're in a hell of a mess. It is a way of minimizing loss." Scapegoating resolves such infernal catastrophes in society, for it reduces loss by eliminating one person or group. The Azazel convention works likewise in bridge. "If you discover that you and your partner are bidding different suits and are at cross purposes and over your heads," Van Dorn elaborates in his own sexist style, "you signal to her that it is better for her to go down in her suit. We'll lose less that way. You do it by bidding your opponents' suit for one round" (61). The grand master of sexual exploitation fully intends the double entendres, which his curious disciple seconds after his night with Ellen by referring to "bidding hearts and going down." When More concludes, "So Azazel can be more than one kind of invitation," he is beginning to recognize how the demon in the waste land is a sign of wide-ranging significance. The Azazel convention makes a game out of all the elements of scapegoating: crisis, exclusion, and solidarity. During a crucial moment of play, the male copies his opponent and thereby casts out the female partner, who goes "down" as a short-term sacrifice for the common good. The sign for victimization in the priestly ritual of Leviticus is also the signal for it in the ritualized aggression of card games—and far beyond. *The Thanatos Syndrome* realizes the convention in spades. Azazel the desert locale stretches across the South and the century, Azazel the demon wears not just a human but a humane face, and Azazel the victim is sacrificed again and again under a host of different names.[2]

READING AGAINST THE PERSECUTION TEXT

Since More's investigation of the Azazel convention leads him to explore what lies hidden behind the triumphant bliss of a newer-than-new South, Percy finds appropriate fictional form for this search by using a mystery-thriller plot. Its origins are as ancient as Greek tragedy. Like Oedipus, More seeks to identify the cause of a baffling plague that afflicts his community. And as Percy's doctor conducts his research, he must avoid becoming the scapegoat for his malaise-filled world—precisely the fate that Oedipus accepts in Girard's radical reinterpretation of Sophocles' drama (*Violence* 68–88). Yet if the novel's exploration of sickness and sacrifice has classical precedent, its models may also be as recent as the films that have long grasped Percy's imagination. *The Thanatos Syndrome* reads like a cross between *Panic in the Streets*, the 1950 film about a potential plague being loosed in New Orleans that Binx Bolling sees in *The Moviegoer*, and *The China Syndrome*, the 1979 film in which a power plant supervisor (played by Jack Lemmon) comes to realize that he must expose the hidden danger of a nuclear meltdown. "Well, what makes you think they're looking for a scapegoat?" the naive Jack Godell asks a colleague early in the film after the investigation of an accident at the plant. His co-worker replies with an answer right out of Girard, "Tradition." As such long-established precedent might have predicted, the whistle-blower becomes the scapegoat. After Lemmon's character takes control of the power plant so that he may reveal its hazards on television, Godell is killed, and his murder is justified by a public relations spokesperson who makes the would-be savior seem drunken and deranged. Percy knew the film that he echoed in his title. In an interview before *The Thanatos Syndrome* was published, he confided to Patrick Samway that "Dr. Thomas More has got himself in a great deal of trouble . . . something is about to happen that is a lot worse than the physical meltdown in *The China Syndrome*" ("Interview" 133).

As More discovers the current meltdown of the spirit and then the cover-up of Van Dorn and Bob Comeaux, *The Thanatos Syndrome* uses the conventions of such pop-culture works to scrutinize the mystifications of the sacrificial order. What Comeaux calls "our little cloak-and-dagger secrecy" (191) reflects how the centrality of scapegoating has been concealed by the very culture that such sacred violence has made possible.[3] Much as both the detective and the analyst look beyond what is superficial and find meaning in what seems misleading or even missing (Žižek 50–57), Percy's therapist-become-sleuth must discover the significance not just of strange details and stray clues but of something more mystifying—a lack of any such signs, an absence of oddness. Like some surrogate for Girard, More must discover how apparent normalcy hides the surrogate victimage mechanism.

Learning the hermeneutics of victimization is especially difficult for More because he has long supported the sacrificial logic that provides the hidden foundation to his culture. In *Love in the Ruins,* Percy's third novel, More adopted such a rationale when he tried to oppose the violence of a decaying and divided America with the violence of his own psychic engineering. However, his deluded efforts to stave off the apocalypse only made it seem more imminent. In *The Thanatos Syndrome* More learns that he has been an unwitting partner to the latest scientific victimization. Comeaux tries to justify the pedeuthanasia routinely practiced at the Qualitarian Center by citing More's own research on how infants do not become conscious of themselves until they begin using language in their second year. And Van Dorn attributes using heavy sodium for social engineering to discoveries More made in isotope brain pharmacology. "So for better or worse, Doctor, it appears you're one of us," Comeaux reasons, and he is not entirely wrong (200). More is so abstracted and alienated throughout the novel that, as Allen Pridgen notes, he seems at once a spiritual colleague of Comeaux and Van Dorn and a victim of the thanatos syndrome (193). Like Comeaux and Van Dorn, More has misused pharmacology; he has recently returned from prison because he sold prescriptions for tranquilizers and amphetamines so that they could be resold at a truck stop. More does not voice disapproval of the Qualitarian Center, admires the success of Comeaux and Van Dorn's scientific utopia, and even agrees with their claim that "society has a right to protect itself against its enemies" (234).

Yet if More is implicated in the current attempt to reestablish the South by scapegoating, he always views that grandiose reconstruction from the very margins of his culture. Having spent two years in prison, More bears the stigma of the victim as exile. He has been subjected to the way that the judicial system reserves violence for its own sovereign use so that it may prevent further violence (Girard, *Violence* 20–27). And although the doctor has ostensibly been healed by such confinement, More is often reminded by Comeaux and Van Dorn that he can easily be remanded to Fort Pelham if he threatens their creation of an ideal society. Wearing his "Bruno Hauptmann double-breasted seersucker," the ex-con wonders why he reminds himself "of an ungainly German executed fifty years ago" (55), but the answer is the one-word title of Anthony Scaduto's book on the alleged kidnapper of the Lindberg baby—*Scapegoat.* More risks duplicating that fate if he sides with those whom Comeaux and Van Dorn would eliminate, if he sees by the light of the victim.

More's interpretive journey in *The Thanatos Syndrome* is essentially a discovery of how *Azazel* signifies the whole world of victimization. At the end of the novel More demonstrates what he has learned about the sacrificial order in America when he tries to answer Comeaux's question about why Father Smith, the doctor's eventual model for opposing scapegoating, is "so dead set against us." Puzzled for a moment, More finally replies in a way that distinctly separates him from Comeaux's presumptive first-person plural, "He thinks you'll end by killing Jews" (351). Since the response only baffles his Jewish friend Max as well as Comeaux, More continues, "He claims it will eventually end as it did with the Germans, starting out with euthanasia for justifiable medical, psychiatric, and economic reasons. But in the end the majority always gets in trouble, needs a scapegoat, and gets rid of an unsubsumable minority" (352).

More could hardly have summarized more concisely what Girard in *The Scapegoat* calls the "stereotypes of persecution"—crisis, accusation, victimization, and violence (12–23)—that underwrite such "persecution texts" as Guillaume de Machaut's fourteenth-century anti-Semitic *Judgment of the King of Navarre* (*Scapegoat* 1–11). Such histories record scapegoating from the self-justifying viewpoint of the community that benefited from it. Hence, they hide the innocence of the victim and the guilt of the victimizers, and they make it seem as if legitimate violence rather than arbitrary oppression has taken place. Yet precisely because the victimizers naively utter the most far-fetched assertions about their enemies, Girard claims that they actually indict themselves rather than those formally accused. As More investigates the thanatos syndrome, he slowly learns Girard's way of dismantling the persecution texts. He reads against the official story to reveal the scapegoating that it seeks to hide. Indeed, More comes to see lots of "things hidden" since the "foundation" of his world—the whole design of the covert Project Blue Boy, the concealed pipeline that adds heavy sodium to the Feliciana water supply, the secret cache of pictures and videos that show how children are being sexually abused at Belle Ame.

All of these signs disclose how the neo-fascist New South, like the slaveholding Old South or the genocidal Third Reich, is based on victimization.

More discovers that such collective persecution is mimetic. It is a violent response to a violent crisis that seems to undermine the civil order. Just as Guillaume de Machaut writes in reaction to an almost apocalyptic outbreak of illness, the Black Death that left behind twenty million casualties, the authors of Project Blue Boy feel that they are confronting a similar kind of medical emergency. Van Dorn itemizes "three social plagues which are going to wreck us just as surely as the bubonic plague wrecked fourteenth-century Europe": crime, teenage suicides and drug abuse, and AIDS (218). Comeaux fears a similar catastrophe when he claims, "We're not even talking medicine, Tom. We're talking about the decay of the social fabric" (265). Although Guillaume de Machaut faces a public health disaster and the planners of Blue Boy feel threatened by societal chaos, the two forms of plague easily merge into each other in the ancient and medieval worlds. "Until the Renaissance, wherever 'real' epidemics occurred, they disrupted social relations," Girard explains. "Wherever social relations were disrupted, epidemics could occur" (*I See Satan* 52). Whether in Europe of the Middle Ages or in modern America, the plague causes a breakdown of differences that makes the body and the body politic virtually interchangeable sites of contagion.

Girard explains that when societies are faced with their own undoing, members often seek to avoid assuming responsibility or investigating the proper causes for the crisis (*Scapegoat* 15–16). Instead of such research and self-reflection, they may blame some other person or group for the progressive dissolution in which they themselves play a part. Although the selection of the guilty party is entirely arbitrary, the community never admits this randomness because it needs to believe that the actual reason for the malaise has been discovered. The accused, according to Girard, are typically found among those marginalized for physical, religious, social, political, or ethnic reasons. The supposed transgressors are denounced for not respecting difference enough, for violating cultural boundaries through an almost standardized list of offenses—incest, sacrilege, infanticide, and bestiality. Seeking a culprit for the devastation of the plague, Guillaume de Machaut blamed the Jews for poisoning the rivers and fountains. Although Comeaux first targets the elderly, the unwanted unborn, and those with physical disabilities, he joins Van Dorn in Project Blue Boy to victimize prisoners, inner city youths, homosexuals, teenaged women, as well as anyone who is too angry or afraid, too ironic or acrimonious. Comeaux and Van

Dorn do not even accuse these groups of any particular wrongdoing; their very existence challenges the social order, as if they were themselves the wrong.

Once this illusion of causality has been established between the crisis and the accused, societies may resort to violence against the alleged offenders. Guillaume de Machaut thus justified hanging, burning, drowning, and beheading Jews because they were the agents of the Black Death. Van Dorn rationalizes a similar form of severity: "In time of war and in time of plague you have to be Draconian" (218). Since he and Comeaux feel like victims of a social epidemic, they become victimizers in what is a very old pattern. Just as the Israelites drove out the goat for Azazel, the high priests of science consign all who disturb their ideal order to various forms of death. As director of the Fedville Qualitarian Center, Comeaux presides over the quarantine of AIDS patients and the elimination of the young who are deformed as well as of the elderly who are deemed useless. Van Dorn helps Comeaux to carry these exclusions even further through a pilot program for social engineering. The designers of Project Blue Boy secretly put heavy sodium (Na-24) in the local water supply to create the kind of new cultural order that scapegoating always seems to promise. The additive reduces crime, teenage pregnancy, and cases of AIDS, and it eliminates the rage, depression, and anxiety that More is used to diagnosing in his patients. However, Blue Boy relies upon a pharmacology of violence that More describes when he charges it with "assaulting the cortex of an individual without the knowledge or consent of the assaultee" (193). Since Comeaux believes that part of the neocortex is "the scourge and curse of life on this earth, the source of wars, insanities, perversions" (195), he does violence to what causes violence. However, Comeaux seems shocked by More's frank description of such assault; Van Dorn later protests, "I abhor violence of any kind" and rejects the very principle of scapegoating when he prates of how "conflict resolution by means of violence is a contradiction in terms" (307). The lip servants to liberal values know that Blue Boy can succeed only if its violence is hidden in deed and in speech.

Although Comeaux and Van Dorn imagine that Blue Boy will herald the newest version of the New South, its offerings to Azazel actually date back to the past that Uncle Jimbilly exposed in Porter's "The Witness." The pilot project in Louisiana repeats how the entire old order was founded on scapegoating. It is appropriate that when Tom first hears a sleepy Ellen refer to the Azazel convention, he thinks that she says, "Azalea," for the mispronunciation suggests that there is something demonic behind this region of show gardens, where the *Robert E. Lee* brings tourists to the landing at Belle Ame for the Azalea Festival and the Plantation Parade. Azalea and Azazel signify the contrasting sides of the Day of Atonement rituals that Orlando Patterson has seen as shaping southern religion. Patterson argues that the goat sacrificed in the temple as an expiation might image a triumphant Christianity in which Jesus is the victor over sin and darkness. The southern master class identified with this Christ as if he were the glorified justification of their own political power. However, the goat taken away to Azazel provides the sign for a more woeful Christianity in which Jesus is the despised and humiliated victim. The planter class tried to impose this image of defeat and dejection on the enslaved as a way of maintaining their subservience (*Rituals of Blood* 218–24). If the Azalea Festival nostalgically celebrates the power structure of the plantation past, Azazel names the way the South's primal scape-goating is continually remembered and re-presented in the novel. When More and his cousin Lucy Lipscomb visit the grave of their common ancestor at Pantherburn, the present chatelaine of the family manor recalls that their fore-bear bequeathed an eleven-year-old mulatto girl to serve his thirteen-year-old daughter. And during his fantasy-filled night at the plantation, More dreams of Miss Bett reading from her grandmother's journal: "For Christmas Daddy gave a little darky to all seven brothers, each to become a body servant" (163).

Such victimization has not been relegated to the family past. Rather, it con-tinues in the many forms of racism and bondage that are the legacy of slavery and the institutionalized counterpart of Blue Boy. Lucy wishes that, like her an-cestors, she too had a personal slave, and she begrudges the brilliant African American Vergil, her only help on the farm, his salary. Resentful of Vergil as well, her uncle complains, "You can't hardly get one of them to do anything these days" (141). More's wife and mother have profiteered from renovating the cramped dwellings of former slaves and marketing them as the pricey and pic-turesque The Quarters. Comeaux boasts of how he has created apprenticeships for Baton Rouge youths who would probably otherwise face a future in prison, but the work really exploits them in largely unskilled and subservient jobs. Al-though Comeaux protests, "We're not talking about old massa and his niggers. We're not talking about Uncle Tom" (198), his denial is unconvincing, for he stages just such plantation scenes among the prisoners at Angola. Made docile and cheerful by heavy sodium in the water, the bare-chested black men and ker-chiefed black women harvest cotton on the prison farm while singing "Swing Low, Sweet Chariot." Azalea, Azazel: from "A" to "Z," from the old order to the new old order, the cult and cultivation of the South is founded on a victim.

The Thanatos Syndrome makes such slavery continually overshadow its

Dixie utopia to suggest how Comeaux and Van Dorn are not pursuing some unique and private obsession. Rather, their plan to renew Feliciana through victimization is only the latest version of a long-held collective desire for what Comeaux calls "the best of the Southern Way of Life" (197). Blue Boy is not so much innovative as imitative. The current form of scapegoating realizes what Clarence Cason in 1930 observed as a strong southern desire for social reconstruction through enchantment. Just as alchemists sought a philosopher's stone to transmute base metals into gold, "certain coteries of southerners today appear to be searching for a magic formula—or perhaps an opiate—by means of which the disagreeable problems of the South may be caused to vanish from their consciousness, leaving there only visions of a Utopia far more elegant and refined than anything Sir Thomas More dared hope for as he dreamed in sixteenth-century England" (171). Cason's contemporaries could only fantasize a solution to the social and economic devastation of the Depression era South. However, Comeaux and Van Dorn out-More Sir Thomas More and even Dr. Tom More, who attempted to heal the sundered self and dis-United States in *Love in the Ruins*. These hermetic scientists have discovered the "magic formula" to "make vanish from their consciousness" the ills that More associates with consciousness itself. The southern wonder drug is Na-24.

PLATO'S PHARMACY IN PERCY'S FELICIANA

Drs. Comeaux and Van Dorn use Na-24 to turn the cultural bequest of scapegoating into the means to perpetuate scapegoating. In explaining how a communal killing forms the hidden foundation for cultural institutions, Girard observes that pharmacology depends on the principle of scapegoating; however, like surgery and immunization, it adapts that mechanism from society at large to the world of the body (*Violence* 287–90). Drugs work by therapeutic victimization. Plato appreciates the violence in medicines when he describes them as aggravating a disease and thereby provoking a more violent reaction from the enemy within (Derrida, *Dissemination* 100–102). Yet just as scapegoating makes it possible for a violence-plagued society to discover a salutary communion, the pharmaceutical attack helps to restore the flesh to health. Precisely because drugs may hurt and heal, Dr. More admits that he seldom prescribes them. The *pharmakon* may bring peace to the troubled patient, but it may also hide and ignore the inner conflicts responsible for the crisis.

The connection between drugs and scapegoating is made clear by a story that Plato recalls in the *Phaedrus* (sec. 229). It was Pharmacia who was playing near a stream with Oreithyia when Boreas drove the latter maiden over a cliff and ravished her away with his winds. The myth of divine assault conceals the fact that Oreithyia suffers the death that was a common climax to the surrogate victimage mechanism in the ancient world (Girard, *Scapegoat* 176). Outside the time of legend, she might just as readily have fallen from the Tarpeian rock in Rome or the sea cliffs of Marseille, favorite sites for ritual executions. Socrates appropriately notes that an altar to Boreas commemorates the spot where the victim was rapt away, as if the initial loss of life needed to be repeated through subsequent sacrifice. Yet if one maiden falls prey to the depredations of sacred violence, the other, Pharmacia, is spared any such onslaught. Pharmacia—the namesake of all that is tonic and toxic—survives to translate the saving death of scapegoating into the promise and peril of the pharmacy.

Comeaux and Van Dorn exploit the connection between medicine and collective murder by using the *pharmakon* against the *pharmakos*, the scapegoat. Since the surrogate victim is typically seen as infecting a society, Comeaux and Van Dorn develop a cure that eliminates the pestilence of all who are deemed socially undesirable. Yet if Na-24 seems to heal society of its violent ills, the drug actually spreads one disease to control another. Comeaux and Van Dorn commit the outrage that medieval victimizers blamed on the Jews: they poison the waters with the sickness unto death. Whereas the Jews were victimized for causing the Black Death, Comeaux and Van Dorn victimize Feliciana by creating what More imagines as a modern version of the bubonic plague, the thanatos syndrome.

The use of such potions that cure and kill repeats in medicine the violence that may date back to the foundations of Western metaphysics. Although the thriller plot of *The Thanatos Syndrome* makes it seem as if the novel "has more action and less philosophy than Percy's previous works" (Hobson, *Understanding Percy* 134), the novel's "philosophy" really gets enacted through its somewhat melodramatic story about crisis, conspiracy, and persecution. "Let's skip the metaphysics," Comeaux advises when More suggests that a patient has a prefrontal cortical deficit. "You get into the prefrontal, you get into metaphysics" (97). More's diagnosis seems as "physical" as any neurologist might want, yet Percy's psychiatrist cannot completely ignore the metaphysical implications that his colleague dismisses. The philosopher's stone of Na-24 is really a stumbling stone. The masterminds of Blue Boy concoct in their pharmacy a more heinous form of the exclusion that Derrida has exposed as endemic to Western philosophy since its origins in what he titles "Plato's Pharmacy" (*Dissemination* 61–171).[4]

The fathers of Blue Boy are the decadent sons of the thinker who established the privileged position of the logos in Western philosophy by an act of scapegoating. Much as Comeaux and Van Dorn resort to ostracism to achieve their vision of the ideal state and ideal academy, Plato's writings, according to Derrida, seek to exclude writing in order to champion speaking. Plato associates orality with all that is primary, vital, and immediate, but he finds literacy much more problematic. Writing is a *pharmakon,* a drug that may be helpful in improving human recollection but harmful in weakening the power of memory itself. Plato fears that readers will not need to remember what writing can always call to mind. Writing has such power to re-present because it is nothing in itself, nothing but a potential double for everything. It only works because of its nondifference, its utter ability to become like anything else. Since writing is so protean, it challenges the identity that depends on being "this" rather than "that" and the structure that is defined by making distinctions. Writing can play the substitute so effortlessly that it may replace and displace, leaving victims in its wake. Hence, Plato associates writing with whatever destabilizes—with death, patricide, usurpation, mob rule. Precisely because it inscribes violence, it must be excluded lest the dangerous possibilities of its mimesis be given free reign (*Dissemination* 89–94). Like Derrida, Girard traces fundamental forms of cultural exclusion back to Plato. Just as Derrida views Plato as wanting to expel writing because of its subversive nonidentity, Girard views Plato as wanting to purify or suppress myths because of their mimetic violence. Their telltale traces of collective bloodshed impugn the moral grandeur of the gods and disrupt the rational culture to which the philosopher is dedicated (*Scapegoat* 76–79).[5] As if taking Plato for their model, Comeaux and Van Dorn are almost science-fiction mutations of Derrida's arch-proscriber and Girard's preeminent censor. Their quest for a southern utopia leads them to exclude the threat of upheaval that Plato feared in the violence of writing and of myth.

Although Comeaux and Van Dorn imitate Plato's policies of rejection and repression, they do not view themselves in any such oppressive role. Indeed, these scientific humanists value Na-24 for all of the reasons that Plato devalues writing. Prescribing the drug as a veritable panacea, literally "writing" it "before" their sample population even seeks such a healing script, Percy's technocrats seem like the counterparts of Theuth, the divine inventor of arithmetic, geometry, and astronomy, who, as Derrida remembers, offers the drug of writing to the King of Egypt in the *Phaedrus.* Comeaux and Van Dorn imagine heavy sodium as precisely such a *pharmakon.* Just as Derrida associates the *pharmakon* with liquidity—water, ink, sperm—because it penetrates, gets absorbed, and blends opposites easily (*Dissemination* 152), heavy sodium infiltrates the water of Feliciana, invades the body, and pervades the victim so that it becomes a fatal counterpart to the elemental nihilism that O'Connor described as permeating her age. Whereas she thought that the noxious gas filled the air people breathe (*Habit* 97), Comeaux and Van Dorn let their deadly drug be disseminated in the water people drink.

Once Na-24 gets deep into the heart of the person, the drug, like Plato's writing, like Derrida's promising yet pernicious philter, has an equivocal effect on memory. Much as the *pharmakon* of writing improved the capacity of memory over what was possible in the culture of orality, the *pharmakon* of Na-24 quickens the cache of memory that is now possible in the ensuing culture of print. Heavy sodium imparts computerlike powers of recall so that mnemonicists can recite amazing calculations of time and distance. Its beneficiaries have become so textualized that they often seem to scan computer printouts before they speak, as if quoting a spread sheet or consulting a graphic. Yet, like writing, the additive stimulates not re-presentation but rote repetition, not truth and knowledge but forgetfulness and dissimulation. It does not enable victims to recover their past, as does Porter's Miranda, but fosters personal and regional amnesia. Under the influence of Na-24, Mickey LaFaye, More's first patient in the novel, has forgotten her recurrent dream about awaiting a stranger in the cellar of her grandmother's farmhouse. Feliciana is plagued by the same temporal dislocation. More's fellow citizens do not cultivate memory as a way of placing past and present in dialogue with each other; rather, they tend to connect with history only to the extent that it offers a nostalgic model that can be copied, commodified, and commercialized. Feliciana's renovated manors and gentrified slave quarters stage a faux version of the past to gratify those deluded by mimetic desire for Porter's old order.

Since writing provides a similar kind of fabrication in letters, Plato associates it with pretense, with a lack of original seriousness, with play (Derrida, *Dissemination* 156–58). Much as the *pharmakon* shares in such artifice and levity, Na-24 authorizes every form of sport and sportiveness. Ellen wins at bridge, the students at Belle Ame excel at soccer, and the LSU football team has not lost a game in three years. Such play—with its competition, crisis, and chance resolution—repeats in stylized form the process by which mimetic strife was once ended through the arbitrary selection of a victim (Girard, *Violence* 311–15). Na-24 heightens the festive legacy of surrogate victimage and distills its wildness into play, especially into the sexual gamesmanship played out in private. Since heavy sodium subverts the carnal restraint that Van Dorn traces back to St. Paul, it encourages the kind of license that Derrida associates with the *pharmakon*'s festival-like reversal of values (*Dissemination* 150, 152): the seductive posturing of Mickey, the deft bedtime positioning of Ellen, the liaison of More and Lucy at Pantherburn, the carnival of licentiousness at Belle Ame. Such fleshliness, along with the equally rampant abstraction of More's roboticized patients, is symptomatic of a far wider syndrome. When Percy's doctor observes that sufferers from the thanatos syndrome seem to have become as mindful as computers and as instinctual as animals, More is not simply diagnosing the extremes that in *Love in the Ruins* he called angelism and bestialism. More is recognizing that all of the ill seem to have lost their peculiar identities as humans and become mere replicas of each other.

Just as the *pharmakon* of writing has no inherent identity of its own but serves to make possible a potentially unlimited number of duplications, the self-effacing Na-24 creates a society of doubles in which all follow to the letter the same script. It alleviates the anxiety, opposition, and anger that Girard views as the effects of mimetic desire and leaves what More terms "a sameness here, a flatness of affect" (85). All of the sufferers show a vacancy that makes them less like their former disturbed selves and more like each other. Such a proliferation of imitation erases the variety that was so endemic to Feliciana. As described in the novel's opening note, this section of Louisiana was a community founded on diversity and divergence. True to its historical origins, "it still harbors all manner of fractious folk . . . [who], for all their differences and contrariness, have an affection for one another" (viii). Na-24 suspends this amiable opposition and replaces it with a bland indistinctness in which everyone is identically empty and undisturbed.

The signal difference in the patients that puzzle More with their strange symptoms is a lack of the differences that once defined them so uniquely. This uniformity is the quintessence of the plague. Noting a similarity in the descriptions of pestilence across eras and countries, Girard detects the very meaning of such illness in precisely this sameness. "The plague is universally presented as a process of undifferentiation, a destruction of specificities," he writes. "The plague overcomes all obstacles, disregards all frontiers. All life, finally, is turned into death, which is the supreme undifferentiation" (*Double Business* 136, 137). To call Percy's plague "the thanatos syndrome" is almost a tautology, for it spreads thanatos precisely to the extent that it constitutes a syndrome. Its deadliness is its similarity, its "running together"—in the root meaning of *syndrome*—of what was once so varied and vital. As More reflects on the peculiar behavior shared by Mickey LaFaye and Donna S——, he speculates, "Two cases are too few even to suggest a syndrome, but I am struck by certain likenesses" (21). If the symptoms that the doctor notices—fragmented speech, computerlike memory, loss of context, sexual license—point to a syndrome, the syndrome amounts to a "certain eerie similarity" that has made the sufferers doubles of each other (68).

Because the thanatos syndrome spreads mass imitation, it is a particularly apt illness for the cultural hour in Percy's novel. Percy takes the runaway repetition that Umberto Eco regards as the essence of the postmodern era (84) and then rewrites it deep in the heart of his fiction's stricken selves. In a novel that is itself a sequel, the plague manifests itself in the realm of duplicated psyches. Much as the television soap opera *Dynasty* (which More mentions) essentially retells the same story with minor variations from week to week, much as the fast food chain that More and his family frequent restages the same standardized space from one venue to another, the thanatos syndrome creates serial selves, who, despite the appearances of difference, are actually the same.[6] This sameness is given literary form in the series of numbered case histories that Percy uses in part II to present More's patients. The familiar and formulaic accounts have the effect of reducing their individuality so that each becomes just one more—not one more in any meaningful progression but one more retelling, one more recounting, one more recurrence.

The similarities of the thanatos syndrome amount to a virtual plague of mimesis. The resemblances can be traced back to the doctors who are the engineers of the sickness. Although the Apollonian Comeaux views Blue Boy as a rational means to social reformation and the Dionysian Van Dorn embraces it as a first step toward sexual liberation, they are so mutually genial and genteel that they become almost indistinguishable from each other. Their model is not so much each other as More, whose southern savoir faire they keep trying and failing to imitate. This Dixie version of Tweedledee and Tweedledum, in turn, creates a school of disciples by forcing model conduct upon all in Feliciana. Na-24 spreads the mimesis as if it were a highly communicable disease. "Metaphysical desire is always contagious," Girard writes. "Internal mediation is present when one 'catches' a nearby desire just as one would catch the plague or cholera, simply by contact with an infected person" (*Deceit* 99). The thanatos syndrome causes each fondly contented citizen of Feliciana to become the mere simulacrum of the other blissful fool.

Such simulation repeats itself to death. Just as the *pharmakon* of writing kills speech by eliminating the spoken for the written word, Na-24 empties the self and leaves a lifeless facsimile in its place. The verbal cadaver is stiff with the rigor mortis of what has been fixed on the printed page. Since the logos is what is really alive for Plato, Derrida likens writing to "weakened speech, something not completely dead: a living-dead, a reprieved corpse, a deferred life, a semblance of breath" (*Dissemination* 143). It may even be a device for mortuary magic, for *pharmakon* may also mean perfume or a painter's colors. Writing is "a cosmetic concealing the dead under the appearance of the living. The *pharmakon* introduces and harbors death. It makes the corpse presentable, masks it, makes it up, perfumes it with its essence" (*Dissemination* 142). The thanatos syndrome transforms Dr. More's quirky clientele into a single type, flagrantly normal and nondescript, endlessly re-typed, ever the same. And so, dead. Socrates criticizes writing precisely because of its moribund repetition. It remembers not the vital truth that the soul knew before its imprisonment in the body but recalls what the person has already called to mind. And it keeps saying itself over and over without ever being able to answer an interlocutor. "Pure repetition, absolute self-repetition, repetition of a self that is already reference and repetition, repetition of the signifier," Derrida graphically repeats as he writes, "repetition that is null or annulling, repetition of death—it's all one" (*Dissemination* 136). Blue Boy inscribes this grim reiteration in all who drink its elixir of life.

Freud viewed such repetition as a sign of thanatos, for it annihilated the essential diversity and multiplicity of life. More supplies the Freudian gloss for the title of Percy's novel while he is reading about World War I, the very conflict that provided the background for Miranda's deadly syndrome in "Pale Horse, Pale Rider." At the Battle of the Somme and Verdun, "two million young men were killed toward no discernible end." More reflects, "As Dr. Freud might have said, the age of thanatos had begun" (86).[7] Deeply disturbed by World War I, Freud believed that thanatos was a drive away from change and toward recovering an earlier inanimate state (*Beyond the Pleasure Principle* 30–33). Repetition promoted that stasis because it impeded difference and development, and it fostered a recurrent sameness. The thanatos syndrome is such mimesis on a mass scale, mimesis upon mimesis, mimesis unto death. However, Freud may not have gone far enough in understanding his destructive century. Although the pioneering psychiatrist recognized how such repetition could be fatal, Girard criticizes Freud for making thanatos into a separate instinct rather than understanding it as a result of imitation and rivalry. The desiring self may seek the death of the model that has become the obstacle to its mimesis. The disciple may even seek its own death as it pursues models that are desirable precisely because they are distant and indifferent. In both cases the self desires death only because it first desires imitation (*Things Hidden* 410–13). Yet if Freud overlooked the crucial role that the mediator played in the rush toward mortality, he provided Percy with an imaginative name to link the death and sameness that More discovers. The thanatos syndrome spreads this lethal confluence, for the afflicted are delivered from the disturbances that Freud associated with living and are made to imitate a quiescence whose ultimate model is death.

Na-24 is so deadly that it even takes its toll on Percy's fiction. Like O'Connor, Percy was increasingly drawn to an aesthetics of violence as a way to expose and attack the very deadness that More notices around him. Percy's nonfiction senses this banality with particular acuteness when the syndrome infects the images, rituals, and vocabulary of Christianity. Such signs seem no longer able to communicate the sacred in an age when "baptism is already accepted but accepted by and large as a minor tribal rite somewhat secondary in importance to taking the kids to see Santa at the department store" (*Message* 118). Percy notes that O'Connor sought to recover the sacred through her violent artistry, portraying baptism in *The Violent Bear It Away* through the Pauline-inspired image of drowning. Percy likewise cultivates the extremes of characters and situations. Describing the "eschatological novelist," he explains, "The fictional use of violence, shock, comedy, insult, the bizarre, are the everyday tools of his trade" (*Message* 118).

In *The Thanatos Syndrome* Percy's end-of-the-world artistry seeks to render the dead in all of their deadness—stiffened, distorted, and dispirited—so that readers cannot mistake them for the living. His success is to realize the novel's title as the master metaphor for More's world. Percy depicts a city of the dead in which only More and Father Smith seem alive, and even they are not unscathed. However, like the *pharmakon,* such fictional violence has a contradictory effect. Because Percy is determined to expose the sacrificial logic, he sacrifices some of the force of his fiction in order to shout the truth about communal persecution. Victims and victimizers are so clearly demarcated in the novel that they wear their status with a capital "V." More's case study patients, the generic children violated at Belle Ame, the nameless and faceless citizens of Feliciana who have been drinking the tainted water—all are either abstracted into ideas or felt only as flesh. Comeaux and Van Dorn, the masterminds responsible for such victimization, are more concepts than characters, as if the syndrome had hollowed out the heart of their mystery. None of the innocent has the poignancy of O'Connor's Bishop; none of the guilty has the complexity of her Rayber or the concreteness of McCarthy's Ballard. And so *The Thanatos Syndrome* never quite escapes its own title and completely comes to life.

Although *The Thanatos Syndrome* may sometimes suffer as fiction, Percy writes into the novel the very problem of writing and the thanatos syndrome, as if he understands what is at stake despite his inability always to achieve it. Heavy sodium may seem like another version of Plato's *pharmakon*, but there is a significant difference between the recipes of Plato and his modern disciples— a difference that undermines significance itself. The drug of Na-24 actually attacks the drug of writing. Much as Plato would proscribe what seems to threaten the culture of orality, Comeaux would exclude texts of all kinds, whether they require verbal or visual literacy. The genius behind Blue Boy boasts that McGuffey Readers, themes on summer vacations, comic books, and *Star Wars* are passé for the new wunderkinder: "They're into graphic and binary communication— which after all is a lot more accurate than once upon a time there lived a wicked queen" (197).

Comeaux's flippant dismissal of a whole genre of folk narratives is symptomatic of his deadly abstraction. Walter Benjamin views such fairy tales as teaching audiences how "to meet the forces of the mythical world with cunning and with high spirits"; however, he considers the modern world as more concerned with data that can be verified than with wise counsel for life (*Illuminations* 102). In eliminating the need for "Snow White" and its kind, the thanatos syndrome is the information age as epidemic. Death, for Benjamin, authorizes humans to compose life stories that offer morals and meanings (*Illuminations* 94–101). Indeed, in that *The Thanatos Syndrome* was published only three years before Percy's own death, it was probably driven by the fierce pressure of mortality upon an aging novelist to leave behind one last testament. However, the living death in Percy's novel prompts no such reflection on and sharing of noteworthy experiences, only the mindless transmission of factoids. These bare exchanges point to how the absolute dichotomy of communal violence has become a foundation of the novel's cyberculture. Since every bit of computerized information results from a stark choice between one and zero, such binary communication is predicated on a logic of constant exclusion. Either/or: in the instant of scapegoating, when crisis is resolved through the most simplistic contrast, either one is a victimizer or one is annulled, erased, reduced to being a victim.

Comeaux does not just denigrate writing in favor of computerese. He seeks to destroy it. Heavy sodium unwrites writing itself, for it excludes the very multiplicity of meaning that Girard traces to the scapegoat and that Derrida locates in the *pharmakon*. Girard proposes that degree and distinction are established in the calm after the killing of the surrogate victim. Time comes to signify what is "before" or "after" the violence, and space to name what is "inside" or "outside" the group that committed the violence. But the scapegoat cannot be defined by such opposites, for as the very precondition of opposition itself, it antedates, includes, and transcends every antonym (*Things Hidden* 102). Derrida describes precisely such indeterminacy in his own reflection on the *pharmakos:* "Beneficial insofar as he cures—and for that, venerated and cared for—harmful insofar as he incarnates the powers of evil—and for that, feared and treated with caution. Alarming and calming. Sacred and accursed. The conjunction, the *coincidentia oppositorum,* ceaselessly undoes itself in the passage to decision or crisis" (*Dissemination* 133). Derrida observes in the victim the same ambiguity and polysemy that he detects in the drug of writing. Indeed, Girard has commented that in Derrida's reading of the *Phaedrus* "the Platonic *pharmakon* functions like the human pharmakos and leads to similar results" (*Violence* 296). Like Girard's *pharmakos,* Derrida's *pharmakon* cannot be reduced to any single element in an antithesis, for it comprehends them both.

Since the *pharmakon* is the prerequisite of every difference and division, it must first be excluded before opposites can be defined. As long as the *pharmakon* remains, its disquieting mixture of distinctions makes impossible any inner stability and tranquility. To achieve such constancy, Plato scapegoats the *pharmakon,* rejecting writing in favor of logos. However, Derrida contends that Plato actually contradicts himself, for he relies upon the very writing that he excommunicates. Plato commits his Socratic dialogues to writing, and his own writing uses writing as a metaphor for the kind of responsive and responsible discourse that voices the truth inscribed in the soul (*Dissemination* 148–49, 153–54).[8] Derrida argues that Plato's opposition between writing and speech actually breaks down into a contrast between two forms of writing, one that is vital and full of knowledge and another that is dead and devoid of insight. Thus, Plato does not so much exclude writing in favor of speech as prefer one form of writing to another.

The violent pharmacology of Blue Boy would exclude Derrida's *pharmakon* in excluding Girard's *pharmakos*. For what Na-24 eliminates is the very possibility of ambivalence that Derrida identifies in the poison/cure and that Girard traces to the outcast savior. "There is no such thing as a harmless remedy," Derrida declares. "The *pharmakon* can never be simply beneficial" (*Dissemination* 99). Yet Comeaux and Van Dorn explain to More the social engineering and sexual liberation made possible by Blue Boy without any understanding of its dangers, as if some thaumaturge, some *pharmakeus*, had precipitated out of the *pharmakon* the deadly threat implicit in the word. Percy's doctor knows that there is rarely "a single magic bullet one can aim at the tiny villain" of disease (4), but the wizards of Blue Boy think Na-24 is so simple and salutary. For them, the venom/antidote heals without hurting. However, in attacking the *pharmakon* as the very nexus of opposition, Na-24 compromises the individual complexity that for Percy always makes humans most human. Although heavy sodium seems to calm the rages and terrors that once afflicted More's patients, it undermines the very potential for difference. Comeaux and Van Dorn consecrate a single model of mental health and then use the drug to impose a bland and uniform vacancy on all who deviate from their norm. Azazel gets his due once more.

THE SCAPEGOAT AND THE SIGN THAT COULD NOT BE EVACUATED

As More works to discover the connection between pharmacology and victimization, he must be careful that his very best intentions do not become co-opted and corrupted by the very scapegoating that he is beginning to expose. So beguiling is surrogate victimage, captivating new servants even while keeping secret its workings, that the mechanism always has the possibility of duping the well-meaning More. Throughout the doctor's research, readers might wonder whether More is pursuing legitimate concerns about public health, suffering from delusions of persecution, or arousing persecution delusions in others. Since communal exclusion depends on the collective error that the scapegoat is guilty, it flourishes under every variation on this untruth: under the delusion that the self is being wracked and wronged, under the delusion that others are being afflicted, under the delusion that oppression justifies counteroppression. All of these deceptions conceal and perpetuate scapegoating because they legitimatize violence and divert concern away from the true victim.

Although More has abandoned the megalomania that made him want to save America in *Love in the Ruins*, he must guard against such messianism returning in the form of grandiose fantasies that he is being persecuted. When More shares with Max Gottlieb his early observations about the thanatos syndrome, his friend and former therapist worries that More may be suffering from paranoia. Gottlieb apparently has good reasons for such speculation. More suspects conspiracy, fears that he is being pursued, senses possible menace behind the affability of colleagues, and wonders whether everyone he meets is secretly dead. If More were paranoid, he would have shifted the scapegoating mechanism from society to psyche. Paranoia affirms the centrality of communal exclusion. However, it substitutes a band of hostile phantoms for genuine persecutors, and it converts being tormented into a privileged position to glorify the self as the sublime outcast. To be sure that he is not making a diagnosis out of paranoia, More must conduct rigorous firsthand observations, gather ever more data, and hesitate about making conclusions. Above all, he must find a confidant who can help him confirm and interpret his findings about the violence of the thanatos syndrome.

Just as More must guard against falsely imagining that he is the victim, he must also be wary of deceiving others into thinking that they are victims. More needs to be certain that he is not fostering the kind of mass delusion that Elaine Showalter finds so common in the crisis-laden society of late-twentieth-century America. She argues that such syndromes of the 1980s and 1990s as chronic fatigue syndrome, Gulf War syndrome, and multiple personality syndrome (along with cases of recovered memory, satanic cults, and alien abductions) may actually result from the "mimetic disorder" of hysteria (15).[9] Showalter claims that these hysterias develop when anxiety about sexuality and frustrations about gender restraints are converted into symptoms and stories that eventually gain professional legitimatization. A theorist gives the complex an explanation and a name, often through emphasizing some facts, de-emphasizing others, and eliciting, coaxing, and sometimes even suggesting testimony that is missing (15–20). Once this syndrome is identified, sufferers are encouraged to view themselves as victims of mysterious powers that are responsible for their malaise. Showalter contends that this interpretation then becomes the pattern that experts use to understand not just the initially troubled patients but future sufferers, who may even be attracted by the publicity surrounding the prototypes. Disseminated in the media, the syndrome is popularized by books, television, films, newspapers, self-help groups, government studies, Internet sites, and even literary criticism (17–20). The mass duplication of the dis-ease may lead to a familiar and violent climax. "As the panic reaches epidemic proportions," Showalter writes, "hysteria seeks out scapegoats and enemies" (5). The targets may range from governments that are accused of not telling citizens the truth about various hazards to parents who are charged with abusing their children.

The thanatos syndrome actually results from a variant of the mimesis run amok that Showalter analyzes. It is masterminded by Drs. Comeaux and Van Dorn, foisted upon a vulnerable and unsuspecting population, and spread by a medium more pervasive than all the media in the culture of mechanical reproduction. However, since More does not at first understand how the illness originates in such imitation, he must be sure that he is diagnosing a genuine syndrome rather than disseminating his own strain of mimetic contagion. Indeed, when More first begins his investigations, it seems possible that he may simply be spreading hysteria. His discoveries—toxic substances, collusion, possible government involvement, rumors of pedophilia—sound like a compendium of tropes from the "hystories" that Showalter critiques. To guard against infecting others with an epidemic of his own devising, More must avoid simplifying a complex phenomenon to fit a predetermined theory. He must avoid influencing his patients so that they become disciples of a self-promoting master narrative projected onto them. Above all, More must scrutinize his own concern for the victim to be sure that he is not suffering from the mania that has been denounced as victimism.

Although Girard claims that scapegoating, like the social engineering of Project Blue Boy, is a hidden mechanism for the foundation and preservation of culture, some critics have charged that scapegoating has increasingly become all too obvious and exploited in American society. Charles J. Sykes argues that the American tendency to absolve the self of responsibility and to explain its behavior in terms of disease, psychological disorder, or social oppression has created, as his title terms it, "a nation of victims." In *Victims and Values* Joseph Amato claims that such politics of the tender heart may actually contribute to victimization. The violated may lodge false accusations against innocent people while the true source of the violence may remain hidden. The proliferating claims of victims may dull the ability of even the sympathetic to respond and may provoke a competition among the persecuted (151–74). Indeed, victims may resort to violence against those who oppress them or against others who seem like rivals as they too seek justice after having been oppressed.

Such critiques of victimism may be dangerous if they undermine the kind of rightful concern for the victim that gradually makes More oppose Comeaux and Van Dorn. They risk dismissing all accusations of discrimination and violence as if they were mythic fantasies, and they risk hiding the scapegoat once again by apathy, incredulity, and cynicism. These complaints do not invalidate Girard's work on collective violence but confirm it, for they speak with a mimetic predictability. Any stance in favor of the victim can be expected to engender an argument that too much attention has been paid to the victim, especially when it is advanced under the name of actually speaking for the victim. However, critics of the contemporary victim culture provide important cautions for More's investigation and for Girardian interpretation. They call attention to how scapegoating can easily be trivialized or manufactured so that the new American myth is not the concealment of the victim but the revelation that victims are everywhere and everyone. They point to how the status of being a victim may foster self-pity, impotence, arrogance, or rage. They emphasize how the mere perception of victimization can easily be turned into a pretext that the vanquished use to justify further violence. More must avoid being caught up in just such delusions of scapegoating lest he mistakenly blame those who are innocent or, once he has found the real source of the malady, victimize the victimizers.

Dr. Lucy Lipscomb helps More with many of the challenges raised by the possibility of paranoia or hysteria. As an epidemiologist, she provides credible scientific information that enables More to trace the etiology of his patients' unusual behavior. During More's evening at Pantherburn, Lucy's approach is as illuminating as her name implies. Her training in how disease may affect a community, expertise with computers, and access to classified health data make it clear that the thanatos syndrome is not a private fantasy or a public delusion that More has fostered. Rather, it is a condition spread by consuming water tainted with heavy sodium. If scapegoating thrives on secrecy, Lucy uses the techniques of the information age to help More bring its methodology to light.

Lucy is so resourceful that the chauvinistic More may feel threatened by her intelligence and self-assertion (Hardy 238–39). However, Percy's researcher has more valid reasons for being wary of her. Lucy helps More to expose the victimization but not, finally, to oppose it. After eagerly providing him with the information that he needs to solve the medical mystery, Lucy becomes disengaged from the quest when she has to consider who is responsible for spreading the syndrome. She shows the same moral reluctance after she conducts perineal exams on the students at Belle Ame. Although Lucy is rendered almost speechless by discovering signs of sexual abuse, she does not believe that headmaster Van Dorn knew about the pedophilia. Lucy can understand the thanatos syndrome as a fascinating exercise in public health, but she cannot move from the plea-sures of scientific abstraction to the imperatives of the ethical life. Hence, she encourages More to forget about the victim by accepting the position that Comeaux offers in Fedville and by dallying with her at Pantherburn.

Reminding More of the spirited "Southern women in old novels" (104), the mistress of the manor entices her cousin with a romance out of the Old South. Lucy is as rivalrous as any of the belles denounced by Eva in Porter's "Old Mor-tality." She seeks to win More's wandering affections by making him doubt Ellen's fidelity and by offering him a seductive stay at Pantherburn. More's night with his kinswoman revives the regional past—with its plantation setting, fe-male coquettishness, male license to fornicate, and attraction between cousins. It is not surprising that at the end of the novel More imagines that marriage to Lucy might have driven him to imitate their eighteenth-century American an-cestor by committing suicide. For life with Lucy would mean a repetition of old mortality, a dispiriting compromise with the culture of violence that the hon-orable gentleman might have escaped only in a fatal version of the thanatos syn-drome. More would have become his own victim.

Whereas Lucy cannot turn information about victims into opposition to-ward the victimizers, Father Smith helps More to take a stand against the sur-rogate victimage mechanism. Although the seemingly zany clergyman has been dismissed by some readers as a mere mouthpiece for Percy, he is more than a surrogate polemicist. Father Smith's oracular pronouncements about signs and victimization during More's first interview with him and his confession of vio-lent desire during More's second interview make the priest a prophetic critic of his bloody century, a self-acknowledged exemplar of what he condemns, and a compelling model for how to get beyond the bloodshed. Like a Girardian de-constructor, Father Smith sees history and culture by the light of the victim. The most recent examples are the patients in his hospice. Three weeks ago the priest learned that the government would fund the euthanasia of Comeaux's Quali-tarian centers but not the palliative care of the church-sponsored St. Margaret's. So, the modern stylite has taken up residence atop his fire tower, not as a private retreat for the righteous but as a protest against a culture of death. The current victimization has a long bloodline. Father Smith mentions the violations of Robespierre, Stalin, Soviet psychiatrists, all of those idealists who believe in the sacrificial logic of "millions dead for the good of Mankind" (129). But for Father Smith the ultimate precedent in the twentieth century is Hitler's attempt to an-nihilate the Jews.

Father Smith understands the social engineering of Comeaux and Van Dorn by way of Hitler's attempts to create an ideal Aryan nation. Although the seemingly absurd analogy may sound like proof of the priest's delirium, it identifies a disquieting tendency in the South that observers of the region have noted since the rise of Hitlerism. In 1941 Cash wrote that Reconstruction established the "savage ideal" in the South "almost as truly as it is established today in Fascist Italy, in Nazi Germany, in Soviet Russia" and that the Ku Klux Klan was as much "an authentic folk movement" as was Nazism (134, 335). Clarence Cason regarded such demagogues as Cotton Tom Heflin, Theodore G. Bilbo, and Huey Long (whose rise to power, Father Smith remembers, his dreamy father seems to have ignored) as representing a southern form of fascism. He even feared that if the "Putsch" in Louisiana culminated in gaining power over the entire South, Long might one day put his critics into concentration camps (89, 107). Robert Penn Warren exposed Long's power-hungry populism in *All the King's Men,* but Katherine Anne Porter, who, like Father Smith, witnessed the rise of Nazism in 1930s Germany and even met Goering at a dinner party, denounced Warren's portrayal of the Long-like Willie Stark as "a sentimental apology for the worst sort of Fascist demagogue" (qtd. in Givner, *A Life* 355). In "The Leaning Tower" Porter herself explored what might have driven a dispirited Germany to follow such a rabble-rouser. And she gave a southern resonance to Charles Upton's sojourn abroad by making the Aryan dedication to violent honor recall similar ideals from the Texas of his family past. Porter found in Germany what Thomas Wolfe detected there as well, a "plague of the spirit—invisible but as unmistakable as death"—the same thanatos syndrome that is taking its fatal toll in Father Smith's Feliciana (qtd. in Wertham 73).

As if to emphasize the continuity between the Newest South and Nazi Germany, Father Smith predicts that the utopian dreams of Comeaux and Van Dorn will eventually lead to the destruction of the Jews. Such a murderous climax suggests that the thanatos syndrome functions as plagues frequently do in literature according to Girard—as a metaphor for the harmful spread of violence (*Double Business* 136–54). The remedy for such violence is always more violence. The priest anticipates that just as German physicians once sought to purify the race, first through forced sterilization and euthanasia of undesirables and then later through selecting concentration camp inmates for extermination, Comeaux and Van Dorn have begun a program of scapegoating that will culminate in another Holocaust. If Father Smith is right, Leo Frank will be hanged again and again and again.

Father Smith's warning understands that southern violence is more than just southern. He places Blue Boy in the wider context of surrogate victimage that extends from myth to the Holocaust. "People have the wrong idea about the Holocaust. The Holocaust, as people see it, is a myth," he shocks More by proclaiming. "What I'm trying to tell you is that the origins of the Holocaust are a myth" (126–27).[10] Unlike the so-called "revisionists," Father Smith is not trying to question the historicity of the murder of six million Jews. He is no Arthur Butz, the engineering professor at Northwestern University whose 1975 *The Hoax of the Twentieth Century* claimed that the Jews were not the victims of genocide but of widespread outbreaks of typhus in the concentration camps. Nor is he any Paul Rassinier, a former inmate at Buchenwald, whose 1977 *Debunking the Genocide Myth* asserted that the number of Jews killed has been exaggerated, denied that gas chambers were used in the concentration camps, and charged that the testimony of accused war criminals was coerced. When Father Smith claims that the Holocaust originated in a myth, he could not be more opposed to such perverse distortions of history. Indeed, while a lieutenant in the infantry, Smith himself was an eyewitness to Dachau, and he helped to liberate Eglfing-Haar, the hospital where children were murdered under the supervision of the esteemed Dr. Jäger.

Whereas Lucy tries to seduce More with an essentially mythic view of time that encourages him to repeat the old southern past (Desmond, *At the Crossroads* 102–17), Father Smith calls upon More to escape the cyclic time of yore that helped to produce the Holocaust.[11] The priest understands that the Nazi genocide as well as Blue Boy and the Qualitarian Center have their genesis in the myth that lurks behind so many myths—the myth of origins, the myth of surrogate victimage. Girard views myth not as the means to express poetic fancy, unconscious desires, or deep mental structures but as the way to suppress the truth about collective violence. As the very origin of the word suggests, myths literally "close" or "keep secret" (Bailie 30–35). What they hide—through repression, misrepresentation, and fabrication—is the communal murder of the innocent. Behind the Greek myth of Oedipus, the Aztec myth of Tecuciztecatl and Nanauatzin, and the Scandinavian myth of Baldr is the victim (*Scapegoat* 24–44, 57–70).[12]

Those pseudo-historians who deny the Holocaust perpetuate the myth in which it originated. Their canards are almost predictable because scapegoating languishes without deception and delusion. Yet whereas Guillaume de Machaut acknowledges that Jews were victimized during the Black Death but hides the real reason, the modern persecution texts carry that dissimulation to a new level of denial. The ultimate myth is that the genocide never happened. Father Smith challenges all such falsehoods, for his provocative claim about the origins of the Holocaust is closer to Eliade's view in *Myth and Reality* than to any work by those who deny the signal event in modern Jewish history. Eliade considers Aryanism a modern myth because it sought to bring a new and supposedly noble order to birth by returning to the time of the origin. Clearly understanding the role of mimetic desire in such a re-creation of the golden era, Eliade writes that "The 'Aryan' was the exemplary model that must be imitated in order to recover racial 'purity,' physical strength, nobility, the heroic 'ethics' of the glorious and creative 'beginnings'" (183). The Holocaust might be interpreted as mythic because it resulted from pursuing such transcendent aspirations so far that they led to mass murder. Girard helps to deepen the connection between the Holocaust and myth because he reveals the scapegoating that took place even before Eliade's time of sacred origins. Like Girard, Father Smith historicizes myth and demythologizes history to reveal the victim that is common to both. When the priest claims that the Holocaust has a mythic foundation, he appreciates how it was justified by the supreme narrative imposture of all time. The belief that a society must expel and exterminate some allegedly guilty member to gain renewal is the arch-myth of all culture.

Father Smith claims that the Nazis acted out this myth in the Holocaust after it could not be completely enacted in language. Like the practitioners of *Sprachkritik* before and between the world wars (Steiner 110–14), Percy has long heard the malady of modern civilization in the unsoundness of its talk: its evacuated clichés, evasive jargon, and deceptive circumlocutions.[13] In *The Thanatos Syndrome* More has begun to notice a more advanced form of this infirmity. The very name of Comeaux and Van Dorn's project sounds this malaise. Although Blue Boy may evoke innocuous nursery rhymes and well-known Gainsborough portraiture, the innocent connotations actually conceal pharmacological violence. Comeaux's drug puts the self into a sleep faster than any boy's under a haystack, and Van Dorn's academy victimizes boys as well as girls with blue variations on children's games. The designers of Blue Boy practice the same deception when they prate of "pedeuthanasia" and "gereuthanasia" to hide how they kill the young and the old who have been deemed expendable. Those victims of their utopian schemes who are not killed can utter only the most deadened form of speech. They speak in fragmented sentences and use words more as if they were a series of mechanical transactions than a Percyan affirmation of the community between speaker and listener.

Hearing how the thanatos syndrome enervates words, Father Smith challenges More, "Can you name one word sign which has not been evacuated of meaning, that is, deprived?" (120). Father Smith listens to a linguistic version of the expulsion that takes place in scapegoating. He hears how significance is muted, driven out, and made void, how the *pharmakon* is excluded. If this widespread deprivation of words points to the work of a depriver, as Father Smith suggests, More has already stumbled upon the demon behind such semiotic violence. At the end of part I he recalls that in *Paradise Lost* Milton made Azazel the ensign-bearer for all of Satan's rebellious angels (I.534–40). Azazel lifts high the imperial *signum* for the infernal force that undermines all signs. The demon in the desert spells death to language because it is the name for the violence that the community rejects as its own and projects onto the scapegoat and the sacred. The depriver is really not devilish at all but, like the stranger in *The Violent Bear It Away*, all too human.

Father Smith maintains that amid such attacks on language, the sign *Jew* held its meaning with a rare integrity. The Jews are a people of the word. The God of Judaism creates by the word, gives his words as the Decalogue, and recalls the heedless to the covenant through the words of his prophetic spokespeople. As Father Smith asserts, "Since the Jews were the original chosen people of God, a tribe of people who are still here, they are a sign of God's presence which cannot be evacuated" (123). *Jew* has not been deprived of significance because it bears ongoing witness to the God who is supremely significant. However, the devotees of Azazel have never stopped trying to evacuate this sign. Like Father Smith, Edmond Jabès clearly hears this assault in *The Book of Questions.* His narrative meditation on writing after the Holocaust notices an identity between the troubled fate of the Jew and of the word. Both are perpetually under question—beset, imperiled, contingent, problematic. Both bear the marks of the victim: "Every Jew lives within a personified word which allows him to enter into all written words. Every Jew lives in a key-word, a word of pain, a password, which the rabbis comment on" (Jabès 100).

Hitler tried to assault the Jews in word and flesh. The rhetoric of *Mein Kampf,* as Kenneth Burke has shown, is founded on the age-old institution of the scapegoat. It convinced Germany to become a victimizer because the fatherland had been a victim of World War I. Like Guillaume de Machaut's *Judg-*

ment of the King of Navarre, it sought to unify a fragmented community around demonizing the Jews as the disease infecting society and then destroying them as the way to restore health (Burke 165–67, 173–74). Hitler's rhetoric cast the Jews out in words and by words. Its imagery emptied a people of their sacredness and left them only as the bearers of violence—from financial ruin to physical contamination and moral pollution—against whom violence must be used. It murdered Jews on the page.

Despite a history of such depredations, the Jews perdured as a people chosen by God. So, as Kathleen Scullin-Esser explains, they became "the natural targets of those who deny the signs of God and subvert the posture of the symbol-user, subsuming the other who is deemed valueless" (75). Unable to evacuate the Jews as a signifier, Hitler effaced six million of the signified.[14] He committed what signs had not yet even signified—*genocide,* a word dating from 1944 and given currency at the Nuremberg war crime trials—to get as close as possible to emptying that one sign of its long-standing significance. "The Holocaust was a consequence of the sign which could not be evacuated," Father Smith announces (126), for it sought to put this divine mark under erasure. Against the word *Jew,* Hitler spoke the logos of violence, the counter-word, counter-order, that affirms scapegoating as the central, organizing principle of all community.[15]

If Hitler and his disciples could not evacuate the Jews in language, they would evacuate the Jews as a people by emptying other words and then turning these eviscerated signs into tools for victimization. Their communiqués depleted language to avoid calling violence by its rightful name. They favored the passive voice in order to avoid responsibility and used bland bywords, like "action," "treatment," and "measures," to conceal mass murder (Dawidowicz, "Introduction" 14–16). The ultimate of these circumlocutions was the "Final Solution," which transformed the Jews into a problem that would be resolved for all time. Through such verbal evasion Hitler would have the last word, for the Holocaust would leave a world of voided signs, a world devoid of the one sign that had resisted deprivation. Nothing but the silence of violence and the violence of silence.

Hitler's assault on the sign through the victimization of the Jews at once restages and reverses what Girard imagines as the origin of sign-use in primordial victimization. Girard proposes that language, like all symbolic thought, begins in the reflective calm that follows surrogate victimage (*Violence* 235–36; *Things Hidden* 99–104). The contrast between the ensuing harmony and the preceding mayhem makes the victim the focus of intense attention in the community that is a community only because it killed one of those held in common. Gathered around the corpse, the community attributes to the victim the entire complex of distinctions that have emerged because of it. Once there was mass undifferentiation, but now the society can recognize violence and peace, life-giving death and death-bringing life. Since the corpse is the very center of all that is double and contradictory, the victim becomes the single bearer of all signification. Derrida's protean Theuth and indeterminate *pharmakon* are but later manifestations of its quicksilvery polysemy (*Dissemination* 92–94, 97–100). Like those fundamental tropes of deconstruction, the victim is beyond any antonyms, for it is the very possibility of antithesis, the all-inclusive figure around whom all difference is configured. Yet despite the similar ambivalence behind the Girardian *pharmakos* and Derridean *pharmakon,* there is, for Girard as for Father Smith, no ambivalence about the victimization itself. "The signifier is the victim," Girard summarizes. "The signified constitutes all actual and potential meaning the community confers on to the victim and, through its intermediacy, on to all things" (*Things Hidden* 103). Although the sacrificial crisis virtually eludes language because it is the epitome of undifferentiation, the peace of the scapegoat makes room for language as a system of differences (*Violence* 64).

As the first sign, the victim is not only the site of all significance but also the basis of all substitution. Girard contends that since the community seeks to preserve the unity and tranquility gained by the founding murder, it reproduces the signs and repeats the surrogate victimage in ritualized killings. These offerings depend on the very principles of meaningfulness and mediation that made the first victim a transcendental signifier. Just as the scapegoat was a substitute for everyone else in the community, each sacrifice is another surrogate, a substitute for a substitute, which can represent the group and be made supremely significant—sacred—by violence.[16] This proxy might at first be another human, but then as the basic principle of displacement and replacement takes hold, it might be an animal, fruits of the field, or even money. The victim thus establishes the precedent for the symbolic replication from which all culture emerges, including the sign-system of language. Girard suggests that speech might have developed from the cries that were sounded during the original mimetic crisis. These shouts were copied in later ritualized reenactments because they were regarded as necessary to the salutary effect of victimization. Since participants in such rituals are normally joined in a spirit of communal cooperation, the ceremonies would have provided a forum for these vocables to become standardized by repetition and disseminated among the faithful (*Things Hidden* 103–4).

Such cries might even have been ways to designate the victim. In *The Origin of Language* Eric Gans modifies Girard's work to focus on the foundational role of the victim as signified rather than as signifier. He imagines that after a primal hunt and killing, members of the community might have reached out toward the victim but then aborted the gesture of appropriation out of fear.[17] They would have hesitated to seize it because if they actually took possession of the victim, they might have suffered the same violent fate at the hands of the other like-minded onlookers. When this gesture of desire and deferral eventually became understood as designating the victim, the intended but intangible object of attention, it created the possibility for the ostensive in language. Gans speculates that this rudimentary linguistic form might first have been used to refer to the sacred object and then to profane objects that manifested one side of the sacred—threats ("Fire!") or benefits ("Water!").

Whereas Girard emphasizes the ritual origins of language in recalling the generative conflict, Gans emphasizes the formal nature of language as creating a reproducible model of reality, of the victim. However, both view language as being born out of violence, as bearing bloody traces, as speaking of the slain. And just as speech repeats, in however distanced a form, the victim, the ongoing process of substitution makes it possible for literacy to become a surrogate for orality. The victim who is earmarked for murder and is the beginning of all subsequent demarcation underwrites every mark on the page. Behind the word, the oral and written vicar, is the vicarious victim—the victim as foremost repository of meaning, the victim as founding principle of representation, the victim as first vocable, the victim as pre-text and subtext for all writing.

If language develops after surrogate victimage, the Holocaust might be understood as repeating and revoking this founding moment of culture. It reenacted scapegoating but on such a catastrophic scale that speech might seem impossible. Father Smith has fittingly lapsed into silence when More first visits him in the fire tower, for the Holocaust to which the priest eventually bears witness attempted to strike at signification itself. It unleashed sacred violence upon the Jew as sign, upon the victim as bearer of meaning, upon the system of differences that was made possible by the victim. "Being made up of differences," Girard explains, "language finds it almost impossible to express undifferentiation directly" (*Violence* 64). Since the Holocaust returned its world to the chaos that preceded scapegoating, its violence eludes and overpowers speech. Elie Wiesel voices the helplessness of the voice before the Holocaust, the almost obligatory words for so many survivors and commentators before any other words may be said, when he wonders, "How does one describe the indescribable? How does one use restraint in re-creating the fall of mankind and the eclipse of the gods? And then, how can one be sure that the words, once uttered, will not betray, distort the message they bear?" (15). Like so many in Wiesel's fiction, Father Smith has virtually given up speaking because he has given up on speech. The question after the Holocaust is not "what can be said?" but "how can anything be said at all?" Silence seems like the only proper response to violence, especially violence of such heinousness and magnitude, for violence attacks the very order and distinctions that make speech possible.

Yet Father Smith does speak. Indeed, Father Smith must speak, for as Wiesel claims, "whosoever contributes to oblivion finishes the killer's work" (199). Not to speak is to expel and silence the Jews once again, in effect, to evacuate the sign that Hitler sought to eliminate. The Holocaust cries out for words. And so if the Nazis attempted to annihilate the sign, Father Smith proclaims the significance of the Jews. His conversations with More and his sustained recollections of pre- and postwar Germany do not just expose victimization but begin to reverse it. In an age when the word seems to bear nothing but its own necrosis, Father Smith's words resist being emptied because they witness to the kind of plenitude that the Holocaust sought to destroy.

Jabès's analogy between the beleaguered Jew and the beleaguered word does not tell the whole story for Father Smith. For if both are exiled and endangered, both also endure in their self-assertion. Berel Lang suggests how *The Book of Questions* needs to be questioned in precisely this way. He argues that just as at the heart of Jewish history there is "the singular desire of the Jew to exist, and to exist *as* Jew," there is in language "the way of affirmation, of securing a foothold where before there was none" (254, 257). Lang's objection echoes two concerns central to all of Percy's work. Percy's writings on semiotics have frequently described language in just such tenacious terms as Lang uses, and his fiction has long meditated on the Jew, wandering and abiding, as sign. In *The Thanatos Syndrome* both language and Jew come together under the auspices of the victim. Percy conceives of both language and Jews, signs and the victim underlying them, in terms of asserting and averring, of what he calls in "Naming and Being," "yes-saying" (*Signposts* 133). What Father Smith hears in the Jews is not privation but perdurance. Or as he contends, the Jews "are still here," and they "are a sign of God's presence which cannot be evacuated" (123). Different is Derrida, who celebrates *The Book of Questions* for singing of absence, absence, above all, of God, whose self-silencing and separation are necessary for the human word to be heard (*Writing and Difference* 67). For Percy, there is a sign that cannot be evacuated, and in *The Thanatos Syndrome* it is the signal victim, the Jew.

Although the Holocaust sought to eradicate the word and the people, it only confirmed the original import of the sign. To speak about such victimization is to speak about the very sign-ificance of the Jew. Amid the violence, amid the meaninglessness, the victimized signifier signified the victim six million times. In repeating the process of victimization by which signs came into being, the Holocaust made the Jews into the sign of signs for the twentieth century. Percy himself suggests this connection between Jews and signification when at the end of "Why Are You a Catholic?" he wonders, "Semitic? Semiotic?" (*Signposts* 314). Percy's essay claims that the Jews point the way out of "the enchanted mists of the mythical past, the Roman and Arthurian and Confederate past, lovely as it is. For, whatever else the Jews are, they are not mythical. Myths are stories which did not happen. But the Jews were there then and are here now" (*Signposts* 314). The Jews demythify what Percy associates with these heroic epochs—the unflinching warrior with hands on his broadsword, the crusading knight killing Jews en route to liberate the Holy Land, the gray-clad soldier who inherited both the stoic and chivalric legacy—because they expose the violence behind the hazy mystique of valor. All of these legendary ages, like the glorious Third Reich, are myths, "stories which did not happen," to the extent that their noble ideals and apologias hide what really did happen—the persecution of the innocent. As the heir in the novel to the Judeo-Christian tradition, Father Smith knows that Jews were elected, abide, and defy annihilation because they testify not to the God of victimizers sanctioned by myth but to the God of victims revealed by Moses and the prophets.

Speaking from a fire tower, like Ezekiel warning Israel from his watchtower (Ezek. 33:1–9), Father Smith typifies the way that biblical prophets might oppose the cult of sacred violence so vehemently that they became the victimized. Elijah was threatened by Jezebel; Jeremiah was flogged, imprisoned, and thrown into a cistern; John the Baptizer was executed. Indeed, Father Smith is almost too perfect a prophetic successor to these scapegoats. The loony old man has taken himself away from the shiny Fedville complex and restored plantations that house the world of Comeaux and Van Dorn. And he has secluded himself high above the wilderness of the pine forest, as if sentencing himself to the very expulsion that he criticizes in the Qualitarian Center and the whole death-plagued century. When one parishioner suggests that the latter-day stylite "could be doing vicarious penance for the awful state of the world," she glances at how Father Smith might be deliberately playing out the role of surrogate victim (113).

After More's first interview with Father Smith, Percy's psychiatrist is inclined to marginalize the priest even further by writing him off as mad. If More recommends that Smith be confined to a mental hospital, he will prove himself a worthy disciple of Bob Comeaux. The master doctor who is supervising More's probation models the psychiatry of violence that indiscriminately resorts to drugs or institutionalization as a way of suppressing all maladjustment. Comeaux would like More to help him eliminate Father Smith so that the wily doctor can silence the critic of his utopian New South and convert the priest's hospice into a private nursing home. Father Smith's retreat into the fire tower and into his memories of the past may seem like symptoms of the fugue state that unsettles so many of Percy's seekers,[18] but Dr. More's initial diagnosis is too facile if he thinks that the priest requires care in a secure facility. It overlooks Girard's claim that "many psychic catastrophes misunderstood by the psychoanalyst result from an inchoate, obstinate reaction against the violence and falsehood found in any human society" (*Violence* 177–78). Yet the doctor seems singularly disinterested in any of the priest's revelations about scapegoating. More grows from potentially victimizing Father Smith to taking a stand in behalf of victims only after his second interview at the fire tower, when the priest confesses how he came to make a similar conversion.

"Father Smith's Confession" and his subsequent "Footnote" take over the first-person narration of the novel much as Lawrence Langer has described Holocaust memory as forever destabilizing and disrupting the flow of chronological time for its witnesses (13–23). Just as the fragments of Father Smith's memories have been randomly breaking into More's consciousness and even into his dreams at Pantherburn, the priest's memories now break into the story proper. Although the doctor only pays restless attention to this seemingly aimless narrative intrusion, Father Smith actually tells a story parallel to More's own life, an autobiographical fragment meant to decenter and then recenter his ambivalent listener. For as the priest keeps his vigil in the fire tower, he speaks not just as a prophet but as a penitent. Father Smith performs the same spiritual exercise that Thomas Merton, the Trappist monk who might have been a model for Percy's secluded priest, recounts in "Fire Watch, July 4, 1952," his essay on patrolling Gethsemani Abbey at night to keep it safe from burning. As Merton travels from the cellar to the tower of the monastery, he realizes that "the fire watch is an examination of conscience in which your task as watchman suddenly appears in its true light: a pretext devised by God to isolate you, and to search your soul with lamps and questions, in the heart of darkness" (352).[19] Likewise searching himself in the fire tower, the penitent Father Smith reveals what made him change from desiring to be a Nazi double to demythologizing all forms of victimization.

"Father Smith's Confession" acknowledges how desire led to the baleful mimesis for which he needs to be shriven. It discloses how the young Simon Smith discovered early models for his desires when he and his father visited distant relatives in 1930s Germany. The youth had not found such mediation in his own parents—in the feckless romanticism of his abstracted father or in the Catholic piety of his vicious mother. Yet while vacationing in Germany, Smith was impressed by his host Dr. Hans Jäger, who seemed manly without being mean-spirited. Jäger and his professional circle were seen as demonstrating their humanity in debating whether euthanasia should be reserved for medical reasons or be allowed for social engineering. Their discussion was not purely academic, for more than 275,000 psychiatric patients—from the psychotic to the aged and unproductive—would eventually be victims of such state-sponsored death (Wertham 158). The teenager so admired the eminent and immensely cultured child psychiatrist that he considered imitating this model doctor by studying at Tübingen and going to medical school.

Smith found, however, an even more compelling model in the fascist cult of the doctor's younger son. Whereas Dr. Jäger scorned Hitler, Helmut committed himself to the twentieth-century sect that consecrated the Volk with violence. He had completed the Hitler Jugend and would soon start training to be an officer in the SS. Nazism is actually a political recrudescence of archaic religion; indeed, Robert Jay Lifton has appropriately compared the mass killings in Hitler's Germany to the ritualized murders of Aztec Mexico (484–85). If the ancient rites guaranteed cultural order through sacrifice, Nazism sought to enshrine a rabid nationalism through excluding whoever might adulterate the purity of the German race. Helmut became a disciple of Nazism, and Simon became a disciple of Helmut.

The young Smith desired what the fiercely dedicated Helmut desired. He sought devotion to a cause so absolute that he might die for it. Nazism made violence the sign of the sublime, for it glorified the shedding of blood—the blood of soldiers like Helmut, of victims like the Jews—to keep the bloodlines pure. The young Jäger ratified his cousin's spiritual blood kinship when he staged a parallel dedication rite for Simon on the very day that he himself completed his final "test of courage" at the Hitler Jugend. Claiming "I think I know you. We are comrades," Helmut entrusted his bayonet to his disciple and double "in a kind of ceremony." On its blade was engraved what might have been the shibboleth of old Dixie, "*Blut und Ehre.*" The pubescent Smith could barely resist such alluring hypermasculinity. He had become so completely Helmut's devotee that at the climax of his "Confession" the priest admits, "If I had been German not American, I would have joined him" (248).

When Father Smith reveals his early fascination with a Nazi model, Percy is not merely justifying the penitential title of this section. Rather, the novelist is conducting his own examination of conscience.[20] After his first year at the University of North Carolina, Percy visited Germany in the summer of 1934 as part of a student tour group led by his German professor. While staying with a family in Bonn, he was impressed by the fifteen-year-old son of the household, who was graduating from the Hitler Jugend and planning to enter the Schutzstaffel. The adolescent became the model for Helmut Jäger and perhaps nearly for the young American abroad as well. Percy found an ardor and energy in the early stages of National Socialism that were especially attractive. Jay Tolson suggests that Percy was captivated by Nazism because the movement did not simply dare death but seemed to desire it (*Pilgrim* 118–19). To the son and grandson of suicides, this dark love might have beckoned as the enticing obstacle, the ultimate mediator of transcendence, the skandalon. But while later convalescing from tuberculosis during World War II, Percy discovered an alternative to the thanatos syndrome that touched his own life and sickened Western culture. Much like Porter after her confrontation with the pale rider of the influenza epidemic, Percy was changed at heart. His readings in existential philosophy and fiction converted the death-haunted physician to a deeply reflective appreciation of being alive in every moment. And over the next decade his vocation as a Christian and a writer confirmed his choice to be an "ex-suicide" (*Signposts* 404). Although Father Smith's memories did not even appear in the first manuscript or typescript of the novel (Samway, "Two Conversations" 25), they actually form the pre-text for the entire book. For if a novel is made possible by its author's renunciation of mimetic desire, the priest's confession is a surrogate for Percy's own self-reckoning with the beguiling power of sacred violence.

More is ill-disposed to engage in such scrutiny as he listens to Father Smith's testimony in the fire tower. Instead, he responds clinically to the priest's confession of mimetic desire toward his Nazi cousin. He views his patient's unsettling memories as possible symptoms of temporal-lobe epilepsy rather than as signs of the thanatos syndrome, and he dismisses his wacky confidant's earlier infatuation with Helmut and Hitler as mere youthful folly. So, Father Smith appends a postscript that reveals how such imitation might have led to participating in mass murder. Although the priest's addendum is modestly entitled "Father Smith's Footnote" and begun just as More is ready to leave, it is no pedantic bit of marginalia. Rather, the unassuming supplement discloses not just the bloody consequences of Nazi marginalization but the sacrificial origins of the entire Third Reich. Girard argues that just as the supplement, for Derrida, is indispensable to the origin that rejects it, the victim constitutes the community that expelled the one who seemed merely extra ("Origins" 27–34). Father Smith's footnote brings together this fundamental trope of deconstruction and the founding truth of the culture of violence. The priest's adjunct narrative announces itself as if it were a somewhat inconsequential afterthought to his confession, a mere addition that extends what was already self-sufficient and self-contained. However, the codicil actually completes his earlier speech by divulging the logic of the supplement: scapegoating made Nazi Germany possible. Its distinctly minor standing is its message. Set apart, relegated to the subordinate position of an ancillary apparatus reached only by way of a superscript, rating no more attention as a source of information than a lowly appendage to the body of the priest's confession, the appendix cautions against setting aside what seems merely extraneous and insignificant. Since Percy's title for this auxiliary section treats the priest's speech as if it were writing, "Father Smith's Footnote" is the kind of unpretentious text that undermines all persecution texts from Guillaume de Machaut's *Judgment* to Hitler's *Mein Kampf.* This postscript records the single word that, post Auschwitz, must be written, the after-word by which all others that come afterward must be read. It is the word of the victim.

"Father Smith's Footnote" tells how Smith witnessed the mechanism for such exclusion and execution when as an army officer he participated in the liberation of Eglfing-Haar, the hospital where Dr. Jäger worked. Some two thousand adults were killed at Eglfing-Haar, mostly by starvation, yet the complete death toll was even higher. Smith recalls that a nurse showed him a room in the *Kinderhaus* where five or six times a month, doctors, usually Jäger, used drugs or gas to kill young patients who were deemed unacceptable.[21] The priest's memory of Eglfing-Haar could easily have compromised Percy's novel, for the destruction of the Jews has become so exploited in fiction and films that Elie Wiesel mourns how the Holocaust has lost some of its ability to provoke awe (200–201). However, "Father Smith's Footnote" does not empty the Holocaust the way Hitler tried to empty the sign that defied evacuation. Although Percy confronts the Holocaust more explicitly in *The Thanatos Syndrome* than in any of his previous novels, as Edward Dupuy shows (106–19), the novelist relies on an obliqueness that he had once foreseen as the only viable artistic strategy for writing about such genocide. In a 1979 letter to fiction writer and longtime friend Shelby Foote, Percy admired William Styron's audacity for facing the Holocaust so directly in *Sophie's Choice* but objected that "it can't be handled, that is, the dead weight and mystery of the horror can't be got hold of by esthetic categories—and when you try, bad things happen, both to the writer and the subject. It would take a Dostoevski to do it, and he would by the utmost guile, indirection and circumspection" (Tolson, ed., *Correspondence* 258). Percy's tact in presenting Father Smith's testimony on the Third Reich avoids the easy sensationalism and sentimentality that often flaws attempts to represent the Holocaust. Using such fictional reticence, Percy lets the death chamber in the children's hospital make a space for absence. The antiseptic room renders the enormity of the Holocaust through a minimalism that bespeaks what has been bereft. Its single decoration is a geranium in the window, a plant whose roots were in the sweet and sunny benevolence with which the doctors murdered their patients. The flower lingers there as a poignant sign of the life that has been lost.

Father Smith's memories of Germany before and after the war inspire him to warn More about the current victimization of Blue Boy. "Do you know where tenderness always leads?" he asks and then provides the startling answer, "To the gas chamber" (128).[22] O'Connor realized the same truth as Father Smith when in her introduction to *A Memoir of Mary Ann* she wrote of a "tenderness which, long since cut off from the person of Christ, is wrapped in theory. When tenderness is detached from the source of tenderness, its logical outcome is terror. It ends in forced-labor camps and in the fumes of the gas chamber" (*Mystery* 227). O'Connor and Percy understand that compassion must be rooted in a community of fellow-suffering.[23] If the tender-hearted regard the victim as merely other, if they cannot identify with a God who identifies with victims, then their compassion can easily degenerate into a benevolent passion for violence. Every surrogate murder depends on the sentimental lie that "it is expedient for us, that one man should die for the people, and that the whole nation perish not" (John 11:50). Theoretical compassion, like that of Jäger's or Comeaux and Van Dorn's, is the ultimate way of concealing such scapegoating because it justifies killing for the good of society under the pretense of killing for the good of the victim. The infirm and outcast are so scandalous that they are better off deadened by the medical establishment or just simply dead.

Having been a witness to the rise of Fascism and to the Holocaust, Father

Smith fears that the well-intentioned scientific humanism of Blue Boy marks the beginning of some future slaughter. The priest scans the forest from his watchtower because he knows that the fires of the Holocaust may burn again. The burnt offerings of Nazi Germany were a sacrifice to the violent god that humanity has continually made in its own bloody image. "Do you think we're different from the Germans?" Father Smith asks More, and he knows well the answer to his own question (256). Although Christianity has a long history of anti-Semitism that helped to make the Holocaust possible, Father Smith opposes such sacred violence and speaks out of a radical biblical faith. The priest enacts this scriptural concern for victims through his work at the hospice. Girard has traced the modern hospital to *l'Hotel-Dieu* in Paris, where the sick were received without prejudice. "Inventing the hospital," he claims, "meant dissociating for the very first time the idea of victim from all concrete ethnic, regional, or class identity" (*I See Satan* 167). Advocating for an endangered "house of God" in Feliciana, Father Smith lives out a Girardian faith in a God of victims.

Father Smith's compassion for the marginalized serves as an eventual example for More. "He's always been a role model for me," a clerical colleague says of Father Smith (110), but the overworked Father Placide, who cannot comprehend the reasons for the elderly priest's retreat into his fire tower, has no understanding of modeling beyond the inspirational examples purveyed by pop psychology. Father Smith's "Confession" and "Footnote" help More understand how the priest models the care for victims that the doctor must imitate as a disciple. Although the psychiatrist is at first only professionally interested in Father Smith, by the end of the priest's footnote, More asks questions about the fate of Jäger and his colleagues. He learns that many killed themselves, as if the murderers could only find fulfillment in some final version of Freud's thanatos. More's curiosity indicates how he is being drawn into an ongoing dialogue with Father Smith. Indeed, as John Desmond demonstrates, the two are already so bound together that images from the memories, reveries, and déjà vus of the one reappear in the consciousness of the other (*Walker Percy's Search for Community* 229). When More lets this psychic conversation deepen into a colloquy between soul mates, it will finally convince the doctor to take his own stand against the living death of his age.[24]

SCAPEGOATING NO MORE

Much as Father Smith in his fire tower must call on a fellow watcher to help determine the coordinates of the smoke that he might spy in the forest, More needs Father Smith as a semiotic reference point on the plague that has been spreading like fire down below. The priest helps the doctor to interpret the ominous signs of victimization that he has been noticing all around him. More finally takes action against the thanatos syndrome by opposing Van Dorn's academy of pedophiles and Comeaux's murderous Qualitarian Center. The sex and violence at these bastions of the new social order flout the kind of fundamental prohibitions that Girard views as developing to prevent another outbreak of mayhem (*Violence* 218–22). More's success at the end of the novel is that he is able to stop such victimization without using violence.

Founded "on the English model" (45), the school at Van Dorn's plantation imitates the Anglo-imitation of eighteenth-century southerners but perverts such mimicry to provide a lesson in the most deleterious kind of modeling. The headmaster's desire surpasses even Rayber's desire for a model student in *The Violent Bear It Away*. Van Dorn does not just impose a rigid program of academics and physical education to create a corps of young disciples; he uses heavy sodium to make these students so docile that they allow themselves to be sexually abused. When Dr. Lipscomb visits Belle Ame to look for signs of pedophilia, the students actually want to undergo the perineal examination and respond to it as if they were sexually aroused. Whereas Tarwater was outraged by the climactic rape in O'Connor's novel, More notices that the photos of the children being violated at Belle Ame show the victims with pleased looks. Their enjoyment reveals how Na-24 has lowered the resistance of youngsters to being molested by heightening their mimetic desire. Throughout childhood they have heard what Girard describes as a chorus of adult voices that invite, "'Imitate us!' 'Imitate me!' 'I bear the secret of life, of true being!'" (*Violence* 147). Blue Boy compels these boys and girls to comply. They drink the deadly water, watch adults model sexual positions, and learn their anatomy lessons only too well. Like the masochist who cooperates with victimization as a means to gaining the glory of the model and victimizer (*Deceit* 176–77), the young seek to live up to the alluring promise of vitality offered by their adult violators. In a circuit of mimetic and sexual desire, they copy their mentors and are themselves copied in pictures and on videos that document their exploitation for the later titillation of their models. When Sheriff Sharp finally sees the incriminating photos from Belle Ame, he declares, "We've had a regular epidemic of pictures like that all over the pa-ish," as if the thanatos syndrome had caused an outbreak of mimesis—both physical and photographic—to spread its infection across Feliciana (316).

Since such exploitation thrives on being undetected, the violent hide their use of the *pharmakon* by trying to pose as the *pharmakos*. They further the deprivation of signs, heard by Father Smith, by engaging in what Charles Sykes calls Victimspeak, the indignant language of moral superiority that the supposedly powerless use to gain power and to end all further conversation (15–18). Coach charges that the pictures of pedophilia that have been found at Belle Ame are a "setup." Mr. Brunette alleges that the photos are an attempt at blackmail or a practical joke. The self-righteous Comeaux later finds his ultimate exoneration by way of Plato's *Apology*: "Who was accused of this? Of corrupting the youth of Athens? You know who was accused of that" (329). As Derrida notes, Plato depicts Socrates as a *pharmakeus*, a beguiler or sorcerer, who became the *pharmakos* by drinking the *pharmakon*. At his death the sage and scandal of Athens lived up to the sacrificial holiday in the midst of which he was born, the celebration on the sixth day of the Thargelia when Athenians regularly purified the city through scapegoating (*Dissemination* 117–19, 134). Socrates accepted the hemlock, fully aware of its ambivalent power. The drink that would poison him was also a kind of cure that would free his soul for contemplation and immortality (*Dissemination* 126–27). When victimizers, like the agents of the thanatos syndrome, masquerade as victims like Socrates, they resort to the supreme strategy for hiding the violence that Girard and Derrida discover in Western culture: they conceal it by claiming to reveal it.

More liberates Belle Ame from the control of such victimizers. Although the harrowing of this hell might easily have turned into the kind of John Wayne shootout that More remembers from the movies, the doctor acts in the most unheroic fashion. Rather than desiring the divinity that violence so often signifies, More rejects such preeminence by continually striving to minimize the bloodshed at Belle Ame. There is no gentlemanly duel with Van Dorn that might ritualize murder with elaborate formalities. There is no charivari or lynch mob that once perpetuated scapegoating in the Old South (Wyatt-Brown 440–61). There is only the somewhat daft Uncle Hugh Bob to threaten the scourge of archaic justice. Cussing and gun-toting and knife-wielding, the would-be avenger is a throwback to the culture of violent southern manhood that Ted Ownby chronicles from the postbellum era to the 1920s. However, More works to restrain the wrath of this ornery old gunman. At Van Dorn's, he twice asks Hugh Bob to leave behind the double-barrel twelve-gauge Purdy that the aged vindicator has decided to bring against More's wishes. Whereas Hugh Bob is also inclined to use a gelding knife on the child abusers in the bloody belief that punishment should somehow mimic the crime, More favors no such violent reciprocity. Indeed, he only signals his weapon-carrying accomplice to graze Coach's ear when the instructor approaches the uncle with fists raised. And after Hugh Bob of his own accord peppers Mr. Brunette's backside with specks of rubber as he tries to escape, More cares for the pedophile's lacerated flesh. From Dr. Jäger to Dr. Comeaux, medicine has been allied with violence in the novel, but Dr. More tries to return to the founding principle of his profession—doing no harm.

More's refusal to seek retribution enables him to avoid the way zealots for the oppressed can easily imitate the oppressors and victimize the victimizers. In an age when signs seem to have lost their meaning, he understands the saving significance of *A Sign for Cain*, a book that Percy's introductory note to the novel hailed as "remarkable" (viii).[25] Frederic Wertham's study of the social and institutional causes of violence impressed Percy with its account of medical scapegoating in the Weimar Republic and Nazi Germany. *A Sign for Cain* emphasizes that the mark on the first murderer (Gen. 4:15) signifies how even the victimizer must be protected from society's impulse to respond to bloodshed by resorting to more bloodshed (Wertham 2). More honors that sign. Yet if he escapes the mimetic temptation of counterviolence, he also avoids the frequent criticism of nonviolence that its failure to resist oppression promotes collaboration with the oppressor. No indifferent bystander, More finally routs Van Dorn's academy by forcing the staff to drink the very *pharmakon* in molar concentration that had been given to the victimized students. The strategy may seem to turn the poison into the cure and punish the guilty by giving them a taste of their own medicine. However, More does not become like Van Dorn in opposing Van Dorn. Vergil makes clear More's rejection of violence when he confirms that the doctor is seeking "not punishment or revenge" (311) but a way to cause a sufficiently chaotic scene that when the sheriff arrives, he will not hesitate to arrest the pedophiles.

Whereas scapegoating restores the social order through violence, More's tomfoolery creates only comic disorder by throwing a monkey wrench into the workings of Belle Ame. The molar Na-24 accelerates the spread of imitative desire so that the staff regresses to the genus proverbial for mimesis. Although, at first, peace reigns after the apelike Van Dorn has asserted his standing over the other pongid "bachelors," rivalry eventually erupts out of the tendency toward "monkey see, monkey do." Girard explains that when two monkeys fight over a banana, the conflict results merely from the fact that one chose the fruit first, and the other sought it in imitation ("Discussion" 123). Such mimicry leads to violent monkey business at Belle Ame. In the struggle for dominance that Desmond Morris views as motivating aggression in all primates (146–47), the naked apes fight for primacy. Van Dorn bites Sharp's head when he feels that his authority is being challenged by Mrs. Cheney's mating overtures to the sheriff. In the ensuing chaos Mr. Brunette seems to ape Van Dorn's role by positioning himself to become the new patriarch. The monkeyshines are a farcical version of the sacrificial crisis that threatens to destabilize a community when mimetic antagonism runs amok. They even humorously restage the strife among primates that Girard imagines as climaxing in primordial victimization (*Things Hidden* 93–99). However, there is little danger of any scapegoating at Belle Ame, for the antics never escalate to the pitch of catastrophe. The pongid-like staff members have the instinctual brakes that are normally lacking in humans who resort to intraspecific violence, and More provides another check on the mischief by having Hugh Bob call the sheriff. The slapstick conflict is ended not by victimization but by the representative of the judicial system that evolved to prevent scapegoating from happening again (*Violence* 21–27). After More quells the mayhem by using candy bars to distract the faculty and staff of simians, Sheriff Sharp leads the pedophiles into his squad car.

Having closed down the ideal academy at Belle Ame, More brings an end, with even less ado, to the ideal state created by Blue Boy. The coup takes only a meeting with Bob Comeaux. In *The Republic* (books 3 and 10) Plato expelled imitative artists because he regarded their copies as untruthful and feared their power to lead citizens astray. Although More likewise opposes Comeaux as a purveyor of harmful mimesis, he does not seek to exclude his rival from the *polis* of his forever imperfect world. Once again More rejects the shoot-'em-up of the video age as he reasons, "Here's where movies and TV go wrong. You don't shoot X for what he did to Y, even though he deserves shooting. You allow X a way out so he can help Y" (332). So, More tries to foster collaboration rather than the mimetic cycle of retaliation, even if his scheming is never completely free from an aura of violence. While discussing the fate of Blue Boy, he plays a game of "tough cop and softy cop" with his friend Max, a familiar strategy from group therapy, to "stage mock warfare" (332, 333) on Comeaux. More's foe has a passion for argument, but throughout the novel the doctor has rejected the temptation to engage Comeaux in the kind of controversy that binds O'Connor's Tarwater and Rayber in ongoing verbal violence. While talking to Comeaux about closing down Blue Boy, More once again avoids becoming the polemicist's double. He even tries to get Comeaux on his side by resorting to some mild scapegoating of his own. More thinks, "blame Van Dorn for now" (333), as he proposes that St. Margaret's be reopened to care for the victims of Belle Ame. More finally gains what Father Smith has long desired even if his stated rationale is to redress the wrong perpetrated by Comeaux's partner in Blue Boy.

That unity-against-one always carries the risk that More will be ensnared in the sacrificial logic he exposes. Indeed, John Edward Hardy claims that Van Dorn's chronic regression to pongid behavior "might be considered equivalent to banishment into the wilderness" like that of the scapegoat, "until Tom, our vacillating Aaron, hits upon a plan for rescuing him" (244). Yet if More assumes the role of the arch-priest in Mosaic tradition, he shows rare restraint and compassion in dealing with these potential victims. He defeats Comeaux and Van Dorn more through wit than through violence and even finds a way to rehabilitate the apelike director of Belle Ame. More resorts to displacing blame as a momentary strategy, but Comeaux has a more tenacious commitment to scapegoating. After More eventually proposes that all terminal patients, AIDS sufferers, and candidates for pedeuthanasia from the Fedville Center should be transferred to Father Smith's hospice, Comeaux protests to Max, "He's talking about shooting down the entire Qualitarian program in this area" (334). The architect of this deadly health care can only understand such nonviolence in terms of violence. However, More's plan merely follows a tradition, dating back to Plato, of having poisoners make restitution. The *Laws* declares that anyone convicted of putting a *pharmakon* in the water supply should pay a fine and be held responsible for purifying the contaminated spring or reservoir (Derrida, *Dissemination* 152). Since Comeaux has filled the Feliciana waters with death, More gives him a chance to counter the thanatos syndrome and to call the scapegoat home.

Unlike the new mythical order that emerges after scapegoating, no grand and immediate regeneration follows More's nonviolent victory. Although Belle Ame and Blue Boy are closed, neither Comeaux nor Van Dorn ever overcomes the violence of the thanatos syndrome. Comeaux is invited to China to promote pedeuthanasia as a way of controlling the population. Van Dorn creates one more victim when he abandons Eve, the gorilla who helped him overcome regression to a pongid state by teaching him sign language. More still drinks too much, his marriage is still strained, and his patients still seem dazed. Although Percy's science fiction thriller trails off into a series of diffuse and fragmentary final sections, the anticlimax is appropriate to More's unspectacular rejection of salvific violence. Percy records no magical healing of a waste land but a prolonged convalescence from the thanatos syndrome.

Father Smith models the only way to recover good health when he reestablishes St. Margaret's as a haven for the *pharmakoi*. Believing in a God who cares for victims, the priest lives out the revelation of Jewish and Christian Scripture by his solicitude for all the outcasts. Sentenced to work at the hospice, the victimizers at Belle Ame tend to those who could easily have become victims. The Brunettes help Alzheimer's patients, Mrs. Cheney mothers a ward of malformed infants, and Coach heads a soccer team for LAV-positive children. As the staff from Belle Ame serve those already marked by their own mortality, the caretakers recover the humanity that had been deadened by the thanatos syndrome.

Through such ministry, the sinful get beyond the scapegoating ritual described in Leviticus by getting to the heart of the Day of Atonement. It is repentance. The story of Jonah is read during the afternoon service on this most sacred of Jewish days because it focuses on a would-be prophet who cannot repent of not really wanting others to repent. As Sandor Goodhart explains, Jonah would sacrifice the Ninevites to an exclusive conception of Judaism that is ultimately anti-Jewish (155). Father Smith's hospice provides a way for the penitent to reject the exclusions of the sacrificial mechanism. They send no goat to Azazel.

Such a countercultural ethic gets reaffirmed during Father Smith's last conversation with More. The priest and the doctor continue the dialogue, begun in the fire tower, about the century of thanatos. However, the conversation comes to focus on how to live amid so much death when the priest wonders about Mary's recent apparition in Medjugorje. Although Father Smith's fascination with the latest Marian vision risks making him seem a questionable mentor to the scientific More, the priest uses the tradition of folk piety to offer the doctor some final guidance. Father Smith is perplexed by "'one little item [that] has been largely overlooked. . . . Yet I think it highly significant'" (364): Mary appears without the apocalyptic iconography that since the Middle Ages has often been appropriated from the Book of Revelation and used to honor her as the Queen of Heaven. Mary warns about avoiding ultimate catastrophe, but she is not the woman clothed with the sun and standing over a serpent as portrayed in Apocalypse 12. Rather than being garbed in the semiotics of the last days, Mary signifies herself as "an ordinary-looking young red-cheeked Jewish girl" (365). She appears as one who might have been victimized by the Holocaust, and she wonders, according to Father Smith, how this century of death has happened: "The Turks killing two million Armenians, the Holocaust, Hitler killing most of the Jews in Europe, Stalin killing fifteen million Ukrainians, nuclear destruction unleashed, the final war apparently inevitable?" Although the priest uses mythical language to speak of Satan's reign over the age, he recognizes that the demonic is the power of human violence: "All he had to do was leave us alone. We did it." Mary's prescription to avoid ultimate catastrophe—"keep hope and have a loving heart and do not secretly wish for the death of others"— purifies tenderness of any murderous intent by prohibiting the covert desire for violence (365). To keep the world from ending is to renounce the killing that has been hidden since its foundation.

More takes Father Smith as a tentative model in working against this century of violence. The lapsed Catholic minimizes the significance of his occasionally attending Mass or assisting Father Smith at the liturgy, but More's participation indicates an ongoing reorientation toward the God who cares for victims. Indeed, at the end of the novel, when Father Smith sends More a cryptic invitation to serve in church on the Feast of the Epiphany, its signal words— "A Jewish girl, a visit from royalty. Gifts" (370)—connect the Christmastide celebration with the priest's earlier reflections on the sign that could not be eliminated despite the Holocaust. The feast of the gift-bearing kings from the Orient remembers how the son of a Jewish mother was made manifest to the world even as Herod was pursuing a murderous campaign to eliminate his supposed rival. And it shadows forth a time when Jesus would be victimized under a sign that would mockingly reveal him as the King of the Jews. Percy does not make clear how More will answer Father Smith's request to help at Mass, for the spiritual wandering of this would-be disciple is ever open-ended. Instead, the novel leaves More on a journey toward the day that signifies a revelation amid a victimization, indeed a revelation of the whole victimage mechanism.

Dr. More's care for the victims of the foremost syndrome of his time suggests that he seeks to follow Father Smith and live beyond the scapegoating of the thanatos syndrome. As More helps the priest in tending to those dying from AIDS, the sick and the well form a mutually supportive community of talkers and listeners: "We do little more than visit with them, these haggard young men, listen, speak openly, we to them, they to us, and we to each other in front of them, about them and about our own troubles, we being two old drunks and addled besides. They advise us about alcohol, diet, and suchlike. It seems to help them and us. At least they laugh at us" (363). The participants in this ministry find a therapeutic reciprocity in the semiotic bond that Percy studied and celebrated in all of his writing. This healing dialogue victimizes no signs and signifies no victims. The differences between "we" and "they," between "us" and "them," collapse in charity, for both patient and professional need help, give and get help, indeed get help by giving help. There is no mimetic strife, no unity against the excluded other, only a salutary mutuality of all those who are somewhere between life and death. After Father Smith decides to return to his fire tower, More must decide between joining a lucrative medical practice with Max or fostering such community by assuming the directorship of the hospice.

Although the novel never reveals More's decision, the issue confronts him with the Azazel convention once again. At the end of part I, More reflected that Hebrew and Canaanite faith viewed Azazel as "a demon who lived in the Syrian desert, a particularly barren region where even God's life-giving force was in short supply . . . a place of wantonness and freedom from God's commandments" (64). The thanatos syndrome created such a desert in More's Feliciana, where the waters ran with death, victims were regularly sent into the wilderness, and the most sacred laws were violated. More and Father Smith have begun to work toward a South where there are no more offerings for Azazel, no more offerings even for Yahweh, who, as Hosea (6:6) and Jesus (Matt. 9:13) recognized, desires mercy rather than sacrifice. If *The Thanatos Syndrome* ends with a predicament rather than with a definite resolution, perhaps the real decision about desire, violence, and divinity is not just More's alone.

NOTES

CHAPTER 1. THE HANGED MAN AT OLD SARDIS CHURCH

1. In addition to the articles from the *Atlanta Constitution* of July 6 and 7, 1933, about Norris Bendy, see Ginzburg's *100 Years of Lynching* 187, 197–98, and 207–8.

2. Recent work by Nisbett and Cohen indicates that the regional propensity for violence, noted by Redfield and Brearley, has persisted. For example, surveys of white male southerners show that they are more likely than their counterparts outside the region to favor violence to respond to insults, to discipline children, to protect self and home, and to maintain civil order. These attitudes toward violence are supported by laws that are more likely in the South than elsewhere in the country to allow force in defending one's self or property, to be lenient in prosecuting domestic violence, and to accept corporal punishment (Nisbett and Cohen 26–37, 60–69).

3. Hackney (909–19) reviews and critiques numerous theories about southern violence. For particular theories, see Jefferson (162) on slavery, Cash (192–93) on the frontier, McWhiney as well as Nisbett and Cohen (4–8) on Celtic belligerence, and Wyatt-Brown as well as Ayers (9–33) on honor. Arguing for the culture of honor as the continuing cause of violence in the South today, Nisbett and Cohen have demonstrated in laboratory experiments that southern students are more likely than northern ones to feel humiliated by an insult and to respond with aggression (41–55).

Many of the explanations for southern violence have been questioned. Nisbett and Cohen object to poverty as an explanation because rural southern counties with the same income as northern ones had significantly higher homicide rates (84–85). Ayers notes that positing slavery as the sole cause of southern violence does not account for the violence among the large majority of southerners who never owned slaves; nor does it account for the continuation of such violence after slavery ended (11). Nisbett and Cohen add that parts of the South with the greatest amount of slavery show the lowest homicide rates and that the West, which has homicide rates comparable to the South's, was not an area noted for slavery (85). Ayers contends that the frontier thesis does not explain why the frontiers of English colonies in Canada and Australia did not record the same high levels of violence as those in America (12).

Although Cason's temperature theory may seem fanciful, experimental psychologists have shown that moderately hot conditions intensified aggressive behavior in subjects; however, extremely hot conditions did not have the same effect (Siann 142). Brearley's study of homicide rates in the early twentieth century, however, leads him to object to the theory on the basis that the South had more homicides in December than in any other month (685). Nisbett and Cohen challenge the temperature hypothesis because statistics show a less than 20 percent increase in violent crime when the hottest quarter of the year in the South is compared to its three cooler ones. The difference is hardly large enough to explain why the South's homicide rate is so much greater than the North's (84).

4. Girard does not consider such biological explanations for violence as neurological dysfunction, hormonal influence, or genetic transmission. Although biological factors may explain aggressive behavior in some cases (hypoglycemia or limbic lesions, for example), they cannot account for more than a limited number of violent episodes (Siann 47).

5. See Wolfgang and Ferracuti 192–94 for how comparative biology has also challenged the instinctual theory of violence.

6. In "Violence, Difference, Sacrifice: A Conversation with René Girard," Girard emphasizes that mimetic desire can lead to heroism and altruism (Adams 24).

7. Although the relationship between obstacle and violence is not a direct and immediate one of stimulus and response, Girard does not consider under what circumstances this frustration may actually lead to aggression. Berkowitz (chaps. 2–4) may provide some answers when he suggests that violence is more likely to occur if the frustrated have a sense of their own power, do not fear reprisal, do not expect the obstruction, interpret the situation as threatening, have learned to respond with force, feel thwarted for long, frequent, or intense periods, have exhausted alternative ways to resolve the problem, will not violate internalized standards for moral action, and believe that their social group would accept the aggression.

8. Girard's work has been applied in such fields as theology (Alison; Williams, *The Bible, Violence and the Sacred*), scriptural studies (Schwager), psychology (Oughourlian), philosophy (Webb, McKenna), economics (Dumouchel and Dupuy), violence studies (Chidester, Bailie), and literary theory (Bandera, Goodhart). See, in particular, Barge's "René Girard's Categories of Scapegoats and Literature of the South" for an attempt to refine Girard's distinction between mythical and nonmythical scapegoats and then to locate those figures in southern literature.

9. Other criticism has been leveled against Girard. Kearney claims that Girard's critique of the hidden violence behind myths actually scapegoats myths, for it fails to recognize that myths may envision a transformed world (146). Hunsinger objects that Girard's reading of the Bible minimizes the importance of the Incarnation, atonement, and resurrection in favor of turning Jesus into a moral exemplar (28–29). Golsan suggests that Girard's combativeness in *The Scapegoat* makes it seem as if the author were succumbing to the very mimetic antagonism that he seeks to expose ("Sacrificial Violence and Evangelical Message" 176).

10. Montell uses the work of Wolfgang and Ferracuti to document how one small part of the South, four counties in Kentucky and Tennessee, deserves to be described as a "subculture of violence." Loftin and Hill argue that the Gastil-Hackney thesis depends on flawed statistical analysis; hence, culture seems more important than socioeconomic factors in causing southern violence.

11. Reed suggests the pervasiveness of violence in the South when he discusses its role in pop culture—country music songs about quarrels and killings, humor based on grotesque retaliation, and passion for blood sport (147–52).

12. Although most of the violence in the South has been traditionally perpetrated by men, women fostered aggression by expecting their children and husbands to defend the honorable cause and by

occasionally resorting to violence themselves. Women in the South even now are more likely than those in the North to commit murder, oppose gun control, and endorse violence in response to insults and in disciplining children (Nisbett and Cohen 86–88).

13. Schwartz discovers in Jewish Scripture a God of abundance much like Girard's nonviolent deity, but she faults biblical monotheism for the way its logic of scarcity promotes violence. Since the sacred writings of Judaism assume that plenitude always has its limits, they regularly sanction one over and against the other—one God, one brother (Abel, Jacob, Joseph), one nation, one gender. The result of such favoritism is that the opposite is excluded and eliminated. Whereas Schwartz identifies such ostracism with the God of Jewish Scripture, Girard tends to separate Yahweh from this victimization by emphasizing how humans project their violence onto God and how Israel gradually came to understand that violence was not sacred. See Alison, Bailie, Schwager, and Williams for attempts to extend Girard's reading of the Bible and to confront passages in Scripture that imagine a violent deity.

14. In *I See Satan Fall Like Lightning* Girard emphasizes how the Psalms give voice to the victim (116). And in *Job: The Victim of His People* he shows how the scapegoated hero defies the mimetic enticement of the crowd and imagines a God who defends the persecuted.

15. Although Girard has long criticized a sacrificial interpretation of Christianity, he has recently come to accept a qualified description of Jesus' death as a sacrifice: "Because Christ did what he did, grace filled the hearts of the disciples. One person did something for all the others, like Judah to save Benjamin in the Joseph story. Jesus alone acts as God would like all human beings to act. Jesus never yields an inch to mimetic pressure." The sacrifice of Jesus is not an offering to a violent deity but a gift of nonviolent love to a violent humanity. Girard has also come to agree with Raymund Schwager that Jesus is a "scapegoat for all—except now in reverse fashion, for theologically considered the initiative comes from God rather than simply from the human beings with their scapegoat mechanism" (Williams, "Anthropology of the Cross" 280).

16. Preachers on the frontier sometimes needed to take literally the injunction to "fight the good fight of faith" (1 Tim. 6:12) and cuff rowdy members of their congregations into appropriate church behavior. Peter Cartwright was a revivalist so well known for his pugilism that he was widely—but incorrectly—said to have thrashed Mike Fink (Bruce 112).

17. Roof claims that the synergy between religion and culture, described by Hill, has been undermined over the last forty years by religious pluralism, increasing numbers of the unchurched, privatization of religion, and the spread of new organizational structures (15–24).

18. Bandera has shown how Girard's insights on the biblical exposure of victimization may be applied to the history of modern literature. He argues that modern poetic fiction emerged in the Renaissance when Christianity's revelation of sacred violence inspired literature to become self-reflective. The result of this analysis was that it started to expose the sacrificial systems at work in culture. Such literature desacralized violence by exhibiting its human origins in mimetic conflict (29–30).

19. Turner's liminal art anticipates the borderland creations that Anzaldúa also envisions: "I see a hybridization of metaphor, different species of ideas popping up here, popping up there, full of variations and seeming contradictions . . . an assemblage, a montage, a beaded work with several leitmotifs and with a central core, now appearing, now disappearing in a crazy dance" (88). Anzaldúa's

own art is situated precisely along this shifting frontier. She emphasizes the connection between such an aesthetic and violence when she describes her writing as requiring "a blood sacrifice" because it demands the complete surrender of her life, especially that of her body (97).

CHAPTER 2. "GIVEN ONLY ME FOR MODEL"

1. See Stout, *Katherine Anne Porter* 171, for a discussion of Porter's self-presentation in photographs. Oughourlian comments on how mimetic desire drives the world of fashion in the three-way dialogue with Girard and Guy Lefort in *Things Hidden* (298, 300–301). At its extreme, such mimesis might lead to the fashion model as trauma victim, the star so self-obsessed yet self-dispossessed that she or he is one of the walking dead (Seltzer 271).

2. Some critics extend the scope of the "Miranda" stories to include ones in which a Miranda-like character appears. For example, Stout includes "Hacienda" and "Flowering Judas" in the group (*Strategies* 113); Nance considers "Theft" and "The Leaning Tower" as "implicit Miranda stories" (5). DeMouy expands the category further by considering Miranda "the implicit narrator of *Ship of Fools* and at least six other stories, including the most psychologically complex ones" (118). I discuss only those stories that specifically focus on the life and family of Miranda Rhea.

3. Such critics as Flanders (50–51), DeMouy (116–22), Stout (*Katherine Anne Porter* 192–95), and especially Fetterley have noted Miranda's search for a model but not in the context of Porter's concern with mimetic desire and antagonism.

4. See Unrue's "Porter's Sources and Influences" for a discussion of writers who inspired Porter.

5. Gretlund provides the most complete discussion of the manuscript that he cites as "The Man in the Tree." Stout notes how Porter's awareness of racial injustice in this unpublished story dramatically differed from her direct expression of racial bias in the unpublished essay "The Negro Question" (*Katherine Anne Porter* 136–39).

6. Although many readers have viewed Eliza's progressive challenge to the old order as completely salutary, Hendrick and Hendrick question the accuracy of her explanation about the tree frogs and recognize that her scientific approach has not answered all of Miranda's questions about life and death (50–51). Brinkmeyer discusses Eliza's tyranny, abstraction, and self-absorption (*Katherine Anne Porter's Artistic Development* 163–64).

7. For emphasis on the similarities between Sophia Jane and Nannie, see DeMouy (123), Gray (*Literature of Memory* 188), and Levy (154).

8. For a parallel to the relationship between Sophia Jane and Nannie, see "Mabelle and Carrie: 'Nothing . . . Separate from the Thought of Her,'" Mab Segrest's memoir of how her grandmother both befriended and oppressed her black servant Carrie Nichols (*My Mama's Dead Squirrel* 148–56).

9. If Amy took her brothers as models in desire, she would have followed traditional expectations for kinswomen of her time. Foxe-Genovese (211–12) discusses how brothers instructed their sisters in the proprieties of the Old South.

10. Clement suggests a rationale similar to Girard's for why women might try to suppress their menstruation. She notes that although women as wives and mothers are associated with cultural order, they are "allied as well with those natural disturbances, their regular periods, which are the epitome of paradox, order and disorder" (8).

11. Girard does not believe that coquetry is limited to women (*Things Hidden* 371); see also his discussion of dandyism in *Deceit* 162–64.

12. Stout sees in Miranda "the Byronic exaltation of the solitary rebellious spirit" (*Strategies of Reticence* 137). Brinkmeyer (*Katherine Anne Porter's Artistic Development* 173) and Nance (130) likewise view Miranda as suffering from romantic flaws at the novel's end.

13. Porter evokes the dual menace of war and epidemic so effectively that Crosby calls the novel "the most accurate depiction of American society in the fall of 1918 in literature. It synthesizes what is otherwise only obtainable by reading hundreds of pages of newspapers" (318).

14. See Booth, 274–77, for a discussion of how Porter creates sympathy for Miranda by forcing readers to identify with her narrative point of view.

15. Consistently described as "dull," "rotten," and "dreary" (*CS* 285, 289, 292), the theater in "Pale Horse, Pale Rider" has lost its salutary connection with its sacrificial origins. It no longer restores health to society by reenacting the catharsis of surrogate victimage.

16. Girard views the Songs of the Suffering Servant as an incomplete revelation of the scapegoat mechanism because God is still implicated in the sacrificial death of his servant (*Things Hidden* 226–27). In *Katherine Anne Porter* Stout notes how Porter saw herself as a victim and how she could victimize others (12).

17. In "Mourning and Melancholia," Freud might almost be describing Miranda when he observes how the struggle to sever attachments to the dead "can be so intense that a turning away from reality ensues, the object being clung to through the medium of a hallucinatory wish-psychosis" (154).

18. See Unrue (*Truth and Vision* 151–52), Levy (158–60), and Brinkmeyer (*Katherine Anne Porter's Artistic Development* 179–81) for other readings of the final scene in "The Grave" as an epiphany of art.

CHAPTER 3. "LIKE A BOULDER BLOCKING YOUR PATH"

1. Porter clearly understands the attraction and repulsion of the skandalon, for she explores its ambivalent power in "Noon Wine," the short novel that she placed between "Old Mortality" and "Pale Horse, Pale Rider" when the three were published in 1939. O'Connor liked "Noon Wine" more than any of Porter's other stories (*Habit* 485) and wrote her own variation on the short novel in "The Displaced Person."

2. Asals and Desmond have also read O'Connor by way of Girard, but neither focuses on the central importance of scandal. In "Differentiation, Violence, and the Displaced Person" Asals views Mr. Guizac in "The Displaced Person" as the scapegoat that is sacrificed to restore order on Mrs. McIntyre's farm. In "Violence and the Christian Mystery" Desmond emphasizes how O'Connor resembles the prophets in exposing sacred violence in *The Violent Bear It Away*.

3. Wood also views *The Violent Bear It Away* as rejecting the belief that heaven is seized by force. He maintains that Tarwater ultimately receives God's kingdom as a generous gift of grace (105–6). O'Connor never gave much consideration to the titular verse from Matthew until she read that it was a favorite of the Eastern fathers. O'Connor wrote to Betty Hester in mid-1957 that she was uncertain about *The Violent Bear It Away* as the novel's title. She viewed the title as implying, "You have to push as hard as the age that pushes against you" to get the kingdom of heaven. By the time that O'Connor finished the book, she thought the title the best part of the novel (*Habit* 229, 382).

4. Giannone (*Flannery O'Connor: Hermit Novelist* 145–47, 154) views the master-disciple relationship between Mason and Tarwater as exemplifying the tradition of desert spirituality. Such asceticism finds its model in the lives of Elijah, Elisha, and other prophets.

5. Tarwater is not as magnanimous as Moses, who rebuked Joshua when he complained about a similar rivalry for the spirit of God: "Enviest thou for my sake? would God that all the Lord's people were prophets" (Num. 11:29).

6. As McMullen notes, O'Connor's habit of referring to both Mason and Rayber as "uncle" as well as her use of ambiguous pronoun antecedents make the family members seem only more alike (13). Perhaps O'Connor is too successful in blurring the distinction: Walter Sullivan objects that the characters are "too much alike" (25).

7. For two of the best discussions of love in *The Violent Bear It Away*, readers should consult Giannone's *Flannery O'Connor and the Mystery of Love* (115–53) and Srigley's *Flannery O'Connor's Sacramental Art* (91–133).

8. See Howells (61–64) for a summary of the theories about child abuse that have been proposed by M. Fraser, W. Kraemer, and R. Gordon. Girard suggests a mimetic basis for pedophilia in "Narcissism: The Freudian Myth Demythified by Proust." He discusses how Marcel in Proust's *Within a Budding Grove* is attracted to a group of adolescent girls because of their autonomy and self-sufficiency. They model what he desires for himself (366–67).

9. See, for example, Asals, *Flannery O'Connor* 139–40; Brinkmeyer, *Art and Vision* 129; Desmond, *Risen Sons* 90–92; Kilcourse 40–42; Muller 92; Ragen 3; Stephens 5; Walters 101.

10. McMullen imagines O'Connor's God as "a wrathful, Old Testament Yahweh who victimizes the weak and considers 'unnaturalness' noble" (40).

11. Stephens regards O'Connor as wreaking havoc on the self-satisfied infidels in her fiction and senses that she was tempted "to punish and outrage her rationalist readers" (5, 42).

12. See Asals, *Flannery O'Connor* 124–59; Brinkmeyer, *Art and Vision* 189–93; Humphries 95–111; and Kessler 19–49 for especially insightful discussions of O'Connor's fictional violence. Baumgaertner suggests why O'Connor's violence may be so shocking: "We encounter violence daily, but most often at a distance. O'Connor counteracts the desensitizing effect of remote violence by forcing it upon us in a form we cannot escape" (18).

13. Scullin's "Transforming Violence in O'Connor's *The Violent Bear It Away*" provides a nuanced understanding of the relationship between grace and violence in the novel.

14. Several critics have attempted to formulate O'Connor's aesthetics in terms that look beyond its obvious use of violence. Scott argues that O'Connor recorded so relentlessly the desacralized world of her time in the hope that the portrayal of modern negations would lead to a rediscovery of wonder and mystery ("Flannery O'Connor's Testimony"). Desmond views O'Connor as crafting her fiction so that the reader, like many of her characters, may grow toward the prophetic narrative consciousness which orders the story. "Symbol, character, and action all operate to create an encounter with mystery for the reader, an encounter with a world that is open-ended, full of possibility, and free" (*Risen Sons* 105). Gordon shows how William Lynch's view of art as incarnational in *Christ and Apollo* influenced O'Connor's aesthetics, especially in her use of a Hopkins-like lyricism in "The River" (137–52).

15. Tarwater's glimpse of this heavenly meal reveals how his life and the gospels have become co-

extensive. In *The Poetics of Revelation* Culbertson describes this kind of confluence when she writes, "To *hear* the Gospel text is to have heard the Gospel in one's own history, to have read one's own text, and thus to recognize in the Gospel one's own story named anew" (183).

16. Commenting on the martyr as witness, Kristeva suggests the connection between speech and suffering that will take its toll on Tarwater the prophet: "Speech addressed to the other, not sinful speech but the speech of faith, is pain; this is what locates the act of *true communication,* the act of avowal, within the register of persecution and victimization. Communication brings my most intimate subjectivity into being for the other; and this act of judgment and supreme freedom, if it authenticates me, also delivers me over to death" (*Powers of Horror* 129).

CHAPTER 4. MCCARTHY'S ENFANT TERRIBLE

1. Although McCarthy mentions in a rare interview that he was influenced by Faulkner and that he esteems Dostoevsky and Melville (Woodward 31), O'Connor also seems to be in the background of his fiction, especially in its startling brutality and spiritual wastelands. Parrish argues that both O'Connor's and McCarthy's fiction professes a belief in violence as the sacred (26–27, 32). However, Cawelti notes that whereas characters in O'Connor's fiction always have the possibility of discovering transcendence, the wanderers in McCarthy's novels discover only horror and death in a godless world (166–67, 174).

2. Readers differ about the vision at the center of McCarthy's fiction. Bell has argued that McCarthy's fiction shows an "antimetaphysical bias" (2) and is largely nihilistic in mood. Marius believes that the only meaning in McCarthy's fiction lies in the choice to continue living (15). Coles locates McCarthy's religious sensibility in his quest for what is significant in life ("The Stranger" 90). Arnold claims that McCarthy's fiction believes in "the need for moral order" and always holds forth "the possibility of grace and redemption" ("Naming, Knowing and Nothingness" 31). See also Arnold's "Blood and Grace" and "The Mosaic of McCarthy's Fiction" for similar challenges to nihilistic readings of McCarthy's fiction.

3. Commenting on the sense of divine power and transcendence that Vietnam veterans reported feeling during a frenzy of killing, Rhodes observes that "to be like a god is to escape, at least momentarily, human contingency; no wonder berserk, malefic violence feels ecstatic" (308).

4. Parrish reads O'Connor's and McCarthy's fiction by way of Bloom's work on American gnosticism.

5. Grammar discusses how Ballard tries to defend and re-create the timeless world of the pastoral tradition (26–27).

6. Ballard demonstrates "the power of indifference" that Dworkin views as leading to "contempt for the body one is using such that one body can stand in for another without personality; this is the dynamic of mass death, body piled on body, each body breached, antisex, antieroticism, antihumanity, antiwoman, antifemale" (232).

7. Seltzer argues that sexual homicide results from the assailant's radical sense of having a merely generic identity. So, the killer asserts self-difference through a violent affirmation of sexual difference (144). Dworkin likewise claims that men who feel debased "need to degrade women, so that the struggle to subordinate women becomes a basic struggle for male identity as such" (302). Mur-

dering a woman, in effect, is a gendered form of scapegoating, which ends a mimetic crisis in the self rather than in society. The killing reestablishes the difference between self and other as the difference between male and female.

8. In "The Evolution of the Dead Girlfriend Motif in *Outer Dark* and *Child of God*" Sullivan discusses how McCarthy follows Poe in conjoining mortality and sexuality.

9. Ballard illustrates Messerschmidt's argument that men may act out a cultural ideal of masculinity through crime (*Masculinities and Crime* 86).

10. In "Cormac McCarthy and the Text of *Jouissance*" Sullivan analyzes how McCarthy's fiction provides textual pleasure by discomforting the reader.

11. Brutalization, such as the kind that Ballard has suffered, plays a significant role in creating violent criminals. Feeling enraged, humiliated, and powerless, the victim may decide to use serious force if provoked. But to become an ultraviolent criminal, the victim must move beyond even performing such violence to what Lonnie Athens calls virulency. Once the aggressor has been heartened by committing earlier violent acts, he or she may resolve to attack with little or no provocation at all (see Rhodes 126–35, 68–74).

12. Arnold observes how Ballard is positioned to be the surrogate victim: "He is created by those around him, a necessary figure of the community, the scapegoat that embodies their weird alienation and stoked violence but also their terrible sadness, their potential nothingness" ("Naming, Knowing, and Nothingness" 40).

13. McKenna aptly describes the bond between monsters like Ballard and the community: "When they threaten us, they are nothing but the form violence takes in its indifference to difference, the form our own violence takes when we disown it. When vanquished, they are surrogates for the victim, the form violence takes when we sacralize it, the form the victim takes when its destruction reconciles the community" (198).

14. Girard suggests how not even scapegoating provides a lasting and decisive solution to violence when he discusses Jesus's exorcism at Gerasa in Mark 5 and Matthew 8: "As it degenerates ritual loses its precision. The expulsion is not permanent or absolute, and the scapegoat—the possessed—returns to the city between crises. Everything blends, nothing ever ends" (*Scapegoat* 175).

CHAPTER 5. NO MORE FOR AZAZEL

1. *The Thanatos Syndrome* seems to take place in the sunny world of postmodern southern fiction, as Fred Hobson describes it: cheerful, cluttered with pop cultural references, unburdened by a tragic past. However, the novel's awareness of slavery, recognition of guilt, critical stance toward society, and philosophical depth also make it indebted to a tradition that Hobson notes in the Southern Renascence (1–10).

2. Percy makes the Azazel convention central to the structure of *The Thanatos Syndrome*. More notes the role of Azazel in Hebrew and Islamic myth at the end of part I, hears Father Smith speak about scapegoating at the ends of parts II and III, and frees the victims of Belle Ame at the end of part IV.

3. Despite writing a thriller, Percy shows a certain lackadaisical approach to his plotting in *The Thanatos Syndrome*. As Hardy has demonstrated, details about time and place are muddled in the novel (225–33). Moreover, the mystery is not really that difficult to figure out, and More's account

of it lacks the compelling intensity of the narration in Percy's more suspenseful *Lancelot*. These lapses in storytelling as well as the power of the crucial scenes with Father Smith suggest that Percy was sometimes more interested in cultural critique than in his flagging narrative.

4. McKenna has rigorously demonstrated how Girard and Derrida circle around the victim as if they were a pair of rival brothers. Whereas Derrida has been more concerned with the rejection that takes place in systems of signs, Girard has traced this exclusion in history and the process of cultural formation (McKenna 12–13). Girard views deconstruction as driven by an *esprit de contradiction*, but he considers such contrariness the "content" of the literature that fascinates him ("Theory and Its Terrors" 252–53). See Quinlan (196–98) for a discussion of Percy's criticism of deconstruction.

5. Other commentators have noted how Plato obscures the role of violence in culture. Bailie contends that whereas Heraclitus recognized violence as both destructive and generative, Plato began a tradition of philosophical evasion and ambiguity by emphasizing ideas over the blinding realities (241–54). Bandera claims that Plato sought to deny the ambivalence of sacred violence by imagining a philosophical system founded on stability and precise differentiation (50–63).

6. The imitation of TV and film models abounds in *The Thanatos Syndrome*. For example, Sheriff Vernon "Cooter" Sharp wears a western costume and keeps his revolver "on a low-slung belt like Matt Dillon" (315).

7. It is appropriate that More, like Freud, is preoccupied with World War I. In *Deceit, Desire, and the Novel*, Girard observes how Proust "shows that the First World War, far from being the last of the national conflicts, is the first of the great abstract conflicts of the twentieth century. . . . He shows us double mediation crossing national frontiers and acquiring the planetary dimensions which we find that it has today" (224).

8. Melberg notes another contradiction in Plato's position: the philosopher creates a fictional world by mimesis, but in this world, mimesis is condemned (12).

9. Showalter notes that different forms of hysteria have found expression in different genres of pop fiction. Multiple personality disorders call for the confession, disclosures of satanic ritual abuses gravitate toward horror stories, and tales of alien abductions find a home in science fiction (11). The thriller is suited to hysterias about mass contamination because its typical plot about stopping evil agents can give fictional form to a plague of anxiety about covert toxic substances.

10. Appelfeld claims that the utter inhumanity of the Holocaust can make the actual historical event seem "as if it no longer belongs to the experience of our generation, but to mythology" (92).

11. More's eventual escape from Lucy's fondness for things past typifies Percy's attitude to the burdensome example of southern history. O'Gorman argues that Percy, like O'Connor, reveals "the final irrelevance of the past in comparison with the present moment, which, properly seen, eternally bears witness to the goodness and radical newness of an ever-ongoing Creation" (95). O'Gorman demonstrates how O'Connor's and Percy's attentiveness to the mysterious present has influenced the work of later southern writers.

12. Kearney contends that Girard's sacrificial reading of myth actually scapegoats myth. He charges Girard with distrusting the imagination behind myths and with misrepresenting all myths as concerned with victimization. See Golsan's *René Girard and Myth* (119–20) for a discussion of Kearney's critique.

13. Hirsch in *The Deconstruction of Literature: Criticism after Auschwitz* hears this evacuation of signs as being continued by much contemporary literary theory. He charges that such theory has

failed to deal adequately with the Holocaust because its commitment to the evasions of language and the elusiveness of the truth has made it incapable of confronting history. What gets lost is the victim.

14. Unconcerned with mediating the God of victims, Nazis may have victimized Jews out of mimetic rivalry. As Vidal-Naquet claims, Aryanism was actually "a perverse imitation of the *image* of the Jewish people," for members of the master race sought to eliminate their rivals as the chosen people and to establish themselves as the racial destiny of history (123).

15. Bailie discusses the logos of violence in Heraclitus and Heidegger (241–43, 254–58). Hirsch contends that Heidegger's logos of violence underwrote Nazism (80–96).

16. Like Girard's victim, Derrida's Theuth is the principle of substitution. He is the writing that takes the place of speech, the moon that takes the place of the sun (*Dissemination* 89).

17. Whereas Gans in *The Origin of Language* speculates that the aborted gesture of appropriation might have been directed toward a slain animal, Girard places the murder of a human victim at the beginning of sign use. Girard's primordial scene is more compelling. His surrogate victim would be both more desirable and more forbidden because it had just brought an end to the crisis that threatened to destroy the group. The scapegoat might thus have had greater power to inspire the blocked gesture of acquisition, which Gans views as the beginning of all designation. The slain animal seems like a later displacement of the role that the scapegoat might have earlier played.

18. In *Percyscapes* Rudnicki discusses the physical, psychological, and semiotic dislocation of the fugue state in the work of Percy and other modern southern writers.

19. Elie deftly explores the relationships among Percy, Merton, O'Connor, and Dorothy Day. For the Percy-Merton connection, see, in particular, 77, 96, 458. Merton was offered the chance to live in a fire tower at the edge of his Kentucky monastery, but he chose a tool shed in the woods as his hermitage (220).

20. Details on Percy's 1934 visit to Germany are found in *More Conversations* (Lawson and Kramer, eds., 79, 104, 189–90) and in the biographies by Samway (74–8) and Tolson (114–19). Allen argues that Percy was attracted to the intensely masculine world of Nazism as a reaction to the weaknesses he perceived in his father's suicide and his adopted father's ambivalent sexuality (194–96).

21. In addition to killing victims with drugs, the Nazi death industry regularly put the *pharmakos* to the service of the *pharmakon*. Prisoners from concentration camps were used, for example, in experiments to test the effects of new drugs and of poison gas (Wertham 148).

22. Wertham links Germany's early experiments with euthanasia to its later sponsorship of genocide. He notes that some of the gas chambers used in psychiatric hospitals and some of the experts who selected patients for death were subsequently employed in the concentration camps (182).

23. Desmond discusses the response of O'Connor and Percy to the Holocaust in *At the Crossroads* 94–101. Crowley demonstrates how Percy's last novel uses images, themes, and techniques reminiscent of O'Connor's fiction.

24. Kobre shows how, in a novel where speech is contaminated by the thanatos syndrome, More and Father Smith enter into a genuine relationship of Bakhtinian dialogue (208–14).

25. Whereas Wertham views the mark on Cain as a sign of protection for victimizers, Girard interprets God's command immediately beforehand as indicating how culture develops in the aftermath of primal violence. God declares that if Cain is killed, sevenfold vengeance will be taken on the killer; he thus seeks to deter murder by threatening the violent reprisal that culture has institutionalized (*I See Satan* 83–85).

WORKS CITED

Abbott, Shirley. *Womenfolks: Growing Up Down South.* New York: Ticknor and Fields, 1983.

Adams, Rebecca. "Violence, Difference, Sacrifice: A Conversation with René Girard." *Religion and Literature* 25.2 (1993): 11–33.

Alison, James. *Raising Abel: The Recovery of the Eschatological Imagination.* New York: Crossroad, 1996.

Allen, William Rodney. "'Father Smith's Confession' in *The Thanatos Syndrome.*" In Gretlund and Westarp, eds. 189–98.

Amato, Joseph A. *Victims and Values: A History and a Theory of Suffering.* New York: Praeger, 1990.

Anzaldúa, Gloria. *Borderlands / La Frontera: The New Mestiza.* 2nd ed. San Francisco: Aunt Lute Books, 1999.

Appelfeld, Aharon. "After the Holocaust." In Lang, ed. 83–92.

Arnold, Edwin T. "Blood and Grace: The Fiction of Cormac McCarthy." *Commonweal* 4 Nov. 1994, pp. 11+.

———. "The Mosaic of McCarthy's Fiction." In Hall and Wallach, eds. 17–23.

———. "Naming, Knowing, and Nothingness: McCarthy's Moral Parables." *Southern Quarterly* 30.4 (1992): 31–50.

Asals, Frederick. "Differentiation, Violence, and the Displaced Person." *Flannery O'Connor Bulletin* 13 (1984): 1–14.

———. *Flannery O' Connor: The Imagination of Extremity.* Athens: University of Georgia Press, 1982.

Ayers, Edward L. *Vengeance and Justice: Crime and Punishment in the Nineteenth-Century American South.* New York: Oxford University Press, 1984.

Bacon, Jon Lance. *Flannery O'Connor and Cold War Culture.* Cambridge: Cambridge University Press, 1993.

Bailey, Kenneth K. *Southern White Protestantism in the Twentieth Century.* New York: Harper and Row, 1964.

Bailie, Gil. *Violence Unveiled: Humanity at the Crossroads.* New York: Crossroad, 1995.

Bandera, Cesáreo. *The Sacred Game: The Role of the Sacred in the Genesis of Modern Literary Fiction.* University Park: Pennsylvania State University Press, 1991.

Bandura, Albert. *Aggression: A Social Learning Analysis.* Englewood Cliffs, N.J.: Prentice-Hall, 1973.

Barge, Laura. "René Girard's Categories of Scapegoats and Literature of the South." *Christianity and Literature* 50.2 (Winter 2001): 247–68.

Barker, Francis. *The Culture of Violence: Essays on Tragedy and History.* Chicago: University of Chicago Press, 1993.

Bartlett, Andrew. "From Voyeurism to Archaeology: Cormac McCarthy's *Child of God*." *Southern Literary Journal* 24 (Fall 1992): 3–15.

Bataille, Georges. *Erotism: Death and Sensuality.* Trans. Mary Dalwood. San Francisco: City Lights Books, 1986.

Baumgaertner, Jill Peláez. *Flannery O'Connor: A Proper Scaring.* Rev. ed. Chicago: Cornerstone Press, 1999.

Bell, Vereen M. *The Achievement of Cormac McCarthy.* Baton Rouge: Louisiana State University Press, 1988.

Benjamin, Walter. *Illuminations.* Ed. Hannah Arendt. Trans. Harry Zohn. New York: Schocken, 1969.

———. *Reflections: Essays, Aphorisms, Autobiographical Writings.* Ed. Peter Demetz. Trans. Edmund Jephcott. New York: Harcourt Brace Jovanovich, 1978.

Berger, John. *Ways of Seeing.* New York: British Broadcasting Corporation and Penguin Books, 1972.

Berkowitz, Leonard. *Aggression: A Social Psychological Analysis.* New York: McGraw-Hill, 1962.

Black, Joel. *The Aesthetics of Murder: A Study in Romantic Literature and Contemporary Culture.* Baltimore: Johns Hopkins University Press, 1991.

Bleikasten, André. "The Heresy of Flannery O'Connor." In *Les Americanistes: New French Criticism on Modern American Fiction,* ed. Ira D. Johnson and Christiane Johnson. Port Washington, N.Y.: Kennikat, 1978. 53–70.

Bloom, Harold. *The American Religion: The Emergence of the Post-Christian Nation.* New York: Simon and Schuster, 1992.

———. "Introduction." *Flannery O'Connor.* Ed. Harold Bloom. New York: Chelsea House, 1986. 1–8.

Booth, Wayne C. *The Rhetoric of Fiction.* Chicago: University of Chicago Press, 1961.

Brearley, H. C. "The Pattern of Violence." In Couch, ed. 678–92.

Brinkmeyer, Robert H., Jr. *The Art and Vision of Flannery O'Connor.* Baton Rouge: Louisiana State University Press, 1989.

———. *Katherine Anne Porter's Artistic Development: Primitivism, Traditionalism, and Totalitarianism.* Baton Rouge: Louisiana State University Press, 1993.

Brooks, Cleanth. "On 'The Grave.'" In *Katherine Anne Porter: A Critical Symposium,* ed. Lodwick Hartley and George Core. Athens: University of Georgia Press, 1969. 115–19.

Brooks, Gwendolyn. *Selected Poems*. New York: Harper Perennial, 1999.

Brown, Richard Maxwell. *Strain of Violence: Historical Studies of American Violence and Vigilantism*. New York: Oxford University Press, 1975.

Broyard, Anatole. *Aroused by Books*. New York: Random House, 1974.

Bruce, Dickson D., Jr. *Violence and Culture in the Antebellum South*. Austin: University of Texas Press, 1979.

Burke, Kenneth. *The Philosophy of Literary Form: Studies in Symbolic Action*. 1941. rev. ed. New York: Vintage Books, 1957.

Burkert, Walter. *Homo Necans: The Anthropology of Ancient Greek Sacrificial Ritual and Myth*. Trans. Peter Bing. Berkeley: University of California Press, 1983.

Butler, Judith. *Gender Trouble: Feminism and the Subversion of Identity*. New York: Routledge, 1990.

———. "Imitation and Gender Insubordination." In *The Second Wave: A Reader in Feminist Theory*, ed. Linda Nicholson. New York: Routledge, 1997. 300–315.

Butz, A. R. *The Hoax of the Twentieth Century*. Richmond [Eng.]: Historical Review Press, [1975].

Cash, W. J. *The Mind of the South*. New York: Alfred A. Knopf, 1941.

Cason, Clarence. *90° in the Shade*. Chapel Hill: University of North Carolina Press, 1935.

Cawelti, John G. "Cormac McCarthy: Restless Seekers." In *Southern Writers at Century's End*, ed. Jeffrey J. Folks and James A. Perkins. Lexington: University Press of Kentucky, 1997. 164–76.

Chidester, David. *Shots in the Streets: Violence and Religion in South Africa*. Boston: Beacon Press, 1991.

Clement, Catherine. "The Guilty One." *The Newly Born Woman*. Hélène Cixous and Catherine Clement. Trans. Betsy Wing. Theory and History of Literature, Vol. 24. Minneapolis: University of Minnesota Press, 1986. 1–59.

Coles, Robert. "The Stranger." [Review of *Child of God*, by Cormac McCarthy]. *New Yorker* 50 (26 Aug. 1974): 87–90.

Couch, W. T. *Culture in the South*. Chapel Hill: University of North Carolina Press, 1935.

Crosby, Alfred W. *Epidemic and Peace, 1918*. Westport, Conn.: Greenwood Press, 1976.

Crowley, Sue Mitchell. "*The Thanatos Syndrome*: Walker Percy's Tribute to Flannery O'Connor." In Gretlund and Westarp, eds. 225–37.

Culbertson, Diana. *The Poetics of Revelation: Recognition and the Narrative Tradition*. Studies in American Biblical Hermeneutics. Macon, Ga.: Mercer University Press, 1989.

Dawidowicz, Lucy S. "Introduction: On Studying Holocaust Documents." In *A Holocaust Reader*, ed. Lucy S. Dawidowicz. New York: Behrman House, 1976. 1–21.

De León, Arnoldo. *They Called Them Greasers: Anglo Attitudes toward Mexicans in Texas, 1821–1900*. Austin: University of Texas Press, 1983.

DeMouy, Jane Krause. *Katherine Anne Porter's Women: The Eye of Her Fiction*. Austin: University of Texas Press, 1983.

Derrida, Jacques. *Dissemination*. Trans. Barbara Johnson. Chicago: University of Chicago Press, 1981.

———. *Writing and Difference*. Trans. and intro. Alan Bass. Chicago: University of Chicago Press, 1978.

Desmond, John F. *At the Crossroads: Ethical and Religious Themes in the Writings of Walker Percy*. Troy, N.Y.: Whitston Publishing, 1997.

———. *Risen Sons: Flannery O'Connor's Vision of History*. Athens: University of Georgia Press, 1987.

———. "Violence and the Christian Mystery: A Way to Read Flannery O'Connor." *Literature and Belief* 17.1–2 (1997): 129–47.

———. *Walker Percy's Search for Community*. Athens: University of Georgia Press, 2004.

Dickens, Charles. *American Notes*. 1842. New York: St. Martin's Press, 1985.

Dinnerstein, Leonard. *The Leo Frank Case*. New York: Columbia University Press, 1968.

Donaldson, Susan V. "Gender, Race, and Allen Tate's Profession of Letters in the South." In *Haunted Bodies: Gender and Southern Texts*, ed. Anne Goodwyn Jones and Susan V. Donaldson. Charlottesville: University Press of Virginia, 1997. 492–518.

Douglas, Mary. *Purity and Danger: An Analysis of Concepts of Pollution and Taboo*. New York: Praeger, 1966.

Dumouchel, Paul, and Jean-Pierre Dupuy. *L'Enfer Des Choses: René Girard et La Logique de L'Économie*. Paris: Editions du Seul, 1979.

Dupuy, Edward J. *Autobiography in Walker Percy: Repetition, Recovery, and Redemption*. Baton Rouge: Louisiana State University Press, 1996.

Dworkin, Andrea. *Scapegoat: The Jews, Israel, and Women's Liberation*. New York: Free Press, 2000.

Eco, Umberto. *The Limits of Interpretation*. Bloomington: Indiana University Press, 1990.

Eighmy, John Lee. *Churches in Cultural Captivity: A History of the Social Attitudes of Southern Baptists*. Knoxville: University of Tennessee Press, 1972.

Eliade, Mircea. *Myth and Reality*. Trans. Willard R. Trask. New York: Harper, 1963.

Elie, Paul. *The Life You Save May Be Your Own: An American Pilgrimage: Flannery O'Connor, Thomas Merton, Walker Percy, Dorothy Day*. New York: Farrar, Straus, and Giroux, 2003.

Eliot, T. S. *The Complete Poems and Plays, 1909–1950*. New York: Harcourt, 1971.

Faley, Roland J. "Leviticus." In *The Jerome Biblical Commentary*, ed. Raymond E. Brown, Joseph A. Fitzmyer, and Roland E. Murphy. Englewood Cliffs, N.J.: Prentice-Hall, 1968. 67–85.

Faulkner, William. *Absalom, Absalom!* New York: Vintage Books, 1986.

Fetterley, Judith. "The Struggle for Authenticity: Growing Up Female in *The Old Order*." *Kate Chopin Newsletter* 2 (1976): 11–19.

Flanders, Jane. "Katherine Anne Porter and the Ordeal of Southern Womanhood." *Southern Literary Journal* 9 (Fall 1976): 47–60.

Fox-Genovese, Elizabeth. *Within the Plantation Household: Black and White Women of the Old South.* Chapel Hill: University of North Carolina Press, 1988.

Freire, Paulo. *Pedagogy of the Oppressed.* New revised 20th-anniversary edition. Trans. Myra Bergman Ramos. New York: Continuum, 1993.

Freud, Sigmund. *Beyond the Pleasure Principle.* 1920. Trans. and ed. James Strachey. New York: Liveright Publishing, 1961.

———. *Civilization and Its Discontents.* 1930. Trans. and ed. James Strachey. New York: Norton, 1962.

———. "Mourning and Melancholia." *Collected Papers.* Vol. 4. New York: Basic Books, 1959. 152–70.

Friedman, Melvin J., and Lewis A. Lawson, eds. *The Art and Mind of Flannery O'Connor.* 2nd ed. New York: Fordham University Press, 1977.

Frohock, W. M. *The Novel of Violence in America.* 2nd ed. Dallas: Southern Methodist University Press, 1957.

Gans, Eric. *The Origin of Language: A Formal Theory of Representation.* Berkeley: University of California Press, 1981.

Gastil, Raymond D. "Homicide and a Regional Culture of Violence." *American Sociological Review* 36 (1971): 412–27.

Genovese, Eugene D. *Roll, Jordan, Roll: The World the Slaves Made.* New York: Vintage Books, 1976.

Giannone, Richard. *Flannery O'Connor, Hermit Novelist.* Urbana and Chicago: University of Illinois Press, 2000.

———. *Flannery O'Connor and the Mystery of Love.* Urbana and Chicago: University of Illinois Press, 1989.

Gilligan, James. *Violence: Reflections on a National Epidemic.* New York: Vintage Books, 1996.

Ginzburg, Ralph, ed. *100 Years of Lynching.* Baltimore: Black Classic Press, 1988.

Girard, René. *Deceit, Desire, and the Novel: Self and Other in Literary Structure.* Trans. Yvonne Freccero. Baltimore: Johns Hopkins University Press, 1966.

———. "Discussion." In Hammerton-Kelly, ed., 106–45, 206–35.

———. "Generative Scapegoating." In Hammerton-Kelly, ed., 73–105.

———. *I See Satan Fall Like Lightning.* Trans. James G. Williams. Maryknoll, N.Y.: Orbis Books, 2001..

———. *Job: The Victim of His People.* Trans. Yvonne Freccero. Stanford: Stanford University Press, 1987.

———. "Narcissism: The Freudian Myth Demythified by Proust." In *Literature and Psychoanalysis,* ed. Edith Kurzweil and William Phillips. New York: Columbia University Press, 1983. 363–77.

———. "Origins: A View from the Literature." In *Understanding Origins: Contemporary Views on the Origin of Life, Mind, and Society,* ed. Francisco J. Varela and Jean-Pierre Dupuy. Boston: Kluwer Academic, 1992. 27–42.

———. *The Scapegoat*. Trans. Yvonne Freccero. Baltimore: Johns Hopkins University Press, 1986.

———. *A Theater of Envy*. Oxford: Oxford University Press, 1991.

———. "Theory and Its Terrors." In *The Limits of Theory*, ed. and intro. Thomas M. Kavanagh. Stanford: Stanford University Press, 1989. 225–54.

———. *Things Hidden since the Foundation of the World*. Trans. Stephen Bann and Michael Metteer. Stanford: Stanford University Press, 1987.

———. *"To Double Business Bound": Essays on Literature, Mimesis, and Anthropology*. Baltimore: Johns Hopkins University Press, 1978.

———. *Violence and the Sacred*. Trans. Patrick Gregory. Baltimore: Johns Hopkins University Press, 1977.

Givner, Joan. *Katherine Anne Porter: A Life*. New York: Simon and Schuster, 1982.

———, ed. *Katherine Anne Porter: Conversations*. Jackson: University Press of Mississippi, 1987.

Golsan, Richard J. *René Girard and Myth: An Introduction*. 1993. New York: Routledge, 2002.

———. "Sacrificial Violence and Evangelical Message: René Girard's *Le Bouc émissaire*." *Helios* 11.2 (1984): 167–78.

Goodhart, Sandor. *Sacrificing Commentary: Reading the End of Literature*. Baltimore: Johns Hopkins University Press, 1996.

Gordon, Sarah. *Flannery O'Connor: The Obedient Imagination*. Athens: University of Georgia Press, 2000.

Gossett, Louise Y. *Violence in Recent Southern Fiction*. Durham, N.C.: Duke University Press, 1965.

Graham, Don. "A Southern Writer in Texas: Porter and the Texas Literary Tradition." In Machann and Clark, eds. 58–71.

Grammar, John M. "A Thing against Which Time Will Not Prevail: Pastoral and History in Cormac McCarthy's South." *Southern Quarterly* 30.4 (Summer 1992): 19–30.

Gray, Richard. *The Literature of Memory: Modern Writers of the American South*. Baltimore: Johns Hopkins University Press, 1977.

———. *Southern Aberrations: Writers of the American South and the Problems of Regionalism*. Baton Rouge: Louisiana State University Press, 2000.

Gretlund, Jan Nordby. "'The Man in the Tree': Katherine Anne Porter's Unfinished Lynching Story." *Southern Quarterly* 31.3 (1993): 7–16.

Gretlund, Jan Nordby, and Karl-Heinz Westarp, eds. *Walker Percy: Novelist and Philosopher*. Jackson: University Press of Mississippi, 1991.

Grosz, Elizabeth. "Intolerable Ambiguity: Freaks as/at the Limit." In *Freakery: Cultural Spectacles of the Extraordinary Body*, ed. Rosemarie Garland Thompson. New York: New York University Press, 1996. 55–66.

Hackney, Sheldon. "Southern Violence." *American Historical Review* 74 (1969): 906–25.

Hall, Wade, and Rick Wallach, eds. *Sacred Violence: A Reader's Companion to Cormac McCarthy.* El Paso: Texas Western Press, 1995.

Hammerton-Kelly, Robert G., ed. *Violent Origins: Walter Burkert, René Girard, and Jonathan Z. Smith on Ritual Killing and Cultural Formation.* Stanford: Stanford University Press, 1987.

Hardy, John Edward. *The Fiction of Walker Percy.* Urbana: University of Illinois Press, 1987.

Harris, Trudier. *Exorcising Blackness: Historical and Literary Lynching and Burning Rituals.* Bloomington: Indiana University Press, 1984.

Hatty, Suzanne E. *Masculinities, Violence, and Culture.* Thousand Oaks, Calif.: Sage, 2000.

Hawkes, John. "Flannery O'Connor's Devil." *Sewanee Review* 70 (1962): 395–402.

Hegel, G. W. F. *The Phenomenology of Mind.* Trans. and intro. J. B. Baillie. New York: Harper Torchbooks, 1967.

Hendin, Josephine. *The World of Flannery O'Connor.* Bloomington: Indiana University Press, 1970.

Hendrick, Willene, and George Hendrick. *Katherine Anne Porter.* Rev. ed. Boston: Twayne/G. K. Hall, 1988.

Hill, Samuel S., Jr. *The South and the North in American Religion.* Athens: University of Georgia Press, 1980.

Hirsch, David H. *The Deconstruction of Literature: Criticism after Auschwitz.* Hanover, N.H.: Brown University Press/University Press of New England, 1991.

Hobbes, Thomas. *Leviathan.* Ed. and intro. Francis B. Randall. New York: Washington Square Press, 1964.

Hobson, Fred. *The Southern Writer in the Postmodern World.* Mercer University Lamar Memorial Lectures No. 33. Athens: University of Georgia Press, 1991.

Hobson, Linda Whitney. *Understanding Percy.* Columbia: University of South Carolina Press, 1988.

Holifield, E. Brooks. *The Gentlemen Theologians: American Theology in Southern Culture 1795–1860.* Durham, N.C.: Duke University Press, 1978.

Howells, Kevin. "Adult Sexual Interest in Children: Considerations Relevant to Theories of Aetiology." In *Adult Sexual Interest in Children,* ed. Mark Cook and Kevin Howells. New York: Academic, 1981. 55–94.

Hudgins, Andrew. *After the Lost War: A Narrative.* Boston: Houghton Mifflin, 1988.

Huizinga, J. *The Waning of the Middle Ages.* 1924. London: Edward Arnold, 1955.

Humphries, Jefferson. *The Otherness Within: Gnostic Readings in Marcel Proust, Flannery O'Connor, and François Villon.* Baton Rouge: Louisiana State University Press, 1983.

Hunsinger, George. *Disruptive Grace: Studies in the Theology of Karl Barth.* Grand Rapids, Mich.: Eerdmans, 2000.

Hurston, Zora Neale. "The First One." In *Black Female Playwrights: An Anthology of Plays before 1950*, ed. Kathy A. Perkins. Bloomington: Indiana University Press, 1989. 80–88.

Jabès, Edmond. *The Book of Questions.* Trans. Rosmarie Waldrop. Middletown, Conn.: Wesleyan University Press, 1978.

Jacobson, B. S. *Meditations on the Torah: Topical Discourses on the Weekly Portions in the Light of the Commentaries.* Tel Aviv: Sinai Publishing, 1956.

Jefferson, Thomas. *Notes on the State of Virginia.* Ed. and intro. William Peden. Chapel Hill: University of North Carolina Press, 1955.

Jelinek, Estelle C. "Introduction: Women's Autobiography and the Male Tradition." In *Women's Autobiography: Essays in Criticism,* ed. Estelle C. Jelinek. Bloomington: Indiana University Press, 1980. 1–20.

Jones, Anne Goodwyn. *Tomorrow Is Another Day: The Woman Writer in the South, 1859–1936.* Baton Rouge: Louisiana State University Press, 1981.

Kearney, Richard. *Poetics of Modernity: Toward a Hermeneutic Imagination.* Atlantic Highlands, N.J.: Humanities Press, 1995.

Kennedy, David M. *Over Here: The First World War and American Society.* New York: Oxford University Press, 1980.

Kessler, Edward. *Flannery O'Connor and the Language of Apocalypse.* Princeton: Princeton University Press, 1986.

Kilcourse, George A., Jr. *Flannery O'Connor's Religious Imagination: A World with Everything Off Balance.* New York: Paulist Press, 2001.

Kobre, Michael. *Walker Percy's Voices.* Athens: University of Georgia Press, 2000.

Kreyling, Michael. *Inventing Southern Literature.* Jackson: University Press of Mississippi, 1998.

Kristeva, Julia. *Powers of Horror: An Essay on Abjection.* Trans. Leon S. Roudiez. New York: Columbia University Press, 1982.

Lang, Berel. "Writing-the-Holocaust: Jabès and the Measure of History." In Lang, ed. 245–60.

Lang, Berel, ed. *Writing and the Holocaust.* New York: Holmes and Meier, 1988.

Langer, Lawrence L. *Admitting the Holocaust: Collected Essays.* New York: Oxford University Press, 1995.

Lawrence, D. H. *Studies in Classic American Literature.* 1923. New York: Penguin, 1977.

Lawson, Lewis A., and Victor A. Kramer, eds. *More Conversations with Walker Percy.* Jackson: University Press of Mississippi, 1993.

Levy, Helen Fiddyment. *Fiction of the Home Place: Jewett, Cather, Glasgow, Porter, Welty, and Naylor.* Jackson: University Press of Mississippi, 1992.

Lifton, Robert Jay. *The Nazi Doctors: Medical Killing and the Psychology of Genocide.* New York: Basic Books, 1986.

Loftin, Colin, and Robert H. Hill. "Regional Subculture and Homicide: An Examination of the Gastil-Hackney Thesis." *American Sociological Review* 39 (1974): 714–24.

Lorenz, Konrad. *On Aggression.* Trans. Marjorie Kerr Wilson. New York: Harcourt, 1966.

Lytle, Andrew. "The Hind Tit." In Twelve Southerners, *I'll Take My Stand.* 201–45.

Machann, Clinton, and William Bedford Clark, eds. *Katherine Anne Porter and Texas: An Uneasy Relationship.* College Station: Texas A&M University Press, 1990.

Marius, Richard. "*Suttree* as Window into the Soul of Cormac McCarthy." In Hall and Wallach, eds. 1–15.

Matthews, Donald G. *Religion in the Old South.* Chicago: University of Chicago Press, 1977.

———. "The Southern Rite of Human Sacrifice." Parts I—III. *Journal of Southern Religion* 3 (2000). 11 August 2004. <http://jsr.as.wvu.edu/matthews.htm>.

Mauriac, François. *The Stumbling Block.* New York: Philosophical Library, 1952.

McKenna, Andrew J. *Violence and Difference: Girard, Derrida, and Deconstruction.* Urbana: University of Illinois Press, 1992.

McLoughlin, William G. *Revivals, Awakenings, and Reform: An Essay on Religion and Social Change in America, 1607–1977.* Chicago: University of Chicago Press, 1978.

McMullen, Joanne Halleran. *Writing against God: Language as Message in the Literature of Flannery O'Connor.* Macon, Ga.: Mercer University Press, 1996.

McWhiney, Grady. *Cracker Culture: Celtic Ways in the Old South.* Tuscaloosa: University of Alabama Press, 1988.

McWhiney, Grady, and Perry D. Jamieson. *Attack and Die: Civil War Military Tactics and the Southern Heritage.* University, Ala.: University of Alabama Press, 1982.

Melberg, Arne. *Theories of Mimesis.* Cambridge: Cambridge University Press, 1995.

Merton, Thomas. *The Sign of Jonas.* New York: Harcourt, Brace, 1953.

Messerschmidt, James W. *Masculinities and Crime: Critique and Reconceptualization of Theory.* Landham, Md.: Rowman and Littlefield, 1993.

———. "Men Victimizing Men: The Case of Lynching, 1865–1900." In *Masculinities and Violence,* ed. Lee H. Bowker. Thousand Oaks, Calif.: Sage, 1998. 125–51.

Moi, Toril. "The Missing Mother: The Oedipal Rivalries of René Girard." *Diacritics* 12.1 (1982): 21–31.

Montell, William Lynwood. *Killings: Folk Justice in the Upper South.* Lexington: University Press of Kentucky, 1986.

Morris, Desmond. *The Naked Ape: A Zoologist's Study of the Human Animal.* New York: McGraw-Hill, 1967.

Morrison, Toni. *Playing in the Dark: Whiteness and the Literary Imagination.* New York: Vintage Books, 1993.

Muller, Gilbert H. *Nightmares and Visions: Flannery O'Connor and the Catholic Grotesque.* Athens: University of Georgia Press, 1972.

Nance, William L. *Katherine Anne Porter and the Art of Rejection.* Chapel Hill: University of North Carolina Press, 1963.

"Negro Is Lynched For Slaying Trucker." *Atlanta Constitution,* July 6, 1933, p. 10.

Nelli, Humbert. *The Business of Crime: Italians and Syndicate Crime in the United States.* New York: Oxford University Press, 1976.

Nisbett, Richard E., and Dov Cohen. *Culture of Honor: The Psychology of Violence in the South.* Boulder, Colo.: Westview Press, 1996.

O'Connor, Flannery. *The Habit of Being: Letters of Flannery O'Connor.* Ed. Sally Fitzgerald. New York: Farrar, Straus, and Giroux, 1979.

———. *Mystery and Manners: Occasional Prose.* Ed. Sally and Robert Fitzgerald. New York: Farrar, Straus, and Giroux, 1969.

———. *The Violent Bear It Away.* In *Three by Flannery O'Connor.* New York: Signet, 1983. 121–267.

O'Gorman, Farrell. *Peculiar Crossroads: Flannery O'Connor, Walker Percy, and Catholic Vision in Postwar Southern Fiction.* Baton Rouge: Louisiana State University Press, 2004.

Olmsted, Frederick Law. *The Slave States.* 1856. Ed. and intro. Harvey Wish. New York: Capricorn Books, 1959.

Oughourlian, Jean-Michel. *The Puppet of Desire: The Psychology of Hysteria, Possession, and Hypnosis.* Trans. and intro. Eugene Webb. Stanford: Stanford University Press, 1991.

Ownby, Ted. *Subduing Satan: Religion, Recreation, and Manhood in the Rural South, 1865–1920.* Chapel Hill: University of North Carolina Press, 1990.

Parrish, Tim. "The Killer Wears the Halo: Cormac McCarthy, Flannery O'Connor, and the American Religion." In Hall and Wallach, eds. 25–39.

Patterson, Orlando. *Rituals of Blood: Consequences of Slavery in Two American Centuries.* Washington, D.C.: Civitas/Counterpoint, 1998.

———. *Slavery and Social Death: A Comparative Study.* Cambridge: Harvard University Press, 1982.

Percy, Walker. *Lancelot.* New York: Farrar, Straus, and Giroux, 1977.

———. *The Message in the Bottle: How Queer Man Is, How Queer Language Is, and What One Has to Do with the Other.* New York: Farrar, Straus, and Giroux, 1975.

———. *The Second Coming.* New York: Farrar, Straus, and Giroux, 1980.

———. *Signposts in a Strange Land.* Ed. and intro. Patrick Samway. New York: Farrar, Straus, and Giroux, 1991.

———. *The Thanatos Syndrome.* New York: Farrar, Straus, and Giroux, 1987.

Peterson, Thomas Virgil. *Ham and Japheth: The Mythic World of Whites in the Antebellum South.* Metuchen, N.J.: Scarecrow Press and American Theological Library Association, 1978.

"Picnic and Sporting Events to Feature Atlanta's July 4." *Atlanta Constitution,* July 4, 1933, p. 1.

Plato. *Phaedrus.* Trans. W. C. Helmbold and W. G. Rabinowitz. Indianapolis: Bobbs-Merrill Educational Publishing, 1956.

———. *The Republic.* Trans. Benjamin Jowett. Norwalk, Conn.: Heritage Press, 1972.

Porter, Katherine Anne. *The Collected Essays and Occasional Writings of Katherine Anne Porter.* New York: Delacorte Press, 1970.

———. *The Collected Stories of Katherine Anne Porter.* New York: Harvest/Harcourt Brace, 1979.

———. *Letters of Katherine Anne Porter.* Ed. and intro. Isabel Bayley. New York: Atlantic Monthly Press, 1990.

Poteat, Edwin McNeill, Jr. "Religion in the South." In Couch, ed. 248–69.

Price, Reynolds. *Clear Pictures: First Loves, First Guides.* New York: Atheneum, 1989.

Pridgen, Allen. *Walker Percy's Sacramental Landscapes: The Search in the Desert.* Selinsgrove: Susquehanna University Press, 2000.

Prown, Katherine Hemple. *Revising Flannery O'Connor: Southern Literary Culture and the Problem of Female Authorship.* Charlottesville: University Press of Virginia, 2001.

Quinlan, Kieran. *Walker Percy: The Last Catholic Novelist.* Baton Rouge: Louisiana State University Press, 1996.

Raboteau, Albert J. *Slave Religion: The "Invisible Institution" in the Antebellum South.* New York: Oxford University Press, 1978.

Ragen, Brian Abel. *A Wreck on the Road to Damascus: Innocence, Guilt, and Conversion in Flannery O'Connor.* Chicago: Loyola University Press, 1989.

Ransom, John Crowe. *God without Thunder: An Unorthodox Defense of Orthodoxy.* 1930. Hamden, Conn.: Archon Books, 1965.

Rassinier, Paul. *Debunking the Genocide Myth: A Study of the Nazi Concentration Camps and the Alleged Extermination of European Jewry.* Trans. Adam Robbins. Torrance, Calif.: Institute for Historical Review, 1978.

Redfield, H. V. *Homicide, North and South.* 1880. Columbus: Ohio State University Press, 2000.

Reed, John Shelton. *One South: An Ethnic Approach to Regional Culture.* Baton Rouge: Louisiana State University Press, 1982.

Rhodes, Richard. *Why They Kill: The Discoveries of a Maverick Criminologist.* New York: Vintage Books, 2000.

Roland, Charles P. *The Improbable Era: The South since World War II.* Lexington: University Press of Kentucky, 1975.

Roof, Wade Clark. "Southern Protestantism: New Challenges, New Possibilities." In *The Changing Shape of Protestantism in the South,* ed. Marion D. Aldridge and Kevin Lewis. Macon, Ga.: Mercer University Press, 1996. 11–27.

Rudnicki, Robert W. *Percyscapes: The Fugue State in Twentieth-Century Southern Fiction.* Baton Rouge: Louisiana State University Press, 1999.

Samway, Patrick, S. J. "An Interview with Walker Percy." In Lawson and Kramer, eds. 127–33.

———. "Two Conversations in Walker Percy's *The Thanatos Syndrome:* Text and Context." In Gretlund and Westarp, eds. 24–32.

———. *Walker Percy: A Life.* New York: Farrar, Straus, and Giroux, 1997.

Scaduto, Anthony. *Scapegoat: The Lonesome Death of Bruno Richard Hauptmann.* New York: Putnam, 1976.

Schwager, Raymund. *Must There Be Scapegoats? Violence and Redemption in the Bible.* Trans. Maria L. Assad. San Francisco: Harper and Row, 1987.

Schwartz, Regina M. *The Curse of Cain: The Violent Legacy of Monotheism.* Chicago: University of Chicago Press, 1997.

Scott, Anne Firor. *The Southern Lady: From Pedestal to Politics, 1830–1930.* Chicago: University of Chicago Press, 1970.

Scott, Nathan A., Jr. "Flannery O'Connor's Testimony: The Pressure of Glory." In Friedman and Lawson, eds. 138–56.

Scott, Sir Walter. *Old Mortality.* Ed. Andrew Lang. Boston: Dana Estes, 1893.

Scullin, Kathleen. "Transforming Violence in O'Connor's *The Violent Bear It Away.*" In *Wagering on Transcendence: The Search for Meaning in Literature,* ed. Phyllis Carey. Kansas City: Sheed and Ward, 1997. 206–29.

Scullin-Esser, Kathleen. "Connecting the Self with What Is Outside the Self in *The Thanatos Syndrome.*" *Renascence* 40.2 (1987): 67–76.

Sedgwick, Eve Kosofsky. *Between Men: English Literature and Male Homosocial Desire.* New York: Columbia University Press, 1985.

Segrest, Mab. *My Mama's Dead Squirrel: Lesbian Essays on Southern Culture.* Ithaca, N.Y.: Firebrand Books, 1985.

Seidel, Kathryn Lee. *The Southern Belle in the American Novel.* Tampa: University of South Florida Press, 1985.

Seltzer, Mark. *Serial Killers: Death and Life in America's Wound Culture.* New York: Routledge, 1998.

Serres, Michel. *Hermes: Literature, Science, Philosophy.* Ed. Josue V. Harari and David F. Bell. Baltimore: Johns Hopkins University Press, 1982.

Sessions, Gene A. "Myth, Mormonism, and Murder in the South." *South Atlantic Quarterly* 75 (September 1976): 212–25.

Showalter, Elaine. *Hystories: Hysterical Epidemics and Modern Culture.* New York: Columbia University Press, 1997.

Siann, Gerda. *Accounting for Aggression: Perspectives on Aggression and Violence.* Boston: Allen and Unwin, 1985.

Simpson, Lewis P. *The Dispossessed Garden: Pastoral and History in Southern Literature.* Baton Rouge: Louisiana State University Press, 1983.

Slotkin, Richard. *Regeneration through Violence: The Mythology of the American Frontier, 1600–1860.* Middletown, Conn.: Wesleyan University Press, 1973.

Sontag, Susan. *Illness as Metaphor.* New York: Farrar, Straus, and Giroux, 1977.

Srigley, Susan. *Flannery O'Connor's Sacramental Art.* Notre Dame, Ind.: University of Notre Dame Press, 2004.

"State Joins in Probe of Lynching of Negro." *Atlanta Constitution,* July 7, 1933, p. 12.

Steiner, George. *Real Presences.* Chicago: University of Chicago Press, 1989.

Stephens, Martha. *The Question of Flannery O'Connor.* Baton Rouge: Louisiana State University Press, 1973.

Stout, Janis P. *Katherine Anne Porter: A Sense of the Times.* Charlottesville: University Press of Virginia, 1995.

———. *Strategies of Reticence: Silence and Meaning in the Works of Jane Austen, Willa Cather, Katherine Anne Porter, and Joan Didion.* Charlottesville: University Press of Virginia, 1990.

Stowe, Steven M. *Intimacy and Power in the Old South: Ritual in the Lives of the Planters.* Baltimore: Johns Hopkins University Press, 1987.

Sullivan, Nell. "Cormac McCarthy and the Text of *Jouissance.*" In Hall and Wallach, eds. 115–23.

———. "The Evolution of the Dead Girlfriend Motif in *Outer Dark* and *Child of God.*" In *Myth, Legend, Dust: Critical Responses to Cormac McCarthy,* ed. Rick Wallach. Manchester, England: Manchester University Press, 2000. 68–77.

Sullivan, Walter. *A Requiem for the Renascence: The State of Fiction in the Modern South.* Mercer University Lamar Memorial Lectures, No. 18. Athens: University of Georgia Press, 1976.

Sykes, Charles J. *A Nation of Victims: The Decay of the American Character.* New York: St. Martin's, 1992.

Tate, Allen. *Collected Essays.* Denver: Alan Swallow, 1959.

———. *Collected Poems 1919–1976.* Baton Rouge: Louisiana State University Press, 1989.

———. "Remarks on the Southern Religion." In Twelve Southerners, *I'll Take My Stand.* 155–75.

Thompson, Edgar T. "The South's Two Cultures." In *Religion and the Solid South,* ed. Samuel S. Hill, Jr. Nashville: Abingdon Press, 1972. 24–56.

Tolson, Jay. *Pilgrim in the Ruins: A Life of Walker Percy.* New York: Simon and Schuster, 1992.

Tolson, Jay, ed. *The Correspondence of Shelby Foote and Walker Percy.* New York: Double Take/Norton, 1997.

Turner, Victor. *From Ritual to Theatre: The Human Seriousness of Play.* New York: PAJ Publications, 1982.

Twain, Mark. *Life on the Mississippi.* New York: Signet Classic/New American Library, 1961.

———. "The United States of Lyncherdom." In *The Portable Mark Twain,* ed. Bernard De Voto. New York: Viking Press, 1968. 584–93.

Twelve Southerners. *I'll Take My Stand: The South and the Agrarian Tradition.* 1930. Baton Rouge: Louisiana State University Press, 1983.

Unrue, Darlene Harbour. "Porter's Sources and Influences." In Machann and Clark, eds. 102–12.

————. *Truth and Vision in Katherine Anne Porter's Fiction.* Athens: University of Georgia Press, 1985.

Vidal-Naquet, Pierre. *Assassins of Memory: Essays on the Denial of the Holocaust.* Trans. Jeffrey Mehlman. New York: Columbia University Press, 1992.

Walker, Margaret. *Jubilee.* New York: Bantam, 1967.

Walsh, Thomas F. *Katherine Anne Porter and Mexico: The Illusion of Eden.* Austin: University of Texas Press, 1992.

Walters, Dorothy. *Flannery O'Connor.* New York: Twayne, 1973.

Weaver, Richard M. *The Southern Tradition at Bay: A History of Postbellum Thought.* Ed. George Core and M. E. Bradford. Washington, D.C.: Regnery Gateway, 1989.

Webb, Eugene. *Philosophers of Consciousness: Polanyi, Lonergan, Voegelin, Ricoeur, Girard, Kierkegaard.* Seattle: University of Washington Press, 1988.

Welty, Eudora. *Delta Wedding.* New York: Harvest/Harcourt Brace, 1974.

————. *The Eye of the Story: Selected Essays and Reviews.* New York: Random House, 1978.

————. *The Robber Bridegroom.* New York: Harvest/Harcourt, 1970.

Wertham, Fredric. *A Sign for Cain: An Exploration of Human Violence.* New York: Macmillan, 1966.

Westling, Louise. *Sacred Groves and Ravaged Gardens: The Fiction of Eudora Welty, Carson McCullers, and Flannery O'Connor.* Athens: University of Georgia Press, 1985.

Wiesel, Elie. *A Jew Today.* Trans. Marion Wiesel. New York: Random House, 1978.

Williams, James G. "The Anthropology of the Cross: A Conversation with René Girard." In Williams, ed. 262–88.

————. *The Bible, Violence, and the Sacred: Liberation from the Myth of Sanctioned Violence.* Valley Forge, Pa.: Trinity Press International, 1991.

Williams, James G., ed. *The Girard Reader.* New York: Crossroad, 1996.

Wilson, Charles Reagan. *Baptized in Blood: The Religion of the Lost Cause.* Athens: University of Georgia Press, 1980.

Winchell, Mark Royden. "Inner Dark: or, The Place of Cormac McCarthy." *Southern Review* 26.2 (1990): 293–309.

Wolfgang, Marvin E., and Franco Ferracuti. *The Subculture of Violence: Towards an Integrated Theory in Criminology.* London: Tavistock Publications, 1967.

Wood, Ralph C. *The Comedy of Redemption: Christian Faith and Comic Vision in Four American Novelists.* Notre Dame, Ind.: University of Notre Dame Press, 1988.

Woodward, C. Vann. *Origins of the New South, 1877–1913.* Vol. IX, *A History of the South.* Ed. Wendell Holmes Stephenson and E. Merton Coulter. Baton Rouge: Louisiana State University Press, 1951.

Woodward, Richard B. "You Know About Mojave Rattlesnakes?" *New York Times Magazine* 19 April 1992: 28+.

Wright, Richard. "The Ethics of Living Jim Crow." *Uncle Tom's Children.* 1940. New York: Harper and Row, 1965. 3–15.

Wyatt-Brown, Bertram. *Southern Honor: Ethics and Behavior in the Old South*. New York: Oxford University Press, 1982.

Yaeger, Patricia. *Dirt and Desire: Reconstructing Southern Women's Writing, 1930–1990*. Chicago: University of Chicago Press, 2000.

Young, Stark. *The Pavilion: Of People and Times Remembered, Of Stories and Places*. New York: Scribner's, 1951.

Žižek, Slavoj. *Looking Awry: An Introduction to Jacques Lacan through Popular Culture*. Cambridge, Mass.: MIT Press, 1991.

INDEX

Abbott, Shirley, 85

Abel and Cain, 163, 240, 256*n*25

Absalom, Absalom! (Faulkner), 3, 21, 47

Adam and Eve, 182

Adams, Rebecca, 168

The Adventures of Huckleberry Finn (Twain), 25, 26, 48

African Americans: Jim Crow laws on, 30–31, 77; lynching of, 1–3, 13–15, 31–33; in McCarthy's *Child of God*, 175; and miscegenation, 30; Morrison on, in literature, 77, 78; as novelists, 3; in O'Connor's *Violent Bear It Away*, 162; in Percy's *Thanatos Syndrome*, 207–8; in Porter's "Miranda" stories, 57, 63, 64, 76–81, 206; and Reconstruction, 29–30, 42, 223; religion of, 41; white discomfort with African American doubles, 30–31. *See also* Slavery

After the Lost War (Hudgins), 89

Alison, James, 136, 248*n*8

All the King's Men (Warren), 223

Allen, William R., 256*n*20

Amato, Joseph, 220

American Notes (Dickens), 19

Anglicanism, 37–38

"Annabel Lee" (Poe), 178

Anti-Oedipus (Deleuze and Guattari), 6–7

Anti-Semitism, 205, 206, 209, 237. *See also* Holocaust

Anzaldúa, Gloria, 24, 249–50*n*19

Apartheid in South Africa, 39

Apology (Plato), 239

Appelfeld, Aharon, 255*n*10

Aristotle, 18

Arnold, Edwin T., 253*n*2, 254*n*12

Aryanism, 225, 256*n*14

As I Lay Dying (Faulkner), 3, 47

Asals, Frederick, 144, 251*n*2, 252*n*9, 252*n*12

Askesis, 86

Athens, Lonnie, 151, 168–69, 254*n*11

Atlanta Constitution, 1, 2, 13, 14, 32

Atomic bomb, 118

Autobiography by women, 59

Awakenings, 37–38

Ayers, Edward, 3, 21, 31, 32, 33, 247*n*3

Azazel, 200–202, 204, 206–7, 226, 245, 254*n*2

The Bacchae (Euripedes), 166, 198

Bacon, Jon Lance, 121

Bailey, Kenneth K., 45, 123

Bailie, Gil, 224, 248*n*8, 255*n*5, 256*n*15

Bakhtin, Mikhail, 25–26, 182, 256*n*24

Bandera, Cesareo, 248*n*8, 249*n*18, 255*n*5

Bandura, Albert, 6

Baptism: Girard on, 151; in O'Connor's *Violent Bear It Away*, 119, 125, 126, 127, 130, 133, 140, 145, 148, 151, 160, 215; Percy on, 215

Baptists, 37–38, 40, 42

Barge, Laura, 248*n*8

Barker, Francis, 10

Barnes, Roslyn, 155–56

Barth, Karl, 36

Gans, Eric, 229, 256*n*17

Gastil, Raymond, 15, 248*n*10

Gender: and androgyny, 71–72; Butler on, 63, 71–72, 90; and coquetry, 85–91, 115, 251*n*11; culture of manhood, 17, 23; and feminism in Porter's "Miranda" stories, 95–96, 97, 115; Girard on, 57; masculinity and crime, 254*n*9; masculinity in McCarthy's *Child of God*, 173–76; masculinity in O'Connor's *Violent Bear It Away*, 133–34; masculinity in Porter's "Miranda" stories, 73–77, 92–93, 104; and menstruation, 76, 84–85, 250*n*10; and New Woman, 58; and passive-aggression, 87; in Percy's *Thanatos Syndrome*, 221–22; Porter and southern womanhood, 55–56; in Porter's "Miranda" stories, 55, 56, 57–91, 178, 222; southern belle, 48, 57–58, 63, 64, 69, 71–72, 85–91, 94, 95, 174, 222; and violence, 248–49*n*12

Genovese, Eugene, 28, 41

Giannone, Richard, 118, 252*n*4, 252*n*7

Gilligan, James, 6, 189

Ginzburg, Ralph, 247*n*1

Girard, René: on askesis, 86; on baptism, 151; on Cain and Abel, 163, 256*n*25; on Cervantes, 47; charges of sexism against, 57; on chauvinism, 100; on children's play, 171; on comedy, 134–35; on coquetry, 85–87, 251*n*11; on death, 112, 179, 180, 215; on deconstruction, 255*n*4; on desire, 6–9, 98, 168, 169, 170, 174, 177, 178, 212, 213–14; on education, 129; on Faulkner, 2–3, 4, 47; on festivals of misrule, 25–26, 92, 182–83; on foreign wars, 100, 101; on Freud, 215; on god with human face, 61; on hatred and jealousy from internal mediation, 98; on heroism, 88, 114, 248*n*6; on honor, 19; on hospitals, 237; on illness, 212, 213–14; on imitation by children, 238; on incest, 185–86; influence of, on different fields, 12, 248*n*8; on interdividuality, 5, 48, 143; on Jesus, 149, 254*n*14; on kudos, 126; on language, 227, 228, 229; on Logos of Heraclitus versus Logos of John, 135–36, 139; on lynch-

ing, 2–3, 13–15, 33; on masks, 80; on masochism, 82, 169; on medicine, 198; on menstrual taboos, 85; on mimesis, 7–9, 21, 32, 59; on mimesis of apprenticeship, 129; on model-disciple relationship, 67, 116–18; on motif of extravagant offers, 92; on myth, 49, 224, 225, 248*n*9, 255*n*12; on novelistic conclusions, 97, 108, 111, 114; on Oedipal conflict, 170; on pedophilia, 252*n*8; on persecution text, 195, 204; on pestilence and plague as metaphor, 89, 101, 223; on pharmacology, 208; on Plato, 210, 217; on prophets, 156; on psychic catastrophes, 232; on religion and the sacred, 10–12, 34–36, 45, 123, 131, 156, 166, 186, 188, 249*nn*13–15; on Resurrection, 152; on ritual, 167; on sacrificial crisis, 8–10, 30, 51, 70–71, 145; on sadism, 175; on Salome and John the Baptist, 71, 120; on scandal, 115–16, 141, 145; on scandalizing children, 146, 147; on scapegoating, 9–11, 13, 23, 26, 27, 32, 40, 50, 75–76, 106, 107, 132, 152, 189, 193, 195, 204, 205, 208, 217, 220–21, 228, 251*n*16, 256*n*17; on Shakespeare, 91; on shame, 22; on skandalon (stumbling stone), 116–18; on Sophocles, 202; and Southern Renascence, 49; on sparagmos, 198; on stereotypes of persecution, 204; on strife among primates, 241; on Suffering Servant, 123, 251*n*16; on suicide, 171; on symbolic thought, 132; on taboos, 85, 173, 185–86; on tombs, 43; on verbal dueling, 139; on violence, 2–17, 19, 25, 100, 101, 108, 150, 166; on writers' own struggles with imitative desire, 59

Givner, Joan, 111, 113, 114

God. *See* Religion

God without Thunder (Ransom), 45, 46, 130

Golsan, Richard J., 248*n*9, 255*n*12

Gone with the Wind (Mitchell), 28, 88

Goodhart, Sandor, 243, 248*n*8

Gordon, R., 252*n*8

Gordon, Sarah, 252*n*14

Gossett, Louise, 51

Graham, Don, 56